WALKING THIS PATH
TOGETHER

WALKING THIS PATH TOGETHER

Anti-Racist and Anti-Oppressive Child Welfare Practice

THIRD EDITION

EDITED BY

Osowa Askiy Iskwew (Gwendolyn Gosek), Michele Fairbairn, Sohki Aski Esquao (Jeannine Carrière) and Susan Strega

Fernwood Publishing • Halifax & Winnipeg

Copyright © 2025 Gwendolyn Gosek, Michele Fairbairn,
Jeannine Carrière and Susan Strega

All rights reserved. No part of this book may be reproduced or transmitted in
any form by any means without permission in writing from the publisher,
except by a reviewer, who may quote brief passages in a review.

Developmental Editing: Wayne Antony
Copyediting: Lisa Frenette
Cover image: Seletze Delmar Johnnie
Cover design: Lauren Jeanneau
Printed and bound in the UK

Published by Fernwood Publishing
Halifax and Winnipeg
2970 Oxford Street, Halifax, Nova Scotia, B3L 2W4
www.fernwoodpublishing.ca

Fernwood Publishing Company Limited gratefully acknowledges the financial
support of the Government of Canada through the Canada Book Fund and the
Canada Council for the Arts, the Nova Scotia Department of Communities,
Culture and Heritage, the Manitoba Department of Culture, Heritage and Tourism
under the Manitoba Publishers Marketing Assistance Program and the Province of
Manitoba, through the Book Publishing Tax Credit, for our publishing program.

Library and Archives Canada Cataloguing in Publication
Title: Walking this path together : anti-racist and anti-oppressive
child welfare practice / edited by Gwendolyn Gosek, Michele
Fairbairn, Jeannine Carrière, and Susan Strega.
Names: Gosek, Gwendolyn, 1951- editor. | Fairbairn, Michele,
editor. | Carrière, Jeannine, editor | Strega, Susan, editor
Description: Third edition. | Includes bibliographical references and index.
Identifiers: Canadiana 20250135809 | ISBN 9781773637372 (softcover)
Subjects: LCSH: Racism in social services—Canada. | LCSH: Child
welfare—Canada. | LCSH: Indigenous children—Canada—Social
conditions. | LCSH: Indigenous children—Services for—Canada.
| LCSH: Social work with Indigenous peoples—Canada.
Classification: LCC HV745.A6 W36 2025 | DDC 362.7/7897071—dc23

CONTENTS

Acknowledgements x

Contributors xi

1 Decolonial, Anti-Racist and Equitable Child Welfare: An Introduction 1
   by Osowa Askiy Iskwew (Gwendolyn Gosek) and Michele Fairbairn
   Who Are We and Where We Come From 2
   Our Editorial Circle 3
   Who Is Child Welfare For and Why? 3
   A Way Forward 11
   Chapter Summaries 11
   References 14

2 Indigenous Children in the Centre: Indigenous Perspectives on
   Anti-Oppressive Child Welfare Practice 18
   by Qwul'sih'yah'maht (Robina Thomas) and Kundoqk (Jacquie Green)
   Discrimination and Disproportionality 19
   The Medicine Wheel 21
   History of Indigenous Child Welfare in Canada 23
   Anti-Oppressive Practice 26
   Self 27
   Practice 30
   Vision 34
   Notes 36
   Suggested Readings 36
   References 37

3 The Long and Twisted Road to Child Welfare: My Mother's Story
   through Colonization, Trauma and Strength 39
   by Osowa Askiy Iskwew (Gwendolyn Gosek)
   I Was Once Five 40
   Early Canadian Colonial Context 42
   Minnie (Halkett) Paul's Story 45
   The Indian Act and Residential Schools 47
   Parenting and Residential Schools 48
   The Indian Act and Enfranchisement 50
   Considering the Impact of Policy 54
   Nimama 56
   Suggested Readings 57
   References 57

4 **Child Welfare Assessment, Documentation and Recordkeeping:**
   Decolonial, Anti-Racist and Equitable Approaches 61
   by Michele Fairbairn

   The Pitfalls of Current Child Welfare Practices 62
   Colonialism 66
   Building the Settler Nation 68
   Securing the Nation: Contemporary Neoliberal Child Welfare 69
   Assessment in Child Welfare 73
   Documentation and Recordkeeping 74
   Reimagining Assessment, Documentation and Recordkeeping 77
   Suggested Readings 78
   References 78

5 **Giidosendiwag: Walking Together with Indigenous Youth in Care** 83
   by Nancy Stevens and Ziigwanbinesii (Rachel Charles)

   Starting Up the AYIT Program 84
   Historical Context in Ontario 85
   Indigenous Youth, Identity and Culture 89
   AYIT at Niijkiwendidaa 94
   Giidosendiwag: We Walk Together 99
   Notes 100
   Suggested Readings 100
   References 101

6 **Four-Level Model of Consciousness for Family Group Conferences:**
   A Wise Practice for Awareness of Colonization and Decolonization 105
   by Don Robinson

   Awakening to the Four Levels of Consciousness 106
   Who I Am and Where I Come From 108
   The Four-Level Model of Wellness 109
   A Wise Practice 119
   Notes 119
   Suggested Readings 120
   References 120

7 **Recentring Métis Kinship Protocols of Care:**
   Disrupting Colonial Child Welfare Practices 122
   by Julie Mann-Johnson and Angie Tucker

   The Importance of Positioning Ourselves in Child Welfare Practices 123
   The Child Welfare System 127
   Kinship 129
   How Were Children Cared For in the Past? 131
   How Kinship Care Has Been Operationalized Using Western Child Welfare Policies ... 133
   Implications for Practice 133
   Child Welfare Built on Métis Knowledge 136
   Note 136
   Suggested Readings 136
   References 137

8   Decolonizing Prevention: Support and Surveillance in
    Indigenous Child and Family Services 140
    by Erika Finestone
    Finding the "Happy Middle" 141
    Journeys of the Heart: An Introduction to Indigenous Participation in Family Programs 144
    Witnessing or Watching? The Risks and Rewards of Visibility 146
    Doing Your Duty: Liability and the "Duty to Report" in Service Settings 150
    Nothing to Hide: Anonymous Reporting as Colonial Accountability 153
    The Conundrum: Working for or against "The System" 154
    Acknowledgements 157
    Notes 158
    Suggested Readings 158
    References 158

9   "Your Best Can Only Take You to Where the Good Is": Strange Things Black
    Parents Say and Do to Prepare Black Children for a Racist Society 160
    by Paul Banahene Adjei
    Anti-Black Racism in Canada 162
    Parenting Strategies of Black Parents 164
    Anti-Racist Child Welfare Practice 174
    Note 178
    Suggested Readings 178
    References 179

10 "Deportation Is Double Punishment":
    The Neoliberal "Crimmigration" System 182
    by Mandeep Kaur Mucina, Jessica Pratezina and Amira Abdel-Malek
    The "Other" Children in Child Welfare Care 183
    Bordering Practices in the Immigration, Child Welfare and Carceral Systems 185
    The Neoliberal Dichotomy of Undeserving versus Deserving 186
    Individual Responsibility and "Productive" Members of Society 188
    Austerity and Inequity 189
    Bureaucratic Violence and Its Consequences 191
    Critical Approaches to Practice with NCFYC 192
    "Exile Sentence Shouldn't Even Exist Anymore" 195
    "They Should Treat You Like a Human Being" 196
    Suggested Readings 197
    References 197

11 Decolonial Trauma-Informed School-Based Practice:
    Hearing the Voices of Refugee Newcomer Parents 200
    by Mehmoona Moosa-Mitha
    Decolonial Perspectives on Trauma 201
    Refugees in Canada 202
    Schools, Refugee Newcomer Children and Ongoing Trauma 203
    Decolonial and Anti-Racist Trauma-Informed School-Based Child Welfare Practice 211
    Coloniality and School Social Workers 215
    Suggested Readings 215
    References 215

12 Taking Children's Resistance Even More Seriously: A Response-Based Approach to Children Who Have Experienced Violence 220
by Kineweskwêw (Cathy Richardson) and Shelly Dean

The Development of Response-Based Practice 221
Conceptualizing Children's Resistance to Violence 224
Seeing the Wellness of Children through the Slightest Details 226
It Takes a Safe Village 227
Attachment: The Tu Cho Circle 228
Response-Based Contextual Analysis 230
What a Child Is or Isn't Doing Rather than What a Child Ought to Do 237
You Don't Say: Children Who Choose Silence 238
Acknowledgements 240
Suggested Readings 240
References 240

13 Calling All Warriors: Indigenous Social Workers Fighting Inequity within the Child Welfare System 242
by Carolyn Peacock and Brooke Lightning-Montour

Who We Are 243
The Age of "Reconciliation" 243
Approaching Indigenous Child Welfare 245
The Fostering Story 247
Reconciliation — What Does It Really Mean? 251
Have Government Systems Reconciled with Indigenous Communities? 253
Current Reconciliation in Child Services 254
Hopes for a Better Future 260
Suggested Readings 261
References 261

Index 263

ACKNOWLEDGEMENTS

Without the efforts of many helping hands this book would not be possible. As with the previous editions there are many to thank and hold up in the highest honour. We thank the children and families who inspired us to pay attention to our practice as we entered and sometimes stayed in their lives. We hope that through this book we will be able to make a difference for people who need a relationship with a social worker in their journey. We are grateful for the interest and engagement of our colleagues at the University of Victoria and like-minded colleagues, academics and professionals from across Canada. Without the support of Fernwood Publishing this book would not have been possible, so special thanks to Wayne Antony for his patience and encouragement throughout all three editions. We also want to acknowledge all the Fernwood staff who stepped in at critical phases of the publishing process. This book is a collective effort, a true walking together, far beyond being an edited collection. It was a collective vision that we prayed for and we thank the ancestors for giving us another opportunity to share this work and vision with others. All our relations.

CONTRIBUTORS

ABOUT THE COVER ARTIST

Seletze Delmar Johnnie (1946-2012)
Seletze was born and raised in Khenipsen, one of the Cowichan tribes in Duncan, BC. He was one of the most generous people I have ever met. Delmar was a loving husband, father, an artist, a role model and a storyteller. The teachings of his Elders were a sacred part of his own personal transformation. In the 1980s Delmar was one of the first former Kuper Island Residential School students in the Duncan area to speak publicly about his abuse. After years of living with the horrific secrets of his abusive experiences in residential school, Delmar decided it was time to speak out and let go of the dark secret he had carried his whole life. His disclosure was out of sheer selflessness — he wanted to inspire others to also release their residential school secrets (or, more appropriately, nightmares) and learn to live a full life of love. By spirit, Seletze was a trickster. He learned to heal and share through the power of laughter and love. As a renown Coast Salish artist, Seletze very generously mentored many young artists. However if you spoke to these artists, most would acknowledge that what they learned from him was far beyond art; Delmar taught them to live with a good mind and heart — uy'skwuluwun.

— Qwul'sih'yah'maht (Robina Thomas)

ABOUT THE AUTHORS

Amira Abdel-Malek is a graduate of the School of Child and Youth Care's master's program at the University of Victoria. She works with children, youth, adults and families using expressive arts and applied theatre in her eclectic career as a community organizer, artist and counsellor. She currently resides on the Traditional Territory of the Lekwungen People with her daughter and partner.

Paul Banahene Adjei is associate professor and the interim associate vice-president (Indigenous research) at Memorial University of Newfoundland. He was previously the dean of the School of Social Work, Memorial University. His teaching and research interests are in social justice, de/anti-colonialism, Indigenization, critical race theory and critical whiteness studies. Paul draws on his African Indigeneity as rich cultural sources of knowledge to (re)imagine new futures for education. He is the recipient of several awards: In 2021, the Carnegie Diaspora Fellow/Visiting Scholar Award for University of Ghana; in 2022, the Most Inspiring Immigrants in Atlantic Canada; and in 2023, the Black Excellence Award for Lifetime Achievement by the Coalition of Black Communities in Newfoundland and Labrador

Sohki Aski Esquao (Jeannine Carrière) is Métis and was raised in St. Adolphe, Manitoba. She has been teaching social work since 1994, first in Alberta and at the University of Victoria since 2005. Her research interests include Métis children's identity and needs for cultural safety in adoptions and child welfare services. Jeannine has been a practitioner in Indigenous child and family services for over thirty-five years and has a number of publications including a co-edited book, *Calling Our Families Home: Métis Peoples' Experiences with Child Welfare* (2017), which is the first book on Métis child welfare in Canada. She has also been on the production team for the documentary *Lii Michif Niiyanaan: We Are Métis* (2023). She was co-editor for the first two editions of *Walking This Path Together: Anti-racist and Anti-oppressive Child Welfare Practice*. She has received a number of grants and awards including the University of Victoria Provost's Advocacy and Activism Award.

Shelly Dean gratefully lives on the traditional unceded ancestral lands of the Secwépemc Nation, known as Kamloops, BC, Canada. Shelly is a wife, a mother and grandmother. She grew up in Northern British Columbia, in the small community of Moberly Lake. Shelly is a family therapist, clinical supervisor and educator who works with organizations and communities to address issues of violence. She works closely with her colleagues through the Centre for Response-Based Practice, developing and practising a specialized approach to violence and other forms of adversity, with a special interest in working for children who have experienced domestic and institutionalized violence. Her research has focused on children's responses and resistance to violence — specifically understanding their behaviour in context, the nature of social interactions with young people, the connection between violence and mutualizing language, and the social responses that children and their families receive.

Michele Fairbairn is an educator in the School of Social Work at the University of Victoria, located on the unceded territory of the ləkʷəŋən-speaking peoples including the Songhees, Esquimalt and WSÁNEĆ. Michele is a doctoral candidate at Memorial University of Newfoundland. Michele has also completed narrative research with child welfare social workers who were in state care as children and/or were investigated as mothers. She focused on how these experiences impacted their (and her own) social work identity and practice decisions. Michele has practised social work in a variety of child welfare and health-related areas. She has also served as a board member at non-profit community organizations and been an activist in grassroots anti-poverty and anti-violence initiatives.

Erika Finestone is a SSHRC Postdoctoral Fellow at the Centre for Indigenous Research and Community-Led Engagement at the University of Victoria and was trained as a sociocultural anthropologist at the University of Toronto. An Ashkenazi settler scholar with over ten years' experience working in collaboration with Indigenous communities, Erika examines the relationship between kinship, refusal and Indigenous sovereignty in settler-states. Her current research, knowledge mobilization projects, and writing examine the radical and everyday ways Indigenous Peoples refuse the removal of their children into the Canadian child welfare system, and how these practices intersect with Indigenous sovereignty movements locally and globally.

Osowa Askiy Iskwew (Gwendolyn Gosek) is a member of the Lac La Ronge First Nation. She is an assistant professor with the School of Social Work at the University of Victoria located on the unceded territory of the ləkʷəŋən-speaking peoples including the Songhees, Esquimalt and WSÁNEĆ. She has previously worked in frontline and management positions with inner-city services for Indigenous women, children and youth. Her areas of interest include Indigenous child welfare, suicide in Indigenous communities and Indigenous women's leadership roles.

Brooke Lightning-Montour is a member of the Samson Cree Nation located in Treaty 6, Alberta. She grew up in Maskwacis, Alberta, where she lives with her husband and children. Brooke has a master's in social work from the University of Calgary and has worked in the social work field for fifteen years. Her work and personal philosophy is "Nakatemitohtan" ("take care of each other"). For Brooke, the role of an Indigenous social worker encompasses a multifaceted set of responsibilities aimed at supporting Indigenous communities in addressing various social, cultural and economic challenges through an understanding of Indigenous cultures, traditions and world views to their practice.

Julie Mann-Johnson is a mother, wife, daughter, sister, auntie, niece, cousin, friend and neighbour living in Mishitihi Sakaikhan (St. Albert, Alberta) in Treaty 6 Territory. She is the associate director of field education and associate professor (teaching) in the Faculty of Social Work at the University of Calgary's Central and Northern Alberta Region. Julie has worked most of her twenty-five-year social work career in various areas of child welfare practice. This experience has led her to be particularly passionate about supporting feminist, anti-colonizing and anti-racist practice as well as ensuring meaningful kin connections for children and youth within that system. Julie is also particularly interested in socializing new social workers to the social work profession, community partnerships and social work education. Julie also loves spending time in the garden, back country hiking with her husband and family and recently became a yoga teacher focusing on a yoga practice with moms and babies.

Kineweskwêw (Catherine Richardson) is Métis with Gwich'in, Cree and English ancestry. She is the director of First Peoples Studies at Concordia University in Tiohtià:ke/Montréal and a registered clinical counsellor. Cathy holds a research Chair in Indigenous Healing Knowledges, is assistant co-director for the Centre for Oral History and Digital Storytelling and is a co-founder of the Centre for Response-Based Practice. Her research includes colonial and interpersonal violence, Indigenous healing, dignity and decolonization. Cathy's recent research includes the Indigenous Healing Knowledges project. She has published six books, most recently being *Facing the Mountain: Indigenous Healing in the Shadow of Colonialism* in 2021. Recent awards include The President's Media Award for Opinion Leader of the Year and the Dean's Award for Community Outreach and Public Engagement.

Kundoqk (Jacquie Green) is from the Haisla Nation and has Tsmishian/Kemano ancestry. She is the executive director for Indigenous Academic, Community Engagement (IACE) at the First People House, University of Victoria. Her scholarship and leadership are embedded in Indigenous Knowledge, its histories and philosophies, thereby looking at histories, identities, place and language through storytelling. She focuses her research, writing, teaching and leadership to include Indigenous and social justice knowledge, epistemologies, pedagogies and philosophies. Kundoqk did not grow up knowing Haisla Nuuyum due to residential school, however her PhD studies was a combination of Haisla Nuuyum, as shared with her by her late parents, aunts and uncles. An exciting part of the process was Kundoqk defending her dissertation in front of her community and celebrated in a community feast. What keeps her grounded in her scholarship is maintaining connection to family and community; importantly, she ensures that any kind of "sport" is a part of her life. Her vision is to provide mentorship to youth and post-secondary students who will become our next generation of leaders. She believes the work of decolonizing and Indigenizing requires a commitment from all people and in this, this is social justice work.

Mehmoona Moosa-Mitha is professor at the University of Victoria's School of Social Work. She has undertaken extensive community-based action research on global poverty as well as trauma and pain in refugee newcomer communities living in Canada. She has published in citizenship studies, particularly the citizenship rights of children and Muslim citizens living in the West as well as transnational decolonial feminist theories.

Mandeep Kaur Mucina is associate professor in the School of Child and Youth Care at the University of Victoria. Over the course of twenty years, Mandeep has worked with children, youth and families in various contexts, including child protection, gender-based and sexualized violence and with immigrant communities. Mandeep's current research and social justice work focuses on family violence, gender-based violence, critical migration studies and exploring second-generation South Asian women's resistance, identity and encounters with racism in the diaspora. Mandeep is co-leading an SSHRC-funded research grant entitled *Bordering Practices: Systemic Racism, Immigration, and Child Welfare*, a collaborative research project in partnership with child welfare, immigration and gender-based violence service providers.

Jessica Pratezina is a researcher and advocate who studies how people and communities change. She works on issues of abuse in religious groups, gender-based violence, gender equality and reproductive justice.

Don Robinson is originally from Bunibonibee (Oxford House) First Nation. He has a Master of Social Work degree (2001) and was a social work instructor with the University of Manitoba for twenty years. He also delivered professional development training and healing workshops throughout Manitoba and across Canada. Don's work has included play therapy work, individual and family therapy, group therapy sessions and healing and sharing circles. He learned from Elders and Knowledge Keepers about the traditional ways and through participating in ceremonies, such as fasting, Sweat Lodge, and Sundances, along with the Western approaches he was trained in. Don has also been a helper oskabayis in the traditional ways and conducts ceremonies. He is a husband, father of two adult children and a stepson. Ekosani.

Nancy Stevens has worked in the field of Indigenous mental health and wellness and Indigenous women's violence against women programs as a counsellor and coordinator largely in northern and rural southeastern Ontario, and in the Yukon Territory. At the same time, she has worked as a post-secondary educator at various institutions in Ontario. She is currently assistant professor in the Indigenous Studies department at Nipissing University in North Bay, Ontario. Nancy is a mother of four adult children and grandmother of two grandchildren. She was not raised connected to any Indigenous Knowledge or practices because she was adopted as an infant. Her birth mother's family are of European and Mohawk ancestry and her birth father's family are British. Due to living and working largely in Anishinaabe territories as an adult, the bulk of her cultural learning has been from Anishinaabe perspectives that frame Nancy's lens on healing and teaching.

Susan Strega is professor emerita, School of Social Work, University of Victoria. A former youth in care and former child protection worker, she is author and editor of many published works including, with Leslie Brown, *Research as Resistance* (2015).

Qwul'sih'yah'maht (Robina Thomas) is a member of Lyackson First Nation, with Snuneymuxw and Sto:lo roots through her grandparents. She is the vice-president, Indigenous at the University of Victoria where she holds the position of professor in the School of Social Work. Her research interests include storytelling, residential schools, Indigenous women and children, Indigenous ways of knowing and being and anti-racism. Robina holds a PhD in Indigenous Governance from the University of Victoria and has many published academic journal articles, including her book *Protecting the Sacred Cycle: Indigenous Women and Leadership*.

Angie Tucker is a member of the Manitoba Métis Federation and Métis Nation of Alberta and a PhD candidate in the Faculty of Native Studies at the University of Alberta. Her work critiques the role of power found in discourse and the effects that this has on the social fabric of Canadian society. Angie is currently focused on collecting oral stories about the everyday experiences of contemporary Métis women in southwestern Manitoba to uncover how they and their families navigated and responded to the ever-changing social, political and economic pressures of 1940–90. As a Métis Studies scholar, her areas of specialization include presenting and publishing on topics such as land, identity, representation, gender and sexuality, traditional adoption practices, community-based research practices and the importance of visiting, memory and storytelling.

Wa Cheew Wapaguunew Iskew (Carolyn Peacock) is a Cree woman from the Enoch Cree Nation in Alberta. She is currently the director of Kasohkowew Child Wellness Society in Maskwacis, Alberta. She has over twenty-five years of social work practice in First Nations Child and Family Services in Alberta. Her research and practice interests include open custom adoption and First Nations child welfare. In 2008 she received the Adoption Activist Award from the North American Council on Adoptable Children (NACAC).

Ziigwanbinesii (Rachel Charles) is from the Mnjikaning of Rama First Nation, belongs to the Mukwa (Bear) Clan and currently resides in the William's Treaty Territory. Ziigwanbinesii holds an advanced diploma in Child and Youth Care and served on the faculty of the Indigenous Studies Program and the Child and Youth Care Program at Fleming College. In addition to various direct care roles with families and youth, Ziigwanbinesii is an active community educator and consultant.

Chapter 1

DECOLONIAL, ANTI-RACIST AND EQUITABLE CHILD WELFARE
An Introduction

by Osowa Askiy Iskwew (Gwendolyn Gosek) and Michele Fairbairn

As editors of this book, we gratefully acknowledge that we are visitors on the unceded lands of the the ləkʷəŋən-speaking peoples, the WSÁNEĆ (Saanich), Wyomilth (Esquimalt) and (Songhees) peoples of the Coast Salish Nation. We acknowledge and keep in our minds and hearts the ancestors of these territories and their contemporary relatives who have been given sacred responsibility for the land, water and living beings that walk, swim, crawl and fly in the territories they know as home.

Osowa Askiy Iskwew (Gwendolyn Gosek) and Michele Fairbairn feel deeply honoured to have been invited by Sohki Aski Esquao (Jeannine Carrière) and Susan Strega to lead the editorial circle for the third edition of *Walking This Path Together*. We are thankful to them for creating the first two editions, and for their mentorship, collegiality and friendship. We are also appreciative to the authors who have contributed to this edition of the book and shared their knowledge, child welfare experiences and insights from a place of wisdom and deep love for the families they live and work alongside.

Like Sohki Aski Esquao and Susan Strega, we have also been walking a path in child welfare. Our journeys have been long intertwined with child welfare, first as young people in care, then as social workers, and finally as researchers, educators and editors of this book. We have much in common as we are now kokums (grandmothers) of numerous children, some of whom are now young adults. Similar to Sohki Aski Esquao and Susan Strega, one of us walks this path as an Indigenous woman (Gwendolyn) and one as a white woman (Michele), which makes our child welfare involvement interconnected but different. While some of our child welfare experiences and impacts are relatable, they remain incommensurable, because they are shaped by historical and contemporary political agendas and each person's life circumstances are unique.

WHO ARE WE AND WHERE WE COME FROM

Osowa Askiy Iskwew

My home community is Lac La Ronge Indian Band in Treaty 6 Territory. My mother is Minnie (Halkett) Paul (Cree-Dene), my maternal grandmother is Susan Hastings (Dene) and my maternal grandfather is Alexander Halkett (Cree). My father was Norwegian. I was born in Saskatoon, Saskatchewan, and my first memories are from North Battleford, Saskatchewan, where we resided while my mother worked at the Indian Hospital. My two brothers and I went into emergency care a few times but when I was five, my mother became seriously ill so my younger brother and I went into care and stayed in the same foster home for eight years. My older brother was sent out of province to live with our father. While those eight years left indelible memories, that story is still unwritten. The stories that I do share are the ones about what being in care could not take away — my life partner, my seven beautiful children and ten grandchildren, along with four university degrees, and most importantly, my reconnection to the sacred teachings. My time in care taught me many lessons that I am now beginning to understand through the seven sacred teachings. Above all, the experience taught me empathy and the desire to fight for change for the current and future generations of children, so they never have to experience separation from family, community and culture.

Michele

I was born in the Prairies at the confluence of the Red and Assiniboine Rivers, in a hospital established by the Grey Nuns. These are the Ancestral Lands of the Anishinaabeg, Anishininewuk, Dakota Oyate, Denesuline and Nehethowuk Nations. It is also the birthplace and homeland of the Red River Métis. They are commonly referred to as Treaty 1 territories. I am now living on the West Coast on the territories of the lək̓ʷəŋən-speaking peoples, which is the place from where I am writing. British imperial expansion provided conditions making it possible for my ancestors to migrate to these lands named Turtle Island by Indigenous Peoples who have lived here since time immemorial. The ocean surrounding these territories unite me with lands now called the Republic of Ireland, Norway and the United Kingdom. My ancestors migrated from these lands, some under conditions of exile and indentured servitude for agricultural labour, while others migrated and contributed to the creation of a dominant white Anglo-Saxon presence in the prairie landscape.

    I am a mother and a grandmother. I became a practising child welfare social worker after graduating from an inner-city BSW program that emphasized the importance of students drawing from their lived experiences with marginalization to build solidarity to transform unjust social work practice. The inner-city program, together with a program in northern Manitoba (both affiliated with the Faculty of Social Work at University of Manitoba) were primarily intended to educate Indigenous students. I am not Indigenous, but this program also selected a small number of newcomer students, and even fewer poor mothers living in the inner city, a group to which I belonged at the time. I was a former permanent ward of the child welfare system with three young children, and a fourth soon to be born.

OUR EDITORIAL CIRCLE

As an editorial circle for the third edition, we first came together at one of the editor's kitchen table to share ceremony, food and stories. This time spent together not only recognized our common life experiences of being involved in child welfare as children, as social workers and as social work academics, and our connections to the same prairie provinces, but it also consolidated our vision that transforming child welfare requires solidarity. As a result, we have now come together with one another and the contributing authors to realize our vision for this book.

WHO IS CHILD WELFARE FOR AND WHY?

Although all the editors were involved with the child welfare system, the reasons for our involvement differ because they were historically rooted in how the Canadian state conceptualized us as distinct types of problems for the nation. Which young people are targeted for state intervention by child welfare has shifted across time as political forces coalesce around perceived threats to the dominant political order of the day. Indigenous young people were targeted as part of a colonial civilizing mission (Blackstock et al. 2023), while social and moral reformers focused on saving children from becoming degenerate adults by making them into economically productive Christian adult citizens (Chen 2005). That colonial mission was — and is still — being carried out on and against Indigenous young people, with negative effects. Indigenous Peoples have also resisted that colonialization for the whole history of "Canada." Theirs is the oldest resistance movement in this country.

Targeting Marginalization and Degeneracy: The Making of Settler Canada

While the specific focus of social reformers and child savers shifted over time, the child welfare gaze was — and is still — firmly fixed on those who at any specific time are marginalized. For example, between 1869 and 1939, over 100,000 poor and otherwise disadvantaged children, some as young as four years old, were sent from Britain to Canada. They are called "home children" because most went from British children's homes and agencies to Canadian receiving homes (Corbett 2002). These children were not orphans: 98 percent had living parents at the time of transport (Corbett 2002). For Britain, the emigration of white children was an opportunity to further "cement the foundations of the empire for generations to come" (Boucher

2014, 13). For Canada, home children served "as a tool of domestication for the social reproduction of Canadian white settler society, which was paired with the forced removal of Indigenous peoples from their lands" (Johnson 2021, 1). Most home children suffered neglect or abuse or both. They worked as child labourers, the girls in households and hospitals and the boys in farming, forestry, construction and manufacturing (Dunae 2005).

Concerns about class, race and gender infused early child welfare in the dominion of Canada. For example, worries about the impact of poor, racialized and ethnically diverse (i.e., not British) children on society led to the founding of industrial schools between the 1880s and the 1930s. Children of the "dangerous classes" (Thomson 2024) were removed from the influence of their "degenerate" (poor, immigrant, racialized) parents to institutional settings featuring strict discipline and structure. Called "schools," they provided little in the way of education. Children were trained as laborers and domestics in the hope that they would avoid the criminality that was said to be their genetic legacy, and instead become productive members of society (Thomson 2024). While both boys and girls were seen as intellectually deficient, thus making it necessary to educate them for menial employment, there were concerns about the sexual immorality of girls (Sangster 2002). "Sexual immorality" was considered a vice under the 1908 federal Juvenile Delinquents Act, legislation that remained in force until 1984. Underage girls suspected of sexual activity outside of marriage could be categorized as juvenile delinquents and confined to an industrial school until they reached the age of majority. Related concerns about morality led child welfare workers to systematically and sometimes violently remove more than 350,000 babies from their mostly white unwed underage mothers from the mid-1940s into the 1970s. Housed in federally funded church-run facilities, almost all their babies were adopted (Senate of Canada 2018).

One of the most instrumental figures in early Canadian child welfare, Charlotte Whitton, head of the Canadian Council on Child Welfare from 1922 to 1941, vigorously advocated banning "undesirable immigrants" (Central European peasants, British slum children and Jewish refugee children) altogether to prevent the dilution of a white, British state (Rooke and Schnell 1987). A eugenicist, Whitton argued for the widespread sterilization of the "feeble-minded" as well as the elimination of financial support to poor families on the grounds that this support encouraged them to have children (Gölz 1993). From 1953 to 1959 Russian immigrant children whose parents were Sons of Freedom Doukhobors were confined to an institution after being forcibly removed from their religious and cultural community, primarily because their parents had refused to send them to school, or their parents were in jail (BC Ombudsman 1999).

Although it is tempting to believe that the story of Canadian child welfare is linear and progressive, these historical illustrations make clear that at the root of who child welfare is for, and why, have much to do with maintaining social order. Thus, current child welfare policies and practices, while ostensibly grounded in the "best interests of the child," far too often make the lives of young people more precarious because they are deeply entrenched in maintaining Canada as a settler-colonial nation stratified along race and class lines rather than caring for their well-being. There is no universal definition of well-being applied to young people, but the welfare of young people under age eighteen is commonly conceptualized within broad categories equating their well-being with rights and security concepts. UNICEF asserts that obtaining an accurate picture of how nations are attending to the well-being of young people is determined by their safety, health, material security, education and socialization, sense of being loved and valued, and being included in their societies. In the 2023 UNICEF "snapshot" of the Canadian picture,

> there are nearly 8 million children and youth under age 18, about a fifth of our population. They are the most urbanized, diverse and educated generation Canada has ever raised. Three in four (73.0 percent) live in urban centers. They live in more diverse families than any previous generation. And they are unequal, with wide gaps between children based on their ethnicity, legal status, gender and gender identity, disability, economic security and geographic location. Indigenous children, including First Nations, Métis and Inuit, are 7.6 percent of the child population. (7)

The well-being and security of Indigenous young people is linked with their rights as Indigenous Peoples. Decolonial and anti-racist child welfare approaches to well-being and security are required to transform child welfare from its colonial underpinnings. There continue to be dire consequences of child welfare involvement for Indigenous communities, but also for Black, newcomer, noncitizen and poor people who are also disproportionately the primary focus of child welfare. These consequences require not only reconceptualizing practice to redress disproportionality but also to support the rights and well-being of young people within their cultures and religions, families and community settings.

While Indigenous children compared to other all children are overrepresented in child welfare systems (Fallon et al. 2020), a Quebec study found that Black children were five times more likely than white children to be reported to child protective services (Boatswain-Kyte et al. 2020). In 2015, the Children's Aid Society of Toronto revealed that 41 percent of children in child welfare care were Black, while they represented only 8.5 percent of the general population in Canada's largest city (cited in Cénat et al. 2023). Similarly, a recent analysis of Ontario child welfare incidence data found that Latin American children were more than twice as likely to be investigated as white children (King et al. 2024). An analysis of Ontario data found that poverty, especially when combined with being diagnosed with mental or physical illness, also led to disproportionate child welfare involvement (Lefebvre et al. 2024). Recent research in Quebec states these disparities in stark terms: Families in the lowest socioeconomic tier saw the highest prevalence rates of all forms of child protection intervention, those in the highest tier saw the least (Esposito et al. 2023). What unites these disparities is how child welfare focuses on people who, based on Indigeneity and race, and intersections of gender, ability and class are subjected to vicissitudes of law, policies and practices intended to maintain settler colonialism. The effects of these stratifying categorizations are further coupled by racism operating within the social realm.

Anti-Racism

Racism and its impact on Black, Indigenous and people of colour (BIPOC) individuals and communities is a vitally important topic at the centre of this book. Where it is not explicitly named, it is inferred through the stories and critique of racist practices and policies operating in child welfare. Racism is not new to Canada as it has been actively expressed for more than two hundred years at the interpersonal and institutional levels and social work has not been exempt (Dudgeon et al. 2023). Racism's role has been evident in the overrepresentation of Indigenous children and youth in the child welfare system generally, and especially in the Sixties Scoop and current Millennium Scoop. It is also evident in the overrepresentation of Black children in care and minority children from diverse communities who are involved with the child welfare system (Cénat et al. 2020).

In order to demonstrate a sincere effort to reverse the disproportionate number of Indigenous and Black children in care, and youth of colour involved with the child welfare system, social work, as a profession, must begin by owning its own historical "complicity in harmful and racist policies and practices" that are based in antiquated, patriarchal values and belief systems such as Manifest Destiny, Kill the Indian and Save the Man, heterosexual nuclear families, patriarchal women's roles and so on (Lynch 2024; Murray-Lichtman et al. 2023). The profession of social work must be forthright about how these belief systems have supported racist policies which deny BIPOC children, families and communities autonomy to thrive in their own traditional ways of being and doing.

As social workers, we need to understand the complex interplay of racism and white supremacy, which Murray-Lichtman et al. (2023, 8) describe as "a political, economic and cultural system in which whites overwhelmingly control power and material resources." It follows that we must also acknowledge the complexity of society and institutional environments we work, teach and learn within. For example, we need to question to what extent are teaching institutions and field placement agencies willing to support anti-racist policies and pedagogies? Do the students entrusted to placement agencies and work environments feel safe and supported to engage in anti-racist practice?

Students, who may have limited relationships with people from different cultures and have limited anti-racist education, risk going into child welfare field practicums or the work environment lacking important knowledge and the confidence to support BIPOC individuals and families (Gates et al. 2023). Without a strong knowledge base regarding racism, students could perpetuate rather than confront the racist acts that BIPOC people experience on a daily basis (Cane and Tedam 2023). While racism is a difficult topic to discuss as it often brings about feelings of shame, guilt or anger, it is important to remember that those emotions, while real, do not work to resolve peoples' experiences of racism. Racism is unfortunately an ongoing battle that needs to be challenged through the development of critical analytic skills, having the willingness to look inward to assess the influences of our own socially constructed environments and committing to acknowledging and sitting with the discomfort until the necessary knowledge and skills to confront racism guide our interactions (Tyler et al. 2024).

In order to meet the needs of students, social work instructors must develop an in-depth understanding and strong comfort level in teaching students along with being prepared to challenge institutional racism. Often, insufficient time and energy are devoted to the topic of anti-racism, meanwhile it needs to be diligently incorporated throughout the curriculum (Cane and Tedam 2023; Tyler et al. 2024). Knowing that it is BIPOC communities that social workers frequently provide services for, and that racism impacts at every intersection with society negatively affecting life outcomes, it behooves us as social workers to uphold a stronger focus on anti-racist teaching and include "strategies to challenge racism" (Cane and Tedam 2023, 1563).

Indigenous Disproportionality

In their research into placement decisions, Fallon et al. (2020) paint a glaring picture of the disproportional involvement of child welfare in the lives of Indigenous young people. Although according to the 2008 census only 6 percent of Canadian children are Indigenous, more than 50 percent of young people in care are Indigenous (Indigenous Services Canada 2020). According to Trocmé et al. (2013) Indigenous children make up 22 percent of substantiated maltreatment reports and Indigenous young people are overrepresented at every point of child welfare decision-making. In some jurisdictions, Indigenous disproportionality is particularly harsh. More than 90 percent of Manitoba children in care are Indigenous (Government of Manitoba 2018) though Indigenous people make up only 18 percent of Manitoba's population (Statistics Canada 2021). In Alberta, more than 71 percent of children in care are Indigenous (Government of Alberta 2021), while Indigenous people comprise only 6.5 percent of Alberta's population (Government of Canada n.d.). Comparing data from the 2013 and 2018 Ontario Incidence Study (OIS), Quinn et al. (2022, 5) found that Indigenous young people were twice as likely to be placed in out-of-home care as compared to white children. Quinn et al. (2022, 5) observe that "a child being First Nations is a significant predictor of out-of-home placement when controlling for other factors in the investigation."

Research has repeatedly tied such statistics to the conditions of Indigenous Peoples' lives in settler-colonial Canada. Indigenous people are 5 percent of the Canadian population (Government of Canada n.d.) but 26 percent of neglect investigations involve Indigenous young people (Trocmé et al. 2013). Yet as long ago as 1983, researchers acknowledged that child welfare standards related to neglect ignored the depths of poverty disproportionately experienced by Indigenous Peoples (Johnston 1983, 75). Decades later, researchers are still pointing out that factors such as poverty and insecure and/or substandard housing were implicated in disproportional neglect investigations (Trocmé et al. 2013). The OIS notes that neglect continues to be the most common reason for Indigenous young people to come to the attention of child welfare authorities (Quinn et al. 2022, 2). As Fallon et al. (2021, 36) explain, "neglect" is associated with "multiple structural challenges, such as living in unsafe housing conditions, economic hardship, and overcrowded housing that all limit the resources available to them to provide for their families." Landertinger contends that governments both facilitate the conditions of extreme poverty and inadequate housing in which many Indigenous people live, and then present these conditions "back to the settler society as 'proof' of the imagined inadequacy of Indigenous parents" (2016, 4). Of course, however unreal this inadequacy is, it has a strong influence in child welfare decision-making.

Rather than being accidental, Indigenous disproportionality in child welfare is, according to many theorists, an intentional continuation of residential school and Canada's genocidal, assimilationist agenda for Indigenous people. The Sixties Scoop, which is a phrase Patrick Johnston (1983) applied to describe the mass removals of Indigenous children from their families and communities and placed with non-Indigenous foster or adoptive families across Canada and often in other parts of the world during the '60s, '70s and into the '80s, is a prime example of this assimilationist agenda. Kemble (2021, 115) relays that assimilation has not only involved the federal government but also other willing participants:

> Kanata, with skilled sleight-of-hand, turned residential schools into de facto child welfare facilities where it advanced the assimilation agenda through forced removal and illusorily compassionate adoptions. But Kanata couldn't do it alone. It never could. We know now that Indian residential schools needed the help of the church, sweeping and enabling

legislation, and policy. For the Sixties Scoop, we know that Kanata needed help from the provinces, enabling legislation, and uninterrupted standards of care that placed Indigenous parents and communities on the losing edge.

Roxburgh and Sinclair (2024) make clear the role of another group of willing participants — social workers. They note that in 1947, both the Canadian Association of Social Workers (CASW) and the Canada Welfare Council advocated for the Government of Canada to fully commit to the assimilation of Indigenous Peoples. According to Roxburgh and Sinclair (2004, 155) CASW contended that, if it used the child welfare system, the government could achieve full assimilation ... within a generation.

Recent Indigenous Initiatives

Since 2015, the urgent need to reduce the overrepresentation of Indigenous young people caught up in child welfare systems has resulted in three significant initiatives (Ball and Benoit-Jansson 2023). When the Truth and Reconciliation Commission (TRC) released its final report in 2015, it included ninety-four "Calls to Action," of which the first five calls were directed to the need to make changes in child welfare. Briefly summarized, the Calls to Action called on all three levels of government to reduce the number of Indigenous children in care; to prepare and publish information related to Indigenous children in care; to fully implement Jordan's Principle; to enact Indigenous child welfare legislation that establishes national standards for Indigenous child apprehension and custody cases; and to develop culturally appropriate parenting programs for Indigenous families (Crown-Indigenous Relations and Northern Affairs Canada 2024).

On January 26, 2016, the Canadian Human Rights Tribunal issued its decision regarding a complaint filed almost a decade earlier, in which the First Nations Child and Family Caring Society and the Assembly of First Nations stated that the Department of Indian and Northern Affairs' (INAC) provision of First Nations Child and Family Services (FNCFS) and implementation of Jordan's Principle were flawed, inequitable and thus discriminatory under the Canadian Human Rights Act. Jordan's Principle is a child-first principle intended to ensure that Indigenous young people can access the supports and services they need when they need them. When supports or services are requested, the government of first contact is to pay for the service and any jurisdictional or payment disputes will be resolved later. The principle is named in memory of Jordan River Anderson, an Indigenous child with complex medical needs from Norway House Cree Nation in Manitoba. Jordon spent more than two years unnecessarily in hospital while the province of Manitoba and the federal government argued over who should pay for his at-home care. Jordan died in the hospital at age five, never having spent a day in a family home (First Nations Child and Family Caring Society 2016).

The Tribunal found that First Nations children were being discriminated against. It ordered Indian and Northern Affairs to:

1. Cease its discriminatory practices regarding the FNCFS Program;
2. Reform the FNCFS Program;
3. Cease applying the narrow definition of Jordan's Principle; and
4. Take measures to immediately implement the full meaning and scope of Jordan's Principle. (Blaney 2021)

Finally, in 2019, the federal government passed the An Act respecting First Nations, Inuit and Métis children, youth and families. The Act "affirms the rights of First Nations, Inuit and Métis peoples to exercise jurisdiction over child and family services" (Government of Canada, 2021b, cited in Ball and Benoit-Jannson 2023, 2). According to a subsequent December 2022 government report, "over 90 Indigenous communities have started to develop and implement policies and Indigenous laws" with seventeen coordination agreement discussions currently ongoing and an estimated twenty expected to begin annually over the next few years (Crown-Indigenous Relations and Northern Affairs Canada 2024). On July 6, 2021, the very first coordination agreement was signed between the Cowessess First Nation and the province of Saskatchewan (Djuric 2021).

Although Indigenous communities continue to move forward on building community-based child and family services that are Indigenous informed and managed, they do so with both anticipation and an understanding of a colonial history still operating in the present that means the way forward is fraught with obstacles. While the Act preamble speaks positively to the "commitments by Canada to working in partnership, achieving reconciliation" with Indigenous Peoples, the lack of commitment of funding beyond the development of coordination agreements is concerning (Metallic et al. 2019) The inclusion of provincial and territorial governments means that Indigenous communities must not only negotiate with both federal and provincial powers, but they also do so in light of these governments having a poor track record of ensuring Indigenous Peoples, including young people in their care, have access to adequate resources (Metallic et al. 2019).

In the meantime, little has changed for Indigenous people. They continue to live with the legacy and trauma of colonial policies including loss of territories, forced removal onto reserves, residential schools, Sixties Scoop, Millennium Scoop, Indian hospitals and the disruption of culture, traditional governance and consensual decision-making, as well as cultural traditions and languages. Although numerous Indigenous communities have worked within their cultural communities to incorporate Indigenous cultural approaches, the vast majority still do so under the mandate of mainstream child welfare policies. In essence, this means that historical trauma, ongoing poverty and racism continue to impact families resulting in a pervasive overrepresentation of Indigenous children and youth in the care of child welfare (Quinn et al. 2022). To date, the TRC's second call for action for "governments to publish annual reports on the number of First Nations, Métis and Inuit children in care, the reasons for apprehension, the amount spent on services and the effectiveness of interventions" has yet to be realized (Quinn et al. 2022).

A WAY FORWARD

As we wait with anticipation for Indigenous communities to apply the Act to develop and begin implementing child welfare policies and practices based on their cultural traditions, it is important to continue to develop a critical awareness of the insidious ways in which assimilative policies and practices have and continue to result in the overrepresentation of Indigenous children and youth in child welfare. While we have a strong focus on supporting Indigenous rights and self-determination, along with addressing anti-racism and equity within and beyond the child welfare system, it is just as important to apply an anti-racist lens to critically investigate the impact of child welfare involvement on all BIPOC children and youth. The decolonial and anti-racist lens in this book recognizes these ongoing struggles for Indigenous Peoples, while acknowledging the struggles of other communities for whom decolonial and anti-racist approaches are paramount to child well-being and security.

CHAPTER SUMMARIES

The focus of Chapter 2, "Indigenous children in the centre," is on the foregrounding and centring of Indigenous and decolonizing approaches to anti-oppressive social work. In applying an Indigenous lens, Qwul'sih'yah'maht (Robina Thomas) and Kundoqk (Jacquie Green) describe an anti-oppressive approach in terms of "anti-oppressive living" and a Way of Life. The chapter goes on to use the Medicine Wheel teachings to demonstrate how sacred traditional teachings support a way forward to decolonial child welfare.

Chapter 3, "The long and twisted road to child welfare," by Osowa Askiy Iskwew (Gwendolyn Gosek) relates the story of Minnie (Halkett) Paul, a Cree-Dene woman, who journeyed through Canada's systemic colonial barriers to earn her nursing degree from the University of Saskatchewan in 1926, only to lose her children to child welfare. Her story goes on to demonstrate how two policies in the Indian Act influenced this traumatic outcome, namely her experience in residential school and the loss of her Indian Status as a result of graduating with a university degree.

Chapter 4, "Child welfare assessment, documentation and recordkeeping," focuses on how current child welfare approaches and procedures require transformation because they remain embedded in colonial logics. Michele Fairbairn traces how the historical formation of contemporary settler-colonial Canada and child welfare processes involved responding to children's welfare as an economic enterprise that maintains the conditions producing colonial childhoods. Fairbairn also outlines how Indigenous communities are leading the way in decolonial, anti-racist and equitable transformation in child welfare.

Chapter 5, "Walking together with Indigenous youth in care," speaks to challenges and benefits experienced by Indigenous youth in the child welfare system in the context of the Aboriginal Youth in Transition (AYIT) program at Niijkiwendidaa Anishnaabekwewag Services Circle in Ontario. Nancy Stevens and Ziigwanbinesii (Rachel Charles) speak to both the challenges faced by youth in care and the importance of ensuring the shelters meet not only their basic needs, but they also demonstrate the value of connecting them to their cultures and communities in meaningful ways.

In Chapter 6, "Four-level model of consciousness with family group conferences as a wise practice for awareness of colonization and decolonialization," Don Robinson weaves personal life experience and theory to make holistic connections between community and families involved in child welfare. The author presents a four-level model to demonstrate both the four levels of colonization and four levels of wellness and demonstrates how it applies to family group conferencing.

Chapter 7, "Recentering Métis kinship care," challenges what is described as the largely appropriated, simplistic kinship care practices currently defined through provincially legislated models. Julie Mann-Johnson and Angie Tucker argue for an acknowledgement and return to the Cree/Michef axiological teaching known as wahkohtowin that recentres and recalibrates current colonialized processes. Through exploring traditional kinship care, the discussion centres Métis ontologies that provide authentic connections and identity formation for children and families in the child welfare system.

Chapter 8, "Decolonizing prevention," reports on data and stories gathered during longitudinal ethnographic research within and on the margins of Indigenous-led family service agencies on lək̓ʷəŋən Territory. The research findings reported in this chapter illustrate that rather than prevention programs offering neutral support sites, prevention programs are also places where Indigenous participants are disciplined as colonial subjects. In reflecting on the findings, Erika Finestone offers liberatory practices that have the potential to disrupt the colonial violence inherent in state-funded institutions.

Chapter 9, "Your best can only take you to where the good is," focuses on the necessity for child welfare workers to comprehend how a prevailing racist and dangerous social context can shape protective and parental responses of Black parents. Paul Banahene Adjei provides quotes from stories shared by Black parents who have become the focus of child welfare inquiries that have not considered the impact of racism on parental responses. Rather than condemn parents, Adjei explains how workers need to engage with and support parents who are desperate to protect their children from racist and potentially lethal harm.

Chapter 10, "Deportation is double punishment," reveals the consequences of the child welfare system's failure to develop legal or policy mechanisms that protect the rights of children of asylum seekers. Through relaying stories shared by young people from care with precarious citizenship status, Mandeep Kaur Mucina, Jessica Pratezina and Amira Abdel-Malek demonstrate how young people can be subjected to deportation when they are no longer eligible for child welfare services. Mucina, Pratezina and Abdel-Malek outline how child welfare practice obligations include preparing young people for adult transition by protecting them after leaving care from ostracizing state policies.

Chapter 11, "Decolonial trauma-informed school-based practice," centres the voices of a group of Syrian refugee newcomer parents who are concerned for their children within school settings. Mehmoona Moosa-Mitha sets parental fears against the backdrop of colonialism and Islamophobia, further explaining how curriculum content and school policies conflict with parental beliefs and their teachings. Moosa-Mitha demonstrates how child welfare workers in school settings can support parents and resist Islamophobia.

In Chapter 12, "Taking children's resistance even more seriously," Kineweskwêw (Cathy Richardson) and Shelly Dean describe children as spirited, responding agents and not as passive recipients in their resistance to violence and responsiveness to justice and fairness. The chapter speaks to concepts related to understanding children's social reactions in violent interactions, how they orient towards safety and dignity and how the roles and relationship of others can contribute to their well-being.

In Chapter 13, "Indigenous social workers fighting inequality within the child welfare system," Wa Cheew Wapaguunew Iskew (Carolyn Peacock) and Brooke Lightning-Montour speak to the challenges that Indigenous social workers continue to experience as they strive to overcome centuries of colonized institutions and belief systems. They delve into the concepts of attachment theory and cultural connections and conclude with suggestions for strengthening social work practice and ways to work respectfully in community.

The authors who have come together to contribute to this edition of *Walking This Path Together*, bring their work, life and research insights and expertise to support our ongoing learning journey through decolonization and anti-racism. Together with the chapter authors, we are concerned about how child welfare policies and the subsequent practice are enacted. Child welfare is situated within a range of ongoing settler-colonial and racist social conditions and practices shaped by legal, policy and practice responses that ordinarily disregard how those conditions produce inequities. Our vision is to reveal these unjust conditions so that workers can contribute to the ongoing transformation of practice with those who become involved with child protection systems, and in related areas affecting the well-being and security of young people, their families and communities. While the authors come from different walks in life, they demonstrate a sincere desire to change the serious shortcomings in child welfare.

Indigenous Knowledge Keepers remind us that in order to make good decisions and live a good life in supporting people, we must go inward and travel that path from our minds to our hearts. For people raised and schooled in a mainstream perspective in which the concept of professionalism is highly regarded, working from the heart may feel uncomfortable until one comes to realize that what we are doing is often lifesaving and we are working alongside children and families who deserve to feel valued and respected. This transformative vision has been the path that we are walking.

REFERENCES

Ball, Jessica, and Annika Benoit-Jansson. 2023. "Promoting Cultural Connectedness through Indigenous-led Child and Family Services: A Critical Review with a Focus on Canada." *First Peoples Child & Family Review* 18, 1.

BC Ombudsman. 1999 (April). *Writing The Wrong: The Confinement of the Sons of Freedom Doukhobor children.* (Public report no. 38 to the Legislative Assembly of British Columbia).

Blackstock, Cindy, Terri Libesman, Jennifer King, Brittany Mathews, and Wendy Hermeston. 2023. "Decolonizing First Peoples Child Welfare." In *The Routledge International Handbook on Decolonizing Justice*, edited by Chris Cunneen, Antje Deckert, Amanda Porter, Juan Tauri, and Robert Webb. Milton: Taylor & Francis Group.

Blaney, R. 2021. "Insights into Loyalty from Living in Two Worlds." In *Religious Soft Diplomacy and the United Nations: Religious Engagement as Loyal Opposition*, edited by Sherrie M. Steiner and James T Christie. Lexington Books.

Boatswain-Kyte, A., Tonino Esposito, Nico Trocmé, and Alicia Boatswain-Kyte. 2020. "A Longitudinal Jurisdictional Study of Black Children Reported to Child Protection Services in Quebec, Canada." *Children and Youth Services Review* 116, 105219.

Boucher, Ellen. 2014. *Empire's Children: Child Emigration, Welfare, and the Decline of the British World 1869–1967.* Cambridge: Cambridge University Press.

Cane, Tam Chipawe, and Prospera Tedam. 2023. "'We Didn't Learn Enough about Racism and Anti-racist Practice': Newly Qualified Social Workers' Challenge in Wrestling Racism." *Social Work Education* 42, 8.

Cénat, Jude Mary, Pari-Gol Noorishad, Moshirian Farahi, Mahdi Seyed Mohammad, Wina Paul Darius, and Robert J. Flynn. 2023. "Reasons for Admission to Service and Overrepresentation of Black Youth in the Child Welfare System in Ontario, Canada: Does Race Matter?" *Child Abuse & Neglect* 140, 106157.

Cénat, Jude Mary, Pari-Gol Noorishad, Konrad Czechowski, Sara-Emilie McIntee, and Joana N. Mukunzi. 2020. "Racial Disparities in Child Welfare in Ontario (Canada) and Training on Ethnocultural Diversity: An Innovative Mixed-Methods Study." *Child Abuse & Neglect* 108, 104659.

Chen, Xiaobei. 2005. *Tending the Gardens of Citizenship: Child Saving in Toronto, 1880s-1920s*. Toronto: University of Toronto Press.

Corbett, Gail H. 2002. *Nation Builders: Barnardo Children in Canada*. Toronto: Dundurn Press.

Crown-Indigenous Relations and Northern Affairs Canada. 2024. "How the Government of Canada is responding to the Truth and Reconciliation Commission's Calls to Action 1 to 5." https://www.rcaanc-cirnac.gc.ca/eng/1524494530110/1557511412801.

Djuric, Mickey. 2021. "How Cowessess First Nation's Historic Child Welfare Agreement with Canada and Saskatchewan Works: Cowessess First Nation will have Complete Decision-making Power Over its Children and Youth." *CBC Online News*, July 9, 2021. cbc.ca/news/canada/saskatchewan/how-cowessess-first-nation-child-welfare-agreement-works-1.6095470

Dudgeon, Pat, Abigail Bray, and Roz Walker. 2023. "Mitigating the Impacts of Racism on Indigenous Wellbeing through Human Rights, Legislative and Health Policy Reform." *The Medical Journal of Australia* 218, 5.

Dunae, Patrick A. 2005. "Gender, Generations and Social Class: The Fairbridge Society and British Child Migration to Canada, 1930-1960." In *Child and Family Welfare in British Columbia: A History*, edited by Christopher Walmsley and Diane Purvey. Calgary: Detselig Enterprises.

Esposito, Tonino, Johanna Caldwell, Martin Chabot, Sonia Hélie, and Nico Trocmé. 2023. "What if Universal Services Don't Have a Universal Impact? A Spatial Equity Perspective on the Prevalence of Child Protection Intervention in a Canadian Province." *Revue Française Des Affaires Sociales*, 3.

Fallon, Barbara, Rachael Lefebvre, Nico Trocmé, Kenn Richard, Sonia Hélie, Monty H. Montgomery, and Marlyn Bennett et al. 2021. "Denouncing the Continued Overrepresentation of First Nations Children in Canadian Child Welfare: Findings from the First Nations/Canadian Incidence Study of Reported Child Abuse and Neglect-2019." Ontario: Assembly of First Nations.

Fallon, Barbara, John D. Fluke, Martin Chabot, Cindy Blackstock, Vanda Sinha, Kate Allan, and Bruce MacLaurin. 2020. "Exploring Alternate Explanations for Agency-Level Effects in Placement Decisions Regarding Aboriginal Children." In *Decision-Making and Judgment in Child Welfare and Protection: Theory, Research, and Practice*, edited by John D. Fluke, Mónica López López, Rami Benbenishty, Erik J. Knorth, and Donald J. Baumann. New York: Oxford University Press.

First Nations Child and Family Caring Society (FNCFCS). 2023 (May). *Jordan's Principle*. Information Sheet.

First Nations Child and Family Caring Society of Canada. 2016. *Victory for First Nations Children Canadian Human Rights Tribunal Finds Discrimination Against First Nations Children Living On-Reserve*. Information Sheet. https://fncaringsociety.com/sites/default/files/Information%20Sheet%20re%20CHRT%20Decision.pdf.

Gates, T. G., B. Bennett, and D. Baines. 2023. "Strengthening Critical Allyship in Social Work Education: Opportunities in the Context of #BlackLivesMatter and COVID-19." *Social Work Education* 42, 3.

Gölz, Annalee. 1993. "Family Matters: The Canadian Family and the State in the Postwar Period." *Left History: An Interdisciplinary Journal of Historical Inquiry and Debate* 1, 2.

Government of Alberta. 2021. "Child Intervention Statistics: Quarterly Statistics." open.alberta.ca/publications/child-intervention-information-and-statistics-summary-quarter-update.

Government of Canada. n.d. "Indigenous Peoples and Communities." rcaanc-cirnac.gc.ca/eng/1100100013785/1529102490303.

——— Government of Canada. n.d. "Indigenous Peoples in Alberta." sac-isc.gc.ca/eng/1647614714525/1647614742912.

——— Government of Canada. n.d. *An Act respecting First Nations, Inuit and Métis children, youth and families (S.C. 2019, c. 24)*. laws.justice.gc.ca/eng/acts/F-11.73/index.html.

Government of Manitoba. 2018. *Transforming Child Welfare Legislation in Manitoba: Opportunities to improve outcomes for Children and youth. Report of the legislative Review Committee*.

Indigenous Services Canada. 2020. "Reducing the Number of Indigenous Children in Care." First Nations Child and Family Services. sac-isc.gc.ca/eng/1541187352297/1541187392851.

Johnson, Morgan Brie. 2021. "Settler Colonial Structures of Domestication: British Home Children in Canada." *Genealogy* 5, 3.

Johnston, Patrick. 1983. *Native Children and the Child Welfare System*. Toronto: James Lorimer & Company.

Kemble, Tibetha. 2021. "I Want to Tell You a Story." *Aboriginal Policy Studies* 9, 2.

King, Bryn, Henry Parada, Barbara Fallon, Veronica Escobar Olivo, Laura M. Best, and Joanne Filippelli. 2024. "Latin American children in Ontario child welfare: An examination of investigation disparities." *Children and Youth Services Review* 156.

Landertinger, Laura. 2016. "'Hell Holes': Unmapping Settler Colonial Geographies and Child Welfare in Manitoba." *Borderlands* 15, 1.

Lefebvre, Rachael, Barbara Fallon, John Fluke, Nico Trocmé, Tara Black, Tonino Esposito, and David W. Rothwell. 2024. "Distinguishing Profiles of Adversity among Child Protection Investigations in Ontario, Canada: A Latent Class Analysis." *Child Protection and Practice* 1, 100022.

Lynch, Brittany. 2024. "Moving from Dialogue to Demonstration: Assessing Anti-racist Practice in Social Work Education Utilizing Simulation." *Social Work Education* 43, 2.

Metallic, Naiomi, Hadley Friedland, Aimée Craft, Jeffery Hewitt, and Sarah Morales. 2019. *An Act respecting First nations, Inuit and Métis children, youth and families: Does Bill C-92 Make the Grade?* Yellowhead Institute.

Murray-Lichtman, Andrea, Adriana Aldana, Elana Izaksonas, Tauchiana Williams, Mitra Naseh, Anne C. Deepak, Michele A. Rountree. 2023. "Dual Pandemics Awaken Urgent Call to Advance Anti-racism Education in Social Work: Pedagogical Illustrations." *Journal of Ethnic & Cultural Diversity in Social Work*, 31.

Quinn, Ashley, Barbara Fallon, Nicolette Joh-Carnella, and Marie Saint-Girons. 2022. "The Overrepresentation of First Nations Children in the Ontario Child Welfare System: A Call for Systemic Change." *Children and Youth Services Review* 139, 106558.

Rooke, Patricia T., and Rodolph Leslie Schnell. 1987. *No Bleeding Heart: Charlotte Whitton: A Feminist on the Right*. Vancouver: University of British Columbia Press.

Roxburgh, Shelagh, and Megan Sinclair. 2024. "Colonial Constructions: Systemic Racism in Child Welfare Practice." *Journal of Social Work* 24, 1.

Sangster, Joan. 2002. "Creating Social and Moral Citizens: Defining and Treating Delinquent Boys and Girls in English Canada, 1920-65." In *Contesting Canadian Citizenship: Historical Readings*, edited by Robert Adamoski, Dorothy Chunn, and Robert Menzies. Peterborough: Broadview Press.

Senate of Canada. 2018. *The Shame is Ours: Forced Adoptions of the Babies of Unmarried Mothers in Post-war Canada.*

Statistics Canada. 2021. "Focus on Geography Series – Manitoba – Indigenous Peoples." www12.statcan.gc.ca/census-recensement/2021/as-sa/fogs-spg/Page.cfm?lang=E&topic=8&dguid=2021S0503602.

Thomson, Gerald. 2024. ""We Are Making Good under the Honor System": The Social Rehabilitation of Juvenile Males through Militarism, Moral Reform, and Enforced Work Routines at the British Columbia Boy's Industrial School, 1919–1934." *The Journal of the History of Childhood and Youth* 17, 1.

Trocmé, Nico, Barbara Fallon, Vandna Sinha, Melissa Van Wert, Anna Kozlowski, and Bruce MacLaurin. 2013. "Differentiating between Child Protection and Family Support in the Canadian Child Welfare System's Response to Intimate Partner Violence, Corporal Punishment, and Child Neglect." *International Journal of Psychology* 48, 2.

Tyler, Stephanie, Sheliza Ladhani, Mica Pabia, and Mairi McDermott. 2024. "Animating Pedagogies of Discomfort and Affect for Anti-racism and Decolonizing Aims in Social Work Education." *Teaching in Higher Education* 29, 5.

UNICEF. 2023. *UNICEF Report Card 18.* unicef.ca/en/unicef-report-card-18

Chapter 2

INDIGENOUS CHILDREN IN THE CENTRE

Indigenous Perspectives on Anti-Oppressive Child Welfare Practice

by Qwul'sih'yah'maht (Robina Thomas) and Kundoqk (Jacquie Green)

CHAPTER FOCUS

This chapter focuses on and engages in foregrounding and centring Indigenous-centred and decolonizing approaches to anti-oppressive practice. As Indigenous scholars who teach and analyze anti-oppressive theories, knowledge and praxis, we illustrate one way that anti-oppressive practice can take up an Indigenizing lens: holding at its core what we call "anti-oppressive living," which we believe is A Way of Life. We capitalize A Way of Life to demonstrate the significance of Indigenous relationships to all living things as A Way of Life.

Anti-oppressive living is rooted and reflected in our sacred and traditional teachings. We utilize the teachings of the Medicine Wheel to illustrate our examination of anti-oppressive practice within the paradigm of child welfare. Although there have been significant changes to legislation and policies in child welfare, colonial attitudes continue to manifest in the provision of child welfare services. Child welfare attitudes and beliefs must shift; hence, the importance of grounding anti-oppressive practice in child welfare through an Indigenizing lens and decolonizing approaches. The four directions of the Medicine Wheel demonstrate how we can dismantle colonial practices in child welfare.

Our hope is to join with and contribute to the Truth and Reconciliation Commission's (TRC) Calls to Action, in particular, Call 1 (iii) and (iv) (2015, 139–40).[1] We also join with and contribute to the National Inquiry into Missing and Murdered Indigenous Women and Girls (NIMMIWG) Calls for Justice, particularly Call for Justice Number 12 – Calls for Social Workers and those Implicated in Child Welfare (National Inquiry into Missing and Murdered Indigenous Women and Girls 2019, 23–25).

QUESTIONS ADDRESSED IN THIS CHAPTER

1. The authors speak to aspects of anti-oppressive practice within the four directions of the Medicine Wheel. What are ways these aspects could be adapted to your practice wherever you are?
2. The authors express anti-oppressive practice with an Indigenous frame as anti-oppressive living. What does anti-oppressive living mean for you? What do Indigenous traditional teachings look like for you in practice?

DISCRIMINATION AND DISPROPORTIONALITY

A study conducted in 2019 found that "First Nations children (aged 0–15 years) in Canada were 3.6 times as likely to be the subject of a child maltreatment-related investigation compared to non-Indigenous children" (Fallon et al. 2021, 32). First Nations children under one year of age were 5.3 times more likely to be investigated than non-Indigenous children of that age (Fallon et al. 2021, 33). The TRC (2015, 139) writes that the rate of investigations for First Nations children was 4.2 times higher than for non-Indigenous children. Overall, Indigenous children under the age of fourteen constitute 7.7 percent of the population, yet 53.8 percent of children in foster care are Indigenous children (Vanier Institute of the Family 2024). In 2021–22 in British Columbia, the rate of children and youth in care was 35.8 per thousand Indigenous children whereas for non-Indigenous children and youth in care, the rate was 2.0 per thousand children (Ministry of Children and Family Development 2022). This is appalling for Indigenous children. It is even more problematic when we consider that encounters with the child welfare system in British Columbia do not necessarily ensure an improved quality of life for these children, nor does it seem likely that they will experience best child welfare practices.

Alongside these aspects of Indigenous children and families and child welfare agencies, the First Nations Child and Family Caring Society of Canada also filed a complaint with the Canadian Human Rights Commission against Aboriginal and Northern Development Canada. This was due to the woefully inadequate funding provided by the department for on-reserve Indigenous child and family services, thereby denying First Nations children "essential services after a significant and detrimental delay causing real harm to those children and their parents or grandparents caring for them" (*First Nations Child and Family Caring Society of Canada v. Attorney General of Canada,* 2019: 71, para. 226). Indeed, in their decision, the Canadian Human Rights Commission (2019: 73: para 231) held the Government of Canada liable for systemic discrimination determining that Canada's conduct was "devoid of caution with little to no regard to the consequences of its behavior towards First Nations children and their families...Canada was aware of the discrimination and some of its serious consequences."

Other questions arise from these crises in policy and care:

- What are the essential components of best practices with Indigenous children and families?
- What are the methods for social workers to continue to incorporate historical analysis into praxis?
- How would we know if someone was centring living and practising anti-oppressively and with a decolonizing approach?

Anti-Oppressive Practice (AOP)

Anti-oppressive practice (AOP) is an important way to address these disproportionalities. Key elements of AOP include, but are not limited to:

- AOP is necessarily complex and an uncomfortable process because as social workers, we enter and intervene in people's lives. In most cases, the children and families will not know us, but we require them to share intimate aspects of their lives and personal history. How we take up their stories is critical, particularly when we understand how vulnerable their intimate stories and histories make them and how this vulnerability is shaped by the asymmetrical power relationships between social workers and our work with families. We must learn to respect and honour those stories, attending to power differences while holding family stories with care and gentleness, thereby not leaving children and families more damaged than before they become involved with the child welfare system.
- AOP, at its core, must include an analysis of power and strive to work across, throughout and within our differences.
- An underlying premise of AOP is that we critically examine how we know what we know and that we explore our assumptions not only about helping, but also our knowledge about all living things from an Indigenous-centred space. AOP invites us to connect our subjective lived experiences to our diverse knowledges — that is, what we know may be connected to who we are and how we see and experience the world.

Using these key elements, we discuss our collective perspectives of anti-oppressive practice. We focus on practice with Indigenous children and families — as we know they are our future. Many people are seeking a definition of anti-oppressive practice that centres Indigeneity and decolonizing approaches. For us, AOP focused through a decolonizing and Indigenizing frame is A Way of Life, one that values the sacred and traditional teachings of varying Indigenous cultures. We will demonstrate these values through the teachings of the Medicine Wheel to frame and discuss our AOP perspectives and practices.

We begin by situating our understanding of decolonizing and decolonization. We connect with the "decolonizing approach" used in the Final Report of the National Inquiry into Missing and Murdered Indigenous Women and Girls (2019, 2), particularly in its emphasis of sovereignty and self-determination:

> [A decolonizing] approach is a way of doing things differently; it challenges the colonial influence under which we live by making space for Indigenous perspectives that are often cast aside. It involves recognizing inherent rights through the principle that Indigenous Peoples have the right to govern themselves in relation to matters that are internal to their communities; integral to their unique cultures, identities, traditions, languages, and institutions; and with respect to their special relationship to the land. Our approach honours and respects Indigenous values, philosophies, and knowledge systems. It is a strength-based approach, focusing on the resilience and expertise of individuals and communities themselves.

THE MEDICINE WHEEL

The Medicine Wheel is an ancient teaching tool. It has no beginning and no end and teaches us that all things are interrelated. The Wheel is comprised of quadrants that represent all living things. The Medicine Wheel has many different teachings and principles, but our teachings come from our Anishinaabe friend and mentor Gale Cyr, from the east of Turtle Island (Quebec, Canada).

It is critical to remember that each quadrant of the Wheel is interrelated. No quadrant is valued more than any other quadrant: all aspects of our being and place are of equal importance and are positioned in balance and harmony with one another. For example, as human beings, we are composed of spiritual, emotional, physical and mental aspects, collectively and connectively. These four elements make us who we are. In other words, our subjective selves are composed of these four components.

Another important teaching of the Medicine Wheel is that once you have journeyed around the Wheel, you have the opportunity to learn from your experiences; and as you journey around the Wheel again, this time you learn from your mistakes and adjust your practice accordingly. The Wheel teaches us to be conscious of our previous journey and reflect on what we have learned, so that our next journey can be different and more effective. Our teaching tells us that we begin in the eastern direction and working clockwise around the Wheel, we circle and pay attention to the four aspects of all human beings — the spiritual, emotional,

Figure 2.1. Medicine Wheel

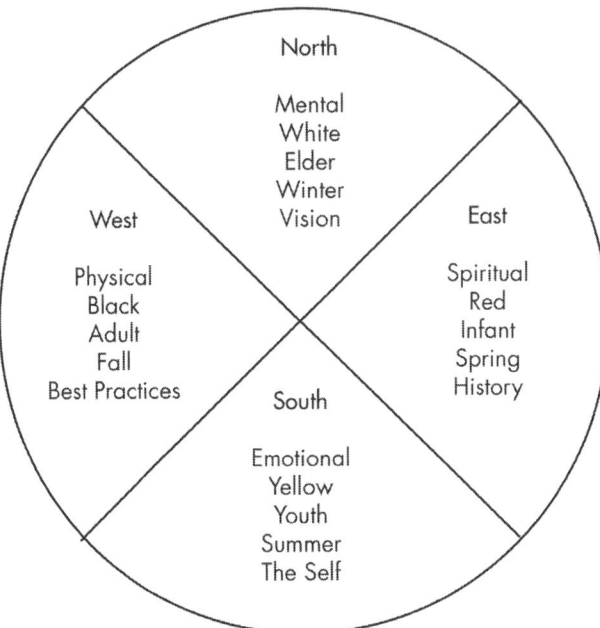

physical and mental (Bopp et al. 1989, 12; Saulis 2003, 294). The Wheel also has four colours that represent all races of Mother Earth: red, yellow, black and white. It also provides us the four stages of the life cycle — infant, youth, adult and Elder — as well as the four seasons: spring, summer, fall and winter (Hart 2002, 40). Each of these representations has particular meanings and interpretations for both life and anti-oppressive practice with Indigenous children and families.

We have been taught to always begin in the East because this is the direction of spirituality. It holds the colour red, the life stage of the infant, the season of springtime, and represents and invites the beginning of all things. This is the direction of daybreak and sunrise. As AOP social workers, we begin in the eastern direction to examine the history of colonization and its relationship to Indigenous child welfare in Canada. It is vital to understand this history to trace and understand the emergence and strategies of Indigenous child welfare. This history is critical if we are to work successfully with Indigenous children and families.

The South is the direction of our emotional being, holds the colour yellow and the life stage of youth. This is the direction of summer, a time filled with lots of activity. For youth, this is a time in their life where they are constantly active and learning much that helps them with their growth. The southern direction is also the place where we recognize and honour teachings of our Elders and spiritual leaders. In this direction, we look at the self and come to ask the question and seek answers to "how we know what we know." Accordingly, we challenge social workers to examine their socialization, their place in the world, to "unlearn and learn" some of the ways they may see the world.

In the West, we have the direction of our physical being, the colour black, the life stage of the adult and the fall/autumn season. This is the direction we look towards when we do our work and our practice. For example, the western direction is where social workers share their knowledge and work within our communities to help strengthen our children and families. In this direction, we focus on the particular skills that AOP requires. We assert that a historical analysis of Indigenous people in Canada is a necessary skill for AOP. We also assert that critical self-examination is another necessary skill. This skill is vital for anti-oppressive practice.

The North is the direction of our mental being, and holds the color white, the life stage of an Elder, and wintertime. When we reach the North, we are reminded to reflect on our work. This is the time to focus on what changes we need to make to our lives, a time to rethink and re-evaluate our actions and behaviours. For social work practice in Indigenous communities, this is the direction of vision. This is the time to dream. We dream that none of our children are in state care and that there is no child welfare system. We dream of a time when our language, culture, and traditions are revived and become a part of our day-to-day lives.

HISTORY OF INDIGENOUS CHILD WELFARE IN CANADA

Given that "colonialism has racism as its ideological rationale," an analysis of the impact of colonization on the lives of Indigenous people in Canada is absolutely necessary if social workers are to practise in an anti-oppressive way (Maracle 1996, 89). Alyssa Couchie (2023, 411) further reminds us, "Only by understanding current child welfare challenges facing Indigenous communities as interwoven with longstanding anti-Indigenous atrocity processes [such as the Indian Residential School System] can we understand what is at stake for affected communities."

However, those of us who live the ongoing assault of colonialism know that it is a much stronger entity than these words reflect. In fact, it is life altering for Indigenous people of Canada and for colonized peoples worldwide. The breadth and depth of colonialism in all of its variegated processes, "includ(ing) geographical incursion, social cultural dislocation, the establishment of external political control and economic dispossession, the provision of low-level social services, and finally the creation of ideological formulations around race and skin colour" are continually shaping and reshaping the quality of Indigenous life and living (Kelm cited in Nelson 2012, 4). Addressing cultural genocide, the TRC Report states, "for over a century, the central goals of Canada's Aboriginal policy were to eliminate Aboriginal governments; ignore Aboriginal rights; terminate the Treaties; and, through a process of assimilation, cause Aboriginal peoples to cease to exist as distinct legal, social, cultural, religious, and racial entities in Canada" (TRC 2015, 1). These definitions enable us to see the complete depth and breadth of control over Indigenous people's lives, livelihood, and Way of Life.

Colonization is about taking control of lives, lands, resources and people at the cost of Indigenous Peoples' lives and livelihood and is an effort to make "taken" lands productive for economic rewards (Tuhiwai Smith 2002, 20–22). In other words, capitalism and colonialism have an intimate and necessary relationship. This link between the subjugation of Indigenous Peoples and capitalism is demonstrated by Brendan Hokowhitu (2021, 134) who states, "one of the pathologies of colonisation was to mark Indigenous peoples as not fully human and the lands they lived upon as unproductive and, thus, empty. These underpinning justifications of colonialism rationalised the usurpation of lands and resources and the killing of Indigenous peoples."

In Canada, the federal government went to great lengths to ensure that capitalism flourished. The government developed extensive legislation that guaranteed that Indigenous people did not get in the way of progress (i.e., capitalism) (Tully 2000, 38). In order to subjugate and oppress Indigenous people, the Canadian settler-state required the creation and maintenance of violence (Hodge 1990, 93). This violence aimed to destroy the mind, body, spirit and humanity of our peoples. Colonial violence was enacted in various ways including the implementation of the Indian Act, in its various manifestations; biological and germ warfare; theft of cultures, knowledges, traditions, languages and identity; residential school policy; child welfare policies; and various treaty processes. The Indian Act is an enforced colonialist, paternalistic legislation that has governed and classified every aspect of the lives of Indigenous Peoples in Canada for well over a hundred years. This broad, sweeping act continues to govern, control, classify, regulate, dictate and define our identity, our movements and the economic, social and political lives of our people today (Lawrence 2003, 4).

While capitalist expansion was critical to colonial enterprise, colonialists were equally interested in the moral and cultural lives of Indigenous people (Tuhiwai Smith 2002, 25–26). The intent of the Indian Residential School System (IRS) was, at its foundation, to assimilate Indigenous Peoples. In his support for the IRS System Prime Minister Sir John A. Macdonald stated in the House of Commons: "Indian children should be withdrawn as much as possible from the parental influence, and the only way to do that would be to put them in central training industrial schools where they will acquire the habits and modes of thought of white men" (TRC 2015, 2). In 1920, Duncan Campbell Scott, who was the deputy superintendent general of the Department of Indian Affairs from 1913 to 1932, made this clear, when he said in 1920, "our object is to continue until there is not a single Indian in Canada that has not been absorbed into the body politic" (TRC, 3).

The TRC Report directly attributes the IRS System as the catalyst for the breakdown between Indigenous children and families:

> In establishing residential schools, the Canadian government essentially declared Aboriginal people to be unfit parents. Aboriginal parents were labelled as being indifferent to the future of their children – a judgment contradicted by the fact that parents often kept their children out of schools because they saw those schools, quite accurately, as dangerous and harsh institutions that sought to raise their children in alien ways. (TRC 2015, 4)

The prohibition on speaking their language, the separation of brothers and sisters, the stripping of their Indigenous names and clothing and the cutting of their sacred braids severed so many ties the children had with their families, kin and communities.

Our children were legislated out of their homes, their families and their communities to be Christianized and civilized (AHF 2003, 27). In these isolated and foreign places, Indigenous children were forced to speak a language they did not know, pray to a god they knew nothing of and be educated in a way that was Eurocentric, alien and purposeless for them. These Indian Act policies degraded the Indigenous people of Canada and positioned them in the lowest strata of society (AHF 2003, 43–44). The education received in those institutions was minimal at best (AHF 2003, 29). The children were, in fact, being trained to become the working class (AHF 2003, 34) — the labourers, housekeepers and maids for the emerging white nation. Subjugation of our people was done in a very deliberate, thoughtful and planned way.

In 1887 the Indian Act was amended to ban Potlatches and Sundances. Traditional ceremonies were, and still are, our traditional governance systems. For example, in the Thi'lelum (Big House) we pass on names, chieftainships, songs, dances and masks; perform marriages; support our families (for example, through funerals); and redistribute our wealth through giveaways. For Indigenous people, ceremonies performed in these sacred places represent both our administrative and governance purposes — in effect, these ceremonies served functions similar to Western structures such as the Department of Vital Statistics and Parliament. By destroying our community governance, the Canadian state attempted to eradicate our communal identity and the status of our nations. Child welfare workers must consider the horrific history of Indigenous communities, policies that are violent, and shift their practice to provide families with a vision of hope.

ANTI-OPPRESSIVE PRACTICE

In many Indigenous languages, there is no word that translates to "anti-oppressive practice." However, there are phrases in our various languages that discuss "A Way of Life." For example, phrases and/or terms such as snuw'uy'u, a Hul'qumi'num Mustimuhw term, roughly translates into our "teachings" — our ways of knowing and being; our governing structures; our cultural traditions; our language; our sacred bathing holes; hunting, fishing and gathering rights; our family; our community; our relationship with Mother Earth and Father Sky. Through banning the Potlatch and other traditional ceremonies, the government specifically and purposefully attacked and attempted to destroy Our Way of Life (Lawrence 2002, 23–24). Indigenous scholar Lee Maracle (1996, 93) captures the spectrum of these ruptures:

> The aims of the colonizer are to break up communities and families, and to destroy the sense of nationhood and the spirit of co-operation among the colonized. A sense of powerlessness is the legacy handed down to the colonized people. Loss of power — the negation of choice, as well as legal and cultural victimization — is the hoped-for result.

Through the development of racist policies that defined "Indians" as inferior, the Canadian state directly attacked Our Way of Life, Our Way of Being (Simpson 2000, 118). Many of our people, both young and old, remember the pain and devastation of the days when the Potlatch and other ceremonies were banned and residential schools were opened.

The state also used education to push forward Eurocentric beliefs. Maracle (1996, 89) believes, "the appropriation of knowledge, its distortion, and in some cases, its destruction, was vital to the colonial process." Education had an assimilationist agenda requiring our people to assume the cultural, social and political belief systems of the colonizer as part of the "civilizing mission" that was directed towards Indigenous Peoples (AHF 2003, 42; Castellano et al. 2000, 25). The intention of the education process was to undermine the knowledges, traditions and Way of Life of Indigenous people, in keeping with the colonialists' hegemonic beliefs that Indigenous epistemologies were inferior to Eurocentric ones (Tuhiwai Smith 2002, 11). In arguing against day schools, the colonial government expressed concern that students would return home and be "re-exposed to their native culture, however diluted, from which the school is trying to separate them" (TRC 2015, 6).

Targeting our knowledge for destruction and forcing our adoption of Western knowledge systems have had significant psychological impact on our people. As a result of Eurocentric educational indoctrination, Indigenous people began (and/or were forced) to forgo their ways of life to be more like the "superior" others. In a similar vein, bell hooks (1996) discusses how colonization impacted Black communities: She claims that through being taught/socialized Eurocentric biases, Black people began to long for the "rewards" that whites had access to (luxury and comfort). To gain access to these rewards, Blacks began assimilating white values. For many people, it was easier and safer to assimilate white values than fight to have the dominant society accept Our Way of Life. The experience of racism has meant that Indigenous people have internalized racism, domination and colonization.

AOP with Indigenous Peoples requires an intimate knowledge and understanding of the colonial history of Canada. Colonization of the lands, resources, psyches and hearts of Indigenous Peoples was an integral part of colonizing processes. The Indian Tribes of Manitoba remind us of the significance of linking history to the present and future, stating, "to deny the past and to refuse to recognize its implications is to distort the present; to distort the present is to take risks with the future that are blatantly irresponsible" (1971, ii). As social workers, we must understand the impact that Canadian policies and practices have had, and continue to have, on the day-to-day lives of the Indigenous children and families we work alongside. It is critical for social workers to ask themselves: What have the experiences of Indigenous children and families been? Did they, their parents and/or grandparents attend residential schools? Have they been involved in the child welfare system and how might they feel about social workers? What is their history with social work? What are their fears? We must always take these questions into account when we work with Indigenous children and families. We must always situate the present within the context of the past, and continuously query how the families we support come to know what they know. As Maracle (1996, 92) states, "Change must be the basis for education."

SELF

Anti-oppressive practice is not enough to centre an Indigenous praxis; it must also include a centring and praxis of decolonization. We cannot decide when or when not to practice in a good way; it must be about living — anti-oppressive living. Indigenous-centred anti-oppressive social work, in essence, is A Way of Life. The central focus for us in relation to a decolonial and Indigenized AOP framework is the questions of how and who we are, and how we want to be in the world. In other words, how we continually create relations and connections between "a good way" and a Way of Life. We believe that the same is true for anti-oppression work, we must live it. Kathy Absolon (2011, 19) illustrates her practice of decolonization and Indigenization as involving rediscovering and nurturing my Anishinaabe Spirit, healing my Anishinaabe heart, decolonizing my mind and creating a critical action plan in my own life. Decolonization and Indigenizing my life include learning and practising my culture; learning my language; speaking my language; fighting ethnocentrism in education, research and writing; battling institutional racism.

In her book *killing rage: Ending Racism*, bell hooks (1996, 263) discusses Martin Luther King's image of a "'beloved community' where race would be transcended, forgotten, where no one would see skin color." We too dream of a "beloved community" where 100 percent of our children are raised in their communities with our families. How can we as social workers engage with this dream? For sure, it has something to do with how we practice and live, our values and beliefs.

Our beloved community would foster Indigenous-centred, anti-racist and anti-oppressive living. The question, then, becomes: What do we need to do to get there? How do we get to living anti-oppression? Every Indigenous culture and tradition has teachings on how to live a good life. The Hul'qumi'num-speaking people have teachings of kwum kwum skwuluwun, which translates into having a strong mind and spirit. If we work from a place of honouring the teachings of walking with a strong mind and spirit, we honour all living things. Kwum kwum skwuluwun teaches us that all human beings are important, but especially the babies and the old ones — they are closest in spirit to each other. The old ones hold the sacred knowledge, and the babies are sacred gifts; both are to be protected at all times.

bell hooks (1996, 271) says, "To live in anti-racist society we must collectively renew our commitment to a democratic vision of racial justice and equality." To do so is not an easy task. Confronting our own teachings, learnings, complicities, biases and assumptions can often be painful and uncomfortable. The knowledges and histories you learn about in AOP and the movement to support a decolonizing framework requires that we engage with difficult knowledges and teachings. It requires our discomfort. It requires a constant process of learning, reflecting, unlearning and relearning. This is where our movement along and around the Medicine Wheel and its four directions provides the guidance to act on these processes.

Anti-oppressive living means we must be committed to justice and equality in all aspects of our lives and be willing to do something about it. Dr. Cindy Blackstock, executive director of the First Nations Child and Family Caring Society of Canada is a fine example. Every time Cindy speaks, she asks the audience, "Now you know the dismal state of Indigenous child welfare in Canada, what are you going to do about it?" Here, Dr. Blackstock is urging a decolonizing practice that takes seriously the work of sovereignty and self-determination as it pertains to child welfare. She believes that it is not enough to merely recognize that inequalities and injustices exist; we must take action. As social workers, if we are committed to the principles of kwum kwum skwuluwun, we too must do something about the inequalities and injustices that exist.

As social workers, what will you do with what you "now" know? In order to strive for social justice, we must begin this process by asking ourselves how we know what we know. Rarely do we have the opportunity to turn inward, look into our life and critique how we have been socialized and what we have internalized from these experiences. We believe that the best helpers are those that know themselves best. Dominelli et al. (1997, 14) believe "[by] getting rid of the injustice perpetrated by racism we will begin reclaiming our own humanity and establishing egalitarian relationships between Black and White people." If anti-oppression is about living, then reclaiming and politicizing our humanity must be a starting point. Seletze, also known by his English name Delmar Johnnie, believed that healing is lifelong and that every day we can strive to be a better person than we were the day before, and a better person the next day than we were today. Yes, we can all heal and become more fully human. Bopp et al. (1984, 75) in *The Sacred Tree: Reflections on Native American Spirituality* include a code of ethics. The first ethic states:

> Each morning upon rising, and each evening before sleeping, give thanks for the life within you and for all life, for the good things the Creator has given you and others and for the opportunity to grow a little more each day. Consider your thoughts and actions of the past day and seek for the courage and strength to be a better person. Seek for the things that will benefit everyone.

We believe that if helpers thought critically every day about their ways of living, then we would be a step closer towards committing to anti-oppressive living and a step closer to keeping our children in our communities and out of the child welfare system.

Indeed, being committed to decolonization as the lens to AOP requires that we examine our values and beliefs and, importantly, we live our values and beliefs as well. As helpers, we must believe that we are good helpers, or we would not be in social work. However, we need to question our intentions and motivations, and ask ourselves: Are we good helpers? Do we truly value all human beings? Do we value parents who neglect their children? Do we care about the poor and the homeless people? Do we understand and care about those with varying (dis)abilities? Do we value the Two-Spirit, gay, lesbian, bisexual, transgender and queer community? These are tough questions, but they must be examined so our biases can be acknowledged and checked. Exploring our values and beliefs is very difficult, but a commitment to anti-oppressive living requires that we do just this.

The eighth code of ethics from *The Sacred Tree* by Bopp et al. (1984, 80) states: "All the races and tribes in the world are like the different coloured flowers of one meadow. All are beautiful. As Children of the Creator they must all be respected." A commitment to continuously examining our values and beliefs can be instrumental in living anti-oppression, which in turn informs how we will practise social work. We must never forget the Children of the Creator — they are our responsibility to protect and nurture.

PRACTICE

For social work with Indigenous children and families, we believe that Indigenous-centred praxis, which is practice based on knowledge and action, must include an understanding of Indigenous histories. We must also commit ourselves to understanding how these histories manifest in the contemporary moment. Often, we think of state policies like the Indian residential school as something that was specific to Canada's past and in doing so, we fail to recognize the ways in which similar processes are at work with the "Millennium Scoop" that is a term that describes the current situation and the alarming rate in which Indigenous children continue to be brought into the child welfare system through child welfare policies and practices. We also believe that praxis must include a continuous reflection of self. A research study on best practices in First Nations communities identified the importance of knowing self in practice:

> One worker talked about always having to remember where she was from and why she was doing this work. It was the personal commitment to her community that kept her strong and wanting to do social work, but also remembering that she was, at the same time, a social worker and a First Nations person. She always had to remember the historical issues that have impacted our people while at the same time remember our traditional ways. (Green and Thomas 2005, 10)

Critical skills in social work practice require an examination and understanding of our assumptions and potential biases. For example, there are assumptions about the importance of Indigenous people living on or off the reserve system. Non-Indigenous people at times assume that Indigenous people who live on reserve are cultural and traditional. However, the reserve system is in fact a colonial regime set up to isolate our people from dominant society (Simpson 2000, 126). Simultaneously, our children were being systematically removed from our reserves and forced to assimilate into dominant society through residential schools and child welfare policies and practices. The result is that there is a spectrum of culture and tradition that varies from person to person. Some people who live on reserve are traditional and follow the teachings of their culture. Others do not. Those who live in urban settings often gravitate towards and are connected with one another. The point here is, that no matter where Indigenous Peoples live, they/we do make connections and nurture relationships with each other and share our traditional teachings or knowledge. For this reason, much of our work is based in the communities in which we live; our work is closely linked to the issues of our community, and we work diligently to pay attention to what our community members tell us. Fostering these relationships is important for the professional and personal growth of child care practitioners; it indeed informs their practice.

Social workers in Indigenous communities must have a fundamental understanding of colonialism and colonial relations. Research by Green and Thomas (2005, 8) shows that social workers believe that they must all have sound knowledge of the history of Indigenous Peoples and knowledge of the geographical area where they are working. By attending to and understanding our histories and lives, social workers will come to understand that, in contrast to colonial policies, traditional teachings are rooted in understanding our connections to Mother Earth, Father Sky and all living things. We are also taught that we are interconnected and interdependent with all living things, and to seek balance in our relationships with all land and life forms. It is through our ceremonies that we understand our identities and our cultures, no matter where we live: these ceremonies are important to our social, political and economic knowledges. Cajete (2000, 183) notes that it is the intimate relationship that people establish with place, with the environment and with all things, that makes them who they are and gives them life. Thus, skills of reflection and locating our histories are integral to unravelling the assumptions we make about Indigenous Peoples and the lives we lead.

Often, assumptions made about Indigenous Peoples are based on racist stereotypes and attitudes. Sinclair (2004, 53) states that, even in the new millennium, standard education (and practice) for social workers is rooted in the literature, world view, life ways and reality of the dominant, white and mainstream society. What helpers must recognize is that, due to racist policies and practices such as residential schools, many Indigenous Peoples have had to deal with multi- and intergenerational trauma. For many, substance misuse is a means of numbing historical pain. It is critical that helpers come to understand this history to see how we can work together to heal from our past and to confront colonial injustices. Many people fail to see the strengths and resilience of Indigenous Peoples. As practitioners, we need to recognize these strengths in order to give families an opportunity to work through their struggles by sharing their stories and creating their own solutions. As social workers, we must be open to changing our beliefs about what helping consists of and stop seeing it as a process of "fixing clients."

Working with families from a strength-based model requires a commitment to valuing and honouring relationships. Underlying these frames is the practice skill of self-determination – that the solutions come from the people themselves and driven by their understanding of their life worlds. Relationships in our practice can be modelled by looking at our own relationships with our families, our teachings and how we engage with Mother Earth and Father Sky. By understanding how we relate to people, we can then model to families what meaningful relationships could look like. King (1990 as cited in Sinclair 2004, 54) speaks to the importance of relationships:

> "All my relations" is a first reminder of who we are and of our relationship with both our family and our relatives. It also reminds us of the extended relationship we share with all human beings. But the relationships that Native people see go further, the web of kinship extending to the animals, to the birds, to the fish, to the plants, to all the animate and inanimate forms that can be seen or imagined. More than that, "all my relations" is an encouragement for us to accept the responsibilities we have within this universal family by living our lives in a harmonious and moral manner.

In our work, we honour our relationships by inviting Elders and cultural Knowledge Keepers to come to our classes to speak to students. Our Elders can share their histories and their experiences and impart an important and different set of learning to students. Elder stories illustrate to students our interconnections to the past, present and future.

We know and believe that children are the heart of communities, and they must be central to how we look at practice, particularly in the child welfare system. Because children are gifts from our Creator, they must be at the centre of love and nurturing from a circle of extended family and community members (Cherrington 2000, 29). More importantly, in practice we must remember how children historically have been traumatized by colonial practices and racism. We know how policies, legislation and other laws have harmed Our Way of Being as Indigenous Peoples. Especially important in social work practice is maintaining relationships with children. Children are precious and must continue to be looked after by our families and extended families. Moreover, children must have strong relationships to people who work with them. Indigenous children are precious to us because they represent our collective future.

Anderson (2000, 159) reminds us that children are not considered possessions of the biological parents; rather, they are understood to be gifts on loan from the Creator. As helpers, it is important to maintain relationships with the children and families with whom we work, most particularly with those children who are in the care of the state. In the past, there were many people involved with children in our communities; these were lifelong relationships. The relationships we forge with children will impact how they must "become" adults: We must therefore be transparent and steadfast, knowing that the children will remember what we do and what we say. For anti-oppressive living we must critically analyze how our own educational teachings and training impact our relationships with children and their families. We must also continuously reflect on how legislation, and organizational policies and practices, could be used to strengthen families rather than to create harm for them.

Social work training and education stress that we must learn how to be objective. We learn that there are certain standards by which to communicate and document what relationships are like between social workers and their "clients." We also learn how to report on the lives of children and families. How can we or how do we shift these relationships of power and authority to work from a decolonizing anti-oppressive lens? This question will be central to your practice throughout your professional life, and our hope is that your answers guide you to work in "the best interest" of Indigenous children, their families, their kin and their community.

Anti-oppressive practitioners who take up a decolonizing lens need to ask: How do we act and write in a way that is resilient and supportive for children? Can we do this ethically? How do our traditional teachings inform how we work within practice standards? What ways can we keep this child connected to their family and community, so they don't experience isolation and their identity becomes fractured or lost? How do I discharge my duties while affirming that Indigenous children and families hold expertise and that families have an inherent right over their children?

We cannot answer the questions fully unless we see the children as human beings and not clients. We as practitioners must journey from our head to our heart. Elders and traditional teachers have taught us that the longest journey anyone makes is from the head to the heart. When we practise from our heart, we understand all the pain and hurt the children and families we work with have felt. We then engage from the place of love and responsibility to protect these children and families. What does this mean for practice? How do we do this? One reason why this head-to-heart journey is important is because social workers are directly involved in and influence relationships with families. Johnson (2000, 133) encourages professionals to believe that personal uniqueness and differences should be valued and respected. It is our responsibility to live our values and beliefs and remember all our relations.

Mainstream social work education and training stresses the importance of being objective: we assess, we recommend, and we implement and then we move onto our next "case file." However, the heart in our practice teaches us and encourages us to practice differently because we as people, as social workers, are responsible for and to the relations and connections we make. In our classrooms, the journey from the head to the heart is at times brought together and made present when we share ceremony with our students. Ceremony collectively connects each person, each student and ourselves as instructors, with the past, present and future and helps us to connect the head to the heart. When we engage in sacred ceremonies together, relationships are solidified and our spiritual, emotional, physical and mental selves are engaged. As social workers, we need to consider all notes and other forms of communication as sacred, and to realize any documentation must be scrupulously respected. Rather than emphasizing professional objectivity, we need to remember that we are communicating about our community members, our families, and not our "cases."

In a report titled *Skye's Legacy: A Focus on Belonging*, the BC Representative for Children and Youth (2021, 94) states,

> We continue to see situations in which children are disconnected from their families of origin and communities due to what is often perceived or presented as a problem with the parents and family members, rather than understanding their vulnerabilities in the context of historical and contemporary trauma, racism, stigma, shame, poverty and lack of timely, accessible and culturally-attuned opportunities to heal.

Creating spaces and opportunities for connection and relations are central to any good practice and to practising in A Good Way.

VISION

The northern direction always reminds us of vision. How do we want our lives to be? We remember the ancestors and old ones and how they fought for everything that we have today. We remember our teachings and how they have the ability to show us how to live a good life. We also remember the strength and resilience of our grandparents, ancestors and children who have been warriors throughout history; we too hope to be remembered in a similar way. Despite the imposition of racist policies such as residential schools and child welfare, our people have survived. Indigenous people continue to reclaim our traditional teachings and regenerate our culture, language and ceremonies.

In the book *The Sacred Tree* (Bopp et al. 1984) we are taught that the only thing we can always count on is that there will be change. We are at a time of immense change in our child welfare practice. We know how policies and practice have affected the lives of so many Indigenous children. Today, we want to recreate policies and practices that ensure that our children are protected. Our vision includes a dream of a time when our children will be raised in their home communities. Our teachings tell us the children are sacred. We must relearn our traditional ways to uphold that teaching.

Graveline (1998, 43) believes, "resistance is essential to our survival." We agree; Indigenous Peoples have resisted assimilating and have survived. We must continue to resist, because we know that what we do today will affect the next seven generations. We know that historically, culture and tradition were instrumental to healthy communities:

> Acknowledging and recognizing that, although our lives, our lessons and our students are steeped in colonial mentality, we still must accept responsibility to teach, and we can rely on traditional forms to do so. I stand strong in my ability and my willingness to accept personal responsibility for understanding power and relationships and to share what I have learned through my own experiences and voice. (Graveline 1998, 48)

Our buddy, Gord Bruyere, used to tell his students, "I teach because I do not want to see any more of our children harmed." Gord's words resonate in our work today. We too do not want to see any more of our children harmed. Her Excellency, Mary Simon (2023, para. 3) encapsulates the Indigenous world view of children and her words capture its essence and spirit:

> Everything we do, we do for our children. We work to build a better world for them. We give them a home, a community. We devote ourselves to their well-being as parents, grandparents, loved ones, friends or neighbours. We pass down identity, language, traditions and culture. We love them and they look to us to keep them safe. All that we do, we do for our children.

We have reflected and shared aspects of child welfare practice through the framework of the Medicine Wheel to provide you with tools and skills of what child welfare could look like in your practice. A hundred years of legislation and policies have not worked for Indigenous children. The most recent legislative shift, the federal Bill C-92 An Act Respecting First Nations, Inuit and Métis Children, Youth and Families, will take time to manifest and become actioned. We ask that you as child welfare workers collaborate with Indigenous helpers to break the cycle of colonialism. We all have an opportunity to create change for the next seven generations. As child welfare workers, this is our responsibility.

We believe practice that is rooted in teachings is A Way of Life. We have watched as our children continue to be apprehended at alarming rates. We must now be the warriors who protect them. The Mohawk people believe that a warrior is one who bears the burden of peace. If we are to bear the burden of peace, we must live our culture and tradition. We must never forget the children, the Elders, those who have gone on before us and those coming up after us. As we pursue best practices for Indigenous children and families, it is possible to be social work warriors for our children. They are our Vision.

All My Relations!
Qwul'sih'yah'maht (Robina Thomas)
Kundoqk (Jacquie Green)

NOTES

1 In their Calls to Justice for Social Workers and Those Implicated in Child Welfare, the Commissioners make the following points:
   - That the "best interest of the child" is based on an Indigenous world view and perspectives, and includes the perspectives of children and youth;
   - That all levels of government recognize Indigenous self-determination and inherent jurisdiction over child welfare;
   - That all levels of governments transform current child welfare systems so that Indigenous communities have control over the design, and delivery of services for families and children;
   - That all governments are responsible for ensuring that children are not apprehended on the basis of poverty and cultural bias;
   - That where apprehension is not avoidable, that family and community members are prioritized to assume care of Indigenous children and that these caregivers be provided the same financial supports available to foster families;
   - That governments ensure the availability and accessibility of culturally safe and language programs for children in the care of child welfare;
   - That provincial governments and child welfare services immediately end the practice of targeting and apprehending infants from Indigenous mothers right after they give birth;
   - That all governments immediately adopt and implement Jordan's Principle in relation to Indigenous children, prioritizing family support, reunification, and prevention of harms;
   - That all governments and child welfare agencies reform its laws and obligations to youth "aging out" of the system and ensuring a network of support from childhood to adulthood based on needs, which can include education, housing and other related supports;
   - That child welfare agencies promote the intensive and ongoing training of social workers and staff on the history of the child welfare system in the oppression and genocide of Indigenous Peoples, training on anti-racism, training on local culture and languages, and training recognizing the signs of sexual exploitation and trafficking and developing a specialized response;
   - That all governments and child welfare agencies fully implement the Spirit Bear Plan; and
   - That child welfare agencies and governments fully investigate deaths of Indigenous children in care.
   - For all of the above points, the Commission calls on all levels of government to ensure that each of these Calls are adequately funded and resourced to ensure the success of children and families.

SUGGESTED READINGS

National Inquiry into Missing and Murdered Indigenous Women and Girls (Canada). 2019. *Reclaiming Power and Place: The Final Report of the National Inquiry into Missing and Murdered Indigenous Women and Girls, Vol. 1a*.

Truth and Reconciliation Commission of Canada (TRC). 2015. *Honouring the Truth, Reconciling for the Future: Summary of the Final Report of the Truth and Reconciliation Commission of Canada*.

hooks, bell. 1996. *killing rage: Ending Racism*. New York: Henry Holt & Co.

Sinclair, Raven. 2004. "Aboriginal Social Work Education in Canada: Decolonizing Pedagogy for the Seventh Generation." *First Peoples Child & Family Review* 1, 1.

REFERENCES

Absolon, Kathy. 2011. *Kaandossiwin: How We Come to Know*. Winnipeg: Fernwood Publishing.
Aboriginal Healing Foundation (AHF). 2003. *Aboriginal People, Resilience and the Residential School Legacy*. Ottawa: Aboriginal Healing Foundation.
Anderson, Kim. 2000. *A Recognition of Being: Reconstructing Native Womanhood*. Toronto: Second Story Press.
APTN. 2021. "Remains of 215 Children Found at Former Residential School in British Columbia." May 28, 2021. www.aptnnews.ca/national-news/remains-of-215-children-found-at-former-residential-school-in-british-columbia/.
British Columbia Representative for Children and Youth. 2021. *Skye's Legacy: A Focus on Belonging*.
Bopp, Judie, Michael Bopp, Lee Brown and Phil Lane. 1984. *The Sacred Tree: Reflections on Native American Spirituality*. Twin Lakes, WI: Lotus Light Publications.
Cajete, Gregory. 2000. "Indigenous Knowledge: The Pueblo Metaphor of Indigenous Education." In *Reclaiming Indigenous Voice and Vision*, edited by Marie Battiste. Vancouver: UBC Press.
Canadian Human Rights Tribunal. 2019. *First Nations Child and Family Caring Society of Canada et al. v. Attorney General of Canada*. CHRT 39 (September 6).
Castellano, Marlene Brant, Lynne Davis and Louise Lahache (eds.). 2000. *Aboriginal Education: Fulfilling the Promise*. Vancouver: UBC Press.
Cherrington, K. 2000. "Building a Child-Centered Model: An Indigenous Model Must Look to the Future." In *Indigenous Educational Models for Contemporary Practice: In Our Mother's Voice*, edited by Maenette Kape'ahiokalani Padeken Ah Nee-Benham and Joanne Elizabeth Cooper. Mahwah, NJ: Lawrence Erlbaum Associates.
Couchie, Alyssa. 2023. "Rebraiding Frayed Sweetgrass for Niijaansinaanik (Our Children): Understanding Canadian Indigenous Child Welfare Issues as International Atrocity Crimes." *Michigan Journal of International Law* 44, 3.
Dominelli, Lena. 1997. "Introduction: Anti-Racist Social Work — A Critical Issue for White People." In *Anti-Racist Social Work: A Challenge for White Practitioners and Educators*.
Fallon, Barbara, Racheal Lefebvre, Nico Trocmé, Kenn Richard, Sonia Hélie, H. Monty Montgomery, Marlyn Bennett et al. 2021. "Denouncing the Continued Overrepresentation of First Nations Children in Canadian Child Welfare: Findings from the First Nations/Canadian Incidence Study of Reported Child Abuse and Neglect-2019." Ontario: Assembly of First Nations.
Graveline, Jean. 1998. *Circleworks: Transforming Euro-Centric Consciousness*. Halifax: Fernwood Publishing.
Green, Jacquie and Robina Thomas. 2005. "Learning Through Our Children, Healing for Our Children: Best Practice in First Nations Communities." In *Communities in a Globalizing World: Theory and Practice for Community Empowerment*, edited by Lena Dominelli. Aldershot, UK: Ashgate.
Hart, Michael. 2002. *Seeking Mino-Pimatisiwin: An Aboriginal Approach to Helping*. Halifax: Fernwood Publishing.
Hodge, David Leo. 1990. "Equality: Beyond Dualism and Oppression." In *Anatomy of Racism*, edited by D. Theo Goldberg. Minneapolis: University of Minnesota Press.
Hokowhitu, Brendan. 2021. "The Emperor's 'New' Materialisms: Indigenous Materialisms and Disciplinary Colonialism." In *Routledge Handbook of Critical Indigenous Studies*, edited by Hokowhitu, Brendan, Aileen Moreton-Robinson, Linda Tuhiwai Smith, Chris Andersen and Steve Larkin. New York: Routledge.

hooks, bell. 1996. *killing rage: Ending Racism*. New York: Henry Holt & Co.
Indian Tribes of Manitoba. 1971. *Wahbung: Our Tomorrows*. Winnipeg: Manitoba Indian Brotherhood.
Johnson, Paul. 2000. "Envisioning a Community-Centered Education: We Do Not Own Our Children, We Must Honor Them in All Ways." In *Indigenous Educational Models for Contemporary Practice: In Our Mother's Voice, Volume II*, edited by Maenette Kape'ahiokalani Padeken Ah Nee-Benham. Mawah, NJ: Lawrence Earlbam Associates.
Lawrence, Bonita. 2002. "Rewriting Histories of the Land: Colonization and Indigenous Resistance in Eastern Canada." In *Race, Space, and the Law: Unmapping a White Settler Society*, edited by Sherene Razack, Malinda Smith and Sunera Thobani. Toronto: Between the Lines.
___. 2003. "Gender, Race, and the Regulation of Native Identity in Canada and the United States: An Overview." *Hypatia* 18, 2.
Maracle, Lee. 1996. *I am Woman: A Native Perspective on Sociology and Feminism*. Vancouver: Press Gang Publishers.
Ministry of Children and Family Development. 2022. "Children and Youth in Care (CYIC)." mcfd.gov.bc.ca/reporting/services/child-protection/permanency-for-children-and-youth/performance-indicators/children-in-care#Children-and-Youth-in-Care-CYIC.
National Inquiry into Missing and Murdered Indigenous Women and Girls (Canada). 2019. *Reclaiming Power and Place: The Final Report of the National Inquiry into Missing and Murdered Indigenous Women and Girls, Vol. 1a*.
Nelson, Sarah E. 2012. "Challenging Hidden Assumptions: Colonial Ideologies as Determinants of Aboriginal Mental Health." National Collaborating Centre for Aboriginal Health (NCCAH).
Saulis, Malcolm. 2003. "Program and Policy Development from a Holistic Aboriginal Perspective." In *Canadian Social Policy: Issues and Perspective*, third edition, edited by Anne Westhues.Waterloo: Wilfrid Laurier Press.
Simon, Mary. 2023. "National Gathering on Unmarked Burials." The Governor General of Canada. gg.ca/en/media/news/2023/national-gathering-unmarked-burials.
Simpson, Audra. 2000. "Paths Toward a Mohawk Nation: Narratives of Citizenship and Nationhood in Kahnawake." In *Political Theory and the Rights of Indigenous Peoples*, edited by Duncan Ivison, Paul Patton and Will Sanders. Cambridge, UK: Cambridge University Press.
Sinclair, Raven. 2004. "Aboriginal Social Work Education in Canada: Decolonizing Pedagogy for the Seventh Generation." *First Peoples Child & Family Review* 1, 1.
Truth and Reconciliation Commission of Canada (TRC). 2015. *Honouring the Truth, Reconciling for the Future: Summary of the Final Report of the Truth and Reconciliation Commission of Canada*.
Tuhiwai Smith, Linda. 2002. *Decolonizing Methodologies: Research and Indigenous Peoples*. London: Zed Press.
Tully, Jim. 2000. "The Struggles of Indigenous Peoples for and of Freedom." In *Political Theory and the Rights of Indigenous Peoples*, edited by Duncan Ivison, Paul Patton and Will Sanders. Cambridge, UK: Cambridge University Press.
Vanier Institute of the Family. 2024. "Families count 2024." vanierinstitute.ca/families-count-2024/.

Chapter 3

THE LONG AND TWISTED ROAD TO CHILD WELFARE

My Mother's Story through Colonization, Trauma and Strength

by Osowa Askiy Iskwew (Gwendolyn Gosek)

CHAPTER FOCUS

This chapter takes a storytelling approach to demonstrate that Indigenous families' involvement in the child welfare system has its roots in systemic forces related to colonial historic trauma and government policies. A portion of Minnie Paul's story tells of her manoeuvring through a colonialized society and illustrates how two policies embedded in the Indian Act, mandatory residential school attendance and enfranchisement, influenced the author's family involvement with the child welfare system. The story is one of strength and determination in the face of overwhelming odds and is intended to draw attention to the challenges of parenting in a society that isolates and separates families through colonial policies.

QUESTIONS ADDRESSED IN THIS CHAPTER

1. Two particular policies in the Indian Act (1876) separated families with the intent to "civilize" and separate Indigenous people from their land, culture, communities and languages. What relevance do policies have in today's society for social workers in terms of understanding the intent, development and application of child welfare policy and its impact on families and communities?
2. In what ways can storytelling inform social work theory and practice?

I WAS ONCE FIVE

I was five and going on fifty

Baby brother two days from turning three

August sun dancing on white clouds

Sitting silently in the spotless back seat

Watching fields of grain passing by the window

The well dressed social worker

Now waiting outside while the deal was done

Baby brother swinging on the gate, crying

Mom's sick but she'll come and get us soon …

"You need to be strong, take care of your brother"

So strong I was

For eight long years

Beatings with the Jonny board

Bruises and welts up and down my body

Abject poverty

Filth

Screaming

Name calling

YOU'RE

    NOT

        MY

            REAL

                MOM

You're not my real mom …

My mother, Minnie Paul (née Halkett), like so many survivors of residential school, turned her back on that part of her childhood and never wanted to look back or speak about her experiences. It was only by being present while she was interviewed for her residential school survivor's benefit in her later years that I learned that she had a younger sister, Ruth, who had died in residential school after a fall down the stairs when she was only ten years old. I have spent many hours over the years since first learning about colonialism, trying to put together the pieces that would somehow make sense of my family's and the families' lives that I have worked alongside. Like so many people who spent time in the child welfare system in foster homes, group homes or adoption, I have questioned, "Why, why my family?" Even as a child, I knew it was complicated; after all, my kind, intelligent Cree-Dene mother was my hero.

I use a storytelling approach to describe some of the life circumstances created by government policies that my Cree and Dene grandparents and mother's generations not only survived but also used to prepare the way for the future generations who came after them. One of the stories my mother shared illustrates that colonization was not just something that *happened to* Indigenous people. Instead, Minnie's story, parts of which she shared with *The Northerner*, La Ronge's local newspaper, demonstrates how Indigenous people used their ways of being, knowing and doing to navigate and overcome obstacles placed on their path and continued to thrive despite the odds (Needham 2000). Canadian colonial policies had a traumatic impact on Indigenous Peoples. The story I share illustrates how two policies embedded in the Indian Act, mandatory residential school attendance and enfranchisement, influenced my family's subsequent involvement with the child welfare system.

The choice to use storytelling is both personal and political. It is personal in that I am personally invested in remembering, representing and respecting my family history. It is political in that I am speaking back to the colonial Indian Act, which is steeped in patriarchy that was designed to rob Indigenous women and their families of their voices and the power to name their truths. In writing our stories, "Indigenous women identify the poisons that threaten to destroy us." In order to "promote survival we must name our enemies" and "the moment we are able to identify the source of pain, [the enemy], we are free of its power over us" (Archuleta 2006, 92–93). In looking back and sharing our stories of struggles and victories, we are carving a path forward for the next generations coming behind us, drawing ourselves together in solidarity and reclaiming our history, our families and communities.

The historical and traumatic outcomes of Canadian government policies continue to reverberate throughout the lives of Indigenous Peoples across Canada. Our historical understanding of our past not only informs us of where we come from but it also informs both our present and our future. For that reason, the concept of historical trauma and Indigenous people, which first appeared in 1998 in the book chapter, "Healing the American Indian soul wound" is integral to the narrative (Duran et al. 1998). Historical trauma is the cumulative emotional and psychological wounding across lifespans and generations that emanates from massive group trauma (Brave Heart 2016). Mitchell et al. (2019, 81) explain that historical trauma response has been identified as a group of reactions to multigenerational, collective, historical wounding of the mind, emotions and spirit. Integral to any discussion of historical trauma and survival is the acknowledgement of strength and resilience (Matheson et al. 2022).

This story demonstrates both strength and resilience within the context of overcoming two specific Indian Act policies, residential schools and enfranchisement, and describes how their intent and creation reinforced a colonial pathway for one family's entry into the child welfare system.

EARLY CANADIAN COLONIAL CONTEXT

My grandparents, Alexander Halkett and Susan Hardlott, were born in the 1880s and my mother was born in 1915 and passed to the spirit world nearly a century later. This means that they were alive to witness some of the most devastating outcomes of Canadian colonial policies. When we consider the historical trauma created by colonial policies experienced by these generations, it is truly miraculous that there are survivors.

The 1800s had been a tumultuous century for Indigenous people of the Americas. The situation did not improve as colonization's detrimental impacts and colonial brutality continued into the twentieth century. From the beginning of the nineteenth century, "until to the mid-1950s it was believed that Aboriginal people were destined to disappear" (Frideres et al. 2008, 56). While many of the methods and policies used for colonization would change over time, the underlying rationale, ideology and goals remained the same. Assailed on every front possible, Indigenous people never gave up their fight to survive. Some of the most devastating events formulized through Canadian policy included the numbered treaties signed between 1871 and 1921 that forced Indigenous people onto reserves thereby losing not only their vast territories and freedom, but they also lost their right to travel for hunting, gathering, trading and participating in ceremonies.

Further restrictive changes came through the British North America Act (1867) and Indian Act (1876). The Indian Act and subsequent amendments focused on assimilation and control of every aspect of Indigenous Peoples' lives, including banning their spiritual practices, enforcing colonial governance and denying women their traditional political voices and spiritual roles, to name a few (Anderson 2016). Residential schools were introduced in 1870 with the final school closing in

1996, resulting in 126 years of forced removal, confinement and institutionalization of more than 150,000 Indigenous children (Nagy et al. 2012). In 1885, the North-West Rebellion ended with its political leader, Louis Riel, tragically hung, leaving the Métis people grieving but determined to maintain their cultural and political autonomy (Saunders et al. 2019). It was also during that period (1881–85) when the "state-sponsored" Canadian Pacific Railroad, that resulted in the removal of Indigenous Peoples from their lands reinforcing their vulnerability, was extended from sea to sea (Roberts 2020, 3). It was this push westward across the plains by the railway and settlers that contributed to the bison being slaughtered to the point of near extinction (Moloney et al. 2014). The wanton slaughter of bison to clear the plains and force Indigenous people onto reserves, along with the over trapping of fur-bearing animals, had devastating impacts to the Indigenous Peoples who relied on them as sources of food, clothing, blankets, tools, utensils and housing (Taylor 2011; Daschuk 2013; Moloney et al. 2014; Feir et al. 2022; Comack 2018).

During that period, Indigenous Peoples across North America were also decimated by diseases originating in Europe and for which they had little or no resistance. Indigenous people were even more vulnerable to the newly introduced diseases due to the starvation they endured, along with the disruption of their traditional roles (Lux 2001; Tough 1996; Hackett 2002; Daschuk 2013). Due to the ongoing intentional pressures of colonization, the situation reached the point that, not surprisingly, by the 1900s the deliberately intended extinction of Indigenous Peoples of North America was imminent (Dickason 2009; Frideres et al. 2012).

It is estimated that 90 to 95 percent of North American Indigenous people perished in the period after contact (Kirkmayer et al. 2000). While there are no officially confirmed statistics, it is estimated that the North American Indigenous population at contact was "upward from 7 million" (Kirmayer et al. 2000, 608). According to Statistics Canada (2015), in 1871 there were 102,358 Indigenous people living in Canada. Seventy-five years later, in 1946, there were an estimated 126,000 Indigenous people, indicating a slow but steady gain in population (Moore et al. 1946). Less than eight decades later, in 2021, despite the genocidal policies, Statistics Canada reported the number of Indigenous individuals at 1,807,250 (Statistics Canada 2022).

When one considers the devastating outcomes from policies that have denied Indigenous Peoples a voice in the decisions that were to impact them for seven generations, it is difficult to visualize how they navigated life on a daily basis and continued to support their families. One of the ways to measure the health of a population is to consider the health of the children and in particular, the infant mortality rates (IMR). In Canada, IMR for Indigenous people, since statistics have been recorded, have been consistently higher than for the non-Indigenous population. While health statistics on Indigenous people were generally not organized and recorded before the 1950s, a study of burial records for Fisher River

First Nations in Manitoba estimates that IMR for that area in the period between 1910 and 1939 ranged from 249 to 281 per 1,000 live births (Moffat et al. 1999, 1826), much higher than for the non-Indigenous population. Dr. Moore, who was the acting superintendent of the Medical Services of the Indian Affairs Branch, and his colleagues support this finding in a study of Indigenous Peoples' health conditions in Manitoba in the mid-1940s that included IMR:

> The infant mortality rate among the Indians studied reached the astounding figure in 1942 of slightly under 400 per 1,000 live births, with a comparable figure for the white population of Canada of 52. The crude mortality rate for 1942 was 39.04 per 1,000, in contrast with a rate of 8.3 for the white population in Manitoba. (Moore et al. 1946, 226)

According to Moffat et al. (1999, 1), "Acute respiratory infections were found to be the cause of death in the majority of cases of IMR. These infectious diseases and high rates of post neonatal infant mortality point to conditions of poverty associated with malnutrition as the major precipitating factor in infant death."

While contemporary IMR overall have improved immensely over those reported in the first decades of the twentieth century, as we can see from a Manitoba report on IMR between the years 1991–2000, the infant mortality rate of 9.8 per 1,000 live births for Indigenous people are still nearly double the rate of 5.0 for non-Indigenous Manitobans (Luo et al. 2010, 5). Living conditions for many Indigenous people who were forced off the land to allow for incoming settlers were described in stark terms. For example, Moore et al. (1946, 226) describe typical housing in northern Manitoba in the late 1940s:

> Frequently the conditions are almost - unbelievable - as many as 10 to 12 people living in a shack 12 feet square. The only furniture may consist of a stove in the centre and a small table or stool ... Sometimes there may be one broken-down single bed, but the majority sleep on the floor. The door is seldom more than 5 feet high and is covered by a blanket or old piece of canvas to keep out the wind.

In addition to concerns about housing conditions, Moore et al. (1946) highlighted the damage to health as people went from a traditional hunting, gathering and fishing diet to store-bought foods. People were not getting enough calories or sufficient nutrients as the foods they could afford to purchase consisted mainly of white flour, lard, sugar and jam which made up 85 percent of their daily diet (Moore et al. 1946, 228).

While poverty existed and continues to exist in Canada in different populations, Indigenous Peoples have consistently been identified as the most impoverished people in Canada since the changes brought about by colonization (Power et al. 2020).

Many Indigenous communities continue to experience food insufficiency, inadequate and crowded housing conditions, along with a lack of clean drinking water (Diochon 2013; Cidro et al. 2015; Comack 2018; Bakker et al. 2018; Hanrahan et al. 2017). The twentieth century also saw further assaults on Indigenous people including forced sterilization of Indigenous women, the cruelty of Indian hospitals, the Sixties Scoop and, presently the Millennium Scoop (Geddes 2017; Dooley 2013; Lux 2016). The Sixties Scoop was a phrase coined by Patrick Johnston (1983) to describe mass child welfare apprehensions of Indigenous children starting in the late 1950s and continuing into the 1980s. It is estimated that approximately 20,000 Indigenous children were permanently removed from their homes and placed or adopted out of province and out of country (Gosek 2017). The Sixties Scoop morphed into the Millennium Scoop, a term that refers to the devastating number of Indigenous children and youth who continue to be apprehended. It was under these early conditions which Minnie Paul was born into and went on to navigate her life travels.

MINNIE (HALKETT) PAUL'S STORY

Minnie Halkett was born in 1915 on a small island in Lac La Ronge in northern Saskatchewan where her family engaged in a traditional lifestyle of hunting, trapping, fishing and gathering. Her parents were Susan Hardlott (Dene) and Alexander Halkett (Cree). Minnie Paul was only in her third year of life when tragedy struck — her mother, Susan, became sick with influenza and passed into the spirit world. It was a traumatic time for the family. Minnie related how she stopped talking for a long time so her father, Alexander, who was a Medicine Man, performed a sacred ceremony with his daughter and she began to speak again. The ceremony connected her heart to the spirit of the chickadees, and she maintained that love for chickadees for the rest of her life. Her children and grandchildren now carry memories of her singing to the chickadees and having them come to eat from her outstretched hand.

Like so many of her relatives, Minnie Paul and her family were determined survivors of historical trauma. Her maternal grandparents, who belonged to a small family-based Dene community, perished in a bout of influenza. This left her mother, Susan Hardlott, and her orphaned siblings, who had lost not only their parents but also their small community to the dreaded disease. As a result, the Cree community of Lac La Ronge adopted Susan and her two siblings and raised them as their own. At three years of age, when Minnie Paul's mother passed away from influenza, her father, who was known throughout the North as a hunter, trapper and medicine person, was left to care for them.

Minnie Paul, her brother and two sisters attended the All Saints Indian Residential School in La Ronge, Saskatchewan. During the ten years Minnie attended residential school, she lived through the death of her ten-year-old sister from "a fall down the stairs" while at school. The reason for her fall and her final resting place was never shared with immediate family members. Although the school was located close to their community, children were only allowed to go home for the summer holidays. It was during those school breaks that Minnie developed deep relationships with her aunts, uncles and cousins. She also maintained her Cree language. Minnie was never one to dwell on the difficult times in her life and if she was relating a traumatic story, she spoke about it in determined tones that relayed her resolve to overcome whatever obstacles she encountered in life.

It was this determination that led to a career in nursing. Since residential schools never intended to produce Grade 12 graduates, Minnie, who described herself as studious and an avid reader, was determined to complete Grade 12 and go on to university to become a nurse. When she was offered support from an Anglican minister to reach her goal to continue her education, she eagerly agreed to move in with his family in Saskatoon and continue with her studies. The first challenge was to get from a small, isolated cabin in the remote northern community of Nemeiben Lake to the city of Saskatoon during January winter conditions. Travel was difficult in the 1930s with roads in the North consisting of little more than trails. It took a great deal of determination for a young single woman, living in a northern remote area without access to modern transportation, to make the journey south. Minnie Paul made the decision to make that journey on foot.

She often described a vivid memory of that part of the trip. She said it was the end of the day and she was exhausted, and her mukluks were frozen from the melting snow, so she stopped to make a fire, thinking she was not going to make it. Soon she described what she thought looked like a pack of wolves coming towards her in the distance and in her utter exhaustion, she did not know how she would survive. As the wolf pack came closer, she could see it was a dog team and as they got closer she recognized her older cousin and his sled dogs. Her cousin then accompanied her to her aunt and uncle's cabin in Sucker River to rest up before completing the remainder of the trip.

Minnie Paul went on to finish Grade 12 and graduated from the University of Saskatchewan with a registered nursing degree in 1942 at twenty-six years of age. Her dream of obtaining a nursing career and working as a registered nurse finally came to fruition. Over the next decades, she worked as a registered nurse and nursing supervisor in hospitals throughout Saskatchewan and BC including the Indian Hospital in North Battleford, and hospitals in Edam, Turtleford, Winnipeg, Vancouver and La Ronge. During her career she became mother to three children, two boys and one girl and grandmother to fifteen and great-grandmother to thirteen. Despite many personal and societal obstacles, including being left alone to raise her children, Minnie Paul lived her life with gentle dignity and powerful determination to be the best she could be.

In many ways, this story is also the story of my two brothers and me, as her role as our mother and survivor of residential school influenced many of our life decisions and the paths we eventually chose to walk. It is also her grandchildren's story as Minnie Paul modelled her cultural values including love, strength, compassion and determination to them. I have long understood that the personal cannot be separated from the public and it was through studying and coming to know Canada's history that I came to better understand my family history. Even today as I research and teach Indigenous courses, I pause as I make the personal connection, contemplating where my grandparents or my mother were when these policy decisions were made and how they survived them. Minnie Paul lived through almost a century of colonial policies and practices that pushed Indigenous Peoples to the margins of society. Yet, she, like so many others, thrived despite the ongoing genocidal policies. Two policy outcomes from the Indian Act, residential schools and enfranchisement, directly impacted Minnie Paul's life and her family's lives for the next generations. The next sections will highlight how Minnie Paul navigated the loss of her Indian Status as a result of obtaining her nursing degree and built up her family despite her experience in residential school.

THE INDIAN ACT AND RESIDENTIAL SCHOOLS

Residential schools' horrific history including the Canadian government goals, treatment of Indigenous children and impacts on generations of families have been described in detail in numerous sources including the Truth and Reconciliation Commission Report (2015) (Truth and Reconciliation 2012, 2015; Dyck 1997; Fournier et al. 1997; Grant 1996; Miller 2000; Milloy 1999; Milloy 2017; Knockwood 2001; MacDonald 2019). The Indian Act of 1876 made school attendance mandatory for Indigenous children and imposed fines and jail sentences for parents who did not comply (Chrisjohn et al. 2002). Further amendments not only made attendance compulsory but also assigned Indian Agents and the Royal Canadian Mounted Police (RCMP) the responsibility to "collect and transport unwilling students" (Kelm et al. 2018, 7). The operation of the schools was subcontracted to the churches who were eager to convert the Indigenous children who were now in their charge.

Lac La Ronge All Saints Indian Residential School was built in 1907 under the supervision of the Anglican archdeacon, J.A. MacKay, who then became the first principal of the school (Dyck 1997). Minnie Paul started residential school in 1921 when she was six years of age and stayed until she completed Grade 10. Over the years, Minnie Paul often shared engaging stories of her relatives, but she spoke very little about her school experiences other than explaining that as she got older, she would "take her little cousins under her wing to protect them." During her interview, in her early nineties, to prove her identity for residential school compensation, she described the building, its interior, the outbuildings, the location and a description of the daily schedule. She also indicated that her school number was 108, her sister Ruth's number was 107, and her older sister Flora's number was 109.

In 1947, the Lac La Ronge All Saints Indian Residential School was burned down in minus 55 degrees Fahrenheit by a twelve-year-old boy who had been given matches by a fifteen-year-old male adolescent (Miller 2000; Dyck 1997). The twelve-year-old was sentenced to two years in a reformatory at the behest of the principal, Reverend Wickenden, who believed the children needed to have instilled into them "a healthy respect for the white man's justice" (Dyck 1997, 39). At the end of his two-year imprisonment, the then fourteen-year-old adolescent, was reported to be the best student in his grade at the reformatory (Dyck 1997).

History indicates that residential schools burned down frequently as it has been reported that the Lac La Ronge Residential School was one of ten residential schools to be burned down over an eight-year span (Hamilton 2021). The cause of the fires was attributed to acts of arson by desperate students and to the condition of dilapidated, run-down buildings that were aptly described as fire hazards (Hamilton 2021; Miller 2000; Milloy 1999; Dyck 1997).

Parents of the children in residential school, who were aware of the ongoing concerns, made repeated attempts to have changes made through verbal and written appeals to those responsible for running the schools (Milloy 1999). According to Miller (2000, 347), in 1934 the Anglican missionary body responsible for the Lac La Ronge Residential School received a petition signed by forty-four concerned parents requesting a change in principals. This protest would have occurred during the time Minnie Paul attended the school.

PARENTING AND RESIDENTIAL SCHOOLS

Indigenous people did not object to providing education to their children as long as the schooling was to be offered in their communities. They recognized the dramatic implications of colonization that swiftly changed lives across the territories of the Americas. They understood that their children, who were the future leaders, would need the colonizers' knowledge to fight for their peoples' rights. In agreeing to the schools, their vision was completely at odds with the government's determination to "kill the Indian in the child" through their colonial resocialization programming (Christian 2010, 11). Publicly, government officials presented their "vision" of residential schools as providing a homelike environment with Christian caregivers to guide and care for the children that conflicted with their stated goal of destroying all aspects of Indigenous culture in the children. Their efforts to remove every vestige of Indigeneity turned into a cruel and punishing attack on the children and children's culture including denying their right to speak their languages, use their traditional names, wear traditional clothing or practise their spirituality, all of which was intended to shame them and rupture their relationships to family and community (Sanderson 2012). The children's reality while in school was that they were often at the mercy of cruel adults who sexually assaulted, beat, starved and tortured them.

According to Robertson (2015, 306), in his discussion of historic trauma and residential school in Lac La Ronge, "the churches plan to pay for school maintenance costs through the labour of the students was unsuccessful, and this resulted in cutbacks to diet impacting the children's health. In 1941 a study found that half the children who entered residential schools prior to that date did not survive to adulthood." This timeline describing the horrendous loss of children's lives coincides with the same time period Minnie Paul attended Lac La Ronge Residential School.

The churches, who were given responsibility for residential schools and oversight of the children, used their religions to manipulate and frighten them. Children were threatened with eternal hell fire if they resorted to their "savage" ways and were told their parents would experience the same if they continued to practise their Indigenous spirituality. In their efforts to convert the children, the churches were intentionally interfering with the transmission of Indigenous culture and alienating them from family and community relationships (de Leeuw 2009).

Within their own communities, children experienced a nonviolent parenting style wherein parents and relatives "never struck a child in their lives" because traditionally children were taught through example, teasing and storytelling (Milloy 1999, 43). Shortly after children learned to walk, they participated in a walking out ceremony and were considered autonomous human beings (Jolly et al. 2011; Makokis et al. 2020). They were encouraged to explore and learn under the watchful eyes of relatives and community members. This parenting style contrasted with the cruel residential school parenting practices thus adding to the confusion and devastating trauma. In comparing parenting approaches, Manual et al. (1974, cited in Milloy 1999, 43) reported, "the priests taught us to respect them by whipping us (while) our mothers and fathers, aunts and uncles and grandparents, failed to represent themselves as a threat, when that was the only thing we had been taught to understand."

While not all residential school personnel were violent, survivors' stories of their confinement in residential schools across Canada indicate cruelty and violence was extremely widespread, atrocious and life altering. Minnie Paul would not talk about her experience other than mentioning the need to protect the younger children and sharing that one teacher had been kind to her and brought her books to read. The unfortunate reality is that she spent the majority of her childhood in an institutional setting where the goal was to "civilize" the children using oppressive and often cruel measures. Although her father was a Medicine Man and she talked about his plant knowledge and ceremonies, she learned to follow Christian advice and warned her own children to "stay away from those things" (traditional spirituality) because they are "bad medicine." She also refused to teach her children Cree as she had been taught in residential school that knowing and using the Indigenous languages would interfere with success in school and acceptance in adulthood generally.

Children were deprived of the opportunity to experience safe hugs and affection in an institutional environment that was known for being overcrowded, understaffed and where contact between male and female siblings and cousins was disallowed. It is little wonder that for many residential school survivors, physical demonstrations of affection did not come easily, if at all. In addition to the violent environments involving physical, mental, emotional and spiritual abuse, residential schools were underfunded, often run by unfit and untrained teachers where children experienced hunger, and lacked proper nutrition, clean clothing and suitable lodging. Although the girls were taught basic homemaking skills such as cooking, cleaning and sewing and the boys were taught farming skills, parenting was neither taught nor modelled. This experience thereby denied successive generations the opportunity to learn and pass on parenting skills normally modelled by the adults in their lives and vital to the dynamic challenges of raising children (Makokis et al. 2020). While residential schools interfered with the passing on of healthy parenting skills, and created a hesitancy for physical closeness, it did not deny the children the innate ability to receive and give love and to demonstrate love for the next generations.

THE INDIAN ACT AND ENFRANCHISEMENT

A second important policy from the Indian Act of 1876 is the section under which Minnie Paul was enfranchised and lost all her rights as a Status Indian under the Act. Minnie Paul was the first graduate from her community and when she graduated in 1942 with a registered nursing degree from the University of Saskatchewan, the government rewarded her by enfranchising her. Enfranchisement involved granting Canadian citizenship, which automatically meant the termination of Indigenous people's legal rights under the Indian Act. The loss of Indigenous rights under the Indian Act had major implications for all individuals who lost their Status, as it basically separated individuals and their families from both the formal and informal rights granted through the Indian Act and their bands. This had particularly far-reaching impacts on women and their children, as they could not longer reside in their home community and were denied any benefits extended through their bands leaving them more vulnerable to poverty.

Section 99(1) of the 1880 revision of the Indian Act details the categories of individuals who would lose their Indian Status if they chose to attend higher education:

> Any Indian who may be admitted to the degree of Doctor of Medicine, or to any other degree by any University of Learning, or who may be admitted in any Province of the Dominion to practise law either as an Advocate or as a Barrister or Counsellor, or Solicitor or Attorney or to be a Notary Public, or who may enter Holy Orders, or who may be licensed by any denomination of Christians as a Minister of the Gospel, may upon petition to the Superintendent-General, ipso facto become and be enfranchised under the provisions of this Act; and the Superintendent-General may give him a suitable allotment of land from the lands belonging to the band of which he is a member. (cited in Kelm et al. 2018, 98)

The Indian Act, immersed in European world views of patriarchy, also privileged men to the detriment of women. This is evident in the fact that the Indian Act only recognized women through their marriage to a man or as a child of a Status male since the Indian Act defined "Indian" (a Status Indian) as "a male Indian, the wife of male Indian, or the child of a male Indian," which was in direct contradiction to the matriarchal relationships adhered to by a majority of Indigenous communities (Day 2018, 175; Bhandar 2016). Furthermore, enfranchisement was automatically applied to the women and children of men who were enfranchised regardless of the reason for enfranchisement. For example, men who joined the army or chose to enfranchise for personal reasons were enfranchised and their wives and children were automatically enfranchised along with them.

The most frequent loss of Status occurred when Indigenous women married non-Status men, at which time both the women and all children born to her lost their Indian Status under the Act. On the other hand, men with Status could marry a non-Status woman and both her and her children were granted Status. Other means of losing Status included children born to a mother who did not register the father's name. In those circumstances the government then considered the child "illegitimate" and the child would not be registered as Status. It is reported that before the passage of Bill C-31, "Approximately 16,000 women lost their Status and tens of thousands of children were also affected" under this provision (Palmater 2014, 36). These numbers are multiplied with each successive generation creating barriers to self-identity, family connections, language and cultural knowledge acquisition.

The government's primary reason for enfranchisement was the same reason for legalizing residential schools, which was in effect to assimilate and "civilize" Indigenous people, disperse them into colonial society and eliminate reserves as opposed to honouring their treaty promises to the First Peoples of Turtle Island (Brownlie 2006). Just as the government's goal for residential schools was to "remove the Indian from the child," enfranchisement had a similar goal which was "to get rid of the Indian problem" (Kelm et al. 2018, 114). Both residential schools and enfranchisement policies applied the principle of divide and conquer through separation of families and removal from communities and culture to achieve their goals. Kelm et al. (2018, 19) note the disruptive process of enfranchisement from an Indigenous lens, "When viewed from the perspective of Indigenous law, the Indian Act's breaking of relationships and communities is even more troubling."

In devising their enfranchisement policy, the government assumed all Indigenous people would desire Canadian citizenship and therefore leave the reserves when offered legal opportunities for enfranchisement. What they did not count on was that Indigenous people recognized that as small as the parcels of land "reserved" for them, the First Peoples valued their home, their relationships to each other and the land, as well as their cultural connections, and their sense of community and autonomy. Their home communities provided a measure of protection from racism versus being scattered and isolated throughout urban areas (Peach 2012). Brownlie (2006, 31) describes the lack of desire to take up enfranchisement in these words: "Perhaps most importantly, it demonstrates one of the greatest successes of Aboriginal resistance: the defeat of the original enfranchisement policy and its provision for dissolving reserves."

Under the Indian Act, Indigenous people were considered wards of the state and non-persons. Until amendments to the Indian Act in 1951, the Act defined a "'person' as an individual other than an 'Indian'" (Joseph 2018, 27). As Cornet (2007, 146) explains, "Indian Status meant 'not a person'" and denoted a legal incapacity regarding many civil and political rights and freedoms. Once they were enfranchised, Indigenous people were officially recognized as Canadian citizens with the right to vote since it was not until 1960 that the vote was open to all Indigenous adults.

In 1985, Indigenous women's long struggle for equity in relation to women's Indian Status was recognized in the passing of Bill C-31 A Bill to Amend the Indian Act. Unfortunately, Bill C-31 did not address all the discriminatory aspects of the Act. Therefore, in response to a legal challenge known as *McIvor v. Canada* filed in 1987, which challenged registration provisions under the Canadian Charter of Rights and Freedoms, Bill C-3 the Gender Equity in Indian Registration Act came into effect January 2011. Bill C-31 had reversed the discriminatory double mother clause that stipulated, in the 1951 Indian Act, that the grandchildren of the mothers and paternal grandmothers who had acquired Status through marriage to a Status Indian, would lose their Status at the age of twenty-one years, but it did not go far enough. The goal of Bill C-3 was to challenge the historical limitations that remained after Bill C-31 became law, with the result being Bill S-3 An Act to amend the Indian Act in response to the Supreme Court of Quebec decision in *Descheneaux v. Canada* that received royal assent December 2017. In essence it addressed the discrimination due to the double mother clause and extended the option for great-grandchildren to apply for Status. While the amendments fell seriously short of addressing longstanding equity concerns, it did allow for reinstatement for a number of women and their children who had lost Status through marriage to men who did not have Status. It also allowed for individuals who had lost Status under other provisions in the original Indian Act to regain their Status.

The ongoing fight against discrimination for Indigenous women and their children that began in the early seventies spearheaded by women warriors such as Mary Two-Axe Earley, Jeannette Corbiere Lavell, Yvonne Bedard, Sandra Lovelace and Sharon McIvor, has been ongoing. Bill C-31, Bill C-3 and Bill S-3 did not resolve all discrimination for Indigenous people in the Indian Act as Bill C-31 had added more categories of registered Indigenous people, but these categories limited the opportunities for individuals to pass on Status to future generations. The new Bill C-31 categories included sections 6(1) and 6(2) and these categories were not changed in more recent legislation. Rather than increase the number of opportunities for future generations to apply for Status, it narrowed the field. This is related to the section a person is designated under, 6(1) or 6(2), as the designation the individual and their children are defined under gives them different rights that impact not only their individual rights but also the rights of future generations since the different categories each carry different rights that they can pass down to the next generation. In other words, having Status does not guarantee a person will be able to pass on full Status rights. It is anticipated that the ability to register under the Indian Act will continue to be limited as only children with both parents designated a 6(1) or alternatively having one parent who is a 6(1) and the other parent a 6(2) will be able to gain Status. This means that if one parent has 6(2) Status and one parent does not have Status, the children are denied Status. As a result, it is anticipated that the population of Status individuals will decline over time (Hartley 2007; Hamill 2010; Day 2018; Clatworthy 2007).

This means the fight to gain or maintain their rights under the Indian Act does not stop here. It was projected in 2004 that Bill C-31 was expected to temporarily increase growth in the population entitled to Status under the Act for "about two more generations (50 years), adding about 327,000 individuals *after which time, the registered population will decline*" (Clatworthy 2004, ix, 44–48, emphasis added; Clatworthy 2007). In other words, the federal government's original goal of forced assimilation of Indigenous people remains a real threat as Indigenous people will eventually lose all rights to the lands set aside for them and the Treaty Rights that their bands negotiated at the time of original treaty negotiations. As Palmater (2014, 34, 43) states, "The Indian Act contains laws designed to define, control, and ultimately eliminate federally recognized Indians in Canada" and once Status Indians are legislatively "extinct" the government will no longer be obligated to live up to their legal and financial commitments.

In view of the ongoing fight to address inequity and regain Status under the Indian Act there can be little doubt that regaining Status represents meaningful and important personal value for Indigenous activists who have fought for it, and for those individuals who have either applied or intend to apply to regain their Status. Overall, it is a powerful testament to the importance Status continues to have for Indigenous people.

In speaking to the benefits of gaining registration under the Indian Act and band membership, it is important to emphasize that the majority of individuals cite personal identity, culture and belonging as the driving forces to gain Status as opposed to a desire to maintain a colonial relationship (Palmater 2014). Briefly, other benefits under the Indian Act and fought for by their ancestors through the treaty process, and of course depending on which category of registration and band membership one falls under, could include: the right to live in their home reserve, the right to be buried on their reserve, the right to participate in the band's political and economic decisions, the right to participate in self-government negotiations, and in some provinces, the right to hunting and gathering (Palmater 2014).

Losing or being denied Indian Status for many individuals and their families has meant that they could not live or stay in their home community, be buried alongside their relatives, or participate in any band decision-making; all of which contribute to a sense of belonging and cultural identity (Palmater 2022).

CONSIDERING THE IMPACT OF POLICY

As citizens of a democratic society, we generally live our daily lives navigating a multitude of policies whether they are school policies, work-related policies, traffic laws, criminal and civil laws, taxation and so forth and often do not consider the extent to which our lives are influenced by these policies. Minnie Paul's circumstances were unique to her situation in the late 1950s and early 1960s. She was an educated Cree woman who lost her Status as a result of the Indian Act's stipulation that if you earn a university degree you automatically lose your Status. Then suddenly she found herself abandoned in an unfamiliar city, socially isolated with three children under the age of four and in a society that frowned upon single mothers. She once spoke about how desperately difficult that first winter was as she tried to keep her home warm and children fed. She remembered very little beyond being grateful for a neighbour who chopped wood for her and left baskets of food on her steps. Canada's safety net as we know it today was in the very early stages of being established and the Sixties Scoop had just swung into effect. After accepting a nursing position at the North Battleford Indian Hospital working shift work and struggling to find reliable child care, she fell ill and made the decision to relinquish her children to child welfare. This was not a decision taken lightly or without deep regret. If she had not lost her Status, she could have returned home to her relatives and found support and comfort with family. Instead, it was a long winding path consisting of difficult personal circumstances and government policies that she had no control over and that isolated her from her natural support network hundreds of miles away.

The Indian Act with its residential school policy and its goal to "remove the Indian from the child" paved the path with estrangement of students from family and community relationships, "severing the ties" that bound them to identity, spirituality and belongingness (Pettipas 1994). The policy to enfranchise individuals had a similar effect using a different approach. At a time in her life when she most needed her relatives and community, Minnie Paul believed she no longer had the option of reaching out to her relatives as distance, lack of financial support and the knowledge that she was only allowed to visit her home community during daylight hours kept her isolated. When she accepted a nursing position in La Ronge Hospital in 1964, she returned to live and work in the town of La Ronge with her young family as she had no Status, which meant she did not have the legal right to reside in her community. Having lost her Status, she was unable to stay on her home reserve for even one night to sit with one of her dying Elders as the RCMP had the power under the Act to remove all persons not registered as a band member. Regardless of her government-induced change in Status, she was warmly welcomed home by her relatives. Two decades later, she followed the news about Bill C-31 closely and as soon as the Bill was finalized, she applied for her Status and her children's Status. She should never have lost it.

Policies govern our day-to-day world and while policies are important and have utility in complex societies, we are responsible for learning why the policies were developed, who was involved in the policy development and whose interest the policies serve. As social workers we need to question the utility and fairness of policies that we apply in our service to others and advocate to not only change the offending policy but also to change the policy development process to include the voices and insights of the people that are impacted by the policies. Finally, we need to recognize that everyone has a story, and it is our responsibility to listen attentively and allow those stories to guide our work with the people we have made the commitment to serve.

NIMAMA

You always said 'walk with your head up high' Be **Brave**

You knew the value of putting on that armour

And never dropping your eyes to insults

And so you did just that

You held your head up high even as time wore your body down

You taught me **Love** through your kindness and gentleness

You tenderly cared for each of my newborns, singing them welcome songs

I learned of your love through the stories told and retold

By neighbours and relatives of how you cared for them in sickness

You taught me **Humility** in sharing 'because, my girl, what goes around comes around'

Through acts large and small, selfless acts of kindness

Taking your gloves off for your adult granddaughter to keep HER hands warm in the prairie winter

You taught us **Truth** and **Honesty** by always standing strong in what you believed

You carried the **Wisdom** of our ancestors and never stopped searching for knowledge

You taught **Respect** by loving and caring for everyone in your life

Policies may have changed the trajectory of your life, our lives

But they never changed your ancestral values and who you are

YOU have always been my real mom

SUGGESTED READINGS

Comack, Elizabeth. 2018. "Corporate Colonialism and the 'Crimes of the Powerful' Committed Against the Indigenous Peoples of Canada." *Critical Criminology* 26.

Fortier, Craig and Edward Hon-Sing Wong. 2018. "The Settler Colonialism of Social Work and the Social Work of Settler Colonialism." *Settler Colonial Studies* 9, 4.

Mitchell, Terry. 2019. "Colonial Trauma: Complex, Continuous, Collective, Cumulative and Compounding Effects on the Health of Indigenous Peoples in Canada and Beyond." *International Journal of Indigenous Health* 14, 2.

REFERENCES

Anderson, Kim. 2016. *A Recognition of Being: Reconstructing Native Womanhood*, second edition. Toronto: Women's Press.

Archuleta, Elizabeth. 2006. "'I Give You Back': Indigenous Women Writing to Survive." *Studies in American Indian Literatures* 18, 4.

Bakker, Karen J., Rosie Simms, Nadia Joe and Leila Harris. 2018. *Indigenous Peoples and Water Governance in Canada: Regulatory Injustice and Prospects for Reform*. Cambridge, UK: Cambridge University Press.

Bhandar, Brenna. 2016. "Status as Property: Identity, Land and the Dispossession of First Nations Women in Canada." *darkmatter Journal* 14.

Brave Heart, Maria Yellow Horse and Josephine Chase. 2016. "Historical Trauma Among Indigenous Peoples of The Americas: Concepts, Research, and Clinical Considerations." *Wounds of History*.

Brownlie, Robin. 2006. "'A Better Citizen than Lots of White Men': First Nations Enfranchisement – An Ontario Case Study, 1918-1940." *The Canadian Historical Review* 87, 1.

Chrisjohn, Roland D., Tanya Wasacase, Lisa Nussey, Andrea Smith, Marc Legault, Pierre Loiselle and Mathieu Bourgeois. 2002. "Genocide and Indian Residential Schooling: The Past is Present. Canada and International Humanitarian Law: Peacekeeping and War Crimes in the Modern Era." In *Canada and International Humanitarian Law: Peacekeeping and War Crimes in the Modern Era*, edited by Richard D. Wiggers, L. Ann and Ann Lynn. Halifax: Dalhousie University Press.

Christian, Wayne. 2010. "Voice of a Leader: If You Truly Believe Children Are Our Future - The Future Is Now!" *First Peoples Child & Family Review* 5, 1.

Cidro, Jaime, Bamidele Adekunle, Evelyn Peters and Tabitha Martens. 2015. "Beyond Food Security: Understanding Access to Cultural Food for Urban Indigenous People in Winnipeg as Indigenous Food Sovereignty." *Canadian Journal of Urban Research* 24, 1.

Clatworthy, Stewart Joseph. 2004. *Re-assessing the Population Impacts of Bill C-31*. Ottawa: Indian and Northern Affairs Canada.

____. 2007. "Indian Registration, Membership, and Population Change in First Nations Communities." *Aboriginal Policy Research Consortium International (APRCI)*, 94.

Comack, Elizabeth. 2018. "Corporate Colonialism and the "Crimes of the Powerful" Committed Against the Indigenous Peoples of Canada." *Critical Criminology* 26.

Cornet, Wendy. 2007. "Indian Status, Band Membership, First Nation Citizenship, Kinship, Gender, and Race: Reconsidering the Role of Federal Law." *Aboriginal Policy Research Consortium International (APRCI)*, 92.

Daschuk, James. 2013. *Clearing the Plains: Disease, Politics of Starvation, and the Loss of Aboriginal Life*. Regina: University of Regina Press.

Day, Shelagh. 2018. "Equal Status for Indigenous Women—Sometime, Not Now: The Indian Act and Bill S-3." *Canadian Woman Studies/les cahiers de la femme* 33, 1 & 2.

de Leeuw, Sarah. 2009. "'If Anything Is to Be Done with the Indian, We Must Catch Him Very Young': Colonial Constructions of Aboriginal Children and the Geographies of Indian Residential Schooling in British Columbia, Canada." *Children's Geographies* 7, 2.

Dickason, Olive Patricia. 2009. *Canada's First Nations: A History of Founding Peoples from Earliest Times*. New York: Oxford University Press.

Diochon, Monica. 2013. "Social Entrepreneurship and Effectiveness in Poverty Alleviation: A Case Study of a Canadian First Nations Community." *Journal of Social Entrepreneurship* 4, 3.

Dooley, Chris. 2013. "Healing Histories: Stories from Canada's Indian Hospitals." In *Oral History Forum d'histoire orale* 33.

Duran, Eduardo, Bonnie Duran, Maria Yellow Horse Brave Heart and Susan Yellow Horse-Davis. 1998. "Healing the American Indian Soul Wound." In *International Handbook of Multigenerational Legacies of Trauma*, edited by Yael Danieli. Boston: Springer US.

Dyck, Noel. 1997. *Differing Visions: Administering Indian Residential Schooling in Prince Albert, 1867-1995*. Fernwood Publishing.

Feir, Donn L., Rob Gillezeau and Maggie E.C. Jones. 2022. *The Slaughter of the Bison and Reversal of Fortunes on the Great Plains* (No. w30368). Cambridge: National Bureau of Economic Research.

Fournier, Suzanne, David Neel and Ernie Crey. 1997. *Stolen From Our Embrace: The Abduction of First Nations Children and the Restoration of Aboriginal Communities*. Vancouver: Douglas & McIntyre.

Frideres, James, and René Gadacz (eds.). 2008. *Aboriginal Peoples in Canada*, eighth edition. Toronto: Pearson Prentice Hall.

____. 2012. *Aboriginal Peoples in Canada*, ninth edition. Toronto: Pearson.

Geddes, Gary. 2017. *Medicine Unbundled: A Journey Through the Minefields of Indigenous Health Care*. Victoria: Heritage House Publishing Co.

Gosek, Gwendolyn. 2017. "The Aboriginal Justice Inquiry-Child Welfare Initiative in Manitoba: A Study of the Process and Outcomes for Indigenous Families and Communities from a Frontline Perspective." Doctoral dissertation, University of Victoria.

Grant, Agnes. 1996. *No End of Grief: Indian Residential Schools in Canada*. Winnipeg: Pemmican Publications, Inc.

Hackett, Paul. 2002. *A Very Remarkable Sickness: Epidemics in the Petit Nord, 1670 to 1846* (Vol. 14). Winnipeg: University of Manitoba Press.

Hamill, Sarah E. 2010. "McIvor v. Canada and the 2010 Amendments to the Indian Act: A Half-hearted Remedy to Historical Injustice." *Constitutional Forum* 19.

Hamilton, Scott. 2021. "Where are the Children Buried?" *Higher Education Learners*.

Hanrahan, Maura. 2017. "Water (In)security in Canada: National Identity and the Exclusion of Indigenous Peoples." *British Journal of Canadian Studies* 30, 1.

Hartley, Gerard. 2007. "The Search for Consensus: A Legislative History of Bill C-31, 1969–1985." *Aboriginal Policy Research Consortium International (APRCi)*, 98.

Johnston, Patrick. 1983. *Native Children and the Child Welfare System*. Toronto: James Lorimer & Company.

Jolly, Freddy, Gail Whiteman, Miriam Atkinson and Ioana Radu. 2011. "Managing and Educating Outside: A Cree Hunter's Perspective on Management Education." *Journal of Management Education* 35, 1.

Joseph, Bob. 2018. *21 Things You May Not Know about the Indian Act: Helping Canadians Make Reconciliation with Indigenous Peoples a Reality*. Port Coquitlam: Indigenous Relations Press.

Kelm, Mary-Ellen and Keith D. Smith. 2018. *Talking Back to the Indian Act: Critical Readings in Settler Colonial Histories*. Toronto: University of Toronto Press.

Kirmayer, Laurence J., Gregory M. Brass and Caroline L. Tait. 2000. "The Mental Health of Aboriginal Peoples: Transformations of Identity and Community." *The Canadian Journal of Psychiatry* 45, 7.

Knockwood, Isabelle. 2001. *Out of the Depths: Experiences of Mi'Kmaw Children at the Indian Residential School at Shubenacadie, Nova Scotia*. Halifax: Fernwood Publishing.

Luo, Zhong-Cheng, Russell Wilkins, Maureen Heaman, Patricia Martens, Janet Smylie, Lyna Hart, Spogmai Wassimi, Fabienne Simonet, Yuquan Wu and William D. Fraser. 2010. "Neighborhood Socioeconomic Characteristics, Birth Outcomes and Infant Mortality Among First Nations and non-First Nations in Manitoba, Canada." *The Open Women's Health Journal* 4, 55.

Lux, Maureen Katherine. 2001. *Medicine that Talks: Disease, Medicine, and Canadian Plains Native People 1880 – 1940*. Toronto: University of Toronto Press.

____. 2016. *Separate Beds: A History of Indian Hospitals in Canada, 1920s-1980s*. Toronto: University of Toronto Press.

MacDonald, David B. 2019. *The Sleeping Giant Awakens: Genocide, Indian Residential Schools, and the Challenge of Conciliation*. Toronto: University of Toronto Press.

Makokis, Leona, Kristina Kopp, Ralph Bodor, Ariel Veldhuisen and Amanda Torres. 2020. "Cree Relationship Mapping: Nêhiyaw kesi wâhkotohk – How We Are Related." *First Peoples Child & Family Review* 15, 1.

Matheson, Kimberly, Ann Seymour, Jyllenna Landry, Katelyn Ventura, Emily Arsenault and Hymie Anisman. 2022. "Canada's Colonial Genocide of Indigenous Peoples: A Review of the Psychosocial and Neurobiological Processes Linking Trauma and Intergenerational Outcomes." *International Journal of Environmental Research and Public Health* 19, 1.

Miller, James Rodger. 2000. *Shingwauk's Vision: A History of Native Residential Schools*. Toronto: University of Toronto Press.

Milloy, John S. 1999. *A National Crime: The Canadian Government and the Residential School System*. Winnipeg: University of Manitoba Press.

____. 2017. *A National Crime: The Canadian Government and the Residential School System*, second edition. Winnipeg: University of Manitoba Press.

Mitchell, Terry. 2019. "Colonial Trauma: Complex, Continuous, Collective, Cumulative and Compounding Effects on the Health of Indigenous Peoples in Canada and Beyond." *International Journal of Indigenous Health* 14, 2.

Moffat, Tina and Ann Herring. 1999. "The Historical Roots of High Rates of Infant Death in Aboriginal Communities in Canada in the Early Twentieth Century: The Case of Fisher River, Manitoba." *Social Science & Medicine* 48, 12.

Moloney, Christopher and William Chambliss. 2014. "Slaughtering the Bison, Controlling Native Americans: A State Crime and Green Criminology Synthesis." *Critical Criminology* 22.

Moore, Percy Elmer, H.D. Kruse, F.F. Tisdall and R.S.C. Corrigan. 1946. "Nutrition among the Northern Manitoba Indians." *Canadian Medical Association Journal* 54, 3.

Nagy, Rosemary and Robinder Kaur Sehdev. 2012. "Introduction: Residential Schools and Decolonization." *Canadian Journal of Law and Society/La Revue Canadienne Droit et Société* 27, 1.

Needham, Fraser. 2000. "Northerner Pursued Dream Despite Odds." *The Northerner.*

Palmater, Pamela. 2014. "Genocide, Indian Policy, and Legislated Elimination of Indians in Canada." *Aboriginal Policy Studies* 3, 3.

———. 2022. "Death by Poverty: The Lethal Impacts of Colonialism." In *Power and Resistance: Critical Thinking About Canadian Social Issues*, edited by Jessica Anthony and Wayne Anthony. Winnipeg: Fernwood Publishers.

Peach, Ian. 2012. "Section 15 of the Canadian Charter of Rights and Freedoms and the Future of Federal Regulation of Indian Status." *University of British Columbia Law Review* 45, 1.

Pettipas, Katherine. 1994. *Severing the Ties that Bind: Government Repression of Indigenous Religious Ceremonies on the Prairies* (Vol. 7). Winnipeg: University of Manitoba Press.

Power, Tamara, Denise Wilson, Odette Best, Teresa Brockie, Lisa Bourque Bearskin, Eugenia Millender and John Lowe. 2020. "COVID-19 and Indigenous Peoples: An Imperative for Action." *Journal of Clinical Nursing* 29, 15–16.

Roberts, Zachary. 2020. "The Ways They Went: Justifications Behind Settler Dispossession of Indigenous Life in Western Canadian Expansion." *Prandium: The Journal of Historical Studies at U of T Mississauga* 9, 1.

Robertson, Lloyd Hawkeye. 2015. "The Trauma of Colonization: A Psycho-historical Analysis of One Aboriginal Community in the North American 'North-West.'" *Revista Interamericana de Psicología/Interamerican Journal of Psychology* 4, 3.

Sanderson, Joan. 2012. "Women for Women: Stories of Empowerment Activism in Northern Saskatchewan." *Pimatisiwin* 10, 1.

Saunders, Kelly and Janique Dubois. 2019. *Métis Politics and Governance in Canada*. Vancouver: UBC Press.

Statistics Canada. 2022. "The Daily: Indigenous Population." statcan.gc.ca/en/census/census-engagement/community-supporter/indigenous-peoples.

Statistics Canada. 2015. "First Nations people, Métis and Inuit in Canada." 150.statcan.gc.ca/n1/pub/89-659-x/89-659-x2018001-eng.htm.

Taylor, M. Scott. 2011. "Buffalo Hunt: International Trade and the Virtual Extinction of the North American Bison." *American Economic Review* 101, 7.

Tough, Frank. 1996. *"As their Natural Resources Fail": Native Peoples and the Economic History of Northern Manitoba, 1870-1930.* Vancouver: UBC Press.

Truth and Reconciliation Commission of Canada (TRC). 2012. *Canada, Aboriginal Peoples, and Residential Schools: They Came for the Children.* Truth and Reconciliation Commission.

———. 2015. *Canada's Residential Schools: The Final Report of the Truth and Reconciliation Commission of Canada* (Vol. 1). McGill-Queen's Press-MQUP.

Chapter 4

CHILD WELFARE ASSESSMENT, DOCUMENTATION AND RECORDKEEPING

Decolonial, Anti-Racist and Equitable Approaches

by Michele Fairbairn

CHAPTER FOCUS

This chapter critiques current child welfare assessment, documentation and recordkeeping practices and proposes decolonial, anti-racist and equitable alternatives. It outlines how dominant approaches to these practices are deeply embedded in political, economic, social and technological contexts that obscure the depth and breadth of social inequities. Through tracing the historical formation of Canada, this chapter demonstrates how colonialism has been and remains implicated in child welfare practices.

Protection approaches primarily conceptualize child welfare as an individual matter and thus fail to redress political and socioeconomic sources of inequities impacting young people. Rather than practice being centrally focused on identifying and redressing social and material inequities that contribute to people being involved with child welfare, workers are increasingly tasked with gathering information to complete standardized assessments and documentation requirements. This chapter explains how assessments can be completed *together* with young people and their families, rather than about them, while including other significant people and supports. Decolonial, anti-racist and equitable approaches to child welfare practice also involve ascertaining ways to recognize and respond to important contextual matters beyond the limits imposed by dominant assessment and documentation processes.

QUESTIONS ADDRESSED IN THIS CHAPTER

1. How can workers prepare to engage in solidarity when undertaking decolonial and anti-racist responsibilities in child welfare practice?
2. What are some of the shortcomings of currently dominant approaches to assessment, documentation and recordkeeping, and how they are applied?
3. How can a decolonial, anti-racist and equity lens be applied throughout all child welfare assessment, documentation and recordkeeping procedures?
4. How do decolonial, anti-racist and equity approaches contribute to developing working relationships with people entangled in child welfare systems?

THE PITFALLS OF CURRENT CHILD WELFARE PRACTICES

Assessment, documentation and recordkeeping are common practices within most areas of Canadian child welfare practice and are required in child protection. They involve gathering, comprehending and recording information that is central to decision-making and planning in the lives of young people involved with child welfare. Assessments are often completed at critical junctures, and sometimes result in life-altering decisions. Child protection assessments can result in decisions such as whether children remain living with a parent or if they are temporarily or permanently removed, and new legal guardianship arrangements are organized. Assessments also inform safety, health, education and related plans impacting the lives of young people. Documented records archive information that embodies rationales for these decisions and plans. They provide accounts about what has been deemed relevant to know and to remember, which also convey how child welfare practice is conceptualized and undertaken.

Assessment, documentation and recordkeeping are never apolitical practices. They are historically situated practices originally shaped by colonial and racist knowledges that have merged with current political and neoliberal socioeconomic rationalities. Although colonial histories are multifaceted and non-linear, the ongoing effects of British imperialism and colonialism still shape child welfare and protection practice in the neoliberal settler-colonial Canadian present. These practices are implicated in creating the inequitable conditions of childhood for young people, and their future lives. Decolonial, anti-racist, equitable and socially just alternatives to current child welfare assessment, documentation and recordkeeping practices are required to transform these conditions. This transformation is a necessary precursor to the decolonization of the childhoods these conditions produce and the future lives on offer.

Recordkeeping was a fundamental colonial technology (Stoler 2002) that enabled the British Empire to gather, monitor and keep a record of information within its colonies (Richards 1993). Current recordkeeping and archiving in child welfare continue this historically embedded practice of monitoring information to uphold social order by authorizing institutions to determine "what is recorded, how records are managed (or often mismanaged), what is destroyed, and who has access to the surviving fragments" (McKemmish et al. 2020, 22). Linda Tuhiwai Smith (2012, 29) reminds us that imperialism fragmented Indigenous Peoples by dislocating them from their histories and everything meaningful to sustain them as collective nations and peoples. The imperial system of slavery dislocated "millions of Indigenous peoples by ripping them from their lands" and shipping them to other colonially seized lands (Tuhiwai Smith 2012, 28). From 1869 until the 1930s Britain also sent more than 100,000 British children to lands now called Canada, many of whom were taken from their parents only because they were poor (Rosman 2016). These children performed farm and domestic labour, often under harsh conditions and significant maltreatment. Their decedents now comprise 11.5 percent of the Canadian population, around four million people (Roseman 2016).

In the 1880s, Indigenous children were removed from their communities and sent to government-sponsored Protestant and Catholic church-run residential schools. Residential schools in Canada were designed as a civilizing and Christian indoctrinating mission that would also prepare children for domestic and agricultural labour. As a strategy of colonial genocide, Spencer and Sinclair (2017, 247) explain how residential schools operated as "death worlds" for Indigenous children, many of whom were subjected to abuse, malnutrition and medical experimentation. Thousands of children died. The imperial practice of dislocation by severing young people from connections vital to sustain their identities and cultures by removing them from their homes, families and communities has continued through child welfare practices (Blackstock et al. 2023; Fortier and Hon-Sing Wong 2018). Child welfare broadly does not just involve removing children, as it focuses on intervening with young people and families in a variety of ways and settings, but contemporary practice remains imbued with the rationalities of colonial legacies. McKemmish et al. (2020) relay that classist, heteropatriarchal, sexist and racist colonial practices persist in child welfare systems. They propose that decolonizing child welfare would contribute to decolonizing the childhoods of the young people who are caught up in this system.

The childhoods that are both produced and denied to young people are politically and socially engineered, and mediated through the assessment, documentation and recordkeeping practices conducted by child welfare workers. These practices might *seem* to be entirely within the control of individual workers, but they are actually constituted by rationalities operating through workers, who are situated within historical and contemporary colonial contexts that constitute certain thoughts and actions. Workers may be aware of the colonial formation of laws and policies and how they are constrained by them but may not realize the extent of what is un/knowable and un/contestable within their practice domain. This un/learning is ongoing. Our knowledge and understanding of the settler-colonial and neoliberal context in which child welfare practice is situated, and how its logics operate, can only ever be partial because it is simply not possible to either know or convey the entirety of a matter. Moreover, perspectives and conclusions are contested rather than settled matters. They can differ in part because of our positionalities; where and how we are situated within systems of social stratification such as colonialism, race, class, among others.

These are not the only influences that have implications for child welfare assessment and documentation practices. Listening, reading, thinking, interpreting and telling are historically constituted practices shaped by relations of power. For example, people and their situations are often extracted from relevant social contexts and their own versions of themselves and events, or some other telling, by professional knowledges and institutional categories framing what is required in child welfare assessment and documentation (de Montigny 1995; Swift 1995). We are not entirely restricted from grasping or relaying another viewpoint when listening or documenting, and we can comprehend what documents are conveying, but only through a filtered lens. Since there is no route to a single or absolute truth, we cannot assume to know or understand people and the entirety of their situations. Consequently, our narrations when documenting, no matter if we are writing a report or entering standardized information into a database, resides in a contested social sphere. These accounts are contextually situated, thus partial and contestable because they are socially shaped and not absolute.

Decolonial, anti-racist and equitable solutions to child welfare assessment, documentation and recordkeeping are also undertaken within contested legal and policy terrains that undermine the inherent rights and sovereignty of Indigenous Peoples. Indigenous Peoples have upheld their rights, including the right to be self-determining in child welfare. Child welfare workers have ethical responsibilities to challenge oppression and make social justice contributions, but they cannot impose their individual definitive solutions, nor individually outline the processes for defining solutions on other people or communities. Contributions can include recognizing, considering and reworking the tools and devices through which both colonial and neoliberal logics harm within and beyond child welfare. Making such contributions are both individual and shared responsibilities.

In practice, solidarity is not individually decided and imposed on those to whom our practice is accountable because solidarity is relational. It is tendered in respectful relationships that account for how hierarchically ordered stratification systems socially sort us, resulting in a mix of unevenly distributed benefits and harms because of what these systems have produced, imposed, taken and attempted to eradicate. In this view, we can recognize and account for how history impacts the present, how contemporary injustices are enacted and what individual and collective actions can be taken. Solidarity recognizes how settler colonialism, as a stratifying system with ongoing workings and effects, is implicated in dispossessing Indigenous Peoples from their lands, cultures and resources. It ascertains commonalities while differentiating between the forms of racism and classism targeting Indigenous Peoples and those directed towards other people and communities whose lives are entangled with child welfare systems. Solidarity recognizes racism and classism as colonial effects but also realizes how these effects have been used to justify occupation and rule of Indigenous lands and peoples, systems of slavery, class systems and other exploitative systems that impact the well-being of young people.

Social workers are often the main occupational group employed within child welfare settings. Like all child welfare workers, their practice is governed by legislation and policy pertaining specifically to child welfare, but law and policy nests in interconnected ways. Jongbloed et al. (2023) draw on a net metaphor, inspired by the installation of artist Janet Echelman, to illustrate how Indigenous Peoples have been entangled by settler-colonial laws and policies comprised of thousands of colonial knots that restrict Indigenous sovereignty and self-determination. While their focus is on healthcare systems, Jongbloed et al. (2023, 229) propose that "untying the colonial knots" within our "spheres of influence" make significant contributions to redressing anti-Indigenous racism and white supremacy. They further propose that healthcare settings have clear legal obligations to recognize and enact Indigenous rights and have responsibilities to stop perpetuating colonial harm. Even when practising within a defined area such as child welfare that may seem unrelated to health or other settings, recognizing how practice areas are all interrelated extends our thinking and responsibilities beyond the limits these separations impose.

Preparing to practice social work specifically involves critically reflecting about how thinking and doing practice is shaped by knowledges and practices that are embedded in governing political and socioeconomic conditions that benefit some, while harming others. These preparations also involve learning how to foster equity by applying anti-colonial and anti-racist approaches that adhere to principles of social justice (CASWE 2021). While social workers can sometimes bend rules to ameliorate injustices, transformative decolonial change requires a collective response. To decolonize child welfare requires a commitment to "bring about the repatriation of Indigenous land and life," because land and life are inseparable (Tuck and Yang 2012, 1). Decolonization requires a historical lens as well as a critical inquiry focused on how the historical and contemporary colonial context operates in the present in ways that may seem ordinary and even necessary, and to what effect.

COLONIALISM

There are differences between anti-colonialism as a struggle against imperial and colonial rule in post-colonial nations and those struggles in settler-colonial contexts like Canada. These differing but related contexts are significant to decolonizing child welfare practice within Canada as a former British colony. Although Canada is both a French and British settler society, as a former British colony its decolonial and anti-racist struggles are different from nations that re/gained their self-governance through the United Nations (UN) nation-state framework. In the UN decolonial framework, the British colonial regime has purportedly withdrawn its rule, and the formerly colonized country is awarded autonomy as a post-colonial nation-state.

Canada, like other former British colonies, is defined as a nation-state housed within the United Nations. Britain has fought, invaded, or occupied 171 of the current 193 United Nation member states (Laycock 2012). The United Nations 1960 decolonizing "transnational blueprint" enabled a transition from empire, and conceptualized nation-state sovereignty and self-determination as the post-colonial future (Kennedy 2016, 81). Establishing post-colonial nation-states has in many instances involved redrawing borders that have created internal strife and instability between ethnic groups within these newly bounded territories, resulting in significant violence and mass migration (Kennedy 2016).

Violence is also prevalent in settler colonies such as Canada, where laws, policies and governing social institutions form a security apparatus that is deeply entrenched in all the ways a territory remains occupied, and order is maintained. In settler-colonial Canada, one way the security state maintains order is by repressing Indigenous dissent even while resources are extracted from Indigenous lands (Crosby and Monaghan 2018). The state's ability to impose order in this way is simultaneously repressing and dispossessing. It is deeply rooted in Christian theology entangled with state-driven historical colonialism declaring lands in present-day settler-colonial nations such as Canada unoccupied because Indigenous Peoples were not Christians (Barker 2018).

Many Indigenous lands, including within Canada, were deemed uncultivated and appropriated by the British Crown. Under colonialism and the rule of law, lands were made into private property, enabled through a legal pretense of treaty-making, though much of the land now occupied was never surrendered by Indigenous Peoples. Individual and corporate entitlement to legally own land, water and other resources for personal and commercial use is common in Canada. State and market formation imposed a legal definition that turns land into property, for private use or exchange between persons and corporations, systematically dispossessing and obstructing the access and relationships Indigenous Peoples had with the land

(Nichols 2020, 35). The violence that Canada has permitted and executed towards Indigenous Peoples, including state-sanctioned genocide, is not separate from how child welfare social work has contributed to the Canadian nation-building project by assimilating, exploiting and removing Indigenous children from their communities, cultures and lands (Blackstock et al. 2023; Fortier and Hon-Sing Wong 2018; Landertinger 2016). Just as child welfare work remains embedded within the colonial legacies of yesteryear, it is not yet untangled from the present-day security operations of the settler-state.

Why Is Decolonizing Difficult?

A settler-state is particularly resistant to decolonization in part because settlers remain on the land and then define a national narrative (Veracini 2010). In Canada, like other settler-colonial nation-states, the national narrative has been premised on a claim to being a sole sovereign, so colonial rule by a separate nation from afar, as with Britain, has seemingly vanished. Indigenous nations resist the narrative that Canada is a sole sovereign, and similarly resist how nation-state sovereignty and self-determination is defined. Indigenous scholar Leanne Betasamosake Simpson (2011, 101) reminds us, "as long as there has been colonialism on our lands, there has been resistance."

Settler societies (commonly referred to as CANZUS — Canada, Australia, Aotearoa/New Zealand and the United States of America) are discernible by ongoing Indigenous resistance to colonial dispossession from lands, law, culture and resources, including how Indigenous Peoples assert self-determination in child welfare (Anderson et al. 2022). Barker (2016, 19) tells us how Indigenous nations in settler-states have made a political claim to being sovereign, but the meaning of sovereignty is embedded within Indigenous epistemologies relating to interconnections of law, governance, culture and land. Audra Simpson (2020, 689) explains that Indigenous Peoples do not adhere to notions of sovereignty emerging from Western histories of legal rule within a jurisdiction but define themselves through collective relatedness and "in relationship to territory ... [that] ... render sovereignty as a form of relationality rather than a violent claim of property."

Canada has claimed legal jurisdiction over land and has etched law into all aspects of life and everything and everyone that exists within imagined nation-state borders. However, Canada is rightfully named part of Turtle Island by the Indigenous Peoples who have lived on these lands since time immemorial and were self-governing before colonial invasion. To date, Canada has not honoured many of its treaty obligations (Keefer 2020) nor its founding document of forming a nation-to-nation relationship with Indigenous Peoples (Government of Canada 2017).

BUILDING THE SETTLER NATION

The British began granting former colonies, including Canada, self-government during the late nineteenth and early twentieth century. Canada gained full legal autonomy from Britain in 1931 but did not adopt its own constitution until 1982. Canada remains part of the British Commonwealth insofar that it officially recognizes the monarch as its own. Nation-building was a project intent on establishing a white British dominion reliant on Anglo-Saxon Protestant moral superiority. Once Canada gained legal authority over its own immigration system, it continued to advance racially restrictive immigration policies favoring white British settlers over all other groups. Many social workers and social reformers were enthusiastic supporters of racialized immigration strategies that would cultivate a white Protestant nation-state (Johnstone and Lee 2020).

Inherently racist, nation-building relied on and reproduced binary notions of superiority and respectability that contrasted with inferiority and degeneracy as an effect and justification for how child welfare was conceptualized and undertaken as a moral and economic project. This racist colonial binary operated to maintain false notions of Indigenous inferiority and degeneracy of racialized peoples, who were then made into moral problems pertaining to their children. The Canadian state focused on colonial management of both Indigenous and settler children (Landertinger 2016). There is ample evidence of child welfare's predominant focus on Indigenous, Black and poor children, albeit in different ways. As Strong-Boag (2011, 53) asserts, Indigenous parenting was deemed "naturally inferior," while Black and Irish Catholic parents were "assumed to embody primitive promiscuity, indolence, and irresponsibility" that required assimilation to enforce respectability.

Child welfare in Canada was not only embedded within settler colonialism; it also produced and governed the types of childhoods and future lives made possible for young people. Children were a preoccupation of social reformers and child rescuers within the emerging Canadian nation (Chen 2005; Landertinger 2016). The function of child welfare in nation-building involved governing the family and operated within other institutions, such as schools, clinics and hospitals, that were involved with children. Child welfare has not emerged from a unitary vision. However, it has involved being a child rescue enterprise in which the childhoods of young people were molded to conform to the inequitable socioeconomic realities that reflected the aspirations of the Canadian nation.

Many current child welfare realities in Canada are shaped by historical factors, driven by colonial and socioeconomic interests. These intermingle with moral and nation-building aspirations, transported across time and place. Having emerged during the rapid industrialization of the Victorian era and circulated through literature, religious organizations and social reform movements, child rescue was premised on removing children from destitute and immoral circumstances, and "served as a barometer for the moral standing of the nation" (Swain and Hillel 2010, 4). Linking poverty to immorality in this way positioned individual parents, rather than stratified political, social and economic arrangements, as solely responsible for their impoverished circumstances. Child rescuers in Canada had little or no interest in challenging the social inequities in society from which children had to be rescued (Adamoski 2002, 316).

Child removal thrived in the former British colonies that became Canada, Australia and the United States. According to Swain and Hillel (2010, 151) child removal was premised on romanticized notions of rescuing "lost childhoods" that were infused with "imperial and racialized assumptions" that it was in the "best interests" of children to remove them from "parents or guardians found wanting." Some child rescuers in Canada believed that if they were transplanted to the right environment, namely to white Christian families, some children could rise above their earlier station in life, or at least not become criminals (Chen 2005). However, many rescued children were "... cut off from their families and communities and trained for a life of servitude, their childhoods were shaped by labour, with love dependent on chance or good fortune" (Swain and Hillel 2010, 151). Residential schools also cut Indigenous children in Canada off from love and connection with their families and communities by targeting them to be assimilated and become sources of menial labour. Overlapping with the closure of residential schools in Canada, social workers began subjecting Indigenous children to removal from their families and communities in the 1960s (Fortier and Hon-Sing Wong 2019). Masquerading as child rescue, social workers arranged foster and adoption placements through the child welfare system, primarily with white families. In other words, the practices of genocide enacted through residential schools continued under the guise of child rescue by the child welfare system. Social workers in Canada continue to remove Indigenous children from their families and communities at alarming rates.

SECURING THE NATION: CONTEMPORARY NEOLIBERAL CHILD WELFARE

Canada is no longer settling the nation through mass migration nor is it still granting citizenship in exchange for a period of indentured labour (Dauvergne 2016). Child labour laws also restrict employers from exploiting young people for their labour, both domestically and through noncitizen migration. However, Canada relies extensively on temporary noncitizen adult workers who may not be able to obtain citizenship. Children of temporary migrant workers typically only join parents who obtain permanent resident status (Taylor and Foster 2015). Canada is an adopter of the United Nations Convention on the Rights of the Child, which stresses that keeping families together is in the best interest of children (United Nations n.d.). Parents who become temporary noncitizen workers in Canada are held individually responsible for their decision; they are not provided with support to bring their children. Despite international human rights instruments identifying the obligations of nations to protect the family unit, Canada has not developed pathways for children to accompany parents who are temporary labour migrants (Nakache 2018). The mobility of these families across nation borders is governed through policies with roots in the British Empire that remake and rework colonial rule "to manage, expel and include/exclude people through modern citizenship" (Turner 2020, 13). These governing strategies not only securitize the nation by controlling migration across borders. These strategies also articulate how the family was a colonial formation and is now governed to conceal racialized violence within liberal nations (Turner 2020).

Colonial nation-building established the groundwork for child welfare social work to occupy an essential place in securing the nation through its focus on intervening with families. State security includes economic security. In more recent times, securing the state is undertaken through establishing neoliberal economies. Although upholding human rights, including those of children, is part of preserving the nation, neoliberalism has shaped the central role of the state as sustaining the economy (Murphy 2020), but without providing the collective social protections and benefits government policy briefly emphasized during the post–Second World War era. Although neoliberalism is not a uniform project, it began shaping social-economic policies in Canada during the 1980s. Schram (2018, 308) explains that through neoliberal reforms, public policy is imbued with market logics emphasizing personal responsibility, in that individuals must "make themselves less of a burden on society as a whole or face the consequences of a heightened disciplinary regime" (see also Hall 2011). Neoliberalism as the default logic for contemporary public policy making resulted in significant cuts to social and income benefits impacting the poorest Canadians. The ways in which Canadian child welfare is conceptualized, and resources are distributed, has always optimized and advanced some lives and ways of living while denying others. Neoliberalism has intensified inequities.

Since the advent of neoliberalism, public-private partnerships and privatization of services have become a common reality in Canadian child welfare. Even when resources exist in the public realm, or must be provided, there are often long waiting periods to obtain supports. Young people are languishing on lengthy waiting lists for substance use and mental health care (Kourgiantakis et al. 2023), while desperate families either pay out of pocket when they can afford private services, or they must simply wait. Needham (2024) reports that upward to eighty thousand

First Nations children in Canada are waiting to receive needed supports through Jordan's Principle, many of which are urgent requests that are not being processed according to required timelines. Jordan's Principle is supposed to redress human rights violations enacted by the federal government for inequitably funding child welfare services for First Nations children by making sure they can now access and receive needed supports.

The reduction of funded benefits and services also has significant implications for the well-being of young people in Canada in terms of their access to material resources such as food, housing, clothing and other basic needs. Although child poverty decreased by 57.3 percent between the years 2006 to 2018 (Hillel 2020), increased poverty levels since 2021 have significantly impacted the daily lives of Canadian young people, where food insecurity impacts 21.3 to 35.1 percent of families (UNICEF 2023). As Stefanick and Tait (2024) explain, these forms of structural poverty created by neoliberal economic and social policies lead to and support disproportional involvement in statutory child welfare for poor, Indigenous and racialized families. Child welfare is not intended to make a stratified society more equitable, and it continues to hold individual parents responsible for circumstances beyond their control, such as poverty, the inability to acquire resources for their children or obtain basic resources like food and housing. Rates of child poverty are persistently high and poor children and families have little access to social protection. UNICEF (2023) reported that in 2021 there were more than one million Canadian children living in poverty. Statutory child welfare approaches, where a prevailing focus remains on intervening with families, nevertheless claim to operate in the best interest of children.

"Best Interests" and Rights

By the end of the twentieth century, a conception of the "best interests" of the child was firmly positioned as child welfare's paramount consideration for intervening in families. Increasingly, children were treated as individual and independent with their own interests and rights (Gilbert et al. 2011; Hennum 2014). Indeed, the United Nations Convention on the Rights of the Child identifies children as having both protection and participation rights. Similarly, the Canadian Charter of Rights and Freedoms extends life, liberty and security of persons to children. The rights of children to personal safety and participation in matters affecting them are mediated in child protection through risk ideology, which is typically premised on scientific claims about predicting probabilities of children being harmed in the future. This approach aligns with a neoliberal rationality of reducing public welfare services by establishing thresholds for services. In the absence of universally available publicly funded supports, meeting eligibility criteria or thresholds for child protection services relies on reporting suspected child maltreatment or neglect.

When a report of suspected maltreatment or neglect of a young person is received, a child protection worker undertakes an investigation that typically includes conducting an assessment and making a safety plan. These risk-oriented safety assessments calculate the likelihood of young people being seriously harmed. Assessments formulated by risk ideology, a premise that the level of likelihood that children will be maltreated or neglected in the future based on identifying the presence or absence of certain indicators, has been criticized for inducing risk-averse workplace climates and adversarial interactions with caregivers (Munro 2009). They have also been criticized for obscuring unjust and inequitable structural factors that disproportionately bring Indigenous, Black, poor people and those from other marginalized communities to the attention of child protection authorities. When children's participation rights (i.e., the right of children to participate in and be heard in judicial or administrative proceedings and processes) are coupled together with an individualized conception of the "best interests" principle, workers are led to consider a child's best interests as though these are separate from the interests of the child's family, extended family or community (Hennum 2014).

When rights and best interests are individualized rather than seen as collective, children can be too easily disconnected from significant relationships and community ties that facilitate their collective, relational and cultural identities (Featherstone et al. 2014). Although these are important considerations for all young people, they are centrally important considerations for Indigenous young people, some of whom may not have connections to a nation or culture and require the opportunity to develop them. These disconnections have particularly negative consequences for Indigenous children (Carrière 2008) and racialized children (Reinoso et al. 2013) and their families. Moreover, as Raby (2014) cautions, to avoid these conceptualizations of individual rights that in effect subjugate children, social workers must see children as embedded in their relational and collective interests. Research demonstrating that the development and maintenance of respectful relationships between workers and families in child welfare processes are always in children's best interests (Fairbairn and Strega 2015).

Child Welfare Law

Laws pertaining to the protection of young people are part of an interrelated statutory and policy framework that emphasizes their personal safety with little to no focus on social protection, often to the exclusion of attending to other important aspects of their well-being. Statutory child welfare overwhelmingly takes a protection stance, which sometimes involves medico-legal forensic investigations that criminalize parental child maltreatment (Gurevich 2010) and child neglect. In Canada, both provincial/territorial child protection laws and the federal Criminal Code hold legal guardians responsible to protect and care for their children. All

Canadian children are legally entitled to these statutory child welfare services, as well as to some state-funded health, education and income-related supports. The effects of these entitlements, however, are neither universal nor equitable. Inequities are due to more than socioeconomic differences. The lives of young people are entangled with laws and policies that regulate Indigeneity, race, class, gender and other social categories. Only about 2 percent of Canadian young people are caught up in the child welfare system, though Indigenous young people are significantly overrepresented (Fairbairn et al. 2019).

ASSESSMENT IN CHILD WELFARE

Michael Hart (2002) shares that an Indigenist framework for assessment features helping values like engaging in non-hierarchical relationships, focusing on healing, ceremony and storytelling. In contrast, dominant approaches to child welfare assessment are typically initiated when there are concerns reported to child protection organizations about children being abused or neglected, or being at risk for abuse or neglect. Reporting is mandatory across Canada and reports can be made by anyone. Disproportionality in reporting, sometimes referred to as referent bias, is well-documented and remains prevalent in neoliberal contexts where very few resources are offered to support parents and communities. In neoliberal risk adverse contexts, protectionist child welfare approaches operate together with "racialized inequities" rooted in "colonialism, class inequity and racism" to intensify reporting disproportionality (Keddell et al. 2024, 107532). Assessments also reproduce gendered, classed, raced and ableist constructions of parenting emerging from imperial and colonial constructions of families, motherhood and childhood (Clarke et al. 2021; Johnstone 2020). Child rescue, the imposition of heteropatriarchal and monogamous family forms as preferred places to raise children, binary constructions of good as opposed to bad mothers and notions of childhood innocence are among the many colonial artifacts that have merged with racism and white (and middle-class) superiority to shape how child welfare has been undertaken. Good parenting is constituted by white middle-class values and norms, which emphasizes parenting practices extensively derived from psychological research and professional knowledge about child development and parent-child relationships (Fairbairn and Strega 2015).

Standardized assessments can normalize dominant parenting practices, conceal racism and privilege professional knowledges that are not relevant to the reasons people are involved with child welfare. These approaches are not just unhelpful, they can reproduce racist and colonial harms. Workers must be alert to how these constructions may be embedded in assessment requirements and processes so they can challenge their own perspectives and consider how they will gather and assess information in ways that resist them. Workers also need to collaborate to advocate for system-level change. While each Canadian jurisdiction has its own standardized assessment framework that workers must follow, these share many similarities, including that redressing or reducing risks and increasing safety for young people are conceptualized as individual caregiver responsibilities. Child protection workers gather information about the adults who are legally responsible for young people to determine whether these adults are both willing and capable of providing required protection and care. Another routine requirement is the development of plans focusing on strengths to redress or reduce risks of harm and increase safety for children, which may include engaging with young people, their caregivers, families and other people with whom they are connected in their communities. Other professionals such as teachers, doctors, therapists and support workers can also provide needed input into child welfare assessments and plans. Indigenous Elders and Knowledge Keepers may contribute essential cultural knowledge to support assessment and planning.

Listening skills are crucial to assessment. From the beginning, it is important to work at understanding everyone's point of view, including differences in perception among family members. The relationships we forge with people provide the foundation for gathering a depth and breadth of understanding about what is important to know *with* children, family members and their communities, thus allowing workers to comprehend how seemingly individual situations are influenced by individual, family and community strengths and resources (Stanley and Mills 2014). It is through relationship and engagement that workers might also come to understand how troubles for young people are aggravated by the effects of political and socioeconomic conditions such as colonialism, poverty, racism, stigma, lack of resources and other inequities. Just as people may be more willing to share their stories when workers are actually listening to them rather than extracting and filtering information through predetermined problem categories, workers may hear how seemingly individual problems are generated in the social realm, including how they have a direct bearing on people's child welfare involvement.

DOCUMENTATION AND RECORDKEEPING

While policies and standards governing documentation and recordkeeping vary between child welfare practice settings, there are very few areas of practice where they are not legally required. Records themselves are legal documents governed under various statutes such as provincial/territorial freedom of information and protection of privacy laws. Workers must be familiar with applicable laws and policies and explain them to young people and their parents, including letting them know with whom and in what circumstances their information can be shared. In addition to documentation requirements in public services like child protection and other non-profit child welfare organizations, regulated social workers employed in public settings and those working in private organizations or practice are also required to follow the documentation and recordkeeping standards outlined by their provincial/territorial regulatory body.

Recordkeeping is required in child welfare for several reasons, including the need for up-to-date contact information for everyone involved; the organization of complex information to facilitate ongoing decision-making and care planning; enabling the sharing of information within and outside the practice setting; the identification of specific details regarding the provision of care; and for current and future legal purposes. Since workers across child welfare practice areas frequently work with many people at the same time, they need accessible, accurate and well-organized information (e.g., name, contact information, age, reason for involvement) about each young person and everyone involved with them. In addition to family members and kin, child welfare matters typically involve other service providers. Since these matters are often complicated and sometimes highly complex, it is important to have a chronology of events and service involvement, including meetings, decisions, interventions and referrals. Documenting details and responses to care plans, including any agreements made together with young people and parents to participate in assessments and services, contributes to evaluating service needs.

Another reason to keep records is because young people and families can be involved with or move to different parts of the child welfare system or be transferred between workers. For example, child welfare services are often divided into separate departments such as intake/investigation, foster care and family services. High worker turnover rates in child protection are common due to high caseloads and stressful work environments. New workers who need to quickly become familiar with relevant information commonly do so through reviewing records. Workers may also need to refer to records in court or records may be subpoenaed for use in legal proceedings. Child welfare, more frequently than other area of social work practice, may involve court proceedings. These include not only child protection hearings and guardianship disputes between parents, but also occasions when children testify as victims or witnesses in child abuse criminal cases. Child protection, parental separation and criminal matters are contentious areas that require workers to rely on detailed notes about assessments and care plans regarding interventions, referrals and recommendations. Records provide evidence demonstrating accountability for service provision and funding audits and may be used in public inquiries and litigation when it is believed services were mismanaged.

Young people themselves or sometimes their parents or guardians may call upon their records to know what workers have documented about them. They may require information pertaining to their medical histories, birth families or to simply understand the events and rationale for decisions impacting their lives. Requests to obtain information from records may even come years later to piece together missing information from their life histories that would otherwise be unknowable. Records may contain emotionally challenging information, or may not include the information people are seeking, which can take an emotional toll. While there are laws in place prescribing how and what information people are entitled to obtain from their records, it is essential for organizations to have processes in place to emotionally support people through the process of obtaining and reviewing their records (Gorin et al. 2024).

Documentation and records can include handwritten or electronic notes taken by social workers pertaining to meetings and telephone contacts; emails, letters and reports completed by other service providers such as parent capacity assessments; and medical, psychological and educational reports pertaining to young people. Records may also include copies of standardized child welfare risk and safety assessments and related forms and checklists. Together with other information, these records may be kept in physical files or entered or uploaded into databases commonly used by public services to store and share information. As Parton (2008) observed, technological systems designed to store information gathered about service users have transformed social work from a relational activity into an informational one. What young people and their families deem important to share can be diminished or excluded when workers are required to gather and record standardized information. The perspectives of young people can be excluded when workers fail to consider children's rights to be included in decisions affecting them, and also when workers disregard the legitimacy of their input simply because they are children (Kosher and Ben-Arieh 2020). Parents not only express concern that records exclude their input but say records can also contain harmful inaccuracies that paint them unfavorably, which can then be used against them in dealings with and decisions made by child welfare workers (Gorin et al. 2024).

Coinciding with neoliberal restructuring focused on increasing efficiency, fiscal management and accountability in public services (Himelfarb 2024), information management systems have resulted in new forms of governing workers and communities. Data-driven electronic documentation systems featuring predetermined check boxes for entering information organize what workers are supposed to be thinking about and doing, thereby dictating how practice encounters are to be undertaken. While these systems have become a mainstay in social welfare contexts, digitalization broadly and in child welfare conceals how conditions of poverty, racism, sexism and other forms of discrimination in the social realm contribute to maintaining inequities for marginalized communities involved with child welfare. Nichols et al. (2024) caution that storing information in databases and other information sharing systems engenders ethical concerns related to increased surveillance created by predictive modelling in risk assessment that targets people from communities that are already overrepresented in child welfare. For example, counter to making services more inclusive and culturally appropriate for Indigenous, Black and 2SLGBTQ+ communities who are overrepresented in child welfare services, the infrastructure of Ontario information systems fails to enable strategies to redress discrimination in workers' decision-making, clinical practice or recording (Nichols and McAuliffe 2024, 3). Similarly, Nichols et al. (2024) explain that when people are made knowable and calculable through standardized digital categories, the means for marginalized communities to represent themselves and their histories in records is subjugated. Although workers could resist whenever possible by extending their assessments and entering additional information beyond standardized categories when more is needed. A decolonial and anti-racist transformation of assessment, documentation and recordkeeping systems is required.

REIMAGINING ASSESSMENT, DOCUMENTATION AND RECORDKEEPING

As a former British colony superseded by an emerging Canadian settler nation, many areas of social work practice were founded and developed alongside colonial social institutions and their administrative infrastructures. According to Sanghera (2024), present-day political, economic and legal methods, just like prevailing cultural norms, remain aligned with those originally established by the British Empire. An empire can seemingly end, but its systems and their workings remain lodged in the infrastructure left behind. This infrastructure not only includes societal institutions, laws and policies and conceptualizations of families and childhood, it extends to our aspirations and hearts and minds and all the ways we think and do. The colonial logics of empire remain deeply entrenched within all aspects of life. This means that most everything about how child welfare is conceptualized must be questioned and rethought, and everything done and how it is done must be reconsidered to decolonize childhood and the future lives on offer for all young people. Solidarity requires child welfare workers to become deeply acquainted with the workings of assessment, documentation and recordkeeping, their historical and contemporary contexts, how they are undertaken and to what effects. In this view, we do not learn to do child welfare assessment, documentation and recordkeeping through a procedure of colonial inheritance; child welfare must be reimagined. The ways of undertaking transformation must also be reimagined and require solidarity to bring about needed change. Just as Indigenous Peoples have not stopped resisting colonial violence, they have never stopped imagining and are already decolonizing child welfare practice.

The United Nations Declaration on the Rights of Indigenous Peoples asserts that Indigenous Peoples are self-determining in relation to family and child welfare. In January 2020, the Canadian government passed Bill C-92, An Act Respecting First

Nations, Inuit and Métis Children, Youth and Families (Government of Canada n.d.). This Act endorses Indigenous jurisdiction over family and child welfare and acknowledges the inherent right of Indigenous Peoples to self-govern family and child welfare rather than operate under provincial/territorial legislation (Walqwan Metallic et al. 2019). The Act also identifies national standards in relation to the best interests of Indigenous children and for provision of services for Indigenous young people and their families.

Indigenous-led child welfare organizations and child welfare practices are not new in Canada. Although some child welfare organizations have provided statutory child protection circumscribed by provincial/territorial legislation, as they and more Indigenous communities assume jurisdiction over child welfare, practice will increasingly be designed according to the distinct protocols of Indigenous nations and communities. Indigenous women have already made extensive inroads into transforming child welfare; they have cared for and educated Indigenous children, established cultural resources and services for Indigenous youth and mothers and their children and developed strategies to abolish carceral and violent policing targeting Indigenous Peoples (MacKinnon and Mallett 2023). Just as Indigenous women have long engaged in resistance to colonialism through being community leaders, decolonial, anti-racist and equitable child welfare approaches require transformative resistance to colonialism.

SUGGESTED READINGS

Nakache, Delphine. 2018. "Migrant Workers and the Right to Family Accompaniment: A Case for Family Rights in International Law and in Canada." *International Migration* 56, 6.

Nichols, Naomi and Jessa McAuliffe. 2024. "The Socio-Technical Organization of Equity, Diversity, and Inclusion (EDI) in Child Welfare." *Journal of Public Child Welfare*, 1–26.

Spencer, Dale and Raven Sinclair. 2017. "Settler Colonialism, Biopolitics, and Indigenous Children in Canada." In *The Sociology of Childhood and Youth in Canada*, edited by Xiaobei Chen, Rebecca Raby and Patrizia Albanese. Toronto: Canadian Scholars Press.

REFERENCES

Adamoski, Robert. 2002. "The Child – The Citizen – The Nation: The Rhetoric and Experience of Wardship in Early Twentieth-Century British Columbia." In *Contesting Canadian Citizenship: Historical Readings*, edited by Robert J. Menzies, Robert L. Adamoski and Dorothy E. Chunn. Peterborough: Broadview Press.

Anderson, Kate, Elaina Elder-Robinson, Alana Gall, Khwanruethai Ngampromwongse, Michele Connolly, Angeline Letendre, Esther Willing et al. 2022. "Aspects of Wellbeing for Indigenous Youth in CANZUS Countries: A Systematic Review." *International Journal of Environmental Research and Public Health* 19, 20.

Barker, Joanne. 2018. "Decolonizing the Mind." *Rethinking Marxism* 30, 2.

Blackstock, Cindy, Terri Libesman, Jennifer King, Brittany Mathews and Wendy Hermeston. 2023. "Decolonizing First Peoples Child Welfare." *The Routledge International Handbook on Decolonizing Justice*, 313.
Carrière, Jeannine. 2008. "Maintaining Identities: The Soul Work of Adoption and Aboriginal Children." *Pimatisiwin: A Journal of Aboriginal and Aboriginal Community Health* 6, 1.
CASWE. 2021. Accreditation Standards. caswe-acfts.ca/our-activities/accreditation/.
Chen, Xiaobei. 2005. *Tending the Gardens of Citizenship: Child Saving in Toronto, 1880s-1920s*. Toronto: University of Toronto Press.
Clarke, Jennifer, Gordon Pon and Doret Phillips. 2021. "The Colour of Child Welfare." In *Africentric Social Work*, edited by Delores V. Mullings, Jennifer Clarke, Wanda Thomas Bernard, David Este and Sulaimon Giwa. Fernwood Publishing.
Crosby, Andrew and Jeffrey Monaghan. 2018. *Policing Indigenous Movements: Dissent and the Security State*. Winnipeg: Fernwood Publishing.
Dauvergne, Catherine. 2016. *The New Politics of Immigration and the End of Settler Societies*. New York: Cambridge University Press.
de Montigny, Gerald. 1995. *Social Working: An Ethnography of Front-line Practice*. Toronto: University of Toronto Press.
Fairbairn, Michele, Susan Strega, and Christopher Walmsley. 2019. "Child and Youth Policy: Building Equality or Buttressing Inequities?" In *Canadian Social Policy for Social Workers*, edited by Robert Harding and Daphne Jeyapal. Toronto: Oxford University Press.
Fairbairn, Michele and Susan Strega. 2015. "Anti-oppressive Approaches to Child Welfare Assessment and File Recording." In *Walking This Path Together: Anti-racist and Anti-oppressive Practice in Child Welfare*, second edition, edited by Jeannine Carrière and Susan Strega. Black Point/Winnipeg: Fernwood Publishing.
Fortier, Craig, and Edward Hon-Sing Wong. 2018. "The Settler Colonialism of Social Work and the Social Work of Settler Colonialism." *Settler Colonial Studies* 9, 4.
Featherstone, Brid, Sue White and Kate Morris. 2014. *Re-imagining Child Protection: Towards Humane Social Work with Families*. Bristol: Polity Press.
Gilbert, Neil, Nigel Parton and Marit Skivenes. 2011. *Child Protection Systems: International Trends and Orientations*. Oxford: Oxford University Press.
Gorin, Sarah, Rosalind Edwards, Val Gillies and Helene Vannier Ducasse. 2024. "'Seen' Through Records: Parents' Access to Children's Social Care Records in an Age of Increasing Datafication." *The British Journal of Social Work*, 54, 1.
Government of Canada, n.d. "An Act respecting First Nations, Inuit and Métis children, youth and families." Justice Laws Website. laws.justice.gc.ca/eng/acts/f-11.73/index.html.
____. 2017. "Realizing a nation-to-nation relationship with the Indigenous Peoples of Canada." canada.ca/en/department-justice/news/2017/07/realizing_a_nation-to-nationrelation shipwiththeindigenouspeoples.html.
____. 2018. "Provincial and territorial child protection legislation and policy." canada.ca/en/public-health/services/publications/health-risks-safety/provincial-territorial-child-protection-legislation-policy-2018.html.
Gurevich, Liena. 2010. "Parental Child Murder and Child Abuse in Anglo-American Legal System." *Trauma, Violence & Abuse* 11, 1.
Hall, Stuart. 2011. "The Neo-liberal Revolution." *Cultural Studies* 25, 6.
Hart, Michael. 2002. *Seeking Mino-Pimatisiwin: An Aboriginal Approach to Helping*. Black Point/Winnipeg: Fernwood Publishing.

Hennum, Nicole. 2014. "Developing Child-Centered Social Policies: When Professionalism Takes Over." *Social Sciences* 3, 3.

Hillel, Inez. 2020. *Holes in the Social Safety Net: Poverty, Inequality and Social Assistance in Canada.* No. 2020-06. Ottawa: Centre for the Study of Living Standards.

Himelfarb, Alex. 2024. *Breaking Free of Neoliberalism: Canada's Challenge.* Toronto: James Lorimer & Company.

Johnstone, Marjorie. 2020. "Epistemic (In)Justice in Child Welfare Risk Assessment." In *Critical Clinical Social Work: Counterstorying for Social Justice,* edited by Catrina Brown and Judy E. MacDonald. Toronto: Canadian Scholars' Press.

Johnstone, Marjorie, and Eunjung Lee. 2020. "Shaping Canadian Citizens: A Historical Study of Canadian Multiculturalism and Social Work during the Period from 1900 to 1999." *International Journal of Social Welfare* 29, 1.

Jongbloed, Kate, Jorden Hendry, Danièle Behn Smith and Joe Kʷunuhmen Gallagher. 2023. "Towards Untying Colonial Knots in Canadian Health Systems: A Net Metaphor for Settler-Colonialism." *Healthcare Management Forum* 36, 4.

Keddell, Emily, Sarah Colhoun, Pauline Norris, and Esther Willing. 2004. "The Heuristic Divergence Between Community Reporters and Child Protection Agencies: Negotiating Risk Amidst Shifting Sands." *Children and Youth Services Review* 159, 107532.

Keefer, Michael. 2020. "Indigenous Human Rights in Canada." In *Gender and Rights,* edited by G.N. Devy and Geoffrey Davis. New York: Routledge.

Kennedy, Dane. 2016. *Decolonization: A Very Short Introduction.* New York: Oxford University Press.

Kosher, Hanita, and Asher Ben-Arieh. 2020. "Social Workers' Perceptions of Children's Right to Participation." *Child & Family Social Work* 25, 2.

Kourgiantakis, Toula, Roula Markoulakis, Eunjung Lee, Amina Hussain, Carrie Lau, Rachelle Ashcroft, Abby L. Goldstein, Sugy Kodeeswaran, Charmaine C. Williams and Anthony Levitt. 2023. "Access to Mental Health and Addiction Services for Youth and Their Families in Ontario: Perspectives of Parents, Youth, and Service Providers." *International Journal of Mental Health Systems* 17, 1.

Landertinger, Laura. 2021. "Settler Colonialism and The Canadian Child Welfare System." In *The Routledge Companion to Sexuality and Colonialism,* edited by Chelsea Schields and Dagmar Herzog. New York: Routledge.

Laycock, Stuart. 2012. *All the Countries We've Ever Invaded: And the Few We Never Got Round to.* England: The History Press.

MacKinnon, Shauna and Kathy Mallett. 2023. *Indigenous Resistance and Development in Winnipeg: 1960-2000.* Winnipeg: Arbeiter Ring Publishing.

McKemmish, Sue, Jane Bone, Joanne Evans, Frank Golding, Antonina Lewis, Gregory Rolan, Kirsten Thorpe, and Jacqueline Wilson. 2020. "Decolonizing Recordkeeping and Archival Praxis in Childhood Out-of-Home Care and Indigenous Archival Collections." *Archival Science* 20, 1.

McLaughlin, Janet, Don Wells, Aaraón Díaz Mendiburo, André Lyn, and Biljana Vasilevska. 2017. "'Temporary Workers,' Temporary Fathers: Transnational Family Impacts of Canada's Seasonal Agricultural Worker Program." *Relations Industrielles* 72, 4.

Munro, Eileen. 2009. "Managing Societal and Institutional Risk in Child Protection." *Risk Analysis* 29, 7.

Murphy, Michelle. 2020. "Some keywords toward decolonial methods: Studying settler colonial histories and environmental violence from Tkaronto." *History and Theory: Studies in the Philosophy of History* 59, 3.

Nakache, Delphine. 2018. "Migrant Workers and the Right to Family Accompaniment: A Case for Family Rights in International Law and in Canada." *International Migration* 56, 6.

Needham, Fraser. 2024. "Human Rights Tribunal Hears Feds Failing to Meet Jordan's Principle Commitments." *APTN News Online*. September 10, 2024. aptnnews.ca/national-news/human-rights-tribunal-hears-feds-failing-to-meet-jordans-principle-commitments/

Nichols, Robert. 2020. *Theft is Property*. Durham, NC: Duke University Press.

Nichols, Naomi and Jessa McAuliffe. 2024. "The Socio-Technical Organization of Equity, Diversity, and Inclusion (EDI) in Child Welfare." *Journal of Public Child Welfare*, 1–26.

Nichols, Naomi, Kody Crowell, Michael Lenczner and Jessa Bourns. 2024. "Data Justice for Youth in and Leaving Care: Mapping the Child Welfare Data Landscape in Ontario." *Information, Communication & Society*, 27, 2.

Parton, Nigel. 2008. "Changes in the Form of Knowledge in Social Work: From the 'Social' to the 'Informational'?" *The British Journal of Social Work*, 38, 2.

Raby, Rebecca. 2014. "Children's Participation as Neo-Liberal Governance?" *Discourse* 35, 1.

Reinoso, Marta, Femmie Juffer and Wendy Tieman. 2013. "Children's and Parents' Thoughts and Feelings about Adoption, Birth Culture Identity and Discrimination in Families with Internationally Adopted Children." *Child & Family Social Work* 18, 3.

Richards, Thomas. 1993. *The Imperial Archive: Knowledge and the Fantasy of Empire*. London/New York: Verso.

Roseman, Sharon. 2016. "Children's Literature and Memory Activism: British Child Labor Migrants' Passage to Canada." In *Migration by Boat: Discourses of Trauma, Exclusion and Survival*, edited by Lynda Mannik. Berghahn Books. Sanghera, Sathnam. 2024. *Empireworld: How British Imperialism Has Shaped the Globe*. New York: Viking Press.

Schram, Sandford. 2018. "Neoliberalizing the Welfare State: Marketizing Social Policy/Disciplining Clients." In *The SAGE Handbook of Neoliberalism*, edited by Damien Cahill, Melinda Cooper, Martijn Konings and David Primrose. Sage.

Spencer, Dale and Raven Sinclair. 2017. "Settler Colonialism, Biopolitics, and Indigenous Children in Canada." In *The Sociology of Childhood and Youth in Canada*, edited by Xiaobei Chen, Rebecca Raby and Patrizia Albanese. Toronto: Canadian Scholars Press.

Simpson, Audra. 2020. "The Sovereignty of Critique." *The South Atlantic Quarterly* 119, 4.

Simpson, Leanne Betasamosake. 2011. *Dancing on our Turtle's Back: Stories of Nishnaabeg Recreation, Resurgence, and a New Emergence*. Arbeiter Ring Publishing.

Stanley Tony and Rob Mills. 2014. "Signs of Safety Practice at the Health and Social Care Interface." *Practice: Social Work in Action* 26, 1.

Stefanick, Lorna and Myra J. Tait. 2024. "Crisis in Care: Structural Poverty, Colonization and Child Apprehensions in Canada." *Canadian Journal of Political Science/Revue canadienne de science politique* 57, 1.

Stoler, Ann Laura. 2002. "Colonial Archives and the Arts of Governance." *Archival Science* 2, 1–2.

Strong-Boag, Veronica Jane. 2011. *Fostering Nation?: Canada Confronts Its History of Childhood Disadvantage*. Waterloo, Ontario: Wilfred Laurier University Press.

Swain, Shurlee and Margot Hillel. 2010. *Child, Nation, Race and Empire: Child Rescue Discourse, England, Canada and Australia, 1850-1915*. Manchester and New York: Manchester University Press.

Swift, Karen. 1995. *Manufacturing 'Bad Mothers': A Critical Perspective on Child Neglect*. Toronto: University of Toronto Press.

Taylor, Alison and Jason Foster. 2015. Migrant Workers and the Problem of Social Cohesion in Canada. *Journal of International Migration and Integration* 16, 1.

Tuck, Eve and K. Wayne Yang. 2012. "Decolonization is not a Metaphor." *Education and Society* 1, 1.

Tuhiwai Smith, Linda. 2012. *Decolonizing Methodologies: Research and Indigenous Peoples*. London/New York: Zed Books.

Turner, Joe. 2020. *Bordering Intimacy: Postcolonial Governance and the Policing of Family*. Manchester: Manchester University Press.

UNICEF. 2023. *UNICEF Report Card 18: Child poverty in Canada*. unicef.ca/sites/default/files/2023-12/UNICEFReportCard18CanadianCompanion.pdf.

Walqwan Metallic, Naiomi, Hadley Friedland and Sarah Morales. 2019. *The Promise and Pitfalls of C-92: An Act Respecting First Nations, Inuit, and Métis Children, Youth and Families*. Toronto: Yellowhead Institute. yellowheadinstitute.org/wp-content/uploads/2019/07/the-promise-and-pitfalls-of-c-92-report.pdf.

Chapter 5

GIIDOSENDIWAG
Walking Together with Indigenous Youth in Care

by Nancy Stevens and Ziigwanbinesii (Rachel Charles)

> Plates make vibrations
> If you smash them
> Against the wall
> But you can't hear the sound
> If your cry is louder
> Than the china

(Poem by a youth at Niijkiwendidaa Anishnaabekwewag Services Circle, shared with permission, 2016.)

CHAPTER FOCUS

Indigenous youth across Canada are disproportionately impacted by the child welfare system, and those transitioning out of care continue to experience challenges specific to their relationships with their families, communities and cultures. In this chapter, we explore some key issues we encountered during the first two years of providing the AYIT program at Niijkiwendidaa Anishnaabekwewag Services Circle in Peterborough, Ontario, Canada. The Youth in Transition (YIT) program, which was launched in 2014 by the Ontario Ministry of Children, Community and Social Services, aimed to better support youth aging out of the system (Ontario Ministry of Children, Community and Social Services 2014). We invited the youth, through a group creative activity, to share how they felt about being in care, their experiences with the AYIT and whether it supported them in ways that strengthened their sense of identity and culture. We share some of their perceptions here.

QUESTIONS ADDRESSED IN THIS CHAPTER

1. What are some of the key challenges that Indigenous youth in Ontario encounter when they are brought into the child protection or child welfare system?
2. What are some examples of how culture can become the foundation of support to Indigenous youth in care?
3. Why is it important that Indigenous youth have access to Indigenous supports as a core principle of their care?

STARTING UP THE AYIT PROGRAM

Niijkiwendidaa Anishnaabekwewag Services Circle is a small non-profit organization[1] that has provided services to Indigenous[2] women and their families since 1992 (Niijkiwendidaa Anishnaabekwewag Services Circle 2016). The services offered have evolved over time, but violence against women funding has been a staple service since Niijkiwendidaa's inception. Niijkiwendidaa's catchment area is substantial and includes the city of Peterborough; the counties of Haliburton, Northumberland, and Peterborough; the city of Kawartha Lakes and the Durham Region. Within this huge area, there are three Children's Aid Societies (Kawartha-Haliburton, Highland Shores and Durham), as well as several private foster care agencies that advertise themselves as specialized treatment agencies for children and youth.

The challenges of starting up a new program not directly connected to either designated, non-profit Children's Aid Societies or for-profit private foster care organizations were considerable. The province required that all youth in care, from age sixteen to the time they exit care, be connected to YIT workers to support the youth's transitions to independent living. But agencies of all types were often unaware that there was such a program or that there were Indigenous-specific YIT programs. Outreach by the AYIT worker was ongoing and substantial in the effort made to create awareness with the various organizations, including private foster care organizations, schools and the Children's Aid Societies within Niijkiwendidaa's catchment area.

Outreach was also necessary to build relationships with local Indigenous Elders and Knowledge Carriers who would become integral to the circle of support offered. The program offered a wide range of supports and activities: individual and crisis counselling; life skills such as budgeting, cooking, and cleaning; networking with community supports; connecting young people to post-secondary education, employment, and housing; linking young people to cultural ceremonies such as smudging, Sweat Lodge, cedar bath, naming ceremonies, full-moon ceremonies, traditional adoption ceremonies and teachings, among others. The AYIT worker also facilitated sharing circles for the youth in the program with invited Elders, Knowledge Holders, Medicine Keepers, storytellers, and drummers. Services were developed from a holistic approach rooted in Indigenous world views. This encompassed looking at mental, emotional, physical and spiritual health and wellness within the context of each person's relationships to family, community and Creation.

Since 2016 there have been several developments, including changes to provincial and federal legislation, that have changed the Indigenous child protection landscape. There are now ten mandated Indigenous-led child welfare agencies across the province, including Dnaagdawenmag Binnoojiiyag Child and Family Services, which provides Indigenous child welfare services in the same region in which Niijkiwendidaa operates. There are more Indigenous-led child and family organizations in line to receive designation, along with more than sixty Indigenous child and family well-being services available across Ontario that do not have designation to apprehend (Association of Native Child and Family Services Agencies of Ontario 2023). Despite funding and policy shifts, Indigenous children and youth remain disproportionately impacted by the child welfare system (Hobson 2022). The YIT programs across the province have grown in number.

HISTORICAL CONTEXT IN ONTARIO

In Canada, the Indian[3] Act of 1876 was imposed on First Nations and has governed all aspects of First Nations identity, land and property access, and more ever since. During the first several decades of its existence, the Indian Act was repeatedly and extensively amended, becoming progressively restrictive and outlawing central aspects of Indigenous life, such as ceremonies and the wearing of traditional clothing. Anyone with Indian Status who wanted to attend post-secondary education lost their Status once they earned a degree. Women were recognized as Indian only through their relationships to men — either their fathers or their husbands — and were stripped of their Status if they married men not recognized as Indian by the federal government. In the 1927 amendments to the Act, Indians were forbidden the right to hire lawyers or to organize politically (Joseph 2018; Shewell 1999). There was substantial pressure by the federal government until the 1970s to force Indians to live on reserves overseen by Indian Agents. The reserve system became a blueprint for later apartheid systems elsewhere, notably in South Africa. The Indian Act also became the legislative vehicle through which residential schools and day schools were launched as official forms of forced assimilation. Funded by the federal government starting in the late 1880s, and operated by Christian churches, residential schools are particularly notorious for their horrific abuses of the children forced to attend them.

From its inception, the Indian Act delineated federal responsibilities for Indians living on reserve. Provinces and territories had no jurisdiction over what happened in First Nations communities, including child welfare, which only later became a provincial responsibility beginning in 1893 in Ontario. Major amendments to the Indian Act in 1951, however, paved the way for the provincial/territorial child welfare systems across Canada to begin apprehending First Nations children living on First Nations lands. Since then, the child welfare system has been integral to perpetuating the assimilation of Indigenous Peoples that was started with the residential school policy amendments in the Indian Act beginning in 1884 (McMahon 2017; Sinha et al. 2021; Truth and Reconciliation Commission of Canada 2015). From the 1960s to the 1980s, First Nations, Métis and Inuit children were apprehended by child welfare workers who advocated and facilitated adoption of these children. According to Sinclair (2016, 9), "By the 1970s, one in three First Nation children was separated from their families by adoption or fostering." This Sixties Scoop evolved into the Millennium Scoop, with exponentially increasing rates of Indigenous children and youth primarily placed in foster care (Fallon et al. 2021; Sinclair 2016).

By the early 1970s in Ontario, First Nations chiefs and groups began demanding that their children be returned to them and any further apprehensions cease (Kozlowski et al. 2012). As a result of these efforts, in 1984 Ontario added provisions into the Child and Family Services Act setting out recognition of the rights of First Nations children and made way for development of the first provincially funded First Nations–run child welfare organizations (Kozlowski et al. 2012). The first of the provinces and territories in Canada to acknowledge the importance of culture, Ontario "also recognized that culturally competent and appropriate services were not optional when working with Native children and families, they were imperative" (Bennett and Blackstock 2002, 52). These legislative changes, however, did not reduce the number of children who came into contact with the system. Rather, rates of apprehension continued to grow apace. The Truth and Reconciliation Commission of Canada (2015, 138) stated, "A 2011 Statistics Canada study found that 14,225 or 3.6% of all First Nations children aged fourteen and under were in foster care, compared with 15,345 or 0.3% of non-Aboriginal children." Ten years later, according to the 2021 Canadian census, Indigenous children make up over half of all children in care under the age of fourteen and yet comprise less than 8 percent of the total child and youth population (Government of Canada 2023). The Ontario Human Rights Commission (2018, 17) notes, "Indigenous children are over-represented at all points of child welfare decision-making. This over-representation increases as service decisions become more intrusive."

Similarly, these changes did little to address the needs of Indigenous children and youth coming into contact with child protection agencies. For example, despite the shifts, Indigenous-run child protection agencies' autonomy to fully function from Indigenous paradigms has been limited by child welfare ministry directives and funding restrictions, essentially forcing them to operate within the same parameters as non-Indigenous agencies (Cameron 2010; Roach 2000). This is seen in aspects such as who was approved to be a foster parent, in kinship care arrangements and in the lack of funding available for extended family members taking on the care of children. Even with more recent changes to provincial and federal legislation, Indigenous child protection agencies too often struggle to access culturally based resources. The recruitment of an adequate number of Indigenous foster families within regions also remains challenging (Aboriginal Children in Care Working Group 2015; Sinha et al. 2013).

Ontario Public and Private Child Welfare Systems

There are many First Nations citizens living off reserve and in urban areas who may be disconnected from their cultural and territorial roots. Similarly, a like number of Indigenous children who are in care and in foster care do not have Indigenous-run organizations as their care provider. Instead, they are placed in non-Indigenous services that offer little, if anything, connected to culture and historical homelands. This disparity is a great concern to Indigenous leaders who believe these children are losing touch with their cultural roots. It is reported that as children's length of care increases, their sense of community and culture becomes more difficult to attain. This disconnect creates despair and confusion as the child ages within the system and eventually leaves it (Beaucage 2011).

Within the publicly funded, non-Indigenous child welfare system in Ontario, efforts to shore up the cultural identity development of children and youth remain inconsistent (Sinha et al. 2013). This factor is even more challenging for Indigenous children and youth who have been raised by their families in urban environments, and who do not have Indian Status when coming into care. For various reasons, their families may not admit they are Indigenous, or the child protection agency may simply not think to ask. This then sets up Indigenous children and youth to be even further disconnected from developing robust cultural identities that would strengthen their overall development into adulthood (Beaucage 2011; Kline 1992; Métis Nation of Ontario 2012). As well, there is substantial evidence that Indigenous youth are more likely to be repeatedly moved from placement to placement than non-Indigenous youth (Doucet 2020; Fallon et al. 2013; Tait et al. 2013). This has the potential to further fragment their sense of identity and belonging.

The for-profit foster system is even more problematic. There are few accountability mechanisms in this system (Ontario Ministry of Children and Youth Services 2016), which raises concerns on many levels, but from Indigenous perspectives, the inconsistent access to cultural supports, activities and services for

Indigenous youth is particularly troubling. Many Indigenous youth, particularly in the for-profit system, are from remote northern communities or out of province. Due to the lack of resources in those areas, they are sent to southern urban areas such as Peterborough, Barrie or Toronto to be raised in cultures that are often vastly different, with very few cultural or familial supports and no real way to remain connected to home. Further compounding this familial and cultural destabilization, the youth's files may not follow them to the new community, and so both care and transition plans rest on the uncertainty that the for-profit agency will facilitate regular, ongoing access to cultural supports for the youth in their care, and that the youth will be connected to YIT workers in preparation for their exit from care. The province has no direct oversight of the private foster care system and so cannot ensure supports that nurture cultural and family continuity.

There have been changes to legislation regarding the ages that children are deemed to be out of care. Although, technically, youth are considered adults on their 18th birthday by the child welfare system, there are some options for youth to remain supported for an additional few years. In 2022, the federal government extended the age of youth aging out of care at their province's age of majority for up to two additional years, but the funds must be applied for. In Ontario, the age of majority is eighteen years. For youth whose file did not follow them to the private foster system, the implications are that there may not be anyone to advocate for the youth and apply for extended funding. This underscores the need for Jordan's Principle to be implemented at all levels of government in its broadest possible interpretation (Aboriginal Children in Care Working Group 2015; Blackstock 2009).

Jordan's Principle is intended to address the discriminatory way in which the Canadian government has underfunded services for First Nations children, including child welfare, healthcare and more. Jordan River Anderson was a child born in 1999 with multiple disabilities who spent all his five years of life in hospital. At age two, his parents were told they could bring him home, but the provincial and federal governments would not agree on who would pay for his out-of-hospital care, resulting in Jordan remaining in hospital. Inspired by the difficulties experienced by Jordan and his family, and by the First Nations Child and Family Caring Society bringing the issue national focus, the principle aims to mitigate chronic disparities faced by First Nations children. There is a long history of protracted disputes between the federal government and the provincial and territorial governments over which body must pay for services for First Nations. This is a result of the differing levels of government having different responsibilities (Sinha et al. 2015). Jordan's Principle was initially adopted by the federal government in 2007 as a child-first principle to "resolve jurisdictional disputes involving the care of First Nations children" (First Nations Child and Family Caring Society 2015, 1–2). In 2007, the Assembly of First Nations and the First Nations Child and Family Caring

Society of Canada brought the issue of inequitable services funding to the Canadian Human Rights Tribunal. The case was found in favour of First Nations children and youth and the Tribunal issued a legally binding decision against the Canadian government. As recently as 2017, the Canadian Human Rights Tribunal has issued decisions requiring the federal government to expand its hitherto extremely narrow criteria for First Nations children and youth to be able to access funds to support their needs (First Nations Child and Family Caring Society 2023).

The impacts of the underfunding on child welfare services were profound, with children and youth being denied services where child welfare agencies were receiving federal funds for First Nations children and youth. Further, for First Nations children and youth with special needs, too often the only way for their parents to access care has been through giving up their children to child welfare agencies (First Nations Child and Family Caring Society 2015). This was prevalent at Niijkiwendidaa, where several youth were in private agency foster homes. Youth with various developmental or other chronic health challenges were more likely to find themselves in care, living in urban areas far from their home communities. We are aware of youth and adult clients in the area who had transitioned out of care and who grappled with the challenges like fetal alcohol spectrum disorder or mental health concerns. The lack of support deeply affects their economic stability, mental well-being and more.

INDIGENOUS YOUTH, IDENTITY AND CULTURE

> As long as I make my bed and follow their rules, they will think I'm doing great even if I have a Wendigo[4] that follows me every night and my dreams are filled with fear. (AYIT youth, sixteen years old, shared with permission)

Indigenous supports that are culturally based are often seen as unimportant by people who interact with the child or youth in the various systems and who are generally not Indigenous themselves (Choate et al. 2019). There is a growing body of literature, however, that articulates the profound importance of a positive sense of one's culture in the formation of a healthy, resilient sense of identity (Chandler and Lalonde 1998; Filbert 2012; Lalonde 2005; Quinn 2020; Hinson et al. 2015). At the same time, research has repeatedly demonstrated that Indigenous youth who have been in the child welfare system are more likely than non-Indigenous youth to end up homeless, criminalized or in other vulnerable situations (Doucet 2020; Kidd et al. 2019; Rampersaud et al. 2021; Sansone et al. 2020). It can be very difficult to understand the immersive and vital role of culture in identity formation unless one steps outside of their own culture. It should not be difficult to understand that children and youth require stable relationships within their families and communities in order to mature into healthy adults, nor should it be difficult to find ways to support families who are struggling because of the intergenerational and collective traumas they have experienced as a direct result of ongoing colonialism. It is within the context of family and community as well that culture and language is transmitted and connections nurtured between generations. Fostering youth connectedness through the creation of a family or community "nest" can be one approach to build connections for youth away from their families and communities of origin:

> Given the extent to which culture is constitutive of Indigenous identity and the capacity of Indigenous peoples to be free to conceive and pursue meaningful lives and given the fundamental importance of children to the survival of First Nations and Aboriginal culture, the "best interests of the community" must inform the "best interests of the child" in placement and custody decisions. (Lynch 2001, 506)

Indigenous youth respond positively to being involved in their cultures, such as through ceremony and working with Elders, and thus creating a strong sense of personal, cultural, familial and community identity (Aboriginal Children in Care Working Group 2015; Cameron 2010; Filbert 2012; Lalonde 2005; Office of the Child and Youth Advocate of Alberta 2016; Raman et al. 2012; Tait et al. 2013). Yet mainstream Canadian society and its various institutions, particularly child protection agencies and workers, too often do not understand how to genuinely and authentically incorporate this into a child or youth's daily life (Fraser et al. 2016; Park 2003). Further, there is a deeply problematic and common practice of framing the youth's access to cultural supports as a reward for compliant behaviour (known as the merit system), which negates the integral role positive cultural identity development has in the overall healthy growth of youth (Fraser et al. 2016).

Incorporating Indigenous cultural practices appropriately into an organization can be facilitated through expanding the service lens and by shifting the organizational culture. However, this takes time and a commitment to going beyond superficial measures. Hiring an Indigenous worker to be the "face" of Indigenousness within a child protection agency, for example, does not adequately address the legitimate and comprehensive needs of our youth. One person cannot meet all needs and job description parameters limit the scope of work that any single staff member can take on. As well, the education and training of social workers and child and youth workers remains firmly rooted in Euro-Western ways of thinking (Blackstock 2009; Choate et al. 2022; Sinclair 2004). These ways of thinking focus on the individual rather than on the family and community. Issues that are systemic in nature (e.g., racism, poverty) tend to be framed through a neoliberal, individualistic lens, as though an individual can somehow create necessary systemic shifts in an ongoing colonial context. Culture is rarely addressed in deep or nuanced ways, and the historical experiences of Indigenous Peoples are often glossed over. It is also important to note that being Indigenous is no guarantee of being able to provide culturally based support because of how colonialism has and continues to affect individuals. Non-Indigenous staff may not have any understanding of Indigenous history or cultures or may lack confidence to use what knowledge they have to support youth, which perpetuates cultural disconnections (Choate et al. 2022).

For our youth to be successful, they need to be fully connected with Indigenous community and have access to their respective cultures. This is difficult under normal circumstances. It is even more difficult for children and youth who come from remote northern communities or from other provinces, who may not speak English or French as a first language, and who may be from a cultural group that has no history in the agency's catchment area. The tendency to homogenize Indigenous cultures remains deeply embedded in mainstream discourse and practices. There is a distinct and persistent lack of awareness that Canada is built on the territories of more than fifty culturally distinct peoples. The cultural and linguistic norms even within a single cultural group such as Ojibway can vary substantially between different communities. Our staff were acutely aware of the challenge to respond to diverse cultural needs in ways that acknowledged our limitations. As often as possible, we would attempt to connect youth to mentors who had some familiarity of the youth's culture. Too often this was not possible. We talked with the youth about the challenges of trying to meet their needs with respect to cultural knowledge. To that end, we drew on the many commonalities across Indigenous cultures to support the youth. They were encouraged to think about what it means to create relationships across cultures and clans, extending their own extended family and community connections. Building community away from home helped reduce the sense of isolation that the youth too often experience.

Diverging Views of Identity and Connection

In Ontario as in the rest of Canada, a growing number of Indigenous-run organizations and Indigenous-specific programs within larger non-Indigenous agencies have been developed to meet a range of needs (e.g., mental health, child protection and family support, primary health care). However, there is inconsistency in terms of provincial and federal mandates for the development or ongoing operations maintenance of these services (Sinha et al. 2013). The child protection system, as with other mainstream systems such as education, law and health care, views the world through a Western lens. According to Park (2003, 47),

> For non-Aboriginals, the focus is on the child as an individual member of society whose needs are individually determined, with primary needs such as security being paramount. In contrast, Aboriginal people view the child as a member of the collective whose identity is tied to his heritage.

Although there is clear evidence that youth well-being is positively impacted by connection to family, culture and community, the importance of ensuring this has varying degrees of weight for child protection agencies, depending on a range of factors such as the child protection agency's policies and organizational culture (Fraser et al. 2016). Some child protection agencies have a clear interest in creating those supports, demonstrated through the development of policies and practices that are championed by key members within the organization, including upper administration and the board of directors. Other organizations have advocates but are unable to move the institutional culture because support for change is lacking in key areas. It is also important to consider the willingness and ability of individual workers to work collaboratively with the respective First Nations representatives, as well as the ability of First Nations workers to engage with and advocate for their members, regardless of their geographic location (Raman et al. 2012; Sinclair 2007).

The challenges of supporting identity and community connection are even more pronounced for Métis youth. The issues of identity and maintaining cultural connection is many layered for Métis peoples, centred on historic experiences that led many to suppress their origins or deny them completely. Despite a complex, oppressive history, Métis communities have fought for years to be recognized federally and provincially as having the same inherent rights as First Nations, although they do not fall within the scope of the Indian Act. While those rights have been acknowledged to some degree by the courts, the subsequent development of policies and resourcing by provincial and federal governments is piecemeal at best. To compound problematic government responses, broader Canadian society remains largely unaware of what constitutes Métis culture, history and rights. This lack of knowledge is shared by individual child welfare workers and more generally at organizational levels by Children's Aid Societies. As recently as 2018, child welfare worker training had yet to adequately address issues of identity to ensure that Métis children are included in the "Indian and Native" provisions of the Child and Family Services Act (Métis Nation of Ontario 2012; Ontario Ministry of Children and Youth Services 2016). Our experience with local organizations affirmed the need for a much more robust training for workers in both the public and private systems.

Urban Indigenous youth, whether they have Status or not, represent another challenge. Currently about 45 percent of all Indigenous people now live in urban areas with populations over 100,000 (Statistics Canada 2022). For urban Indigenous people with Status, federal programs offered to First Nations reserve communities are not available to those living off reserve. Distance from a home reserve can impede the First Nation community's involvement in decision-making in child welfare cases. This can take the form of an inability to travel to distant communities, unstable communications technology to participate in child welfare court proceedings or case conferences, or simply the breakdown of relations between the youth's family and their First Nation reserve community over time and lack of involvement (Toth et al. 2018). And, although provincial organizations such as the Ontario Federation of Indigenous Friendship Centres and federal government departments have worked to create policies and programs to support the urban populations, there remain many challenges in meeting the needs of Indigenous families and youth consistently across all regions (Government of Canada 2017; Government of Ontario et al. 2018).

Changes to provincial and federal legislation and practice guidelines since 2018 give some hope that child welfare organizations are adopting practices better suited to meeting the needs of First Nations, Métis, Inuit and non-Status Indigenous children. In an Ontario ministry policy directive, for example, designated agencies are expected follow a set of guiding principles when considering a youth's transition from care. The principles are:

- transition planning is care;
- individualized assessment and planning is most effective when done gradually with strong preparation and individualized supports;
- education and employment pathways can be made more accessible when the right supports are in place for youth;
- youth must be the drivers of their transitions from care, and agencies need to use a trauma-informed approach in supporting the youth;
- concurrent planning is necessary for all options for children;
- connections to culture, identity and community are integral to the well-being of youth;
- culturally appropriate services for First Nations, Inuit and Métis youth should be provided. (Ministry of Children, Community and Social Services 2023)

The challenge for Indigenous youth, however, is in the wording: "should" does not carry the same legal weight as "will," which allows ample room for child welfare organizations to avoid efforts to ensure the cultural needs of youth are met. Too many organizations take advantage of this room.

At the federal level, legislative changes brought about in 2021 also offer some optimism for how changes may be coming to child welfare services. The 2019 Act respecting First Nation, Inuit and Métis children, youth and families represents the first time the federal government has taken steps to exercise its ability to create child welfare legislation and set out the recognition that First Nations, Métis and Inuit have an inherent right to care for their own children (Government of Canada 2019; Walqwan Metallic et al. 2019). Despite this federal recognition, there is a growing list of provinces and territories that are challenging what they believe to fall within their jurisdiction (Stefanovich 2023). Ontario is not one of those challenging the federal government's jurisdiction, perhaps because of its different history with funding agreements with the federal government regarding child welfare. Yet language within the Act, particularly foundational concepts such as "best interests of the child," perpetuate colonial rules and practices in ways dicussed earlier. As noted by Walqwan Metallic et al. (2019) there are substantial concerns regarding national standards, funding, jurisdiction and accountability.

AYIT AT NIIJKIWENDIDAA

> I feel more cultured and I can stand on my own two feet. I feel more open and connected. The drumming, singing and dancing helps me … these are normal activities at Niijkiwendidaa it makes me feel like I am home. I don't have to hide who I really am here. I feel safe. I am aging out of care in three months, and I know that the [AYIT] program won't drop me like CS is going to. I don't feel scared to turn 18 anymore. I know I will have these people in my life for as long as I need them … this is what family means to me, this is community. (Male at Niijkiwendidaa, seventeen, youth in care, shared with permission)

AYIT blends Western therapies with Indigenous practices and teachings. The Circle of Courage model is a culturally based approach to individual counselling and for developing plans of care for the youth. The model is divided into four quadrants: belonging, mastery, independence and generosity (Brendtro et al. 2013). These concepts are consistent with Medicine Wheel teachings and holistic approaches in Indigenous service provision. They reflect universal human needs, creating foundations for psychological resilience and positive youth development. This framework was an effective basis on which to develop programming to reach a deeper level of learning and insight with the Indigenous youth. The model was also used as an assessment tool to identify gaps for the youth and to plan how to bridge those gaps. In practice, the assessment process would explore where the youth felt belonging and what those relationships looked like. Mastery would identify things the youth felt they were good at or that they felt confident about their knowledge. Independence and generosity were considered similarly. In using this as an intervention, belonging was developed through the relationships with other members of the group and with the Elders, community and agency involvement. Mastery came through acquiring new skills, such as drumming or sharing a smudge, and then demonstrated by mentoring new youth coming into the group, and so on.

Supporting youth as they fill these quadrants is a process that takes time and requires support from more than just the AYIT worker. Creating a strong and positive community for the youth is another essential aspect. When the youth have a strong, positive network they are then able to connect with healthy mentors and role models and through them learn about the culture. Through the building of relationships, the youth at Niijkiwendidaa found many skills they excelled at, such as traditional dancing, beading, singing, drumming and cooking. This, in turn, strengthens the youth's abilities so they are not merely surviving. Instead, they are thriving, building their identity and creating a supportive community. By using a strengths-based approach that teaches youth to "do for self," the AYIT worker created a supportive space for every step along the path with each of the youth.

Cultural connection is the foundational philosophy and practice at Niijkiwendidaa, which created opportunities for the youth to build their sense of self while learning more about where they were from. Many of these youth reported feeling culturally numb, which for them meant knowing nothing or very little about their own cultures or the history and impacts of colonization on Indigenous Peoples and cultures. They did not realize how their own family breakdown was often a direct result of colonialism. For example, they did not connect the substance abuse and the physical, mental, emotional or spiritual violence the youth or their family experienced to colonialism. Many of them were not proud to be Indigenous and did not understand the sacredness they held within themselves. Many youth were oblivious to their gifts and roles and responsibilities and had little exposure to traditional practices or teachings. Several AYIT youth indicated that they felt isolated from their culture, their biological family and their community. Bringing in diverse Elders and healthy community members for the youth drop-in group or for cultural activities helped build an inviting space and community for the youth at Niijkiwendidaa. Maintaining the focus on cultural reconnection and belonging proved to be very successful for the AYIT program youth. Many of them reported feeling a sense of home or family at Niijkiwendidaa. And many youth have stated that receiving their traditional spirit name, a ceremony brought to AYIT youth, has helped them feel as though they have a sense of purpose, replacing their former feelings of emptiness or hopelessness.

Challenges

> Before I started learning about my true self, culture and spirituality ... I had a lot of past hurts and trauma to sort through that were constantly holding me back. It felt like a weight I couldn't lift ... turns out I just needed someone to spot me. (Male, seventeen, shared with permission)

In the short first two years of the AYIT program, we saw many challenges and successes. Many of the challenges for the program originated from outside agencies' lack of cultural competency or historical awareness. The importance of Indigenous identity and the history of colonization and its resulting impacts on families is a key factor in child protection, both for the parents and children. Yet many workers in group homes or within the Children's Aid Societies did not understand this. It was not uncommon for the AYIT worker to cross paths with workers who held biased mindsets. For example, we would receive calls, inquiring about services for youth with the worker saying something like, "The youth states that they are Native, but he has no proof of this. He also has blond hair and blue eyes." This type of unexamined bias and racism was experienced frequently; the idea that a person can only be Indigenous if they look like a stereotypical "Indian" or if they carry a Status Card reinforces broader societal attitudes that invalidate the youth's inner knowledge of self. Racism presented itself in ways that were equally as damaging. Too often, if a youth had misbehaved, we would hear that their cultural activities or programming would get taken away, but basketball or cooking class was not. Culturally based activities such as participating in powwows, ceremonies or other Indigenous-specific programming was not looked upon as effective or equal to mainstream supports, religion (i.e., Christianity) or mainstream activities.

> I felt that I was trapped before, in a cocoon before I came to Niijkiwendidaa. I felt isolated ... I felt that I had nobody to help me even though I was surrounded by CAS workers and in a foster home. I feel that I have opened into a butterfly since being involved with the Aboriginal Youth in Transition program. (Male, seventeen, shared with permission)

Another systemic challenge was the lack of referrals received through the child welfare system. YIT programs were not often housed within child protection agencies at that time. Adding a new layer of service takes time to gain momentum, even when it is an in-house program; adding a new layer that is both external and culturally different from the mainstream adds a double burden on the workers trying to move a program forward. Despite the provincial mandate to connect all youth in care from age sixteen to YIT programs, it was our experience that while the AYIT worker was the last to be consulted or brought into plan care meetings and case conferences, they were the first person the youth would call when they were in trouble from being absent without leave from their foster placement or when they needed immediate support. We also noted a distinct lack of consistency in how youth were involved in developing their plans of care. Too often they were not consulted about their own transition plans, or they were forced out of the system, often on their eighteenth birthday, regardless of their actual readiness for independent living.

We encountered additional systemic challenges with respect to youth who were transferred to our region from other areas. Niijkiwendidaa had agreements with child protection agencies such as Tikinagan in northwestern Ontario so that we could more easily step into supporting children and youth being relocated to the Peterborough and Durham regions, as per the Ministry of Child and Youth

Services policy directive. Significantly, the AYIT worker too often was not notified about new Indigenous youth being relocated, so when they arrived, they were left without cultural supports or the means to make community connections. It is important to note that northern and remote organizations are chronically underfunded and under staffed, leading to a lack of capacity for follow through on cases. A compounding issue for the youth, in our experience, was that too often their file did not come with them. This resulted in the AYIT worker being unable to work on transition plans with the youth because there was no official child welfare agency oversight. In essence, the youth were left to fall through the cracks.

A final note regarding challenges: lack of funding for the AYIT program remains a critical issue. The level of funding available to Niijkiwendidaa during the initial period covered the wages of one full-time equivalent worker along with limited funds for other program costs. The cost of travel and the time needed for it was considerable because the catchment area is quite substantial. This left the program financially constrained in its ability to access Elders and Traditional Knowledge Keepers. Land-based programming was not funded, and so unattainable for AYIT, even though spending time on the land is an integral aspect of Indigenous identity. At the same time, we consistently had more youth engaged in the program than our annual targets were set at. Referrals were coming to us through word of mouth among the youth. This is an important reflection of the youth's perceptions of the program and agency, and especially in its role of fostering positive cultural and personal identity development in the youth in care.

Successes

> I feel that I have support and mentors within the community that I didn't have before. I have a close relationship with Rachel and I feel she listens to me and she means it. I have learned that I don't have to be afraid to be Native and I'm proud to be Mohawk. (Male, sixteen, shared with permission)

Despite the challenges, we experienced substantial success. Youth who were part of the AYIT expressed their desire to become mentors and leaders for the Indigenous community as a result. Also, we saw many of the youth graduating high school and considering post-secondary education as a result of being involved in AYIT. They made it onto honour rolls and chalked up academic achievements. They were also picking up traditional knowledge; these youth will eventually be the new Elders. They acquired a deep confidence within themselves and built their self-esteem. Many who had challenges managing their emotions and behaviour learned how to self-regulate. The youth learned that they had the capacity to set and achieve their goals. Perhaps the most moving achievement was that the youth involved in the

AYIT program developed a sense that they mattered and that they had a supportive community wrapped around them.

> What they are helping me with is finding housing, looking after my physical health, and last but not least — getting over my past. (Female, twenty-one, shared with permission)

Increasing widespread knowledge about Indigenous cultures and history in Canada will change and improve Canadians' understanding of the realities of Indigenous lives. Once the youth in our service began to open up, we saw consistent patterns. Many were so isolated from their own cultures and histories that they believed they were to blame, that they were at fault, that they were flawed. Even in our own larger circle, rooted in a heterogeneous urban Indigenous population, there was an alarming lack of understanding that the systemic oppression that is both intergenerational and deliberate is not the fault of a single Indigenous individual and can only be solved through systems-level responses (Menzies 2007). Intergenerational and collective traumas set children and youth up to fail even as their parents and grandparents were robbed of the ability to become healthy adults. We know this runs counter to Indigenous worldviews of children as gifts from Creator on loan to us (Auger 1997; Brendtro et al. 2013; Cajete 2000). When children are raised with love and respect, they grow to understand who they are. The adults in their lives act as the buffers to the more difficult life experiences and provide the stories that connect them firmly to ancestors in dynamic relationships. They see themselves as worthy of respect and love. They become the next generation of healthy, loving adults.

The AYIT worker and the Elders and Knowledge Keepers helped the youth learn about their history and their resilience. The youth learned to see themselves in a much more positive light; no longer the pejorative "Indian," and they understood they are the keepers and protectors with deep ancestral roots and knowledge. They were reminded that the history of residential schools, which many of their relatives were forced to attend, is still very recent. They made connections about how residential schools and similar acts of violence and dispossession have disrupted their grandparents' and parents' abilities to live balanced lives (Aboriginal Children in Care Working Group 2015; Office of the Child and Youth Advocate of Alberta 2016; Truth and Reconciliation Commission of Canada 2015). Once the youth began to see their struggles as collective experiences shared by their ancestors, they began to encourage each other to embody the teachings and knowledge they had gained. At events held by Niijkiwendidaa where different generations intersected, a youth labelled as "troubled" would gladly offer to make tea for a visiting grandmother. It is a seemingly small gesture but it was rooted in a new understanding of respecting Elders; it becomes a contemporary expression of ancestral relations.

The youth also began to have significant conversations with the workers at Niijkiwendidaa about relationships, including explicit talks about dating, intimacy and social conduct. We saw that relatively mundane appropriate physical contact (e.g., touching the arm, giving a hug) were novel and transformative for the youth. They learned about healthy boundaries through many different teachings, allowing them to start breaking the cycle of physical, emotional and sexual abuse. Many of the youth modelled these boundaries as they interacted positively with members in our community, with our counselling staff and our Elders. Some developed formal kinship relationships with community members, adopting surrogate aunties and uncles. Our emphasis was on the youth's overall well-being, their sense of belonging, their personal capacity for changing their circumstances, and their spiritual path and growth. By breaking the intergenerational bonds of trauma, by speaking the unspoken and helping heal the soul, we worked to help youth to feel free to make new choices and live a good life — *mino bimaadiziwin*.

GIIDOSENDIWAG: WE WALK TOGETHER

> Now I am very proud to say that I am Native. I appreciate it and I know what it means. I have been involved with the AYIT program for over a year. I feel confident in myself as a healthy Native man. I have my traditional name, clan, and experienced a Sweat Lodge ceremony for the first time. This for me has fostered a healthy sense of who I am. (Male, seventeen, shared with permission)

This exploration of our experiences with Indigenous youth and the AYIT program at Niijkiwendidaa illustrates how ongoing systemic colonialism is connected to the challenges that confront Indigenous youth and Indigenous services. The positive impacts that occur when the supports we provide are centred in culture have deep implications for youth well-being. As Indigenous services expand provincially and nationally, there remains a clear need for non-Indigenous organizations to ensure they include education for their staff on the history of colonization; modify their practice paradigms to respond to the cultural needs of Indigenous children and youth; and find ways to support Indigenous organizations and communities in their efforts to build capacity and engage in healing from historic and ongoing colonialism.

We hope that we have demonstrated that our youth need more than merely the basics of shelter and food; our youth require connection to their cultures and communities in ways that are substantive, consistent and constant regardless of whom their caregivers are. Even in the extreme cases of a child or youth needing to be completely removed from their family home, retaining cultural and community connections is essential, and can be done through enfolding them in a surrogate community with access to all the relational supports they would normally have access to in their home communities. Regardless of whether the youth has a Status Card or only family stories of ancestry, remaining connected to Indigenous culture and community has long-lasting restorative potential that can see the youth rightfully taking their place as emerging leaders and mentors within broader society. They are the teachers and helpers who will eventually become the new Elders — but only if we support them now as they transition into adulthood. The political and social climate has shifted enough that cultural aspects of Indigeneity, particularly spiritual ceremonies, no longer need to remain hidden. It is not an easy path though. We are confronted with the remnants of our ancestors' knowledge in ways that resemble jigsaw pieces. Repairing the damage takes work and time, in addition to a lot of care, thought, commitment and love. Our work with our youth, regardless of where they come from, is just one step along that path that we all walk along together.

NOTES

1. There are several different ways of spelling Anishinaabe words that have been emerging over the past number of decades. Historically, the language was learned only via oral transmission; the use of writing is quite new and is not yet fully standardized.
2. We use the term "Indigenous," which has generally replaced "Aboriginal" and "Native," and may be used interchangeably with First Nations, Anishinaabe/Anishinaabeg, or similar identifiers. Cultural identity is rooted in particular nations (e.g. Anishinaabe, Kanien'kehá:ka, Métis). In many urban places, such as Peterborough, Ontario, there is a substantial urban Indigenous population who often come from very diverse nations from across Turtle Island/ North America.
3. The term "Indian" was applied by European colonizers to Indigenous Peoples across North, Central and South America. It remains the legal term for First Nations under the Act.
4. A wendigo or windigo is a monster found in many Indigenous cultures, associated with ravening, insatiable hunger and cannibalism.

SUGGESTED READINGS

Absolon, Kathy. 2010. "Indigenous Wholistic Theory: A Knowledge Set for Practice." *First Peoples Child & Family Review* 5, 2.
Ansloos, Jeffrey P. 2017. *The Medicine of Peace: Indigenous Youth Decolonizing Healing and Resisting Violence*. Halifax: Fernwood Publishing.
Baskin, Cyndy. 2022. *Strong Helpers' Teachings: The Value of Indigenous Knowledges in the Helping Professions*, third edition. Toronto: Canadian Scholars Press.
Fortier, Craig and Edward Hon-Sing Wong. 2019. "The Settler Colonialism of Social Work and The Social Work of Settler Colonialism." *Settler Colonial Studies* 9, 4.
James, Cherylanne. 2023. *Indigenous Child and Youth Care: Weaving Two Heart Stories Together*. Toronto: Canadian Scholars Press.
Provincial Advocate for Children and Youth. 2014. *Together We Are Feathers of Hope: A First Nations Youth Action Plan*. Toronto: The Provincial Advocate for Children and Youth.

REFERENCES

Aboriginal Children in Care Working Group. 2015. *Aboriginal Children in Care: Report to the Premiers*. Ottawa: Canada's Premiers Council of the Federation Secretariat.

Association of Native Child and Family Services Agencies of Ontario. 2023. "About." ancfsao.ca

Auger, Dale. 1997. "Empowerment through First Nations Control of Education: A Sakaw Cree Philosophy of Education." In *First Nations in Canada: Perspectives on Opportunity, Empowerment and Self-Determination*, edited by J. Rick Ponting. Toronto: McGraw-Hill Ryerson.

Beaucage, Jean. 2011. *Children First: The Aboriginal Advisor's Report on the Status of Aboriginal Child Welfare in Ontario*. Toronto: Ontario Ministry of Children and Youth Services.

Bennett, Marlyn and Cindy Blackstock. 2002. *A Literature Review and Annotated Bibliography on Aspects of Aboriginal Child Welfare in Canada*. Ottawa: First Nations Child & Family Caring Society.

Blackstock, Cindy. 2009. "The Occasional Evil of Angels: Learning from the Experiences of Aboriginal Peoples and Social Work." *First Peoples Child & Family Review* 4, 1.

Brendtro, Larry, Martin Brokenleg and Steve Van Bockern. 2013. "The Circle of Courage: Developing Resilience and Capacity in Youth." *International Journal for Talent Development and Creativity* 1, 1.

Cajete, Gregory. 2000. "Indigenous Knowledge: The Pueblo Metaphor of Indigenous Education." In *Reclaiming Indigenous Voice and Vision*, edited by Marie Battiste. Vancouver: UBC Press.

Cameron, Rose Ella. 2010. "What Are You in the Dark? The Transformative Powers of the Manitouminasuc upon the Identities of Anishinabeg in the Ontario Child Welfare System." Doctoral dissertation, University of Toronto.

Chandler, Michael and Christopher Lalonde. 1998. "Cultural Continuity as a Hedge Against Suicide in Canada's First Nations." *Transcultural Psychiatry* 35, 2.

Choate, Peter, Taylor Kohler, Felicia Cloete, Brandy CrazyBull, Desi Lindstrom and Parker Tatoulis. 2019. "Rethinking Racine v Woods from a Decolonizing Perspective: Challenging the Applicability of Attachment Theory to Indigenous Families Involved with Child Protection." *Canadian Journal of Law and Society* 34, 1.

Choate, Peter, Natalie St-Denis and Bruce MacLaurin. 2022. "At the Beginning of the Curve: Social Work Education and Indigenous Content." *Journal of Social Work Education* 58, 1.

Doucet, Melanie M. 2020. *Relationships Matter: Examining the Pathways to Long-Term Supportive Relationships for Youth 'Aging Out' of Care*. Montréal: McGill University.

Fallon, Barbara, Martin Chabot, John Fluke, Cindy Blackstock, Bruce MacLaurin and Lil Tonmyr. 2013. "Placement Decisions and Disparities among Aboriginal Children: Further Analysis of the Canadian Incidence Study of Reported Child Abuse and Neglect Part A: Comparisons of the 1998 and 2003 Surveys." *Child Abuse and Neglect* 37, 1.

Fallon, Barbara, Racheal Lefebvre, Nico Trocmé, Kenn Richard, Sonia Hélie, H. Monty Montgomery, Marlyn Bennett, et al. 2021. *Denouncing the Continued Overrepresentation of First Nations Children in Canadian Child Welfare: Findings from the First Nations/Canadian Incidence Study of Reported Child Abuse and Neglect-2019*. Ottawa: Assembly of First Nations.

Filbert, Katherine M. 2012. *Developmental Assets as a Predictor of Resilient Outcomes Among Aboriginal Young People in Out-of-home Care*. Doctoral dissertation, University of Ottawa.

First Nations Child and Family Caring Society. 2015. "Role of Jordan's Principle. Fact Sheet." Ottawa: First Nations Child & Family Caring Society.

First Nations Child and Family Caring Society. 2023. "Background." fncaringsociety.com/i-am-witness/background.

Fraser, Sarah, Melanie Vachon, Ghayda Hassan and Valerie Parent. 2016. "Communicating Power and Resistance: Exploring Interactions between Aboriginal Youth and non-Aboriginal Staff Members in a Residential Child Welfare Facility." *Qualitative Research in Psychology* 13, 1.

Government of Canada. 2017. "Summary of What We Heard in Urban Aboriginal Strategy Engagement 2016." isc-sac.gc.ca/eng/1490291019414/1583690920335

———. 2019. "An Act Respecting First Nations, Inuit and Métis Children, Youth and Families. Ottawa." laws.justice.gc.ca/eng/acts/f-11.73/index.html.

———. 2023. "Reducing the Number of Indigenous Children in Care." *Indigenous Services Canada, Social Programs, First Nations Child and Family Services.* sac-isc.gc.ca/eng/1541187352297/1541187392851.

Government of Ontario, Ontario Federation of Indigenous Friendship Centres, Métis Nation of Ontario, Ontario Native Women's Association. 2018. "The Urban Indigenous Action Plan." ofifc.org/wp-content/uploads/2020/03/Tab-7-The-Urban-Indigenous-Action-Plan-2018.pdf.

Hinson, Riley, Angela Snowshoe, Claire V. Crooks, Paul Tremblay and Wendy Craig. 2015. "Development of a Cultural Connectedness Scale for First Nations Youth." *Psychological Assessment* 27, 1.

Hobson, Brittany. 2022. "More than Half the Children in Care are Indigenous, Census Data Suggests." *CBC News*. September 21, 2022. cbc.ca/news/canada/manitoba/census-indigenous-children-care-1.6590075.

Joseph, Bob. 2018. *21 Things You May Not Know About the Indian Act: Helping Canadians Make Reconciliation with Indigenous Peoples a Reality*. Port Coquitlam: Indigenous Relations Press.

Kidd, Sean A., Jesse Thistle, Tera Beaulieu, Bill O'Grady and Samual Gaetz. 2019. "A National Study of Indigenous Youth Homelessness in Canada." *Public Health* 176.

Kline, Marlee. 1992. "Child Welfare Law, 'Best Interest of the Child' Ideology, and First Nations." *Osgoode Hall Law Journal* 30, 2.

Kozlowski, Anna, Vandna Sinha and Kenn Richard. 2012. "First Nations Child Welfare in Ontario (2011): Information sheet #100." cwrp.ca/information-sheet/first-nations-child-welfare-ontario-2011.

Lalonde, Christopher. 2005. "Identity Formation and Cultural Resilience in Aboriginal Communities." In *Promoting Resilience in Child Welfare*, edited by Robert Flynn, Peter Dudding and James Barber. Ottawa: University of Ottawa Press.

Lynch, Philip. 2001. "Keeping Them Home: The Best Interests of Indigenous Children and Communities in Canada and Australia." *Sydney Law Review* 23, 4.

McMahon, Thomas. 2017. "'We Must Teach the Indian What Law Is': The Laws of Indian Residential Schools in Canada." *SSRN Electronic Journal*. doi:10.2139/ssrn.2954877.

Menzies, Peter, and Sagamok Anishnawbek First Nation. 2007. "Understanding Aboriginal Intergenerational Trauma from a Social Work Perspective." *The Canadian Journal of Native Studies* 27, 2.

Métis Nation of Ontario. 2012. *Métis Nation of Ontario Recommendations Concerning Métis-specific Child and Family Services*. Toronto: Métis Nation of Ontario.

Ministry of Children, Community and Social Services. 2023. "Policy Directive: CW 003-23 — Preparing Youth for Successful Transition from the Care of Children's Aid Societies." ontario.ca/document/child-protection-service-directives-forms-and-guidelines.

Niijkiwendidaa Anishnaabekwewag Services Circle. 2016. "About Us." niijki.com

Office of the Child and Youth Advocate of Alberta. 2016. "Voices for Change: Aboriginal Child Welfare in Alberta. Special Report." Government of Alberta.

Ontario Human Rights Commission. 2018. "Interrupted Childhoods: Over-representation of Indigenous and Black Children in Ontario Child Welfare." Government of Ontario. Toronto: Ontario Human Rights Commission.

Ontario Ministry of Children and Youth Services. 2016. "Because Young People Matter: Report of the Residential Services Review Panel." Government of Ontario. Toronto: Ontario Ministry of Children and Youth Services.

Ontario Ministry of Children, Community and Social Services. 2014. "New supports for youth leaving care: Ontario helping young people prepare for independence." Government of Ontario. February 27, 2014. news.ontario.ca/en/release/1002724/ontario-connecting-youth-leaving-care-with-supports-to-succeed.

____. 2022. "Ontario enhancing access to customary care for Indigenous children and youth." Government of Ontario. March 9, 2022. news.ontario.ca/en/release/1001736/ontario-enhancing-access-to-customary-care-for-indigenous-children-and-youth

Park, Tae Mee. 2003. "In the Best Interests of the Aboriginal Child." *Windsor Review of Legal and Social Issues* 16.

Quinn, Ashley. 2020. "Nurturing Identity Among Indigenous Youth in Care." *Child and Youth Services* 41, 1.

Raman, Shanti and Deborah Rhodes. 2012. "Cultural Issues in Child Maltreatment." *Journal of Paediatrics and Child Health* 48, 1.

Rampersaud, Marsha and Linda Mussell. 2021.*"Half the Time I Felt Like Nobody Loved Me": The Costs of 'Aging Out' of State Guardianship in Ontario.* Toronto.

Roach, D. 2000. "Developing a Pro-active, Unified Approach in Child Welfare." Native Child Welfare Conference Child Welfare Report. Sault Ste. Marie: Anishinabek Nation.

Sansone, Genevieve, Barbara Fallon, Steven P. Miller, Catherine Birken, Avram Denburg, Jennifer Jenkins, Faye Mishna, Marla Sokolowski and Suzanne Stewart. 2020. *Children Aging Out of Care.* Toronto: University of Toronto.

Shewell, Hugh. 1999. "Jules Sioui and Indian Political Radicalism in Canada, 1943–1944." *Journal of Canadian Studies* 34, 3.

Sinclair, Raven. 2004. "Aboriginal Social Work Education in Canada: Decolonizing Pedagogy for the Seventh Generation." *First Peoples Child & Family Review* 1, 1.

____. 2007. "Identity Lost and Found: Lessons from the Sixties Scoop." *First Peoples Child & Family Review* 3, 1.

____. 2016. "The Indigenous Child Removal System in Canada: An Examination of Legal Decision-making and Racial Bias." *First Peoples Child & Family Review* 11, 2.

Sinha, Vandna and Anne Blumenthal. 2015. "No Jordan's Principle Cases in Canada? A Review of the Administrative Response to Jordan's Principle." *International Indigenous Policy Journal* 6, 1.

Sinha, Vandna and Anna Kozlowski. 2013. "The Structure of Aboriginal Child Welfare in Canada." *International Indigenous Policy Journal* 4, 2.

Sinha, Vandna, Johanna Caldwell, Leah Paul and Paula Roberto Fumaneri. 2021. "A Review of Literature on the Involvement of Children from Indigenous Communities in Anglo Child Welfare Systems: 1973–2018." *International Indigenous Policy Journal* 12,1.

Statistics Canada. 2022. "Indigenous Population Continues to Grow and Is Much Younger than the Non-Indigenous Population, Although the Pace of Growth Has Slowed." Ottawa: Statistics Canada.

Stefanovich, Olivia. 2023. "2023 Will be a Pivotal Year for Indigenous Child Welfare on Both Sides of the Border." *CBC News*. January 2, 2023. cbc.ca/news/politics/indigenous-child-welfare-upcoming-decisions-canada-us-1.6694103.

Tait, Caroline L., Robert Henry and Rachel Loewen Walker. 2013. "Child Welfare: A Social Determinant of Health for Canadian First Nations and Métis Children." *Pimatisiwin: A Journal of Aboriginal and Indigenous Community Health* 11, 1.

Toth, Katalina, Daisy Smith and Daphne Giroux. 2018. "Indigenous Peoples and Empowerment via Technology." *First Peoples Child & Family Review* 13, 1.

Truth and Reconciliation Commission of Canada. 2015. *Honouring the Truth, Reconciling for the Future: Summary of the Final Report of the Truth and Reconciliation Commission of Canada*. Winnipeg: Truth and Reconciliation Commission of Canada.

Walqwan Metallic, Naiomi, Hadley Friedland and Sarah Morales. 2019. *The Promise and Pitfalls of C-92: An Act Respecting First Nations, Inuit, and Métis Children, Youth and Families*. Toronto: Yellowhead Institute. yellowheadinstitute.org/wp-content/uploads/2019/07/the-promise-and-pitfalls-of-c-92-report.pdf.

Chapter 6

FOUR-LEVEL MODEL OF CONSCIOUSNESS FOR FAMILY GROUP CONFERENCES

A Wise Practice for Awareness of Colonization and Decolonization

by Don Robinson

CHAPTER FOCUS

This chapter is a story of decolonization and healing based on my life and professional experiences. The story begins with the impacts of colonial policies within my family and moves through the Indian Act, Sixties Scoop and a jagged world view that led to my struggles with chronic alcoholism and homelessness. I slowly woke up, realizing that I was colonized, and began a long healing journey ignited by Mohawk Elder Tom Porter talking about his family and community. I can only write about some significant experiences along this healing journey in the context of sharing the four-level model of colonization and decolonization. As social workers working from the heart, we learn to start from where the person is at and to support their autonomy. I share the Family Group Conference (FGC) model as one wise practice that holistically supports decolonization and healing at the four levels mentioned. The key components of the model include the social worker's role, the child welfare worker's role and the family's responsibility in creating a holistic wellness (mino-pimatisiwin, good life) plan. The FGC model honours the parents, grandparents, extended family members and significant networks involved.

QUESTIONS ADDRESSED IN THIS CHAPTER

1. How can social workers in child welfare let go of social control and power to empower families in FGC to reclaim their autonomy?
2. Child welfare workers often meet parents at the lowest points in their lives, when they are struggling with mental health, addictions and crisis. How can parents be trusted to create wellness (mino-pimatisiwin) plans? Does the answer lay in the strengths of the family group and their wisdom?
3. FGC creates a pathway to healing for individual parents, their family, the community and their nation. What are some ways social workers can investigate FGC as an empowerment model, apply FGC principles and advocate for its use in our field?

AWAKENING TO THE FOUR LEVELS OF CONSCIOUSNESS

In the late 1970s, I attended a gathering organized by the Indian[1] Students Association at the University of Manitoba. Elder and young activist Tom Porter began to talk about his Mohawk Nation, his community, his family and the teachings that were vital for life. He was talking about the development of his consciousness as a Mohawk man and his responsibility to share his knowledge to all people (Porter 2008). I was captivated by this man who spoke to my heart and spirit, reminding me that I grew up in a culture similar to what he described. Reflecting on my life journey, I realized that this event was pivotal to my process of awakening. In my Cree language, waniska means wake up. This was the beginning of a gradual awareness of the four levels of consciousness in the Ma Mawi Wi Chi Itata Centre family group conferencing project in Winnipeg, Manitoba.

The four levels of colonization, illustrated in the figure below, demonstrates that Indigenous people have been impacted by colonization that has affected the four levels of nation, community, family and individual. The first level refers to cumulative and historic trauma from policies such as residential schools, the Sixties Scoop,

FIGURE 6.1. Four levels of colonization

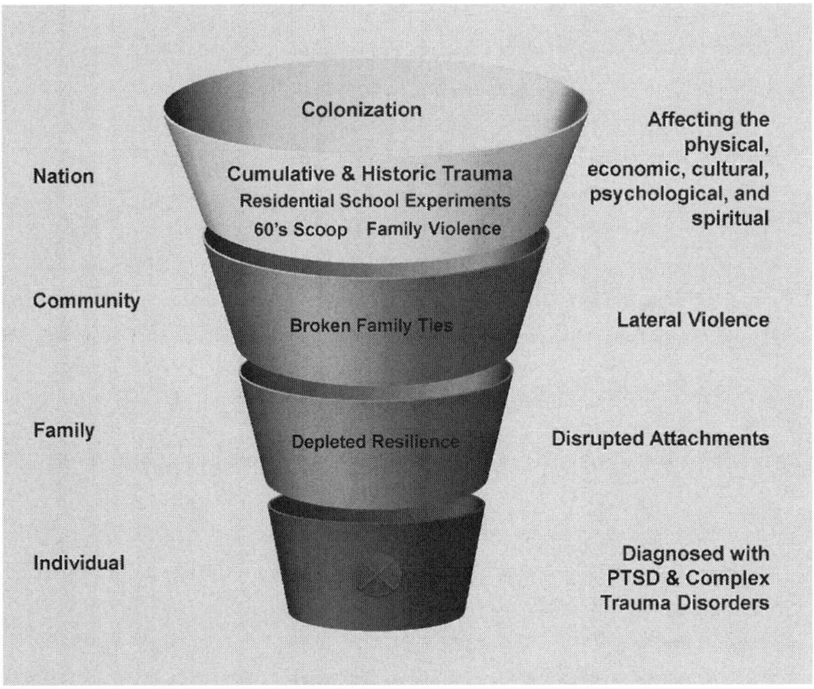

This four-level model is a graphic visual of how colonization has affected nations, communities, families and the individual. For example, I have had to decolonize my thinking (social work education, therapy training and the mainstream) to heal myself. A holistic understanding is essential to healing from the inside out. Image developed by Michael McPherson. Reprinted with permission.

and forced relocations[2] that impacted the physical, economic, cultural, psychological and spiritual wellness of the nations. The second level demonstrates lateral violence that affected the community, resulting in further breaking of family ties. The third level represents colonial trauma that disrupted family attachments, further depleting their resilience. The fourth level represents the individual who has been exposed to colonial trauma on all levels, often resulting in PTSD and complex trauma disorders.

This four-level model begins by briefly exploring the Indian Act, residential school policy and the child welfare practice called "the Sixties Scoop" for their impacts on Indigenous consciousness. The four-level model also envisions a decolonizing strategy that utilizes the FGC model as a wise practice for implementation.

The Indian Act and the Indian Residential Schools

The Indian Act continues to cast a long shadow over the relationship between Indigenous Peoples and Canada. The policy animating the Indian Act had the explicit aim of breaking down and ultimately eliminating the distinct political, social, cultural and economic fabric of Canada's First Nations (Hamilton et al. 2021).

The federal government instituted the Indian residential school policy to remove the Indigenous children separating them from their family, culture and community with the Gradual Civilization Act of 1857. This policy of assimilation evolved into compulsory attendance for all children (six to fifteen years of age) at residential schools often far away from their communities and they also established day schools on reserves where children attended during the day. Between 1883 and 1996, an estimated 150,000 children were placed in these Indian residential schools (Truth and Reconciliation Commission of Canada 2015). Christian churches were involved throughout the process. Both types of schools were designed to remove the child, with distant residential schools being the preferred model. In Manitoba, there were fourteen residential schools[3] throughout the province with students from other provinces attending. Families and communities were left without the child as their centre fire and as a result suffered tremendous grief and losses.

The Sixties Scoop: Child Welfare Policy

Indigenous people in Canada became alarmed about the high number of children they were losing to the child welfare system. In the 1970s, Indigenous people of Ojibway, Cree, Oji-Cree, Dene, Inuit and Métis communities began investigating the situation. Patrick Johnston (1983) first used the term "Sixties Scoop" in his 1983 report entitled *Native Children and the Child Welfare System*. The term refers to the large-scale removal or "scooping" of Indigenous children from their homes, communities and birth families beginning in the 1960s, and their subsequent adoption into predominantly non-Indigenous, middle-class families across Canada, the United States and Europe (Duhamal 2018, 373). The experience left many adoptees with a lost sense of cultural identity. The physical and emotional separation from their birth families continues to affect adult adoptees and Indigenous communities to this day.

The provincial child welfare authority, Children's Aid Society, was the largest child welfare institution in Manitoba working in urban and rural areas. In the 1960s, when the federal government extended child welfare jurisdiction to First Nations in Manitoba, provincial child welfare agencies began to travel to Métis and reserve communities, with the result that many children were removed from their families. In response to concerns brought forward by Indigenous communities, the province of Manitoba was pressed to create a commission of inquiry led by Judge Edwin Kimelman. Kimelman travelled across Manitoba holding hearings in various communities. In his report, called *No Quiet Place*, he stated that Manitoba had failed in its duty to provide care for Indigenous children in care of the child welfare system (Kimelman 1985). Furthermore, he named the practice of placing and adopting children in non-Indigenous homes out of province and country a cultural genocide and ordered an immediate moratorium on these practices. These practices had been in place for twenty years before being challenged.

In Manitoba, the Dakota leaders, Elders and other community people were successful in bringing attention to the serious matter and gained jurisdiction of their own child welfare mandate. Dakota Ojibway Child and Family Services was established in July 1981. This occurred after much lobbying and consultations in communities to bring about the much-needed changes for the Dakota and Ojibway Nations.

WHO I AM AND WHERE I COME FROM

So far, I have only touched the surface of the colonization that penetrated the depths of my psychic world. I have been deeply affected by these colonial forces, as my parents struggled with addictions, family violence and involvement with the child welfare system. My siblings and I became wards of the child welfare system; seven became permanent wards, with the youngest two brothers adopted out of province in the early 1970s. These two brothers returned to Manitoba from Ontario after they both reached the age of majority. My parents loved us but could not overcome their addictions and sadly both passed away before they could see my brothers return home. These events influenced my decision to enter training to be a helping professional in community economic development in 1985. I completed a Bachelor of Social Work in 1991 and a Master of Social Work in 2001 at the University of Manitoba. Additionally, in 2011, I sought training in treating complex post-traumatic stress disorder using Eye Movement Desensitization and Reprocessing. I also found my way to the traditional ceremonial responsibilities of being a pipe carrier and Sweat Lodge conductor. Along the way, I realized that many Indigenous people have experienced complex trauma and have responded to their pain by adopting unhealthy behaviours to cope. Over the years, I have been honoured to hear many of their stories in therapy sessions, sharing/healing circles and in ceremonies.

I am from the Muskwegowak Inninew (Swampy Cree) community of Bunibonibee, also known as Oxford House, in northern Manitoba. I lived there for the first seven years of my life then my family moved to the Métis community of Thicket Portage, Manitoba. After being diagnosed with rheumatoid arthritis (RA) in the mid-1970s, I was sent to Winnipeg because there were no medical specialists in the North. Dealing with the chronic pain of RA as a young man, I discovered the power of alcohol as self-medication and developed a serious addiction. I struggled with addiction and homelessness for almost a decade before finally achieving solid sobriety in 1984. This was achieved by a return to the teachings of my Elders.

THE FOUR-LEVEL MODEL OF WELLNESS

The four levels of wellness represent the healing that occurs on the four levels of nation, community, family and individual. At the nation level there is a focus on intergenerational transmission of knowledge that is passed on through Elders, Knowledge Keepers and grandparents. Restoring Indigenous ways of being, doing and knowing requires a focus on wellness, healing and ceremony, and self-determination. The focus at the community level is building resiliency through applying the values of sharing, healing, teaching circles and cultural and land-based teachings. At the third level, the family level, the focus is to rebuild healthy attachments involving grandparents and Elders' teachings. In the fourth level, the individual learns about the teachings of balance.

As a young community development worker, I became aware that the young people I worked with were dealing with poverty, racism and discrimination. Some of these young ones were attracted to the emerging gangs that promoted the power of belonging. Young people describe feeling important and valued in belonging to a gang (Comack et al. 2020). I learned that their parents were concerned about their futures and wanted opportunities for them. Parents who were involved with the child welfare system in the late 1990s were usually referred for parenting classes, addiction treatment and anger management before they could regain custody of their children. Today, parents are still being referred to this trifecta service model as the transformative solution for families.

FIGURE 6.2. Four levels of wellness

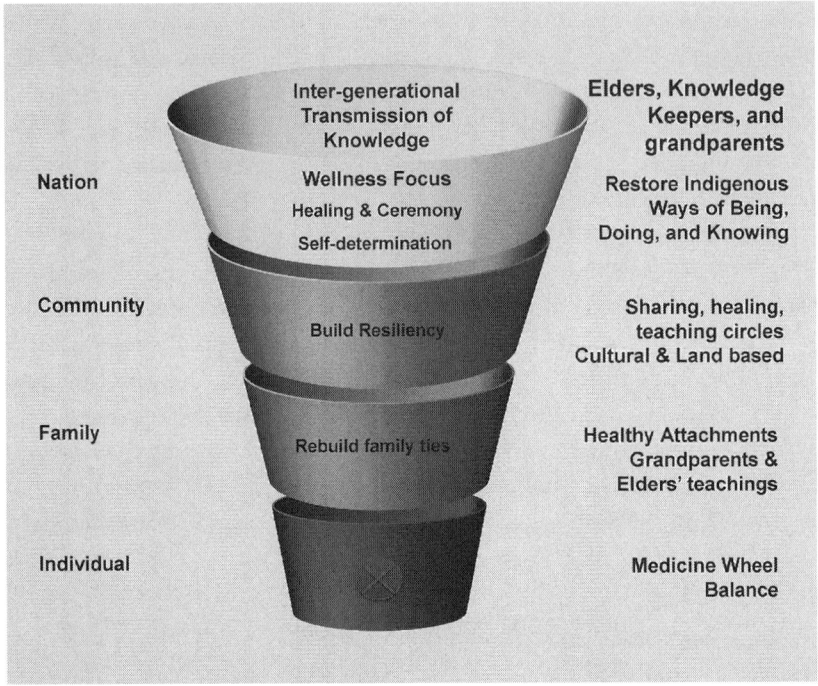

In my healing journey, I had to explore Indigenous ways of being, doing and knowing to decolonize from my social work education and assimilated mindset of the mainstream world. This four-level model is a work in progress in my life as I believe that I am still colonized in subconscious ways.
Image developed by Michael McPherson. Reprinted with permission.

In the late 1990s, I became aware of FGC as an empowerment model that included the extended family and community (Pennell 2009). I began my work as an FGC coordinator and realized the power of this approach and since that time I have witnessed family group decision-making in action. I have been fortunate to once again be witness as part of the evaluation team interviewing family members, community and child welfare workers who participated in the FGC project with Ma Mawi Wi Chi Itata Centre in Winnipeg, Manitoba (Hart et al. 2021).

The FGC model is an approach based upon ancestral values, practices, beliefs and was implemented at Ma Mawi Wi Chi Itata Centre in collaboration with the Maori people from New Zealand where it originates (Robinson 2012). Maori delegates were invited back in March 2018 to Ma Mawi Wi Chi Itata Centre to provide ongoing support that had been in place since 2000. The guests shared their knowledge as the first traditional Maori-based practice in a social service setting and to provide support to the Ma Mawi Wi Chi Itata FGC mentors. I was able to participate in the ceremonies and training with them where they stressed the importance of fidelity to the model to provide culturally responsive services to families. As part of their commitment, Ma Mawi Wi Chi Itata Centre wanted an Indigenous-based evaluation of the program and hired Michael Hart as the principal evaluator. I was also part of the evaluation that informs the concepts in this chapter.

The FGC Process

The FGC process begins with a referral from a child welfare agency, a community organization or a parent who has heard about this service, which then facilitates a connection with one of the FGC mentors. The mentor connects with the person who requests the service and begins the process to provide information about the program to ensure informed consent. The families are offered this voluntary service when there has been an assessment of low to medium risk.

Mandated agencies have developed the following risk criteria for determining protection concerns:

> *High Risk:* A child is likely to be seriously harmed or injured, subjected to immediate and ongoing neglect, abuse, or be permanently disabled or die if left in his or her present circumstances without protective intervention.
>
> *Medium Risk:* A child is likely to suffer some degree of harm if he or she remains in the home without an effective protective intervention plan. Intervention is warranted. However, there is no evidence that the child is at risk of imminent serious injury or death.
>
> *Low Risk:* The home is safe for children. However, there are concerns about the potential for a child to be at risk if services are not provided to prevent the need for protective intervention. (Dakota Ojibway Child and Family Services 2020)

Ma Mawi Wi Chi Itata Centre understands that the child welfare mandate is to provide protection services for children in high-risk situations that require immediate intervention. In working with low- to medium-risk situations, the FGC program provides preventative services that connect the child(ren) with the community, keeps children with their families and promotes kinship care.

The FGC model has four stages: assessment, preparation, family group conference and review and monitoring (Hart et al. 2021; Robinson 2012). When a referral is received either from child welfare agencies, or by self-referral through a Ma Mawi care site, an assessment is begun with the referral source to determine eligibility in terms of risk levels. The Ma Mawi Wi Chi Itata mentor meets with the child welfare agency to obtain information with care to ensure that the family is aware of the referral. In meetings with child welfare workers, the mentor has an opportunity to present information on the FGC process. The mentor then follows up with the community care site regarding the family again to ensure informed consent to the referral. Finally, in the case of self-referral, the mentor begins to meet with the family to engage in a holistic assessment and to fully explain the FGC program. When the assessment determines that the family voluntarily accepts participation in the FGC program, the mentor begins the preparation stage.

All Families Have Unique Strengths and Decision-Making Powers

FGC practice holds that all families have unique strengths and decision-making powers. Families who come to the attention of child welfare often present with a laundry list of problems and few solutions. Sometimes people become discouraged with life's struggles after trying many different solutions. The FGC mentors enter the family circle with the presupposition that the family has wisdom inherent in their own unique world view, strengths and ways of making decisions. From first contact, mentors begin to assess the family's strengths and quality of relationships, and must be proactive in seeking out members of the family, friends and other significant people identified by the family. It is from the larger family group that this information is obtained. Everyone, including the parents, paternal and maternal grandparents and kin, are included to the fullest extent to learn about these strengths as well as more about their challenges. The children's voices are included in the preparation stage and may include their drawings, a written story or video or audio expressing their hopes and fears. Their voices are presented during the FGC stage to the family group. Children twelve years or older may participate in the FGC and request their own support network who may be outside the family group. Based on my experience, young people have requested support persons who they trust and ask for their inclusion in the FGC.

FGC holds the value position that families are the most knowledgeable about their history and family dynamics. Child welfare workers and other professionals are only involved with families for a brief time and are limited in their knowledge of the family's culture, dynamics and history, whereas family members have known each other for many years and have intense relationships. By approaching family members with respectful curiosity and creating trust relationships the mentors can learn this supportive information from the family group. Mentors discover the strengths, values and beliefs that can support the family group in creating their plans. The family group is then prepared for the next stage — the Family Group Conference.

The Family Group Conference

The important value of self-determination inherent in the FGC process speaks to empowerment when families create their own safety and wellness plans. The Family Group Conference is the stage where the family group gathers in ceremony that is conducted in accordance with their cultural beliefs and practices. The family may request a pipe ceremony, songs and prayer with an Elder, or may have their religious practices that they wish to follow. The FGC follows a process of presenting information by child welfare representatives, resource presentations and any relevant service that can help the family with their safety and wellness plans. The family group then has an opportunity to meet in private to discuss all the information and to develop their plan.

FGC holds the value position that families are more likely to implement plans that they have devised on their own. When families create these plans, they have a sense of ownership and pride to be able to reclaim their power. In the FGC process, the family members are assured that the family plan decisions will be respected and honoured. It is understood that many families have a distrust of mandated agencies and will often have a low level of trust at the beginning of the FGC process. The relationship-building with the families promotes the central message that the agency believes in the strengths and wisdom of the family throughout the whole process. It is also understood that families need the appropriate resources in order to implement plans, so the agency has dedicated financial resources to help facilitate family group conferences. It is ideal when the family can use their own capabilities and resources, however they may need other resources to successfully implement their plans. For example, family members may need financial support to travel to Winnipeg where the FGC is being held or have support with concrete issues such as child care and providing for Elder involvement. The mentors need to advocate with families for any such extra resources to facilitate their plan. Once the family plan, which is based on the family's unique history, needs and resources, is developed and presented to everyone involved, the child welfare agency accepts this as their commitment to working through the next stage.

A review meeting is usually held three months after the FGC and is held with family members, the child welfare worker and the FGC mentor. These review meetings are with a smaller family group with the intention to monitor how the plan is working. The family group in reviewing their plan, may revise and adjust components of their work when necessary. The review and monitoring process continues with mentors maintaining connections for up to a year depending on need.

The FGC Model as a Wise Practice

The Family Group Conference model can be described as "a wise practice." A wise practice provides for making space for Indigenous Knowledge and experiences. There is a recognized need to return to and invigorate ancestral wise practices that reassert fundamental belief structures, values and practices (Hamilton et al. 2021). The FGC model as practised by Ma Mawi Wi Chi Itata Centre has an environment that supports a wise practice. The program philosophy is based on creating individual space, family space, cultural space, community space and collaborative space to facilitate learning about nation, community, family and individual. The program involves local Indigenous Elders and Knowledge Keepers to share traditional wise practices for families (Linklater 2014; Ross 2014; Fiola 2021). This environment creates opportunities for the development of critical consciousness, a decolonization that Waziyatawin and Yellow Bird (2012, 3) describe as both an event and a process:

> As an event, decolonization concerns reaching a level of critical consciousness, an active understanding of that you are (or have been) colonized and are thus responding to life circumstances in ways that are limited, destructive, and externally controlled. As a process, decolonizing means engaging in the activities of creating, restoring, and rebirthing … it means restoring cultural practices, thinking, beliefs, and values that were taken away or abandoned but are still relevant and necessary for survival.

The FGC program is one that promotes critical consciousness as families become immersed in the activities and relationship-building process from the beginning.

The Ma Mawi Wi Chi Itata Centre team is comprised of a program coordinator and ten mentors. They represent the community in that they are Ojibway, Cree, Oji-Cree, and Métis and many are parents themselves. The program operates in the north end of Winnipeg in a space that is named the Bear's Den.

The Bear's Den houses the team members and is a family space for all the FGC participants to drop in. The Bear's Den is a safe place for families to gather both on a casual drop-in basis and for program activities. Herman (2015), a noted trauma therapist, supports the idea that healing relationships require safety, opportunities for remembrance and mourning, and reconnection. All the participants in the program are treated as relatives — they are not referred to as "clients." This busy area provides individual and family space for participants who may want to connect with mentors, cook meals and spend time with each other. This site also hosts most of the family group conferences in the "Truth and Reconciliation round room." The site has a child care space that has multiple functions including a play area, child care room for respite or for young children while parents are in conference, and for supervised visits. Families may also utilize the space for playing and bonding with their children. Family members who are being supervised during their visits report that previously they had often been supervised in cramped rooms at the child welfare offices and felt uncomfortable while visiting with their children and preferred this child care space.

The FGC mentors are individuals with lived experience who understand the stresses of life in an urban context. Jackie Anderson, FGC coordinator, and Tammy Hamelin, mentor, both stated in an interview that the mentors hired to work in FGC were vital to its success. The program hired ten individuals with lived experience with racism, discrimination and intergenerational trauma similar to what the families they interact with may have faced (McCallum et al. 2018). For example, families report indifference and racist treatment when dealing with the health system, housing, justice, income security and mainstream organizations. Both Jackie and Tammy stress the importance of respect throughout the whole FGC process. The assessment stage is important to ensure that family members and child welfare workers are fully invested and informed about the FGC process.

Within a trust relationship, mentors learn when to be gentle and when to be directive. The mentors are available to support family members after hours and on weekends. Jackie reports that it is vital to create a tribal (nation) world view and consciousness of the collective responsibility (community and extended family) for children. Both Jackie and Tammy state that the FGC model is a return to the traditional ways when extended family members were involved in parenting and supportive roles (see also Bodor 2011; Makokis et al. 2021; Hart 2002).

The FGC program provides cultural space for families where they can attend activities such as sharing circles, ribbon skirt making, cooking classes and time with Elders and Knowledge Keepers to learn traditional teachings. Male and female Elders and Knowledge Keepers are invited to share their teachings on-site and in land-based activities in which people are encouraged to connect physically, emotionally and spiritually to the land through the teachings that are shared with them. The Elders and Knowledge Keepers provide ceremonies (Sweat Lodge, medicine picking, teachings, naming) on sites owned by Ma Mawi. These land-based activities provide time and a retreat space away from the city to engage in ceremonies. Alfred (2005; 2009; 2023) stresses the importance of creating awareness first in the individual by involving them in land-based activities with Elders and local Knowledge Keepers. He writes about the importance of rebuilding our connections to our heritage, history and culture that can only be learned in ceremony. He also speaks to nation-building and the creation of a warrior mind for the individual man and woman (Alfred 2005; 2009; 2023). Alfred (2009, 181) spoke with a couple about the warrior mind and stressed the four sacred trusts: looking after the land, looking after the people, looking after the spirituality and looking after the culture, which includes language. To us, being a warrior and a leader means being a protector of the four sacred trusts.

FGC participants report learning about their medicines, cultural ways, ceremonies and spirit names. The FGC process creates individual space for trust to develop as participants can reach out to mentors when they are struggling with life. The mentors are available to support individuals through difficult life issues such as parenting, family conflicts, intimate couple relationships, grief and loss, housing and food insecurity. After receiving individual support in the program, participants report that they felt heard, validated and empowered to persevere (Hart et al. 2021).

Unhealed intergenerational trauma often emerges in the FGC process, with the family group creating individual healing strategies for individual members.

Recovery from addictions is a long-term effort and relapse is common. The mentors recognize this fact and support the participants when they have a relapse. The participants report feeling supported and not being judged when they do struggle in recovery (Hart et al. 2021, 55). Jackie and Tammy shared that some participants are still struggling with addictions but have their children in kinship care. They continue to support the parents whenever they reach out to them.

In one instance, a father found out that his family had traditional teachings and practices (critical consciousness) that might help his children (Waziyatawin and Yellow Bird 2012). Another father shared that he was beginning to reconnect through visits with his son who had been in care and while visiting his son, he was busy on his cell phone talking with a friend. His mentor came into the room and quietly spoke to him about his behaviour. The gentle confrontation shook him out of his unconscious state as he realized his tremendous parenting responsibility. Thereafter he focused on building an attachment and bonding relationship with his son. His mentor observed the behaviour and decided that this was a teaching moment in becoming the "tough auntie" who scolded in a gentle way (Hart et al. 2021, 59).

The Family Group Conference itself creates a dynamic where parents come to realize the strengths that they did not know they had but that were always present. Mentors focused on supporting the family group to honour their strengths and decision-making power to create strong plans. Family members come to realize and appreciate their own knowledge. A family member stated, "FGC got the family involved with activities like traditional feasts, doing crafts, and learning traditional teachings" (Hart et al. 2021, 59). She shared that she grew up with traditional teachings and used to dance and sing and shared, "I want to teach my kids our ways and our language. My uncle stays with us, and he speaks fluently to me all the time." She states that the FGC is the traditional way and fits her values (Hart et al. 2021, 65).

The FGC creates community space for participants to connect with services available to support their family plans. FGC participants learn about their culture and their own nation's Elders and Knowledge Keepers that they then can reach out to on their own (Hart et al. 2021, 65). The Elders and Knowledge Keepers who share their nation's teachings invite the participants to their land, their community spaces and to their ceremonies for longer term healing. The family plans created included referrals to community-based organizations providing relevant programs such as parenting, addiction and recovery, grief and loss groups and sharing and teaching circles. The family plans include referrals to mainstream programs such as at the Addictions Foundation that include relapse prevention and psychotherapy resources for children and adults. During the assessment and preparation stages the mentors determine the family's needs in collaboration with the family group and initiate the referral process for the FGC. Many participants on learning about other opportunities become involved with Ma Mawi Chi Itata Centre programs and services for themselves and their children. They also learn about other collateral programs and services that they can and do utilize.

The FGC creates collaborative space with child welfare agencies who participate. Family members and child welfare workers reported improved relationships as the FGC work progressed. The mentors noted that there is much distrust, fear and reluctance to cooperate with the agency that apprehended or could apprehend their children. Mentors develop close working relationships with child welfare workers and parents to respond to issues as they arise. This ongoing collaboration builds success as issues are resolved. Some issues may be related to relapses or family conflicts that occur frequently in recovery. Child and family workers are also included in events that celebrate successes, not just crisis situations. A mentor explained that there will always be challenges in this environment, but the focus is on making the relationship with child welfare agencies smoother. The mentors also stressed that child welfare workers have to do their own development work to realize that families do have decision-making capacities.

The FGC program has been effective in working with families identified as low to moderate risk demonstrating that families can develop plans for reunification and kinship care. These strategies positively impact the child welfare system reducing the time in care when children are returned to their families and communities. The FGC process created a positive collaborative relationship when the parents requested the attendance of a non-Indigenous foster parent at the FGC. The foster parent was seen as a caring ally who was trusted with their children. They did not want their children to be moved to another home to create more trauma for them. FGC has a welcoming home reunification ceremony when the children are returned home. This ceremony includes Elder participation, family members and the child welfare worker to welcome the children home. The child welfare worker, who usually is involved in the traumatic process of apprehension, is involved in a spiritual healing ceremony that includes the gifting of star blankets for the children. There have been many welcoming home reunification ceremonies in the FGC program. I was honoured to participate in two of these events witnessing the power of the family.

Indigenous Evaluation Outcomes

The Indigenous-informed evaluation (Hart et al. 2021) provided some important teachings for everyone in the helping field. Overall, the evaluation demonstrated that a total of 225 families with 635 children were involved in the FGC program, and 258 children were returned to their families, 95 children were placed in kinship care and 41 children were prevented from coming into care (Hart et al. 2021). The first teaching that the evaluation demonstrated is that the FGC program is highly successful in having children returned to families and that this success is related to the fact that it is grounded in the Indigenous ways of helping (Alec 2020; Bodor 2011; Pennell 2009; Simpson 2004). The second teaching is that culturally based programming has been effective when working with families who have or are facing the effects of trauma (Johnson 1983; Linklater 2014; Stonechild 2016). The third teaching is that basing FGC in a non-mandated Indigenous organization versus a mandated child welfare agency, supports the mentors to address the effects of trauma by applying Indigenous world views, values and practices (BC Aboriginal Child Care Society 2010; Duran 2006; Hart 2002). Ma Mawi Wi Chi Itata Centre, for example, is a non-mandated agency meaning the organization does not have legal authority to apprehend or place children in care. The fourth teaching is that FGC positively impacts society and particularly the child welfare system. This voluntary service results in family reunification, meaning that child welfare's involvement is significantly reduced. Mentors advocate for family centred plans that focus on their needs, cultural values and beliefs. The fifth teaching is that family involvement in child welfare is greatly reduced as families stay out of the system.

Based on my work in FGC and more recently as a research interviewer, I can add two more teachings. The FGC process is inclusive, as it empowers families to identify their significant family and community members to help them in this circle of support. The families may include people who they identify as significant in their wellness plans. The process is definitely a wise practice that creates critical consciousness of their own mental, emotional, physical and spiritual powers. The FGC process creates awareness of complex trauma and the traditional ways of healing using their own values, beliefs, and traditional intergenerational trauma that took generations to take root and requires resilience, long-term visioning and commitment.

The other teaching is that the FGC model is a wise practice that addresses the effects of colonization on the nations, all the communities, families and the individuals. For example, a seemingly simple act of getting a spirit name is a commitment that is psychoactive, in that getting a name requires one to seek answers from Elders on the meaning of the name. The act of getting a spirit name evokes action and critical consciousness to realize the responsibility that comes with their name. It means going to ceremonies that can include fasting, Sweat Lodges, and Sundances, all of which are definitely decolonizing actions (Waziyatawin and Yellow Bird 2012).

There are some cautions about FGC. First, those implementing the program need to be committed to helping for the long term as FGC is not a quick fix model. We must remember the words of Leroy Little Bear: "Colonization left a heritage of jagged worldviews among Indigenous peoples. They no longer had an Aboriginal worldview. Their consciousness became a random puzzle, a jigsaw puzzle that each person has to try to understand" (cited in Linklater 2014, 28).

Importantly, the model requires attention to the number of families per FGC mentor, because families cannot be effectively served if the caseloads are high and unmanageable. Prevention programs often deteriorate to crisis responses when caseloads are high. The FGC mentors must be trauma informed, curious and attentive to their cultural biases about family, traditions, values and beliefs.

A WISE PRACTICE

In my experience not only as an FGC coordinator, but also as a therapist in private practice, I believe that the concepts presented in this chapter provide a template for holistic healing. Using the FGC process as the wise practice, I believe in this four-level model to explore healing, starting first at the individual level and then looking at the family. The social work concept of "genogram work" is a good framework for tracing family relationships but individuals, such as me, would need to seek out family historians (grandmothers, grandfathers, Elders) who know them. This work leads to the community level when the individual finds out where she or he comes from (belonging), and finally to the nation. This process of critical consciousness awakening is decolonizing as the individual takes actions by connecting with their family, community and the members of their nation. Although I am retired now, I still use this framework to guide my helping activities as I still am involved with the community and still conduct ceremonies.

I believe that I am still colonized in many ways that may be conscious and subconscious and I am always mindful of these blind spots in my cultural conditioning. As one who has travelled on the traditional path, I realize that I have only been learning since 1984, so I am still a beginner with plenty to experience.

Kinanaskotinow, ni totemak (I thank all my relatives)

Ekosani.

NOTES

1 Indian was the accepted vernacular for the time.
2 There were many relocations: two Manitoba communities will be referenced, the Sayisi Dene were removed from their Traditional Territory and relocated to Churchill to a territory they didn't know with few resources. The results were devastating and genocidal (Bussidor 1997) The Chemawewin community was moved to Easterville for the building of the Grand Rapids Hydro Project (Cromak et. al 2013).
3 Assiniboia (Winnipeg), Birtle, Brandon, Churchill, Cross Lake, Elkhorn, Fort Alexander (Sakgeeng), Guy Hill (The Pas), McKay (Fisher Island and Dauphin), Norway House (Rossville), Notre Dame Hostel (Norway House), Pine Creek (Camperville), Portage LaPraire, and Sandy Bay. (Manitoba – Where were Manitoba's residential schools – and what stands there now.)

SUGGESTED READINGS

Bruyere, Gord, Michael Hart and Raven Sinclair. 2020. *Wicihitowin: Aboriginal Social Work in Canada.* Winnipeg: Fernwood Publishing.

Hart, Michael. 2020. *Seeking Mino-Pimatisiwin: An Aboriginal Approach to Helping.* Winnipeg: Fernwood Publishing.

Simpson, Leanne Betasamosake. 2011. *Dancing on Our Turtle's Back: Stories of Nishnaabeg Re-creation, Resurgence and a New Emergence.* Winnipeg: Arbeiter Ring Publishing.

REFERENCES

Alec, Elaine. 2020. *Calling my Spirit Back.* Victoria: Tellwell Publishers.

Alfred, Taiaiake. 2005. *Wasase: Indigenous Pathways of Action and Freedom.* Toronto: University of Toronto Press.

____. 2009. *Peace, Power, Righteousness: An Indigenous Manifesto,* second edition. Don Mills: Oxford University Press.

____. 2023. *It's All About the Land: Collected Talks and Interviews on Indigenous Resurgence.* Toronto: University of Toronto Press.

Bodor, Ralph. 2011. *Indigenous Social Work Practice: Creating Good Relationships.* St. Paul: Blue Quills College Press.

BC Aboriginal Child Care Society. 2010. *Bringing Tradition Home: Aboriginal Parenting in Today's World.* British Columbia Aboriginal Child Care Society.

Bussidor, Ila and Ustun Bilgen-Reinart. 2000. *Night spirits: The story of the relocation of the Sayisi Dene.* Winnipeg: University of Manitoba Press.

Comack, Elizabeth, Laurie Deane, Vern Morrissette and Jay Silver. 2020. *"Indians Wear Red": Colonialism, Resistance, and Aboriginal Street Gangs.* Winnipeg: Fernwood Publishing.

Dakota Ojibway Child and Family Services. 2020. *Dakota Ojibway Policy Manual.*

Duhamel, Karine. 2018. "Honoring the Eighth Generation: Indigenous Childhood and Indigenous Children at the Canadian Museum for Human Rights." *Journal of the History of Childhood and Youth* 11, 3.

Duran, Eduardo. 2006. *Healing the Soul Wound: Counseling with American Indians and Other Native Peoples.* New York: Teacher's College Press.

Fiola, Chantal. 2021. *Returning to Ceremony.* Winnipeg: University of Manitoba Press.

Hamilton, Robert, John Borrows, Brent Mainprize, Ryan Beaton and Joshua Ben David Nichols (eds.). 2021. *Wise Practices: Exploring Indigenous Economic Justice and Self-Determination.* Toronto: University of Toronto Press.

Hart, Michael. 2002. *Seeking Mino-Pimatisowin: An Aboriginal Approach to Helping.* Winnipeg: Fernwood Publishing.

Hart, Michael, L. Lacerda-Vandenhorn and Don Robinson. 2021. *Ma Mawi Wi Chi Itata Centre Family Group Conference: An Indigenous-Based Evaluation.* Winnipeg: Ma Mawi Wi Chi Itata Centre.

Herman, Judith. 2015. *Trauma and Recovery: The Aftermath of Violence from Domestic Violence to Political Terror.* New York: Penguin Books.

Johnston, Patrick. 1983. *Native Children and the Child Welfare System.* Toronto: James Lorimer & Company.

Kimelman, Edwin C. 1985. *No Safe Place: Review Committee on Indian and Metis Adoptions and Placements.* Manitoba Legislative Library.

Linklater, Renee. 2014. *Decolonizing Trauma Work: Indigenous Stories and Strategies*. Winnipeg: Fernwood Publishing.

Makokis, Leona, Ralph Bodor, Avery Calhoun and Stephanie Tyler (eds.). 2021. *Ohpikawasowin: Growing A Child: Implementing Indigenous Ways of Knowing with Indigenous Families*. Winnipeg: Fernwood Publishing.

McCallum, Mary Jane and Anne Perry. 2018. *Structures of Indifference: An Indigenous Life and Death in a Canadian City*. Winnipeg: University of Manitoba Press.

Pennell, Joan. 2009. "Widening the Circle: Countering Institutional Racism in Child Welfare." In *Walking This Path Together*, edited by Susan Strega and Sohki Aski Esquao (Jeannine Carrière). Winnipeg: Fernwood Publishing.

Porter, Tom. 2008. *And Grandma Said: Iroquois Teachings as Passed Down Through the Oral Traditions*. Library of Congress.

Robinson, Don. 2012. "Awakening the Spirit of Family: The Family Group Conference as a Strengths-Based Assessment Process." In *Awakening the Spirit: Moving Forward in Child Welfare - Voices from the Prairies*, edited by Ivan Brown, Don Fuchs and Sharon McKay. Regina: University of Regina Press.

Ross, Rupert. 2014. *Indigenous Healing: Exploring the Traditional Paths*. London: Penguin Publishers.

Simpson, Leanne Betasamosake. 2004. *Dancing on Our Turtle's Back: Stories of Nishinaabeg Re-creation, Resurgence and a New Emergence*. Winnipeg: Arbiter Ring Publishing.

Stonechild, Blair. 2016. *The Knowledge Seeker: Embracing Indigenous Spirituality*. Regina: University of Regina Press.

Truth and Reconciliation Commission of Canada. 2015. *Canada's Residential Schools: The Final Report of the Truth and Reconciliation Commission of Canada*. Montréal: McGill-Queens University Press.

Waziyatawin and Michael Yellow Bird (eds.). 2012. "Introduction: Decolonizing Our Minds and Actions." In *For Indigenous Minds Only: A Decolonization Handbook*. Santa Fe: SAR.

Chapter 7

RECENTRING MÉTIS KINSHIP PROTOCOLS OF CARE
Disrupting Colonial Child Welfare Practices

by Julie Mann-Johnson and Angie Tucker

CHAPTER FOCUS

The child welfare system has several impacts on Indigenous children, youth, families and communities. Existing processes continue to interrupt Indigenous-centred systems of protection that centre their focus on the relational obligation of collective care. Through residential schools, the Sixties Scoop, and Millennium Scoop, Métis, First Nations, and Inuit children were disproportionately removed from their families and communities. Indigenous children continue to be placed with caregivers whom they do not know. While child welfare systems have recently introduced kinship care placement options appropriated from Indigenous practices, they have imposed their own definitions on these practices. Current legislation surrounding kinship care in Alberta mandates that children in care should receive culturally appropriate placements with approved caregivers who are related or have significant connection with the child (Government of Alberta 2023a). This model is simplistic in its definition and not inclusive of community-centred decision-making. Moreover, this one-size-fits-all model essentializes Indigenous lifeways and experiences and only works to maintain the colonial status quo.

We are reminded in our work to embed the Cree/Michif axiological teaching of wahkohtowin because it recentres who we are and recalibrates the colonized processes of which we are imbued. Centring wahkohtowin in our endeavours reminds us of the importance of our teachings about obligations, respect, reciprocity and generosity. These are foundational to our work with children, youth, families and the communities from which we have come and for whom we work. As we continue to work with Indigenous children, youth and families, Indigenous-centred approaches to kinship care must be privileged and encouraged.

In this chapter, we explore traditional Métis practices of kinship care and consider how contemporary anti-colonizing social work within Métis child welfare practices can privilege Métis ontologies. In what follows, we outline how kinship systems have continued to meet the needs of Métis children, youth and their families. We also consider how colonial systems have co-opted and skewed these ideas into Western policies and practice solutions, furthering its colonial impact and perpetuating ineffective and assimilative systems of care. We strive to find anti-assimilative processes because the disconnection from communities ultimately impact Métis children's emotional, spiritual, emotional and mental well-being. The maintenance of children's and youth's connections to their families, communities, language and culture has long been noted as a protective factor leading to positive outcomes for children and youth that has led to positive outcomes (Chandler and Lalonde 2008). Kinship care provides opportunities for this authentic connection and identity formation. For Métis children, youth and their families to thrive within their communities, we must revisit practices that "fill the spirit" (Richardson 2016, 87) of children while respecting each person from "wherever they stand" (92).

QUESTIONS ADDRESSED IN THIS CHAPTER

1. How have we seen kinship care present itself historically and traditionally?
2. What are the benefits and experiences of kinship caregivers and children and youth placed in kinship care?
3. How can social workers and child welfare practitioners honour these traditional kinship care approaches?

THE IMPORTANCE OF POSITIONING OURSELVES IN CHILD WELFARE PRACTICES

Métis Elder Maria Campbell's keynote at the 2022 Mawachihitotaak Métis Studies Symposium in Winnipeg highlights the importance of positioning ourselves, our ancestors and our beginnings within our research. Campbell claims, "if we want to know who we are, we have to know our own specific land, community, and our own responsibilities to our people" (2022). Her words speak to the importance of our relations, our kin, our communities and our responsibilities to not only others but to ourselves. Therefore, we begin framing this chapter by centring our own belonging within our research because it is our understanding that our work is always relational, multilayered and community based. When focusing on topics that centre on children, youth and their families, we believe that the location of self is required. Locating ourselves reinforces our commitments to anti-colonizing, anti-racist and anti-oppressive practices. With this practice we bring our full selves into the conversation adding openness, vulnerability and thoughtfulness. Furthermore, "when we claim our location, we become congruent with Indigenous world views and knowledge, thus transforming our place within research" (Absolon and Willett 2005, 113). Locating ourselves demonstrates our commitment to centring Indigenous ways of knowing and being within all aspects of our work both professionally and personally.

Angie

Although I now live in modern-day Calgary on Treaty 7 Territory, the area that I come from in Manitoba spreads from modern-day Oakville to MacGregor, through Portage la Prairie, into Poplar Point, up Highway 26 and into St. Francois Xavier — and through Winnipeg into St. Andrews. These are the places where my Spence, Hallett, Murray, Norquay and Parenteau families married into the Fidler, Setter, Bird, Scofield, Garrioch and Foulds families. My paternal Métis grandmothers were Marjorie Murray, Elsie Riggs and MaryAnn Spence. I am a member of both the Manitoba Métis Federation and Métis Nation of Alberta and am currently a PhD candidate in the Faculty of Native Studies at the University of Alberta. I have continued to be interested in the transmission of culture, the operationalization of power, the complexity of identity and the social structure of belonging.

These interests began with my own lived reality. Although growing up in my father's family I understood that we were "Métis," I was never sure what this actually meant. I was born and raised in a blue-collar, white, suburban neighbourhood in Winnipeg during the 1980s and 1990s. I did not recognize myself in the depictions of Métis people in Grade 6 social studies textbooks and was confused by the stereotypical (and inaccurate) descriptions of Métis people as simply half "one" and half "other." At the time I did not see myself as unique from others in our urban community. But I did recognize that my father's family desired to remove themselves from their history and fit in with white society. Despite these desires, we continued to be unique from others within our predominantly white community. We were simply living and creating new stories as a contemporary and urbanized generation of Métis people.

I mourned the loss of this community and connection and considered that my urban identity and general disconnection from the broader Métis community had played a role in my own sense of recognition and belonging. Therefore, as part of my research for a master's degree, I (re)connected with a rural land-based Métis community, Buffalo Lake Métis Settlement in Northern Alberta. I wanted to uncover if living within a land-based Métis community — and the anticipated language and culture found within those spaces — could strengthen one's sense of identity. This research was two-fold. Although some residents were clear about their belonging and had a strong sense of self as Métis, many more had complex issues that affected how they placed themselves in the world. Many children and youth were detached from traditional teachings, ceremony and language, while older residents lamented that their children (and even themselves at some point) were not always interested in learning about the old ways or their family's past. However, despite these more obvious forms of erasure, I was also not able to flatly reject that there were aspects of Métis world view that persevered. I was able to observe, participate and witness through acimowin (stories) and kiyokewin (visiting) how we as Métis people have continued to value our relationships with the land — particularly as we recounted the histories of our own specific territories and landscapes — and our interconnected kinship relationships with each other. We simply began with where individuals were shaped and influenced by unique sets of circumstances that played out within our specific locales. We navigated and survived the political, social and economic pressures of our territories. Despite these complexities, I recognized that the importance of caring for and protecting each other has been deeply engrained and continues to push us together. We strive to remain connected. We are enacting parts of the relational obligation of wahkohtowin — connected not only to each other, but to the land, our communities, our histories and to our ancestors. Our acimowin, whether at Buffalo Lake or in southwestern Manitoba, are not without substance — our identities and belonging are found within them — and when we tell acimowin, we are practicing our relational obligation to share these histories.

I was invited by Dr. Nathalie Kermoal to work as a research assistant for the Rupertsland Centre for Métis Research (RCMR) at the University of Alberta to develop a booklet surrounding customary Métis adoption protocols, child welfare and the introduction of Bill C-92 for the Métis Nation of Alberta (Tucker et al. 2022). I was drawn to this work because of my own community-centred research that focused on the loss of identity, culture, disconnection from land and removal from communities. I recognized the need for anti-assimilative, community-based processes that would allow Métis youth to remain connected and remain empowered by our people. I am grateful to Dr. Kermoal, Kelsey Bradburn and Amber Yamuch from Children and Family Services at Métis Nation of Alberta for the opportunity to work and learn alongside one another.

Julie

It is important to share the world and the kinship ties that have formed my perspective and passion on the issue of kinship care and the welfare of children. For nearly twenty years I worked within the child welfare system, though I suggest it is a system inaptly named as it has often forgotten about the welfare of children. I do not claim Métis citizenship and am aware of the privilege that I have had as an otherwise white settler woman. I have lived as an occupier on Treaty 6 Territory for most of my life. My mother immigrated from Europe following the Second World War. Her father was a political refugee from Ukraine and her mother was a member of the Belgian bourgeoisie. My father grew up with his French Canadian family in

St. Adolphe along the Red River in the Métis homeland with his French Canadian family. Growing up in northern Alberta, I was told we were French Canadian, but noticed we were different. No one else seemed to go berry picking like their lives depended on it. No one else ate rabbit pasta sauce. No one else spoke French using words like my dad did. I was told that his ways of being and his vernacular were due to living in a rural location or due to being francophone, but other francophone families in the area were still not quite the same. No surprise, there would be far more to my father's family's story.

As we have both alluded to, identity is complex. There are many social, political and economic factors that would shape how our families came to know themselves on the Prairies. There were a multitude of reasons why families chose to operate as they did in their localities and their decisions have had impacts on their descendants (Hancock 2017). My paternal grandmother was a fascinating and determined woman. Whenever my father reflects on his childhood he claims, "Were it not for your grandmother, we would have starved." She was a survivor, and she was strong-spirited. But my grandmother also held a secret about her Indigenous ancestry until shortly before she passed. Despite these silences, my father also knew about this past and resisted the narrative of their "public identity." My father was very close with my grandmother's brothers when he was younger. He recalls going to one of his uncles' homes — men he describes as being "real voyageur men" — fur caps, sash and all. He recalls a conversation that he had with one of them about his identity. He said, "I think we might be Indian" and his uncle laughed and said, "Of course you are, your grandmother is an Indian woman." His grandmother, my great-grandmother, was Julie Gervais of Iroquois descent in Quebec. My grandmother, Alice, moved as a young woman with her new husband to the Red River area and settled in St. Adolphe.

Although my grandmother kept her Indigeneity hidden, she also simultaneously lived and raised my father using an Indigenous world view. They quietly spoke Southern Michif. They honoured the land, used its medicines and practised sacred connections with Mother Earth. My grandmother lived in and for her garden just as many of my aunts, uncles and father still do. I will never know if these were her teachings or if her activities are in my blood memory, but I do hear her voice whenever I work in the garden and whenever I learn and embrace speaking Michif. I remember walking with her to visit her Métis girlfriends around town where she would *always* bring vegetables from the garden and then sit down for tea and a lively discussion. I remember them coming for tea and even though she had lots to do in the garden, she would put that work aside to shell peas at the kitchen table over some tea while she listened and cared for her community. When I began to learn about Indigenous world views, it was as if a light bulb went off. I began to understand why I may not have resonated with Western world views. I began to understand why my family was different and the feeling of shame that came from not knowing and embracing our identities.

Although it took me many years to recognize, my grandmother's teachings were truly my first lessons in social work. She was centred in her responsibilities to her community. After receiving a Bachelor of Social Work degree, I began working at an urban child welfare office. After telling my father about my work and a typical day in my life, he commented that he did not understand why we developed these systems of care. He then outlined how informal systems of child welfare operated in his community. If a situation arose in Red River where local children could not be cared for by their parents, the aunties, neighbours and ladies in town would gather around the kitchen table to discuss who would care for the children. They decided where they would live, who would bring the family additional food to help out and who would take the children to the local Catholic church on Sundays. When I first heard this story, the internalized colonial forces of the system within which I was taught led me to conclude that this process was old and outdated. But as time went by, this story never left my mind. Today, as I teach future social workers as a social work educator and researcher, I come back to the idea of collectively gathering around the kitchen table to discuss how to move forward as a community — kiikwookew kwizin (Mann-Johnson 2017). This is a coming together of those who care for children to make decisions in love, care and kinship. Perhaps the shift in my social work practices have been guided by my grandmother. Perhaps she has been whispering the teachings of wahkohtowin in my ear all along and guiding me towards exploring more accurate kinship care practices for Métis children, youth and their families.

THE CHILD WELFARE SYSTEM

The child welfare system has a long and sordid history as an agent of colonization that operated across the political enterprise now called Canada (Strega et al. 2015). This system formally began in 1876 with the creation of the Indian Act and the establishment of assimilative residential schools. The *Final Report of the Truth and Reconciliation Commission of Canada* (2015) affirms that assimilative education was destructive to Indigenous Peoples and has had negative intergenerational effects on Indigenous communities and families in Canada (Batiste and Barman 1995). Two-thirds of Indigenous people across Canada have stated that their lives have been directly or indirectly influenced by the Residential School System (Environics 2010).[1]

The Indian Act was amended in 1951 to provide provincial governments with the authority to enforce provincial child protection laws on First Nations. The amendment led to aggressive adoption/foster care initiatives facilitated by newly appointed social workers who had little to no formal training in working with

Indigenous groups. They were often ignorant about colonialism and the systemic discrimination that Indigenous people faced. Many were unaware of the socioeconomic disparities between Indigenous and non-Indigenous groups. After the 1951 amendment, many Indigenous children were apprehended based solely on their race and/or poverty. This is what we have come to know as the "Sixties Scoop." The rate of Indigenous children in care grew from 1 percent in 1951 to 30–40 percent by the end of the 1960s (Carrière and Strega 2015), disproportionate to the rates of apprehension within any other community or ethnic group in Canada (Bombay et al. 2020). In addition to being removed from their communities, children were not often told about their Indigenous roots. The aim of child welfare was to assimilate Indigenous children and youth into Euro-Canadian society through their placement in white families outside of their original communities. The legacy of these actions has devastated Indigenous culture and history.

Despite all that was learned about the negative impacts of the Sixties Scoop, the number of Indigenous children in care has continued to escalate. By 2002, over 22,000 Indigenous children were in care, more than the number of children adopted during the Sixties Scoop and even more than attended residential schools at the height of forced enrollment (Vowel 2016, 182). Recent statistics are even more striking. In June 2023, 75 percent of children in care in Alberta were Indigenous (Government of Alberta 2023b) despite Indigenous Peoples representing only 6.8 percent of Albertans (Statistics Canada 2021). Half of the children who were in care in 2018 have parents or grandparents who have been in the child welfare system at one time or another (Métis Nation of British Columbia et al. 2018). These statistics demonstrate the ongoing nature of intergenerational trauma for Indigenous Peoples. This trauma is a national epidemic. The current rate of apprehension of Indigenous children has led to what former Grand Chief John Beaucage (2011) describes as the "Millennium Scoop." The Millennium Scoop has been driven in part by practices such as flagging many Indigenous families as perceived at-risk families and the use of so-called birth alerts.

Indigenous children are not only greatly overrepresented in the child welfare system, but also Indigenous families are subjected to more intrusive forms of child welfare involvement (Sinha et al. 2011). These intrusive measures are often directly related to systemic issues such as poverty, violence against women and structural barriers that restrict access to services (NIMMIWG 2019; Brittain and Blackstock 2015). The rate of substantiated investigations is much higher for Indigenous families than for non-Indigenous families, and this is particularly true in cases of suspected neglect. Indigenous families also experience less supportive intervention within their cases. More holistic services such as providing in-home support to work alongside the family is less likely to occur for Indigenous families (Sinha et al. 2011).

Although child welfare systems may have been thought to protect Indigenous children, they were ultimately responsible for a legacy of trauma. Policies and practices were assimilative, oppressive and harmful. Métis survivors of residential schools, the Sixties Scoop and the Millennium Scoop recall culture and language loss in addition to physical, emotional, psychological and spiritual harm (Métis National Council 2019). It is evident that the trajectory for child welfare processes has been far from successful for Indigenous Peoples. Therefore, we argue that new processes that are inclusive of and privileging of Indigenous Knowledge and ways of being and doing must be put in place. As those who work within Métis communities and circles, we bring forward more traditional forms of child care centred on Métis-specific definitions of kinship and the obligations that we all have to each other.

KINSHIP

All societies operate within kinship systems. Kinship is the means through which individuals determine and develop relationships between themselves and other people. Cultural anthropologists have contemplated the definition of kinship from varying standpoints (Overing et al. 2004). Broadly speaking, kinship has been defined as a relatively static network of social bonds (called "affinal kinship") and/or biological (called "blood-tied") networks. These networks are then seen to be the foundation of human relationships, the basis of our alliances and the backbone to the social institutions that continue to intersect with other institutions and organizations within our society. These simplistic definitions have been subjected to several critiques including: the failure to account for the passing of time; linguistic misinterpretation; bias; non-inclusion; oversimplification; and the role that power has played in kinship studies (Wilson 2016). Anthropological kinship definitions are further limited by the reality that kinship is never static. Kinship is socially constructed, reconstituted and culturally practised. Kinship does not always operate within the definitions put forward in the Eurocentric discourse of mainstream cultural anthropology.

Social work understands kinship care through Eurocentric kinship models. For example, the Government of Alberta (2023a) defines kinship care as the full-time care, nurturing and protection of children by relatives or others who have a kinship bond to a child. Although factual, this definition is skeletal. It fails to include how decisions are made and by whom. While kinship care resembles the models of care that have been employed by Métis families, the adoption of kinship care by the government systems is largely appropriative. In their study of kinship care as the preferred placement for Australian Aboriginal youth, James Beaufils (2022) argues the conflation of kinship care has become paternalistic and is inclusive of co-opted notions of Indigenous traditional child rearing. Government policies fail to address the connection to land and extensive bloodlines and community central to Indigenous child rearing and kinship. When governments respond with policies, standards and training, the sacredness and tradition of caring for each other and one's kin becomes sanitized and colonized (Beaufils 2022).

How kinship is understood by Euro-Canadian society differs in several ways from how Métis know and understand their own kinship systems. We argue that this is due to the differential focus on individual versus collective ways of being and knowing. Indigenous communities centre on the collective whole and the responsibilities that they have to their relations within their communities. This reflects a community-based ontology.

Wahkohtowin

The axiological teaching of wahkohtowin informs Cree/Métis kinship and relationship protocols not only with humans but also other animate and inanimate entities. It holds the lessons and laws for how Métis collectively understand their family systems and their continued connections with their ancestors from the past, present and future. Who Métis people are is deeply set within this interconnectedness. Wahkohtowin as a world view that contains the original laws and principles that guide how Métis families are intended to function in our society. Brenda MacDougall (2014) further claims that Métis understand their identity due to their interconnectedness. Métis know themselves through a continued peoplehood from within a specific time and place (Andersen 2014). Couched within genealogy and nationhood, Métis people have also developed and, although complex, maintained specific language, religion, culture and history (Holm et al. 2003, 12) and this has resulted in a unique kinship structure (Devine 2004; MacDougall 2014; Wade 2005) that relies heavily on where and from who you come from. Métis responsibilities have been tied to the land in specific locations. Métis thus have obligations to their kin and extended kin within those territories. Through wahkohtowin, there are laws surrounding all aspects of commitments and obligations to the community and lands of which they are part. These laws include those surrounding childcare and, thus, about child welfare and adoption.

This community-based obligation has been fundamental to the development, perseverance and future of Métis children, youth and families. For Métis peoples, remaining connected to one another has provided them with the opportunity to pass on cultural teachings and language from one generation to the next. Métis community members are obligated to remain connected and care for the Elders and other aging members within their communities, particularly when they have no other family members around. This care can include bringing other community members harvested fish, meat or vegetables from local gardens. Métis understand that nobody should be left without connections. Brenda MacDougall (2010, 10) states, "no individual in a territory or community was to be without any connections, so a place was made for everyone to belong." She is affirming an intended connectedness among people in the community regardless of their background or if they were blood or married kin. Métis people also worked to include newcomers into the social networks within their territories. This was integral to their survival and an important aspect to their perseverance. As we are both familiar with the responsibilities that we have of living alongside Métis people, we continue to practise this sense of community, embrace one another and protect those we are tied to.

HOW WERE CHILDREN CARED FOR IN THE PAST?

For Métis, caring for, protecting, educating and disciplining their children is a community's responsibility. To learn how to care for children is further considered to be an important teaching. Children are unique and each have valuable gifts that they have received from the Creator to bring to the community (Greenwood 2006). Therefore, "it was up to each member of the Métis community to help children explore, discover and strengthen the child's talents and gifts" (Métis Centre 2008, 56). Historically, Métis children were raised by their community. This community was comprised of their parents, their extended family, godparents and other Métis families in their vicinity. Children would more often remain within their own family circle but, at times, it would be necessary for another family or community member to provide support, as Julie described earlier in her story. There are several reasons why this intervention would be necessary. For example, a parent may be deceased, away for an extended period or dealing with their own physical or mental health. For example:

> My Great, Great, Great-Uncle John Norquay was raised by his paternal grandparents (whom we share). John's father was not equipped to raise all of his children and therefore gave his son to his mother, Jane Morwick and her second husband, James Spence, to raise as their own. Clearly this was a good upbringing, because John Norquay would grow up to be the fifth premier of Manitoba (1878-1887).

This was not an isolated experience. Reviewing several nineteenth century Métis genealogical and archival records from southwest Manitoba, it is evident that this type of customary adoption became relatively normalized. The time between 1870–1920 in Red River Territory was complicated by a serious smallpox epidemic and bout of deadly influenza. During these epidemics many children lost one or both of their parents. Although not explicitly drawn out, there were protocols and obligations in place to support the children of those who had passed. Adoption records are virtually non-existent in the area since adopted children would simply be claimed as biological children. However, by reading through genealogical records and archival documents such as birth, baptism and death records it is possible to recreate the experiences of adopted children through birth, baptism and death records. Archival records show that family members such as aunts, uncles, or grandparents would often take on the responsibilities of caring for their own family's children. Living spouses would even at times marry their deceased spouse's brother or sister to reinforce the child's kinship ties.

Sometimes care would be less permanent. At times, parents were temporarily absent or dealing with their own personal issues. Therefore, children would live with another family or community member until their parents were able to return to their child caring responsibilities. This form of caregiving could vary in length from days to years. According to Leah Dorion (2010), this form of apprehension was never considered a failure and was never negatively judged. So, if we revisit the context of the teaching of wahkohtowin as it pertains to families and communities, we can see that Métis people were enacting their relational responsibilities. Furthermore, when Elders or other respected adults in the community requested to raise other people's children, it was considered an honour. Regardless of who took on the responsibilities of caring for the children, the community was obliged to support the person or family who had taken on the role. This practice is called ka oopikihtamashook and was understood and employed to maintain and strengthen Métis kinship ties; provide the opportunity to strengthen the child's existing relationships; reinforce a strong sense of Métis culture, identity, community; and to expand the Métis Nation. Children also forged new relationships through the making of new relatives (Auger 2001; Cross 2014). These practices demonstrate that kinship principles were at the core of what could now be called adoption practices.

An examination of these protocols can also work to recover and reclaim traditional practices surrounding child welfare. It is crucial that we recognize that Indigenous children and youth thrive when family connections and cultural traditions are preserved and protected. Intervening with customary protocols prevents Métis children and youth from losing the connections that they have with their communities and from having to, at times, awkwardly reconnect with their communities as adults. Customary adoption models ensure a fluid experience that respects culture, heritage and the connections that children have with their extended family and is a historically and culturally appropriate response to the needs of Métis children, youth and their families. These historic processes further promote how Métis understand permanency as opposed to formal adoptions that terminate a parent's rights (Cross 2014).

HOW KINSHIP CARE HAS BEEN OPERATIONALIZED USING WESTERN CHILD WELFARE POLICIES

Although kinship care has been common practice within collective societies (Farmer 2009), these processes of kinship care were not considered to be a viable long-term solution in North American child welfare systems until the 1990s (Leos-Urbel et al. 2002). Prior to that time, formal options such as foster or group care were the preferred alternate care models. However, children and youth within these placements were more often than not placed in the homes of strangers from different communities, ethnicities and ways of life unknown to them (Mann-Johnson 2017). This was not always an ideal placement. Navigating another family's way of life was difficult for Indigenous children and recent studies have linked living with strangers to several childhood traumas (Choate et al. 2021; Blackstock et al. 2020).

The rise of kinship care in Westernized models and the recognition of its potential as a legitimate placement option only happened because of the shortage of spaces within formal foster or other group care options. Yet, government bodies began to recognize the positive impacts that kinship placements had on children in care. For example, children who were living in kinship-based arrangements were less stigmatized than those who were placed in formal systems with strangers (Messing 2006). They also experienced healthier identity formation due to their continued connection to their kin and to their community (Ban 2005; de Finney et al. 2015). More notably, children placed in kinship care experienced lower rates of recidivism, meaning that once they returned to their parents or primary caregivers, children were less likely to return to in-care status. It is speculated that this can be attributed to the community-centred system of care, because where kinship caregivers remain in the lives of the children they are able to provide ongoing support (Koh et al. 2011; Perry et al. 2012; Burke et al. 2022). While kinship placements may not always be permanent, they are considered to be more stable (Farmer 2010; Koh 2010), because even if a kinship placement breaks down, children who are placed with kin are more likely to stay connected to their family and community going forward (O'Brien 2012).

IMPLICATIONS FOR PRACTICE

Initially, government systems responded to the rise of kinship care by applying policies, regulations, standards and processes that were similar to those applied in standard foster care and adoption processes. Selwyn and Nandy (2014) suggest this evolution from informal to formal systems of care has been confusing for both caregivers and frontline child welfare practitioners. Confusion leads to challenges for caregivers navigating the child welfare system due to unclear definitions of and boundaries between types of kinship care (formal, informal, permanent, etc.) and variances in levels of support, access to information and system rules and standards.

Furthering the complexity, kinship caregivers are more likely to require support than foster parents, due to structural issues such as poverty, racism and caregivers' health issues (Falconnier et al. 2010; Berrick 2016; McPherson et al. 2022). Kinship providers who are grandparents or are elderly are particularly likely to be impacted by medical issues that restrict their caregiving, and which are compounded by poverty and other social determinants of health (McPherson et al. 2022). Moreover, kinship caregivers are more likely to enter into a kinship agreement following a family crisis. During this time of crisis, an initial assessment of support might be completed where the potential caregiver may also be experiencing a sense of fear or of repercussions from asking for support (McPherson et al. 2022). This fear of the assessment process arises in the context of colonization, racism and lack of cultural safety, yet support during a crisis is most needed. Understanding these structural issues and the power imbalance inherent in assessment procedures is vital to anti-oppressive, anti-racist and fair assessment practices.

Typically, to become approved as a kinship caregiver, prospective caregivers must participate in a home assessment process. This might occur as an initial assessment or a more comprehensive assessment for long-term placement. Although some jurisdictions have amended their home assessment processes for kinship caregivers to be more inclusive of specific cultural processes, many more continue to follow similar processes to those expected of adoptive and foster families (Mann-Johnson 2016). This is problematic because these processes align with the expectations of Western, more affluent middle-class families. For example, children in care are not permitted to share bedrooms, all adults in the home must have clear criminal record checks and all homes require insurance. This is at times difficult for family members who are living below the poverty line. Poverty in turn may become a barrier or be stigmatizing and dissuade potential caregivers creating barriers to placing children within kinship networks.

Navigating government and colonial systems of child welfare is one of the most significant barriers identified by kinship caregivers (Gentles-Gibbs and Zema 2020). Kinship caregivers often mistrust these systems. Métis kinship caregivers have directly or indirectly experienced colonization through the loss of land, culture, language, way of life and community. Due to this experience, it is difficult to trust that the government will support them through their challenges. Punitive responses are often feared when potential caregivers are seeking support, particularly after caregivers have completed a long and intrusive assessment process. Kristina Brant (2022) describes caregivers' experience in losing autonomy in the caregiving of children as the child welfare system retains or gains formal decision-making. This formal process then becomes a trade-off, as caregivers may now access financial and other support from the child welfare system, yet often give up autonomy in caregiving and decision-making power for the child while child welfare retains guardianship. Brant (2022) described this as a fraught process and points out the importance of the caregivers' relationship with the caseworker, as the caseworkers are able to successfully navigate support and resources within the broader child welfare system while empowering caregivers.

Kinship families have unique needs based on their demographics and circumstances. These needs are compounded and complicated by structural issues like poverty and access to resources. These needs do not mean a caregiver is a poor caregiver. It means they may have needs for support that can be met individually or collectively. The community can come together to meet them, as was the case historically. Or in situations of disconnection from community due to the impacts of colonization, a child welfare system may need to support the family.

In her work on the impact that colonial and racist policies have had on Métis children, youth and families, Cathy Richardson states that current child welfare approaches remain "top-down and non-collaborative," and argues that in this post–Truth and Reconciliation era, these approaches should be moving towards "transcending colonial social work practice" (2016, 84). To disrupt these colonial and racist policies she advocates a shift towards social work practices that are "based on reducing isolation and reconnecting children with their family, community, lands and culture" (2016, 92). Citing the framework adopted by New South Wales, Australia, she describes practising from an anti-oppressive approach as a starting point that begins with respecting each person from "wherever they stand" (2016, 92). This framework commits to ensuring "culture is ever-present, language impacts on practice, relationships create change and restore dignity, critique leads to improved practice and ethics and values are integral to good practice" (NSW 2017, 91).

Formalized kinship care is promising if practised in a manner that disrupts colonial notions of top-down approval and rejects Eurocentric standards. Returning to a system of family and community decision-making means honouring the outcomes of these decision-making processes. Too often, child welfare systems override a family's decision, and call into question a family's commitment or ability to identify the best possible option for a child. This is a contemporary manifestation of colonial and paternal practices where the child welfare system imposes its ideas of knowing better than a family.

A system where families lead the process towards child caring arrangements that are child and family centred and are supported through a well-resourced support plan will ensure successful and authentic kinship caregiving that are founded in traditional approaches of care. Caseworkers function as the arm of the child welfare system and must approach families in a manner that is equitable to restore trust and ensure that families are receiving the required support. As outlined previously, it is important to understand that kinship families have a historical mistrust of caseworkers and are reluctant to reach out for support. Knowing this, caseworkers must make it their priority to build relationships and be reflective about the power they carry in these roles and the impact that power has on families and their working relationship. Adopting a principle of understanding and continuously engaging in reflection and reflective supervision is a key component of this authentic, anti-colonizing and anti-racist practice.

CHILD WELFARE BUILT ON MÉTIS KNOWLEDGE

It has become clear that a sense of responsibility and care for their children is integral to Métis culture. We argue that the obligations to children and to communities are already well-rooted within Métis knowledge systems and we do not need to reinvent this foundation. Despite generations of Métis families being removed from their culture, language, history and land, these teachings remain. This is also important because these teachings and protocols continue from the knowledge and ways of doing that came from Métis ancestors. New systems will operate differently than those that occurred in the past, yet child care must be built upon the traditional systems that Métis people have already created from their own perspectives. This must include community-based decision-making. This knowledge reaches into the past, exists within the present and should therefore extend into the future. When building new programs and services for Métis children, youth, their families and communities, we must further reject models that continue to isolate children from their connections. Because without these systems of relationship, Métis children will continue to lose their cultural teachings, language and identity. Children gain a "sense of trust, strength, a sense of purpose, and a sense of commonality within their communities" (Cross 2014, 376). The community is at the centre of who Métis people are, therefore, it is vital that we protect it.

NOTE

1 Métis people are one of three recognized Indigenous people (First Nations, Métis and Inuit) as per Section 35 of the Constitution Act. We include statistics for Indigenous children and families because Métis people are Indigenous people.

SUGGESTED READINGS

Andersen, Chris. 2014. *"Métis": Race, Recognition and the Struggle for Indigenous Peoplehood.* Vancouver: UBC Press.
Carrière, Jeannine and Cathy Richardson. 2017. *Calling our Families Home: Métis Peoples' Experiences with Children Welfare.* Vernon, BC: JCharlton Publishing Ltd.
Richardson, Cathy. 2016. "Metis-Astute Social Work: Shining the Light on Some Helpful Practices." *Journal of Indigenous Social Development* 6, 1.

REFERENCES

Absolon, Kathleen and Cam Willett. 2005. "Putting Ourselves Forward." In *Research as Resistance: Critical, Indigenous, and Anti-Oppressive Approaches*, edited by Leslie Brown and Susan Strega. Toronto: Canadian Scholars Press.

Andersen, Chris. 2014. *"Métis": Race, Recognition and the Struggle for Indigenous Peoplehood*. Vancouver: UBC Press.

Auger, Don. 2001. "The Northern Ojibwe and Their Family Law." Doctoral dissertation, York University.

Ban, Paul. 2005. "Aboriginal Child Placement Principles and Family Group Conferences." *Australian Social Work* 58, 4.

Batiste, Marie and Jean Barman. 1995. *First Nations Education in Canada: The Circle Unfolds*. Vancouver: UBC Press.

Beaucage, John. 2011. "Children First: The Aboriginal Advisor's Report on the Status of Aboriginal Child Welfare in Ontario." Toronto: Ministry of Children and Youth Services.

Beaufils, James. 2022. "'That's the Bloodline': Does Kinship and Care Translate to Kinship Care?" *Australian Journal of Social Issues* 58.

Blackstock, Cindy, Muriel Bamblett and Carlina Black. 2020. "Indigenous Ontology, International Law and the Application of the Convention to the Over-representation of Indigenous Children in out of Home Care in Canada and Australia." *Child Abuse & Neglect* 110, 1

Bombay, Amy, Robyn McQuaid, Janelle Young, Vandna Singa, Vanessa Currie, Hymie Anisman and Kim Matheson. 2020. "Familial Attendance at Indian Residential School and Subsequent Involvement in the Child Welfare System Among Indigenous Adults Born During the Sixties Scoop Era." *First Peoples Child and Family Review* 15, 1.

Brant, Kristina. 2022. "When Mamaw Becomes Mom: Social Capital and Kinship Family Formation Amid the Rural Opioid Crisis." *Journal of the Social Sciences* 8, 3

Brittain, Melisa and Cindy Blackstock. 2015. "First Nations Child Poverty: A Literature Review and Analysis." First Nations Children's Action Research and Education Services.

Burke, Susan, Jane Bouey, Carol Madsen, Louise Costello, Glen Scmidt, Patricia Barkaskas, Nicole White, Caitlin Alder and Rabiah Murium. 2022. "Kinship Care: Evaluating Policy and Practice." *Journal of Public Child Welfare* 17, 3.

Campbell, Maria. 2022. "Respecting Each Other's Bundles." Keynote presentation delivered at Mawachihitotaak Métis Studies Symposium, Winnipeg, Manitoba, May 6, 2022.

Chandler, Michael and Christopher Lalonde. 2008. "Cultural Continuity as a Protective Factor Against Suicide in First Nations Youth." *Horizons* 10.

Choate, Peter, Roy Bear Chief, Desi Lindstrong, Brandy CrazyBull. 2021 "Sustaining Cultural Genocide - A Look at Indigenous Children in Non-Indigenous Placement and the Place of Judicial Decision Making - A Canadian Example." *Laws* 10, 3.

Cross, Terry L. 2014. "Customary Adoption for American Indian and Alaskan Native Children." In *Child Welfare for the Twenty-First Century*, edited by Gerald Mallon and Peg McCartt Hess. New York: Columbia University Press.

de Finney, Sandrina and Lara di Tomasso. 2015. "Creating Places of Belonging: Expanding Notions of Permanency with Indigenous Youth in Care." In *Walking This Path Together: Anti-racist and Anti-oppressive Child Welfare Practice*, second edition, edited by Jeannine Carrière and Susan Strega. Winnipeg: Fernwood Publishing.

Devine, Heather. 2004. *The People Who Own Themselves*. Calgary: University of Calgary Press.

Dorion, Leah Marie. 2010. "Opikinawasowin: The Life Long Process of Growing Cree and Métis Children." Master's thesis, Athabasca University.

Environics. 2010. "Urban Aboriginal Peoples Study: Main Report." Environics Institute, Toronto.

Falconnier, Lydia, Nicole Tomasella, Howard Doueck, Susan Wells, Heather Luckey and Jean Agathen. 2010. "Indicators of Quality in Kinship Foster Care." *Families in Society: The Journal of Contemporary Social Services* 91, 4.

Farmer, Elaine. 2009. "Making Kinship Care Work." *Adoption and Fostering* 33, 3.

———. 2010. "What Outcomes Relate to Good Placement Outcomes in Kinship Care?" *British Journal of Social Work* 40.

Gentles-Gibbs, Natallie and Jordan Zema. 2020. "It's not about them without them: Kinship grandparents' perspectives on family empowerment in public child welfare." *Children and Youth Services Review* 108.

Government of Alberta. 2023a. *Enhancement Policy Manual*.

———. 2023b. *Child Intervention Information and Statistics Summary: Child Intervention Information and Statistics — 2023-24 First Quarter (June) Update*.

Greenwood, Margot. 2006. "Children Are a Gift to Us: Aboriginal-Specific Early Childhood Programs and Services in Canada." *Canadian Journal of Native Education* 29, 1.

Hancock, Robert. 2017. "We Know Who Our Relatives Are." In *Calling our Families Home: Métis Peoples' Experiences with Children Welfare*, edited by Jeannine Carrière and Cathy Richardson. Vernon, BC: JCharlton Publishing Ltd.

Heath Justice, Daniel. 2016. "Reflections on Indigenous Literary Nationalism: On Home Grounds, Singing Hogs, and Cranky Critics." In *Sources and Methods in Indigenous Studies*, edited by Chris Andersen and Jean O'Brien. New York: Routledge.

Hogue, Michel. 2015. *Métis and the Medicine Line: Creating a Border and Dividing a People*. Regina: Regina Press.

Holm, Tom, Diane Pearson and Ben Chavis. 2003. "Peoplehood: A Model for the Extension of Sovereignty in American Indian Studies." *Wicazo Sa Review* 18, 1.

Koh, Eun. 2010. "Permanency Outcomes of Children in Kinship and Non-Kin Foster Homes: Testing the External Validity of Kinship Effects." *Children and Youth Services Review*, 32, 3.

Koh, Eun, and Mark Testa. 2011. "Children Discharged from Kin and non-Kin Foster Homes: Do the Risks of Foster Care re-entry Differ?" *Children and Youth Services Review* 33, 9.

Leos-Urbel, Jacob, Roseanna Bess and Rob Geen. 2002. "The Evolution of Federal and State Policies for Assessing and Supporting Kinship Caregivers." *Children and Youth Services Review* 24, 1/2.

MacDougall, Brenda. 2014. "Speaking of Métis: Reading Family Life into Colonial Records." *Ethnohistory* 61,1.

———. 2010. *One of the Family: Métis Culture in Nineteenth-Century Northern Saskatchewan*. Vancouver: UBC Press.

Mann-Johnson, Julie. 2016. "Decolonizing Home Assessment Practice at the Kitchen Table: A Thematic Analysis Identifying the Crucial Elements in the Assessment of Kinship Caregivers." Unpublished Master's thesis, University of Calgary.

Mann-Johnson, Julie. 2017. "Kiikwookew Kwizin and Kinship Care: Attending to the Hearts of Métis Children." In *Calling Our Families Home: Métis Peoples' Experiences with Children Welfare*, edited by Jeannine Carrière and Cathy Richardson. Vernon, BC: JCharlton Publishing Ltd.

McPherson, Lynne, Kathhomi Gatwiri, Kylie Day, Natalie Parmenter, Janise Mitchell and Noel McNamara. 2022. "'The Most Challenging Aspect of this Journey has been Dealing with Child Protection': Kinship Carers Experiences in Australia." *Children and Youth Services Review* 139.

Messing, Jill. 2006. "From the Child's Perspective: A Qualitative Analysis of Kinship Care Placements." *Children and Youth Services Review* 28.

Métis Centre. 2008. "In the Words of Our Ancestors: Métis Health and Healing." National Aboriginal Health Organization (NAHO). Ottawa.

Métis Nation of British Columbia, Métis Commission for Children and Families of BC, and Ministry of Children and Family Development. 2018. *Métis Children and Youth in Continuing Care: Descriptive Analysis.*

Métis National Council. 2019. "What We Heard: Report of the Métis Nation's Engagement With Métis Sixties Scoop Survivors."

National Inquiry into Missing and Murdered Indigenous Women and Girls (NIMMIWG). 2019. *Reclaiming Power and Place: The Final Report of the National Inquiry into Missing and Murdered Indigenous Women and Girls*, vol. 1a. Ottawa.

O'Brien, Valerie. 2012. "The Benefits and Challenges of Kinship Care." *Child Care in Practice* 18, 2.

Overing, Joanna, Paolo Fortis and Margherita Margiotti. 2004. "Kinship in Anthropology." In *International Encyclopedia of The Social & Behavioral Sciences*, edited by Neil Smelser and Paul Baltes. Elsevier.

Perry, Gretchen, Martin Daly and Jennifer Kotler. 2012. "Placement stability in Kinship and Non-Kin Foster Care: A Canadian Study." *Children and Youth Services Review* 34.

Richardson, Cathy. 2016. "Metis-Astute Social Work: Shining the Light on Some Helpful Practices." *Journal of Indigenous Social Development* 6, 1.

Selwyn, Julie and Shailen Nandy. 2014. "Kinship Care in the UK: Using Census Data to Estimate the Extent of Formal and Informal Care by Relatives." *Child and Family Social Work* 19.

Sinha, Vandna, Nico Trcome, Barbara Fallon, Bruce LacLaurin, Elizabeth Fast, Shelley Thomas Prokop and Kenn Richard. 2011. *"Kiskisik Awasiak": Remember the Children. Understanding the Overrepresentation of First Nations Children in the Child Welfare System.* Ontario: Assembly of First Nations.

Statistics Canada. 2022. "Indigenous Population Continues to Grow and is Much Younger Than the Non-Indigenous Population, Although the Pace of Growth Has Slowed." The Daily.

Strega, Susan and Jeannine Carrière. 2015. "Anti-racist and Anti-oppressive Child Welfare." In *Walking This Path Together: Anti-racist and Anti-oppressive Child Welfare Practice*, second edition, edited by Jeannine Carrière and Susan Strega. Winnipeg: Fernwood Publishing.

Truth and Reconciliation Commission of Canada. 2015. *The Final Report of the Truth and Reconciliation Commission of Canada (vol. 3): Canada's Residential Schools: The Métis Experience.*

Tucker, Angie, Nathalie Kermoal, Kelsey Bradburn and Amber Yamuch. 2022. *Reclaiming Our Children: Exercising Métis child and family services jurisdiction under act C-92.* Pamphlet. Rupertsland Centre for Métis Research and University of Alberta. RCMR/Métis Nation of Alberta.

Vowel, Chelsea. 2016. *Indigenous Writes: A Guide to First Nations, Métis, and Inuit Issues in Canada.* Winnipeg, Manitoba: HighWater Press.

Wade, Peter. 2005. "Hybridity Theory and Kinship Thinking." *Cultural Studies* 19, 5.

Wilson, Robert A. 2016. "Kinship Past, Kinship Present: Bio-Essentialism in the Study of Kinship." *American Anthropologist* 118, 3.

Chapter 8

DECOLONIZING PREVENTION

Support and Surveillance in Indigenous Child and Family Services

by Erika Finestone

CHAPTER FOCUS

This chapter analyzes the benefits and risks experienced by child protection–involved Indigenous caregivers and their children as participants in prevention programs: publicly funded programs intended to support at-risk families in their healing and growth, enhance parenting skills and/or assist children in healthy development. Drawing on data and stories gathered during ethnographic research within and on the margins of Indigenous-led family service agencies on Vancouver Island, I amplify the voices and reflections of Indigenous service providers navigating their responsibilities as professionals and their accountabilities as kin to families in their programs. The stories in this chapter demonstrate that — rather than neutral support sites for families — child welfare prevention programs are places in which Indigenous caregivers and children are disciplined as colonial subjects in the context of child protection surveillance. Woven throughout the chapter are my reflections on the decolonial and liberatory potential of Indigenous participation in prevention programs and the creation/deepening of practices that disrupt colonial violence from within state-funded institutions.

QUESTIONS ADDRESSED IN THIS CHAPTER

1. What are the risks of Indigenous caregivers' participation in state-funded prevention programs, and how can Indigenous and non-Indigenous service providers mitigate those risks?
2. What is the "duty to report" and how does it help or hinder Indigenous self-determination over the family?
3. How might we rethink our responsibility as helpers and caregivers working within and/or on the margins of the child welfare system through a decolonial lens?

FINDING THE "HAPPY MIDDLE"

It was March 2017, and I was sitting in Kendra Gage's[1] office. Kendra is the executive director of the urban Indigenous family service agency Hulitan Family & Community Services Society (henceforth referred to simply as "Hulitan") in Victoria BC. Funded by the provincial Ministry of Children and Family Development, Hulitan is one of the few Indigenous-led family service agencies offering culturally rooted healing and prevention programs and services to Indigenous families who live both on and off reserve in Southern Vancouver Island on the traditional territories of the Lekwungen (Esquimalt and Songhees), Malahat, Scia'new, T'Sou-ke and W̱SÁNEĆ (Pauquachin, Tsartlip, Tsawout, Tseycum) people (Hulitan Family & Community Services Society n.d.).

Most of the families participating in Hulitan's programs are "ministry involved." The term "ministry involved" refers to families who have previous or ongoing involvement with the statutory child welfare system. These families have open case files with the Ministry of Children and Family Development (MCFD) and/or their local Indigenous child and family service agency due to previous or ongoing child protection concerns. Many ministry-involved families accessing services at Hulitan are participating in programs which are technically voluntary and/or preventative but are in many cases mandated by their caseworkers either as an avenue towards reunification with a child in care, or as a stipulation for decreased ministry involvement or less severe interventions, or in rare cases the closure of a case file altogether.

Sitting in Kendra's office that day, I observed walls decorated with artwork and thank-you cards gifted by members of the families she works with, while she laid out the history behind the development of Indigenous-led family services agencies like Hulitan. She was lamenting the difficulty of finding a "happy middle" between intervention and independence when supporting ministry-involved Indigenous families. She explained:

> So, we started with a system of complete oppression [...] you know, basically saying to Indigenous families, "You don't know how to care for your kids, and you're savages, so we're gonna show you!" and the damage that's happened from that .... [Then] you have reconciliation and the apology[2] [Prime Minister of Canada Stephen Harper's 2008 apology to former Indian residential school students] and it's almost like now the pendulum has swung to, "We just need to leave community alone." But that's not good enough either! So, we've gone to this place where we intervene way too much and we cause trauma, we do nothing and we cause trauma, or we do the minimal and we cause trauma. Where's

the happy middle? Where's the grey area of this work? And that's where we [Hulitan] try to sit: in the grey area, where we want to keep families together, but we also want to provide families the opportunity to flourish and grow and be held up, you know?

Kendra's rendering of the complexities of child welfare service delivery to Indigenous families in this passage helps frame a series of questions worth examining in more detail in this chapter, such as:

- What are the generative possibilities of working in the "grey area" between complete independence from the state (and state rules/resources) in the delivery of family services versus the overinvolvement of the state in service delivery?
- How can state-sponsored institutions like Hulitan at once commit to meeting the existing immediate and material needs of Indigenous families and work to uphold those families' self-determination in the context of child welfare involvement?
- In a settler-colonial context, to what extent is Indigenous self-determination expressed as autonomy from or within state-funded child welfare institutions?

These questions feed into broader theoretical debates preoccupying critical scholars of settler-colonial states, namely:

- Does Indigenous participation in state-funded institutions contribute towards or detract from decolonial futurities?
- What, if any, are the emancipatory possibilities that gestate in the liminal spaces between the utter rejection of the state and recognition and/or participation within it?

Some scholars critical of Indigenous Peoples' participation in settler institutions argue that state-funded social programs can be understood as a ventricle of colonial power through which marginalized and racialized bodies are managed, governed and assimilated into the broader body politic (Dhillon 2017; Stevenson 2014; Povinelli 2002). Anti-colonial scholar Dr. Jaskiran Dhillon (2017), for instance, sheds light on the duplicitous nature of some state-led social services that can be "inherently disciplinary while simultaneously positioned as functioning in support of Indigenous [Peoples]." This critique has meaningfully shaped the lens through which I view and understand Indigenous family service environments. However, as you will shortly see in this chapter, I argue that discipline is far from the only thing that happens in Indigenous family service environments. By spending time with Indigenous service providers and child welfare–involved families at Hulitan and other service sites on Vancouver Island, it became evident that colonial child welfare practices, policies and perspectives can be disrupted not only from outside but also from within state-funded institutions.

One of the benefits of having Indigenous providers working within state-funded service sites is that it offers an opportunity to learn the "master's tools" — to observe the nefarious ways state policies and practices work to threaten or dismantle Indigenous self-determination and to manipulate them to do the opposite (Spivak and Morris 2010). As Spivak argues "the only way you can sabotage something is when you are working intimately with it" (Spivak cited in Brohi 2014, n.p.). She continues, "You can only deconstruct that which you know intimately. It is not a weapon of the weak; it can only be done from a position of strength" (n.p.).

In this chapter, I take up Spivak's understanding of "affirmative sabotage" (Spivak and Morris 2010) as a framework for examining the role Indigenous service providers play in the lives of child welfare–involved Indigenous families on Vancouver Island. Using stories and observations gathered during ethnographic hanging out at several Indigenous-led family programs and interviews with Indigenous service providers, I inquire into the politics of Indigenous participation, performance, surveillance and reporting in and on the peripheries of Indigenous family programs. I pay particular attention to Indigenous families' and service providers' social transactions within program environments where they are made "visible" to the state in ways that, I argue, at once challenge and affirm their self-determination. Using stories gathered in these sites, I zoom in on service providers' advocacy, surveillance and reporting practices, demonstrating how participation in program environments can in some instances place child welfare–involved Indigenous participants at heightened risk of child welfare interventions (including child removal), while in other instances can protect them from those interventions. Using these findings, I argue that decolonial care and colonial complicity often operate coterminously in the child welfare context.

Zooming out, this chapter aims to demonstrate how family programs can be at once "educative" (Foucault 1977; Rose 1996; Li 2007) — part of an overarching structure of colonial governmentality and surveillance of marginalized families — while also serving as sites of "everyday resistance" (Scott 1987), "everyday resurgence" (Corntassel et al. 2018), and "affirmative sabotage" (Brohi 2014; Spivak and Morris 2010). I argue that it in these unlikely sites that Indigenous providers can choose to resist colonial intervention and family dislocation and reconstitute ancestral care methods in ways that are inherently decolonial even as they are positioned within institutions of state. Overall, through an examination of the grey areas in Indigenous child welfare, this chapter gives shape to the risks and rewards of Indigenous participation in the family service industry.

JOURNEYS OF THE HEART: AN INTRODUCTION TO INDIGENOUS PARTICIPATION IN FAMILY PROGRAMS

Walking into the room to hang out at the Journeys of the Heart (JOH) program, Hulitan's cultural learning and school readiness program for Indigenous families with young children, I feel big. In a classroom designed to make a toddler feel at ease, complete with miniature tables and chairs, crayons, safety scissors and tiny snacks made for tiny people with tiny stomachs, one can't help but feel a bit bulky, always on the verge of taking up too much space. Though the physical things in the room may be small, the energy emanating from the characters within it is not. The women who run the program are lovingly referred to by colleagues and friends as the "JOH Ladies," and they all bring a different spirit to the work they do.

The participants and staff involved in JOH are, for the most part, Indigenous, though they are from several different nations. Many are descendants of Indian residential school survivors or are themselves survivors of child apprehension by the Canadian child welfare system, either as children, caregivers or close kin. In this sense, both participants and providers are experts of the child welfare system and the practice of colonial child removal, either through personal or professional experience or, in certain cases, both. While it is not explicitly mentioned on the Hulitan web page, the JOH program mainly attracts child welfare–involved Indigenous caregivers who may be participating in the program as a condition of the return of children who have been removed into state care or as a stipulation of the care plans designed to prevent child removal for those with open case files. Though participants can self-refer, which makes JOH technically a "voluntary" program, many caregivers are instructed (i.e., "voluntold") to participate by their caseworkers as a pathway towards decreased child protection involvement.

Participating caregivers at JOH had different reasons for showing up but these reasons were never aired openly in the group, at least while I was present. I attribute this omission to the goal of maintaining a certain level of confidentiality in a group of child welfare–involved families who may be (understandably and rightfully) skeptical of institutional surveillance and who are already, for better or for worse, "known" to the system. Due to many participants having open case files with the ministry, the JOH staff are frequently solicited by social workers and other caseworkers for information about the caregiver and children's progress as it is measured in relation to goals and conditions set out in their case files. Therefore, though it may not be explicitly listed in the job description, advocating for child welfare–involved families is a crucial role played by JOH program staff, placing them on the frontlines of witnessing, resisting and/or complying with Canadian child welfare laws and policies, including child apprehension orders.

While hanging out at JOH, I witnessed and heard stories about this form of advocacy played out by the JOH Ladies. In one instance, Julia, one of the JOH program leads, recounted a story about a JOH participant-caregiver I'll call Marika. Marika had previously attended a counselling session outside of JOH during which she expressed that she suffers from depression and anxiety. When asked by the counsellor whether she was experiencing suicidal ideation, Marika clarified that she would not consider suicide because she "would not want her son to grow up without a mother." Despite Marika's affirmation that she was not considering suicide, directly following this session, the counsellor reported the mother to the MCFD, claiming that "she was depressed" and, in their assessment, was possibly unfit to raise the child. At this point in Julia's retelling of the story she exaggeratedly rolled her eyes. "Can you believe that?!" she said, scoffing at the counsellor's refusal to take this mother at her word.

Luckily, instead of apprehending the child into foster care, a Temporary Care Order (TCO) was put in place that placed the child in the care of her maternal grandmother. Following this intervention, the social worker assigned to Marika's case mandated that she participate in JOH with her son as part of their "return plan." The JOH Ladies all agreed that the TCO was too drastic a response given the circumstances and began actively advocating on the mother's behalf to MCFD by affirming that she was showing up to the program, working well with her child and showing signs of recovery when it came to her experience of depression and anxiety. The JOH Ladies recognized the importance of making the mother's progress known to the social worker as an avenue towards return. Given their knowledge of the mother's everyday struggles as a single parent, they could assist in contextualizing her experience to the social worker instead of using it as evidence against her.

It is in these seemingly small and quiet ways that service providers become witnesses, protectors and advocates for the children and families in their programs. They undergo the long-term and careful work of relationship-building, earning their clients' trust by demonstrating care over time and become these families' protectors in a climate of punitive child welfare (over)involvement. Through their efforts to build relationships with the families in their programs, service providers like Julia have the capacity to render legible certain comments, behaviours or events that may otherwise be deemed suspect by social workers. Left unchecked and decontextualized, these observations could trigger unnecessarily violent child welfare interventions, such as the removal of an Indigenous child from their family of origin and/or keeping a child tied up in the system longer than necessary.

This example helps frame the constraints of paternalistic child welfare surveillance structures. Here, a child welfare–involved caregiver must perform their "progress" (towards parenting goals they themselves did not set) to a room full of child care professionals, who must then verify this progress to the parent's caseworker (i.e., more powerful professionals); all this so a parent might "earn back" their privacy in a system designed to eliminate it. One might question whether this impulse to publicize parenting and this push to have Indigenous parents perform progress is helping or harming the families the child welfare system purports to protect.

WITNESSING OR WATCHING? THE RISKS AND REWARDS OF VISIBILITY

The answer to this question is not so simple. Witnessing and accountability structures embedded within Indigenous family programs can be at once protective and punitive. Some Indigenous caregivers described being wary of participating in family programs because they feared they would be watched and judged as bad parents and subsequently reported to the ministry. In a conversation with a previous JOH staff, Suzanne Jackson (Gisghast Clan [Fireweed], who holds the Gitxsan Feast name Ludow) described this dynamic in very clear terms:

> The main issue is that the kids who are MCFD involved are told that they need to be "visible" so [the parents] are supposed to send their kids to programs and daycare, etc. But then there's sometimes no funding for programs like this, so the system prefers that the kids be in foster homes where they are more "visible" rather than being in their own family's homes in community. The main issue is that sometimes programs aren't available in certain communities and even if they are, some parents are fearful to go because they think they're going to be reported for some behavior ... they fear that MCFD is lurking, and just waiting to find their kid having a tantrum and them not managing it well. This is a fear that holds people back from programs.

Suzanne's words shed light on the challenges of choice within colonial constraint. Indigenous caregivers, particularly those who are child welfare–involved, must weigh the potential benefits and costs of placing themselves inside or outside of the gaze of an army of social service and child welfare professionals who may either help or harm their cases. In other words, they are rolling the dice. In some cases, Indigenous participants in family programs felt uncomfortable being observed and managed by care professionals but participated strategically in family programs to resist or alter undesirable child welfare interventions that were already unfolding. In other cases, child welfare–involved Indigenous caregivers I spent time with described the strain (on both time and resources) of having to run around from one so-called voluntary (really mandated) program to another; some complained that meeting the demands of their social workers' care plans felt like a full-time job. This begs the question: in a context where child welfare–involved parents are made to work to keep their kids, how might participation in family programs become yet another barrier to a family's growth and development rather than a building block towards it?

I will place a caveat around this admittedly leading question by acknowledging that many Indigenous families do come away with positive experiences, teachings and community built within family programs. That said, it is important to also note the political constraints under which some caregivers feel they should or must participate in family programs where they are asked to demonstrate their progress under the child welfare gaze. As Suzanne mentioned in the previous passage, some families avoid participating in voluntary programs because they fear having potential parental missteps observed, judged, reported and punished with unwanted child welfare interventions. In either scenario, a deep-seated fear of the child welfare system often seems to underpin Indigenous caregivers' decisions to participate in or avoid family services that are even loosely tethered to it.

Another issue raised in Suzanne's passage is the idea that the removal and placement of an Indigenous child into state care could be the result of the state's desire to "visibilize" child welfare–involved children who may be considered at risk in their guardian's care. Let me spend a moment unpacking this idea. First, according to data on Indigenous Peoples' experiences in state care, including foster care and group homes (Starr 2016; Johnson 2011; Tilbury 2009; de Finney and Tomasso 2015), and my own conversations with Indigenous survivors/resistors of child removal (Finestone 2024), there is little evidence to suggest that children are generally safer or more visible as wards of the state than with their families of origin (Blackstock 2015; Trocmé et al. 2004). There are countless stories of Indigenous children — and non-Indigenous children for that matter — suffering terrible abuses in state care in which many children feel they had no recourse through the state systems in place for child protection. There are many stories (both reported and unreported) of children experiencing abuse and even dying in foster care, groups homes or other out-of-home care arrangements. In other words, children in state care often don't feel seen at all and too often, they are not. For example, BC's Office of the Representative for Children and Youth in 2015 reported the particularly shocking story of the discovery of the lifeless body of a fifteen-year-old boy who had been placed by his social worker in a motel, alone, as an out-of-home care arrangement. He did not receive check-ins of any kind for ten full days before ending his life (Penner 2020).

It is interesting then that state surveillance is still framed as protective by child welfare system standards. Removing an Indigenous child from their "invisible" place in the home into institutions where they can be "seen" as a tactic of risk management fails to acknowledge that state surveillance is itself a risk. As Miskimmin notes in her exploration of Indigeneity and the culture of risk management in colonial states,

"Risk is the means by which the future is controlled and colonized" (2007, 109). In the child welfare context, risk management strategies fail to acknowledge the impact of the wealth and class inequalities that weave themselves into analyses of risk, disproportionally impacting economically disenfranchised Indigenous caregivers. Here, a "disposition to risk continues to fall along class lines" (Miskimmin 2007) but is masked as a harm-prevention measure for vulnerable children. In other words, being poor/working class is viewed, in and of itself, as a risk factor in child protection cases (Miskimmin 2007).

I once listened to an Indigenous service provider describe the role she played as a mediator between MCFD–involved parents in her program and their social workers as a "reality checker." After hearing a social worker complain about the "risky" living conditions of one of the parents he was supporting, she snapped back:

> "Do you think they have Martha Stewart furniture, and you know ... shelving and ornaments?!" They didn't have beds, but they had sleeping bags. That's what they've adapted to. "You need to open your eyes and see what our people are up against." He was dumbfounded. Yeah, he was just horrified. I said, "You need to come down a little bit ...."

Stories like this show that Indigenous service providers are uniquely positioned to play the role of cultural translators between families and social workers who may have no previous experience, professional or otherwise, working with Indigenous families, especially families with lived experiences of trauma and colonial dispossession. In the situation above, contextualizing and reframing what the social worker saw as a "risky" living environment and focusing instead on the adaptability displayed by the caregiver who is parenting in conditions of socioeconomic constraint becomes a key interjection in an otherwise punitive and frankly racist perspective. This provider turned the social worker's judgement on its head to illuminate its rootedness in Eurocentric logics that punish poor and racialized parents for their social precarity in states where they have and continue to be actively dispossessed of land, resources and kin — where not only poverty but Indigeneity itself is constructed as a risk to children.

Importantly and harmfully, this riskiness is not framed as contextual (i.e., seen as the result of colonial harm) but is framed as a biopolitical fact (i.e., seen as the inherent riskiness of Indigenous Peoples). The demarcation of risk along the lines of race and class weaponizes the surveillance of Indigenous people under the assumption that "if these antecedents or determinants of risk can be found, effective preventative efforts can be implemented" (Miskimmin 2007, 113–14). Yet it is also these "preventative efforts" that expose Indigenous families to the added risk of unwanted and sometimes harmful child welfare interventions that further dislocate Indigenous children from communities of loving kin. It is, thus, necessary to consider how preventative family programs are nested within an ever-growing web of state-funded institutions invented to find and subsequently manage risk in ways that perpetuate racist and Eurocentric perspectives and the forms of systematic dispossession they justify.

Despite Suzanne's clear understanding of the reasons behind Indigenous families avoiding social programs, she works in partnership with Hulitan to "support the development of local partnerships [with] Aboriginal communities" (Hulitan website 2021). At first glance, these goals may appear to contradict her previous critique of Indigenous participation in family programs. However, Suzanne explains that her aim is to change the nature of program environments through what she describes as the incorporation of "Aboriginal histories, issues and cultures, within the context of Early Childhood Development." Through her own unique lens as an Indigenous woman, Suzanne at once empathizes with her peoples' trepidation to participate in programs due to heightened surveillance and the risk of reporting, while also understanding the opportunities these programs could offer to families who have already been disconnected from supportive communities. In these circumstances, a caregiver's participation in a family program could offer them, at minimum, advocates to help them navigate existing child welfare cases, or at best, the opportunity to build community with other caregivers.

This is the paradox of Indigenous participation in family services in the context of child welfare involvement: one is soliciting the participation of MCFD-involved Indigenous families who understandably least trust state institutions and then promising them that, if they partake and progress in the correct ways, they may be granted the right *not* to participate, *not* to be watched. It is necessary to name that the requirement to earn one's privacy is reserved for poor and racialized families, upholding racist logics that frame Indigenous parents as baseline suspect — guilty until proven innocent. In this context of punitive oversurveillance, participation in family programs exposes Indigenous Peoples to material risks experienced at the level of the family (e.g., the risk of punitive child welfare interventions) and social risks experienced at the level of society (e.g., the perpetuation of racist and colonial ideologies that justify the watching and taking of Indigenous children from their families and communities and uphold the dispossessive logics that fester at that system's base).

The question then becomes: given child welfare's overinvolvement in poor, Indigenous and other racialized families' lives, how can care professionals practise in their roles in ways that mitigate rather than maintain the risk of removal? In the coming section, I explore several strategies enacted by Indigenous service providers to resist child removal, specifically examining the ways providers interpret their "duty to report" child welfare concerns to the ministry.

DOING YOUR DUTY: LIABILITY AND THE "DUTY TO REPORT" IN SERVICE SETTINGS

An emphasis on what MCFD calls "crisis prevention" shapes the way service providers interact with child welfare–involved Indigenous families. Though many service providers do their best to create safe spaces for Indigenous children and families, they are still bound by a statutory duty to report any child protection concerns to MCFD. Many Indigenous service providers I spoke with mentioned the ethical uncertainty around reporting, wishing they could at once respect their participants' privacy and honour their "duty" to the state. As described in the *B.C. Handbook for Action on Child Abuse and Neglect: For Service Providers*:

> As a service provider, your role is to be aware of, and alert to, signs of child abuse or neglect. If you have reason to suspect that a child or youth has been, or is likely to be, at risk for abuse or neglect, you have a duty to report your concern to a child welfare worker. If the child or youth is in immediate danger, call police first. Depending on the kinds of services you offer, you may also have an important role to play in responding to child abuse or neglect. This is usually determined on a case-by-case basis" (Ministry of Children and Family Development 2017, 13).

The handbook continues: "In most cases, your duty to report suspected child abuse or neglect overrides your duty to protect the privacy of clients, patients, students, staff or colleagues" (17). Note here the linguistic ambiguity of the "duty to report": "depending on the kinds of services you offer you may …"; "usually determined on a case-by-case basis …"; "in most cases." Given these loose parameters, I was not surprised to find that service providers took very diverse positions on how to enact their "duty," ranging from staunch refusal to complete compliance.

One service provider, whom I'll call Rita, noted that instead of reporting on families in her program as an immediate reaction to observing concerning behaviours, she would "poke and prod 'til they do it right," so she did not have to report the concern to MCFD. Rather than report, Rita used the resources at her disposal to aid the family in repairing and/or correcting their behaviours so that she did not have to involve MCFD. In this way, she side-stepped her duty to the state in favour of her duty to support healing and growth for the families in her care.

Rita also described instances where she felt it necessary to kick child protection workers out of her program when they showed up, often unannounced, to evaluate and report on the families in her program. Rita shared:

> Did I tell you that I never let any professionals into that room? You can't even be sniffing around that door. […] One day I got sick … and I couldn't meet my group. So, my co-worker was doing the group for me,

right? And the social worker paraded right through, and she was all, "I'm not supposed to be here, am I?" [...] My parents [her clients] know her [the social worker]. She's not a nice one, and a few of them had files with her in there, cuz there's still some involvement ... and I said "Crap! What are they gonna think?" Cuz, I've always told them, "I've got your back. No one is ever gonna come in." [...] and I said [to the colleague], "Why didn't you just show her the door?" And she said, "I did tell her she's not supposed to be in here," and I said, "You take her by the arm, and you walk her out. I would kick you like a beach ball out that door ... get out!" I'm a blood hound! I'll phone your supervisor, and I will not stop. Cuz these kids trust me so much.

Again, this is the choice of one kind of protection over another. Note how, at the outset of this passage, Rita specified that she "never lets any professionals into that room," elucidating a perceived difference between the kind of professional she is (a provider of preventative services) and the kind of professionals they are (MCFD social workers). This us/them dynamic between prevention workers and protection workers was at play in many of the programs I visited. Prevention workers like Rita viewed themselves as protectors in ways that diverge significantly from the settler ethic of "child protection"; their aim is to protect parents against the looming threat of MCFD interference. This distinction seems to be formed around disparate understandings of "protection," which is viewed by many protection workers as a duty to the state in service of children (who are framed as decontextualized at-risk people) but is viewed by many Indigenous prevention workers as the duty to protect *caregivers* as the protectors of their own children.

Rita drew the boundaries around a safe and quasi-private space for Indigenous families in the context of colonial oversurveillance. Here we see how Rita's perception of the duty to report is shaped by an understanding of the threat of colonial interference. When MCFD agents arrive as notetakers or evaluators, she often shuts the door because allowing them in could compromise the safety of "her families." Through these practices, Rita makes kin of the families in her program by demonstrating care, protection and loyalty, weighing the real and perceived threat of state surveillance and reporting through a decolonial and relational lens.

But Rita's approach to "duty to report" is not necessarily the norm; it sits on one end of a spectrum that ranges from complete compliance to complete refusal. Taking a more conciliatory approach to reporting, the director of an Indigenous daycare I interviewed shared that their team had collectively decided they would not report to MCFD on their own volition (i.e., they would not go out of their way to make the call) but clarified that they would share information with a social worker if necessary. Clarifying further, the director explained that while they might view a report of neglect as unnecessary, they would not hesitate to report suspected abuse.

Though these boundaries may appear clear in theory, in practice they are not so simple. The director mentioned having "made an oopsy" recently when a social worker called asking about a family from the daycare. Without giving it too much thought, the director discussed the family's progress with the social worker without that family's explicit consent. The director noted:

> I think there should be a clause in the daycare contracts saying that the staff at the daycare will talk to MCFD. Not to make reports per se [...] but to give them updates, to advocate for the parents.

Seemingly having a second thought about the team's interpretation of the "duty to report" the director corrected that if they did have concerns, they would report to MCFD, and added: "We see a lot ... the daycare is an extension of the home." Here, the breaching of a family's privacy is framed as a commonsense response to witnessing potentially risky behaviours. In other words, the duty to report overrides a duty to consult with or a duty to receive consent from a "risky" family before sharing observations with the state. Curiously, the director described feeling like they had, in their words, "made an oopsy," by failing to receive consent from the family to discuss their progress with a social worker but specified that they would have felt entitled to this omission if they "had concerns" (implying child protection concerns).

The notion that the "daycare is an extension of the home" underlines a juxtaposition behind many service delivery sites: though the programs are public, they provide portals into intimate social worlds. Interweaving public and private realms in this way situates service providers at the decision-making table in assessments of parental "fitness," which has particularly dramatic ramifications when caregivers are child welfare–involved or have a history of child welfare involvement. Bearing witness to these extensions of home life, service providers are asked to provide on-the-ground reconnaissance that augments child welfare's gaze into Indigenous families' so-called private lives, leaving them vulnerable to further interventions.

And the state's gaze extends much further than that. Some parenting programs require workers to conduct home visits where they are permitted to enter the homes of participant families to provide evaluations of their parental fitness and home safety. Though these programs are inherently and problematically nosey, this does not preclude service providers from upholding non-punitive approaches to their roles. In a conversation with two Indigenous family support workers running a parenting program, they joked about how "weird" it is to observe the participating families' daily routines (e.g., preparing food, doing the laundry, putting their kids to bed). The workers described attempting to give the families in their program clear expectations to put them at ease in this deeply uncomfortable situation, telling the parents, "Look, we're gonna be all up in your business for the next little while," while assuring them, "We are not looking for problems. We are looking for solutions."

One can see in instances like these that a provider's world view, personal experiences or understandings of colonialism and its intergenerational impact will dramatically shape their approach to surveillance and reporting. Some watch for success using a decolonial and trauma-informed lens while others watch for risk and danger using a settler-imposed lens. Some wade through the murky waters at the intersection of these two approaches, observing material risks while also contextualizing them, attempting to find a path forward that will meet the long-term needs of the child, the family and the community within that family is nested. This requires service providers to navigate the extremely difficult task of measuring the risk of non-interference against the risk of intervention. In either circumstance, service providers' proximity to child welfare–involved families allows them a great deal of power in determining the outcomes of open child welfare cases, and thus the outcome of children's lives; this is not by accident but by design (Miskimmin 2007).

This power is not only held by child welfare professionals but extends to community members as well, who are yet another set of eyes watching and reporting on Indigenous families, a dynamic I discuss in the next section.

NOTHING TO HIDE: ANONYMOUS REPORTING AS COLONIAL ACCOUNTABILITY

Though care professionals have a duty to report child welfare concerns to the child protection authorities, non-professional referrals (i.e., reports made by relatives, parents, neighbours, friends or the child in question, or in other words, those who are not legally bound by a duty to report) led to 31.1 percent of First Nations child maltreatment investigations in Canada (Sinha and Kozlowski 2013, 2). These calls are made anonymously and, though they are sometimes made by concerned citizens (i.e., strangers) who witness what they believe to be child maltreatment and/or neglect, they more often come from people with close relationships to those they are reporting on (Sinha and Kozlowski 2013, 2). Disturbingly, not all reports of this kind are true.

During my research, I was part of many conversations in which service providers discussed the danger of anonymous reporting within marginalized communities. In conditions of severe inter/intracommunal and/or inter/intrafamilial conflict, it is thought that some individuals launch false reports against families or caregivers due to pre-existing feuds, a practice known as "malicious referrals" (Sinha and Kozlowski 2013, 2). Notably, malicious referrals often lead to unfounded maltreatment investigations. Though some of these investigations might amount to nothing more than a slight disturbance to the reported-on family — a relatively brief bureaucratic encounter — in other cases, even if the report is proven to be false, a note may remain on the family's file and the information used against them in future child protection investigations. In a meeting with the former director of the BC Public Service, Priscilla Sabbas-Watts (Nuu-chah-nulth), she explained to me: "Most of us [Indigenous people] will have the MCFD called on us, usually because of anger against a person, and they say they're gonna call and 'I'll show them.'"

While the anonymity of anyone who report a child protection concern is guaranteed, there is no anonymity for the caregiver accused of child maltreatment; their private life is transformed into a "case" to be opened or closed. In these circumstances, service providers with existing connections to the caregiver(s) in question may be solicited by social workers for further information that might confirm or deny the accusations being made. In one such scenario, one of the JOH participants, a mother with a newborn child whom I will call Karen, was anonymously reported to MCFD for a child protection concern. The person who reported to MCFD had apparently overheard Karen saying that she "looked forward to a time where she did not have to hold her babies." Following this event, Julia (one of the JOH Ladies) received a call from a social worker who explained, "I'm just doing my due diligence, but I got this complaint from someone about Karen. Do you have any concerns?" Julia reported that she had no concerns, and added, "Karen is probably just tired! She has a newborn and other kids. She has a partner but he's not doing much there."

Julia went on to confirm to the social worker that Karen had been attending program consistently for nearly two years and had been progressing steadily through the JOH curriculum. The counselor thanked her for the information and hung up. A few weeks later, Julia found out that the case temporarily opened for Karen in response to the report was now closed. Presumably, Julia's advocacy on Karen's behalf and her ability to contextualize the mother's comment provided enough information for the social worker to decide against launching a full maltreatment investigation. It is worthwhile to consider, in this situation, what may have happened to Karen and her children if they did not have Julia advocating on their behalf or if she had not made herself "visible" within the JOH program in the first place.

THE CONUNDRUM: WORKING FOR OR AGAINST "THE SYSTEM"

In this chapter, I raised several questions about the nature of Indigenous participation, surveillance and reporting within and on the peripheries of Indigenous family service agencies. Returning to Kendra's ruminations on Indigenous family service provision at the start of the chapter, it seems the search is still underway for "the happy middle" when it comes to supporting child welfare–involved Indigenous children and families while upholding the self-determination of Indigenous Peoples as caregivers and caretakers of their own kids, communities and nations. The Indigenous family service sector requires providers and community members who are capable of precisely discerning between real and perceived risk; who possess a calculative framework for deciding when it may be helpful or harmful to involve the state (e.g., through reporting, investigating, mandating or intervening) in matters of the family; and who have strategies to foster accountability in ways that respect and uphold Indigenous self-determination.

Though many questions remain unanswered at this point, on this I am clear. Where the state is already a fixture in the lives of child welfare–involved Indigenous families, it is important to consider what tactful acts and relationships can reduce the harm families experience in that system, especially the harm of further unwanted and/or unjustified state interventions. At the same time as we continue to think critically about Indigenous participation in colonial systems, we must also direct attention to the forms of relational solidarity and kinship that exist between Indigenous service providers and their (client) families. It is sometimes through these relationships that Indigenous service providers do the difficult work of parsing when it is necessary to perform to, protect from or preclude the state in matters of child welfare as a method of harm reduction. I have argued, too, that as we witness more and more Indigenous people, many of whom have survived violent child welfare interventions themselves, enter the social work profession and the field of family service provision, we must acknowledge the ways the work is being done differently (i.e., perhaps more sensitively or relationally) while also remaining attentive to the risks of tethering Indigenous care work to states that continue to condone and fund the removal of Indigenous children from their families of origin.

Recognizing that many Indigenous service providers choose, as a harm-reduction strategy, to labour within/on the margins of systems they rightfully mistrust raises new questions about the relationship between Indigenous participation and decolonization in settler-states. For instance, can we rethink what it looks like to care for Indigenous kin in an age of colonial child removal in ways that honour the emancipatory potential of working both from within and outside of settler institutions? Witnessing Indigenous service providers discuss the intended impact of their work, it became clear that many are standing in their roles in ways that uphold ancestral caregiving responsibilities and (re)constitute kinship with the families they serve by working to keep those families together and well. Viewing Indigenous family service work through this lens forces us to rethink the methods by which, and contexts within which, decolonial care is delivered in this moment, and the way it responds to the emergent needs of Indigenous communities disparately impacted by colonial harm. In other words, rather than conforming to settler-built care practices in settler-built systems, perhaps Indigenous service providers are operating with use of customary care practices that, in Spivak's words (cited in Brohi 2014), "sabotage" settler-built systems from below to meet the current needs of their people.

If Indigenous care practices are being adapted to meet the needs of children and families experiencing the intergenerational impacts of colonial violence, this begs the question of what is more important: the institutional, social or geopolitical contexts within which Indigenous children are protected, or the outcome: that the children are protected, that the families are well, that the work is getting done? And what is "the work" anyway? After over a decade of research on the subject, I remain curious whether the purpose of Indigenous family service provision is to protect families *through* the child welfare system or *from* it. To be clear, these are not being posed as rhetorical questions but as very real ones with very real political implications. It is crucial to contemplate the long-term ramifications of Indigenous people labouring within the same systems many ultimately aim to dismantle, the child welfare system being no exception (Coulthard 2007; Lorde 1984). Moreover, we must examine the impact of further entrenching Indigenous families into program environments where they can be observed and managed regardless of whether the "watcher" or "manager" is Indigenous.

Weighing these considerations, it is a matter of debate whether, viewed as a whole, Indigenous participation in the child welfare system (as providers or users) ultimately constricts or advances Indigenous sovereignty. And yet, we know what we know: Indigenous children continue to be removed into state care at shockingly high rates (Statistics Canada 2016) and the specter of state surveillance still especially haunts child welfare–involved Indigenous families, with the looming threat of removal at every turn. This makes the stakes of Indigenous family service provision disturbingly high. Service providers who push back against the practice of punitive child removal thus become frontline resistors of Indigenous erasure. Their small acts of resistance have ripple effects that permeate beyond institutional walls. As I have explored through case studies and stories in this chapter, Indigenous service providers' advocacy on behalf of their client families can result in the interception of child apprehensions; the reunification of children in care with their families of origin; or prevent undesired/unhelpful/unwarranted child welfare interventions of all kinds. Overall, Indigenous service providers' advocacy holds the potential to set into motion decolonial possibilities that might otherwise be out of reach for child welfare–involved Indigenous caregivers.

In a settler-state built on the assumption of Indigenous disappearance and replacement (Kauanui 2016; Wolfe 2006), keeping kin together requires constant vigilance to detail. Some Indigenous service providers have become the guardians of those details, keeping their eyes and ears open for potential threats to the families in their care and, when necessary, mitigating (or, as Spivak might suggest, "sabotaging") those threats from within. Throughout my time visiting and conducting research with Indigenous family service providers and MCFD–involved families on Vancouver Island, the matter of their intimate knowledge of the system was never up for debate. That said, it must be acknowledged that Indigenous service providers occupy a liminal space as both agents and disrupters of settler statehood due to their emplacement within agencies that are largely funded by the state, and thus are (technically) bound by its rules.

Indigenous service providers often work at agencies that receive their core funding from MCFD, the agency that is a key perpetrator of the abuse many of them understand the families in their programs to be experiencing. Though some attempt to shut social workers out of the room and others shut down social workers' assumptions, most cannot (at least at present) completely shut the door on MCFD's fiscal support. It is yet to be seen how policies such as the newly approved Bill C-92, which grants Indigenous nations full jurisdiction over child welfare in their communities, will impact this power dynamic or how this might translate into a more equitable fiscal relationship between Indigenous communities and the state. Perhaps this policy will transform Indigenous-led child welfare as we know it (Minister of Indigenous Services 2019), and in our lifetime.

In the meantime, though it continues to be messy, the grey area of Indigenous family service delivery remains an important site of anti-colonial resistance. Nested in institutional environments, Indigenous service providers can activate decolonial futures from within by wrapping around kin in need, creating blockades around families who may otherwise be reduced to yet another case number in the giant bureaucratic circus we call the child welfare system. This labour builds upon existing kin relations and generates new ones between providers and recipients of care, challenging us to nuance our understanding of how and where Indigenous kinship is expressed in settler-states. These relationships gesture towards lesser-known strategies and solidarities quietly proliferating inside and on the margins of settler-built systems in ways that diminish colonial violence from within.

ACKNOWLEDGEMENTS

I wish to acknowledge the staff and families at Hulitan Family & Community Services Society, as well as the countless other caregivers and practitioners I encountered during this research both within and outside of family service organizations (some named and many unnamed here), who endured my presence in meetings, in interviews, at events and in programs for many years during my doctoral fieldwork. You are all true teachers of what it looks like to "make kin" in unexpected sites. The insights found in this paper were harvested alongside you and are as much yours as mine. HÍSW̱ḴE, ƛ'eeko, thank you!

NOTES

1 All identifying details have been altered for Indigenous caregivers referenced in these program settings to protect the privacy of ministry-involved families with open child welfare cases. Service providers who are named in this paper have consented to being recognized by name in my research outputs. Those who requested to remain anonymous were assigned a pseudonym. Only organizations who have requested to be named are named, otherwise I leave the institution unnamed here.
2 In 2008, Prime Minister Stephen Harper recognized the Indian residential school period as a "sad chapter in our history" and acknowledged that the policies underpinning the schools were "wrong […] caused great harm, and have no place in our country" (Government of Canada 2008).

SUGGESTED READINGS

Corntassel, Jeff, Gerald R. Alfred, Noelani Goodyear-Ka'ōpua, Noenoe K. Silva, Hokulani K. Aikau and Devi Dee Mucina (eds.). 2018. *Everyday Acts of Resurgence: People, Places, Practices*. Olympia, Washington: Daykeeper Press.

Coulthard, Glenn S. 2014. *Red Skin, White Masks: Rejecting the Colonial Politics of Recognition*. University of Minnesota Press.

de Finney, Sandrina, Lena Palacios, Mandeep Kaur Mucina and Anna Chadwick. 2018. "Refusing Band-Aids: Un-Settling "Care" Under the Carceral Settler State." *Journal of the International Child and Youth Care Network* 235.

Dhillon, Jaskiran. 2017. *Prairie Rising: Indigenous Youth, Decolonization, and the Politics of Intervention*. Toronto: University of Toronto Press.

Finestone, Erika. 2024. "Reunification as Refusal: Kin-Making and Unmaking in the Aftermath of Indigenous Child Removal." In *Difficult Attachments: Anxieties of Kinship and Care*, edited by Kathryn E. Goldfarb and Sandra Bamford. Rutgers University Press.

REFERENCES

Blackstock, Cindy. 2015. "Should Governments be Above the Law? The Canadian Human Rights Tribunal on First Nations Child Welfare." *Children Australia* 40, 2.

Brohi, Nazish. 2014. "Herald Exclusive: In Conversation with Gayatri Spivak." *Dawn* (December 23).

Coulthard, Glen S. 2007. "Subjects of Empire: Indigenous Peoples and the 'Politics of Recognition' in Canada." *Contemporary Political Theory* 6, 4.

Dhillon, Jaskiran. 2017. *Prairie Rising: Indigenous Youth, Decolonization, and the Politics of Intervention*. Toronto: University of Toronto Press.

Finestone, Erika. 2024. "Reunification as Refusal: Kin-Making and Unmaking in the Aftermath of Indigenous Child Removal." In *Difficult Attachments: Anxieties of Kinship and Care*, edited by Kathryn E. Goldfarb and Sandra Bamford. Rutgers University Press.

de Finney, Sandrina and Lara di Tomasso. 2015. "Creating Places of Belonging: Expanding Notions of Permanency with Indigenous Youth in Care." *First Peoples Child & Family Review* 10, 1.

Foucault, Michel. 1977. *Discipline and Punish: The Birth of the Prison*. New York: Vintage Books.

Government of Canada (House of Commons). 2019. *C-92 (42-1) - First Reading - An Act Respecting First Nations, Inuit and Métis Children, Youth and Families*. Parliament of Canada.

Hulitan Family & Community Services Society. n.d. "Acknowledgements." hulitan.ca/acknowledgments/.
Johnson, Shelly L. 2011. "'I Screamed Internally for a Long Time': Traumatized Urban Indigenous Children in Canadian Child Protection and Education Systems." Doctoral dissertation, University of British Columbia.
Kauanui, J. Kēhaulani. 2016. "'A Structure, Not an Event': Settler Colonialism and Enduring Indigeneity." *Lateral* 5, 1.
Li, Tania. 2007. *The Will to Improve: Governmentality, Development, and the Practice of Politics*. Durham: Duke University Press.
Lorde, Audre. 1984. "The Master's Tools Will Never Dismantle the Master's House." In *Sister Outsider: Essays and Speeches*. Berkeley: Crossing Press.
Ministry of Children and Family Development. 2017. *The B.C. Handbook for Action on Child Abuse and Neglect: For Service Providers*.
Miskimmin, Susanne. 2007. "When Aboriginal Equals 'at Risk': The Impact of Institutional Discourse on Aboriginal Head Start Families." In *Words, Worlds, and Material Girls: Language, Gender, Globalization*, edited by Bonnie McElhinny. Berlin and New York: Mouton de Gruyter.
Penner, Patrick. 2020. "Foster-Care System Improved Following Abbotsford Teen's 2015 Suicide, Province Says." *Lake Cowichan Gazette*. January 30, 2020. lakecowichangazette.com/news/foster-care-system-improved-following-abbotsford-teens-2015-suicide-province-says-968106.
Povinelli, Elizabeth A. 2002. *The Cunning of Recognition: Indigenous Alterities and the Making of Australian Multiculturalism*. Durham: Duke University Press.
Rose, Nikolas S. 1996. *Inventing our Selves: Psychology, Power, and Personhood*. Cambridge, England: Cambridge University Press.
Scott, James C. 1987. *Weapons of the Weak: Everyday Forms of Peasant Resistance*. New Haven: Yale University Press.
Sinha, Vandna and Anna Kozlowski. 2013. "The Structure of Aboriginal Child Welfare in Canada." *International Indigenous Policy Journal* 4, 2.
Spivak, Gayatri Chakravorty and Rosalind C. Morris. 2010. *Can the Subaltern Speak?: Reflections on the History of an Idea*. New York: Columbia University Press.
Starr, Lenora. 2016. *First Nations Experiences with Adoption and Reunification: A Family and Community Process* Doctoral dissertation, University of Victoria.
Statistics Canada. 2016. Census of Canada.
Stevenson, Lisa. 2014. *Life Beside itself: Imagining Care in the Canadian Arctic*, first edition. Oakland: University of California Press.
Tilbury, Clare. 2009. "The Over-Representation of Indigenous Children in the Australian Child Welfare System." *International Journal of Social Welfare* 18, 1.
Trocmé, Nico, Della Knoke and Cindy Blackstock. 2004. "Pathways to the Overrepresentation of Aboriginal Children in Canada's Child Welfare System." *Social Service Review* 78, 4.
Wolfe, Patrick. 2006. "Settler Colonialism and the Elimination of the Native." *Journal of Genocide Research* 8, 4.

Chapter 9

"YOUR BEST CAN ONLY TAKE YOU TO WHERE THE GOOD IS"

Strange Things Black Parents Say and Do to Prepare Black Children for a Racist Society

by Paul Banahene Adjei

CHAPTER FOCUS

Systemic racism, sexism and classism in North America have informed and shaped the disciplinary practices Black families utilize, fostering approaches to parenting that teach Black children self-esteem, survival, self-respect and methods for responding to threats of racism. "Your best can only take you to where the good is" is the advice a Black parent received from his parents when he came to Canada in his teens. Today, as a parent, he reminds his children about how hard they have to work to be successful as Blacks in Canada. This story is one of many that reveal what some may deem unusual parenting practices, in particular what Black parents say and do to their children. For Black parents who took part in our research study, these "unusual parenting practices" are necessary to prepare Black children to survive a society that blatantly disregards any life that is not white. When child welfare workers fail to appreciate the context of Black parenting in a racist society, their perception of Black parenting styles can lead to tension between Black parents and child welfare. The result is the disproportionate apprehension and out-of-home placement of Black children. When working with Black parents, it is necessary for workers to understand the context of Black parenting practices through both a critical race and an anti-racism lens.

QUESTIONS ADDRESSED IN THIS CHAPTER

1. What are some factors that contribute to Black disproportionality in Canadian child welfare?
2. How does racism shape the strategies that Black parents use to protect their children?
3. How can child welfare workers support the efforts of Black parents to protect their children from racist harm?

On April 29, 2015, Toya Graham, an African American mother, became a national celebrity in the United States during the demonstration-turned-riot of Black youth at Baltimore's Mondawmin Mall following the death of Freddie Gray while in police custody. Ms. Graham was filmed dragging and repeatedly slapping her sixteen-year-old son Michael Singleton for participating in throwing stones at police officers. Ms. Graham's reaction was widely applauded by the media in both the United States and Canada, and she was crowned the "Mother of the Year" (King 2015). A parade of interviews followed, including with Anderson Cooper on CNN, Whoopi Goldberg on *The View*, as well as a phone call from Oprah Winfrey. Baltimore Police Commissioner Anthony Batts wished more Black parents like Ms. Graham would "take control of their kids" (Craven 2015). Rep. Bobby Rush (D-Ill.) went to the floor of the United States Congress with a picture of Ms. Graham in hand, "praising the love whopping" she gave her son (Craven 2015). Rush even suggested that American mothers should wear yellow on Mother's Day to create a "Mothers in Yellow" movement as a symbol and in solidarity of Ms. Graham (Craven 2015). When contributing to a discussion on *Fox News*, Ben Stein described Toya Graham as the "Rosa Parks for 2015" (Pitts Jr. 2015).

Yet, Ms. Graham did not see herself as a national hero to be celebrated. In fact, in her interview with CBS *News*, Ms. Graham explained that she acted instinctively to save her son from a potential tragedy: "He gave me eye contact. And at that point, you know, not even thinking about cameras or anything like that. That's my only son, and at the end of the day, I don't want him to be a Freddie Gray" (CBS News 2015, para. 2). Indeed, given jarring, repetitive and frequent Black homicides at the hands of white police officers in the United States, Ms. Graham knows the fragility of Black lives in the presence of police. Aiyana Stanley-Jones, Breonna Taylor, Tamir Rice, Kurt Reinhold, Philando Castile, Rayshard Brooks, Stephon Clark, George Floyd and others in the United States; Eric Osawe, Abdirahman Abdi, Jean-Pierre Bony, Pierre Coriolan and others in Canada are just a few of the young Blacks who encountered police officers and did not live to tell their stories.

These examples of Black homicides at the hands of mostly white police officers are comprehensible and predictable if situated in the broader context of virulent anti-Black racism. In this context, it makes sense that Ms. Graham acted, to use her own words, "not even thinking," about the consequences of her actions. In her mind, physically assaulting her son, although it could lead to her arrest or/and having her son apprehended and placed in care by Baltimore child protection workers was a necessary evil to save her son from potentially being killed by the police. In short, Ms. Graham acted to protect her son from potential death.

The Black parents we interviewed told us many similar stories of what Black parents say and do to their children while raising them in Canada. Excerpts from their stories appear in this chapter. Their narratives demonstrate that Black parents who have to protect Black children from a racist society that thinks less of Black lives are prepared to use any means necessary to keep them safe. Yet these protective actions could be defined as illegal under Section 43 of Canada's Criminal Code. Under Section 43, parents are allowed to use "reasonable force" to discipline a child. In 2004 the Supreme Court interpreted this to mean that it is illegal for parents to physically discipline teenagers or children under two, or to hit a child with an object, or to slap the head of any child regardless of age (Parliament of Canada n.d.). Similarly, child welfare legislation, although it varies across Canadian jurisdictions, generally defines physical discipline as physical abuse and mandates its investigation. In short, the parenting strategies that Black parents employ to keep their children safe and alive may leave their families vulnerable to the most intrusive forms of state intervention.

Child welfare workers can support parents to successfully resolve this challenging conundrum by understanding the anti-Black context within which parenting decisions are made. This context is the basis for parenting choices and decisions described and explained by the Black parents and Black workers we interviewed in Toronto, Winnipeg and St. John's. Black child welfare workers are in the unique position of living in two worlds: a world of living as a Black person and a world of operating within the rules, regulations and institutional norms and practices of child welfare. Listening to Black child welfare workers deepens the analysis of Black parenting practices by helping us understand how one can navigate the complex world of parenting as Black within the child welfare rules and regulations that are often at variance with the reality of living Black in a white settler society. The insights of both Black parents and child welfare workers helps to chart an anti-racist way forward for child welfare. Child welfare workers are responsible for assessing the safety of young people within the parameters of legislation holding parents/guardians responsible for protecting their children and not maltreating or neglecting them. Anti-racist assessment requires that workers keep the violent/ racist context of Black lives at the forefront of their thinking when talking with Black parents (and young people) about possible parental maltreatment. In particular, workers must avoid decontextualized assessments that all parental use of physical discipline automatically constitutes child maltreatment. These sorts of unreflective conclusions undermine the parent and the parent-child relationship, and can leave parents who face virulent anti-Black racism unsupported.

ANTI-BLACK RACISM IN CANADA

The lives of Black families are fundamentally shaped by lethal violence and the possibility of lethal violence. The Malcolm X Grassroots Movement notes that of the percentage of people killed by either police officers, security guards or vigilantes in five cities of the United States in 2012, Blacks constitute 91 percent in Chicago,

Illinois, 48 percent in Houston, Texas, 87 percent in New York, and 100 percent in Rockford, Illinois and Saginaw, Michigan (Eisen 2014). In Canada, the Ontario Human Rights Commission's (OHRC 2018) analysis of data collected by the Special Investigations Unit shows that between 2013 and 2017 in Toronto, Blacks were nearly twenty times more likely than whites to be involved in fatal shootings by the Toronto Police Service. A CBC report notes Blacks account for 36.5 percent of people killed by police officers in Toronto between 2000 and 2017 although they make up just 8.3 percent of Toronto's population (Dunn 2018). For Black parents attempting to raise their children safely to adulthood, what is most terrifying is the capriciousness of these killings: they happen anywhere and everywhere. Aiyana Stanley-Jones and Breonna Taylor were killed while resting on their beds in their homes. Tamir Rice was killed while playing at a recreational centre. Kurt Reinhold was killed while walking on the street. Philando Castile and Rayshard Brooks were killed while driving. Stephon Clark was killed while standing in his grandmother's backyard. It is as if a message is being sent to Black people through these killings that no space is safe for you. Henry Giroux (2015, 1) describes the phenomenon of white police officers shooting to kill unarmed Black men and women as "the new totalitarianism of the boot in your face racism, one in which the punishing state is the central institution for both controlling poor minorities of race and class and enforcing the rules of the financial elite."

Racism impacts Black people in other ways. In *The Skin We're In: A Year of Black Resistance and Power,* Toronto journalist Desmond Cole describes being racially profiled by police officers in Toronto more than fifty times in seven years (Cole 2022). Analysis of police data of racial profiling cases in Toronto showed that Blacks were stopped and searched seventeen times more often than whites (Winsa and Rankin 2012). As with the policing of Black bodies, the school system in Canada has become a carceral space that is physically, emotionally, spiritually and psychologically harmful to Black learners (Dei et al. 1997; Maynard 2017; Raza 2022). The Ontario Ministry of Education's review of racism within the Peel School Board, for example, documented disturbing incidents of anti-Black racism, including school principals disproportionately suspending Black students for what on the face of it are absurd reasons, such as wearing hoodies or hoop earrings (Raza 2022). The same report noted that Black students, especially Black boys, are perceived as aggressive because their actions are interpreted more negatively than similar actions by white students (Raza 2022). Similarly, disproportionality in Canadian child welfare has been extensively documented. Racialized minorities, and particularly Black parents, are disproportionately investigated and the children of these parents are disproportionately apprehended and placed in care (Boatswain-Kyte 2020; Cénat et al. 2021a; Cénat et al. 2021b; Clarke 2012; Greenbaum 2014; Gosine and Pon 2011; Pon et al. 2011).

Studies of race-based employment discrimination in Canada (Block and Galabuzi 2011; Cooper Brathwaite et al. 2022; Henry 2015; Teelucksingh and Galabuzi 2010) note that when Black and white applicants have the same employment qualifications, white applicants are more likely to be hired than their Black counterparts. Even when Black and white applicants with the same qualifications are hired in the same organization at the same time, white employees are more likely to get a higher salary (Wijesingha 2021; Wright-Kim and Perna 2023). These facts mean that Black parents are faced with the daunting challenge of motivating their children to perform above the average, knowing being average is not enough for a Black person, while simultaneously managing their children's expectations, as they know that being the best as a Black person may only earn one what is reserved for the average white.

PARENTING STRATEGIES OF BLACK PARENTS

Black parents need multiple strategies to ensure not only their children's physical safety but also their emotional and psychological well-being. This is the reality of living in a white space as a Black person (Adjei 2024). These are the everyday, commonplace realities of living Black in a white settler society. Black parents, knowing these realities, attempt to provide their children with the tools to survive them.

For example, given the disproportionate and sometimes lethal violence that Black people experience at the hands of authorities, Black parents are particularly concerned with how their children conduct themselves when interacting with people in authority like police, teachers, social workers and other public officials. Parents understand that raising one's voice when talking or appearing to challenge persons in authority, especially as a Black male, can be deemed threatening enough to invite physical harm. Therefore, at home, Black parents, seeing themselves as the symbol of authority, require Black children to accord them the kind of respect they are expected to show to people in authority at public spaces. Any insubordination of Black children at home is an indication of how they will behave in public. For Black parents, these insubordinations must be rooted out before Black children take them to public spaces where the outcome could be death or incarceration.

Black parenting practices can be summed up as what Gayatri Spivak describes as "the unavoidable usefulness of something that is dangerous" (Spivak 1994, 5). Black parents tell us that systemic racism and colonization shape how they raise their children to survive in a racist society.

Support and Expectations in a Racist Society

Racism and discrimination fundamentally shape the parenting behaviours of Black parents. In a society deeply rooted in anti-Black racism, the first responsibility of a Black parent is to prepare Black children to survive in a hostile, anti-Black environment. Belinda,[1] a single mother originally from Jamaica, explained that the nature of her environment determines how she raises her children. Unlike her country of origin (Jamaica), where she did not concern herself so much about racism, in Canada racism impacts everything Black people do. Therefore, she has to adjust her parenting strategies to offer countermeasures to protect her children:

> I am trying to parent to protect so I have to teach my children that racism impacts me and I know will impact my boys. And so, I cannot just parent because that is what it is here because if I was in Jamaica, I will parent one way but as I mentioned to you my parents' parenting style has to be adjusted to accommodate the impact and force, the negative forces of racism and of under expectation if that makes sense.

Ruby, a single mother originally from Nigeria, agrees with Belinda. She believes Blacks' parental responsibilities include teaching Black children to be aware of the inner workings of racism and its potential impacts on Black lives. Given her own racist experiences in Canada, Ruby considers it a parenting failure if somehow her children are not prepared for the realities of living in a racist society:

> I will be stupid if I don't. So, I went through hell because I had nobody prepare me for challenges for racism that I faced so a lot of one been a good parent is being able to recognise that there is racism and then equip their children to be able to face the challenges. Yes, I do raise my kids to face the challenges of racism in Canada.

Gina, another Black mother originally from Nigeria, states that her parenting goal is to raise her children to be independent and strong. To achieve this, she has created what she calls "pseudo-suffering" parenting strategies to help her children to adapt to living in a racist society:

> We want to raise children who are 'independent' and 'strong.' It is necessary to create 'pseudo-suffering' to help them grow.

For Gina, "pseudo-suffering" is her effort to train her children to be responsible adults. To achieve that she takes actions that may appear unusual and or be interpreted as borderline "abusive" but which she believes will in the long run help her children to become responsible adults. Agnes, a Liberian-Canadian, also subscribes to the "pseudo-suffering" strategy. Agnes believes Black children must be exposed at the early stages of their development to the principle that all actions have consequences:

> I just believe that in life kids need to go through consequences if they do not do the right thing. I try to tell that every good deed pays. That is how

I put it to them. If you behave well .... You are going to get good results. If you behave badly, you get bad rewards.

From the perspective of Gina and Agnes, Black children cannot be raised to be independent and strong minded if they do not understand what taking responsibility means. Teaching Black children the importance of taking responsibility means making them understand actions have consequences. Similarly, many Black parents assign certain duties to their children as a part of their training to become responsible adults. Sophia, a Nigerian-Canadian mother, has a nine-year old son who actively participates in household chores. She teaches her son how to make his bed, clean his room and wash dishes, which she acknowledges will not happen in some families in Canada:

> If you come to my house, my nine-year-old will make the bed, clean his room, and wash dishes ... you understand. So, I'm still an African parent in that way. Like my friends [who are] Canadian will not send their eight years old or nine years old to do these things. They will say, oh no she can't do it. The Canadian ways [are] most of the things I don't like.

Black parents believe that Black children must be motivated to aim higher than the low standard set for them by society. Jackson, a Black father, explained that living in a society in which media representations of Blackness persistently feature images of degeneracy, criminality, deviancy, immorality, pathology and inferiority confer certain parental responsibilities on him. He must offer counter-narratives to these dominant hegemonic constructions by instilling in his Black children the value of excellence. Jackson came to Canada as a teen and his parents taught him to perform above the average if he wanted to succeed as a Black person. Today, as a parent, he offers the same advice to his children:

> When I came here as a teenager my parents telling me that you know you cannot just be good. If you want to go to where the white people go you have to be the best. The best is what will get you to where the good is, you understand ... you need to know that you know where you are coming from. You know your colour fights against you so you need to make sure that you are the best in everything you do. And I think we continue to do the same thing without even thinking about it to be preparing our children that you know the need to be the best in everything that they can be, they need to be careful in everything because very easily you can be labelled you know, identified with so many things just because you are Black.

Jackson's comments reveal how Canadian stereotypes of Black people can inspire a style of parenting where an undue toll is placed on Black children to perform beyond human expectations. Harriet and Belinda, two Black mothers, share Jackson's view. They explain that Black children are not treated fairly so they have to learn to achieve an above average status. Harriet says, "The system, society, expects nothing much, demands nothing much from Black children and so it is the mothers who must remind them that they are to dream and to dream high, the mothers have to remind them of that."

Belinda agrees:

> Absolutely, every day, yeah, if my kids listen to that part of my trying to give them advice, they will be the hardest working people because if you are average that is when you get ignored. Because you are average with the pack, because if they want to pick they can pick anybody that is average. Then they will be able to use the excuses not to pick you. But if you are above average, nobody can ignore you. Nobody, nobody, you are in a better position to challenge them. Not that it is fair, it is wrong. We should be, if we are average we should be where most human beings are, we should be treated fairly. But the reality, it is [not] easier to get you over those hurdles, one of those obstacles, if you are just mediocre, if you are just average.

Parenting for Black Survival

The Black parents who spoke with us were strict with their children. They demanded attitudes and behaviours that they saw as necessary for Black survival in a racist society. For example, some had a dress code that required their children to dress in ways that avoid racial profiling. Hannah, a Black mother in a mixed-race relationship, has a son with a lighter skin colour. She explained that when her son grows a beard or makes a ponytail, he easily passes as an Arab or an individual of Middle Eastern descent. Hannah therefore forbade her son from growing a beard or making a ponytail:

> Yeah, I will say that keeping in mind that my children are mixed so they tend to be Mulatto type coloured, in fact my son does not look Black at all. He looks more Arab and so I tend to, I am more fearful because he looks Arab that he will be discriminated against because of what is going on in the Middle East, right? So anytime I call him, when he tries to leave a beard, I say shave it. Don't put his hair in a ponytail and all that. Because I fear he looks more Arab than Black. Either way it is still racism right.

Hannah's concerns must be situated within the current mainstream politicization of anti-Muslim racism and Islamophobic rhetoric in Euro-American/Canadian society that positions all Arabs, Muslims and Middle Eastern men as people to fear, surveil and harm in the name of national security (Fekete 2006; Moisi 2010; Naber 2006; Wilkins 2009). Hannah did not want her son to fall victim to malicious Islamophobic and anti-Muslim racist campaigns in Canada and the United States.

Wilson, another Black parent, spoke about the physical appearance of Black boys in public spaces, in particular their dress and their reasons for doing so, as a major parental concern for some Black parents. Wilson explained that he intentionally enrolled his children into a Catholic school that has a standard dress code. By sending his children to a Catholic school, Wilson believes he succeeds in eliminating any potential profiling related to dress, as all students dress in the same way. Second, he avoids the burden of spending excessively on clothing for his children:

> I sent my kids to a Catholic school as a protection ... my eldest son and it was purposeful. One, I thought to myself that I didn't want my kids to fall into the materialistic ways that kids in public schools are swayed by. Sorry, but you are all in the same uniform. Those stereotypes within the system and from the teachers are all eliminated. Those biases are seeing everybody as the same. Because of the same clothes. So already I was thinking just from your dressing, your appearance, am gonna eliminate any biases.

Besides clothing, parents were particular about how their children talked and behaved in public spaces when interacting with persons in authority. Within a context in which people in authority have visited harms on Black people because they perceive them to be threatening and dangerous, Black parents teach their children to interact with persons in authority in ways that are non-menacing, non-threatening and unobtrusive. Naomi, a Black mother, raises her children to understand how they should conduct themselves in front of law enforcement officers:

> We raise our children letting them know ... better respect authority because out there if you go out and try to talk back, you know the law enforcement officer are talking to you or you would get yourself killed or you would go to the school system you want to challenge teachers you would get yourself you know dismissed ... because we realize that the system is not that tolerant and has not opened to our children and so training home is a way to prepare them for the reality out there.

Some Black parents also adopt non-verbal cues to support their parenting practices. For example, there is an unspoken rule about a Black mother's "one stern look," a look that implies an unspoken threat of either a grounding or a "whupping" if her request is not immediately met with compliance. Usually, Black mothers utilize this non-verbal cue to warn their children when they are misbehaving in public spaces. Every Black child understands the Black mother's stern look. Julia, a Black mother originally from Ghana, understands that in Canada, the use of physical discipline is prohibited. Nonetheless, she has a firm look, a facial expression that tells her children that they better behave, else the consequences will be unpleasant:

> Whenever they go wrong, I try to correct them but unlike Ghana that you beat them, here I have strategized my own way with them. I use my eyes. I have a certain facial expression that when I show to them, they know what I am talking about and then they stop.

Solomon, having experienced racism in the past in Canada, continues to raise his children to conduct themselves in specific ways in public, especially when they encounter police officers:

> Anytime I talk to my kids ... when you go out there be very mindful of the way you behave. When they [police officers] stop you, don't pick up quarrel with them. Because if you pick up quarrel with them. Whatever they ask you show them and go your way. It doesn't take anything from you. It is kind of painful but that is what thing we live in, so take it or leave it.

Martha, a Nigerian-Canadian mother, similarly tailors her parenting style to respond to Black realities in Canada. She also teaches her children how they should respond to police officers when they are stopped:

> Yeah, I believe that. I will sit with my child even up till now, I always taught her to obey the authorities and anywhere she goes. I'm texting her because I want to know where she is. So, I believe that a lot of parents do raise their kids because you know what, they look at the TV and they see what is going on so you know it's like oh a Black kid is being killed; so the police shot this kid. So, you raise them to say you know what, you have to obey the authority; you know, if a police stops you, try to stay away where you are going to have a conflict with the police and if a police officer stops you try to obey them. So, they kind of put that fear in the kids because of what is going on. Because any time you look at the radio it's always a Black kid being killed, you know, police is always ... you can even be driving by and just being in a good car they can stop you just knowing that there is a Black kid in that car. The first thing is like "Oh, he is Black" so where did you get the money to buy this car. When you look at the news you don't want your child to be in the statistics so you have to raise them the way that you feel they fit the society because you fear what is going to happen.

Many Black parents who migrated to Canada as refugees were exposed to the dangers of living in a war-torn country with children. In such an environment, close supervision of children is not only necessary but also a matter of life and death. Every unaccounted minute of the child's whereabouts could mean something tragic. Such parents are hypervigilant about their children's safety. But an environment of constant threat to Black life, whether those threats originate from Black-on-Black gang violence and/or from police brutality, also motivates parents to closely supervise their children. Marcus, a Trinidadian-Canadian father, spoke about the restrictions Black parents impose on their children, such as not allowing them to go out at certain time or with certain people for fear of their safety:

> I would hear Black parents making comments to me where their Black boys are concerned by saying, "I'm not gonna allow my son to go out at night after eight o'clock because I'm afraid for his safety if he's met by police," or "I'm not gonna allow my daughter to go with a group of friends to this event because I'm afraid that the group may be painted with the same brush and she would have an adverse outcome." So, Black parents, those of African descent, do gauge the community, the environment and parent their kids accordingly, for in their mind the best interest of their children to avoid any adverse outcome whether it be safety or whether it be reputation or whether it be you know psychological kinds of injury.

This authoritarian stance of Black parents has not been appreciated by Black children, who often want to exercise freedom of choice and expression at home. Black parents, however, believe that this freedom of choice and expression that Black children so much desire at home can easily get them killed or arrested in public spaces. The challenges of navigating these sorts of tensions between Black parents and Black children is further complicated by involvement with child protection authorities.

Child Welfare Responses

Black children are disproportionately referred or investigated for child maltreatment concerns compared to white children (Mohamud et al. 2021); a recent Ontario study demonstrated that Black parents' use of physical discipline is a major driver of this disparity. While schools are the main source of the over-reporting of Black families (King et al. 2017), both community service providers and child welfare workers report oversurveillance of Black families by all referral sources (Antwi-Boasiako et al. 2022). Once caught up in the child welfare system, Black families routinely encounter racism from child welfare workers (Phillips and Pon 2018). Workers lack sensitivity to the cultural context in which Black parenting occurs (Antwi-Boasiako et al. 2022).

The Black parents we talked to described how child welfare workers reacted negatively to some of their parenting strategies and styles, while the Black child welfare workers we talked to suggested that these situations could have a different outcome if workers were racially and culturally conscious in their assessment of Black parents. Anita, a Black female worker, shared a case where a white worker failed to take into consideration the unique racial and cultural history and contemporary realities of Black communities when they assessed the family:

> I can say yes, some of the occurrences they express to me clearly, especially when you work on an on-going process with a family and if it happens that the case was investigated by a Caucasian, sometimes it is about the culture because one understands they protect the children but for the children to become a better person. Because society will be taken over by the children, but these children need to have reference, need to have parents. But if we are taking the children away and place them to foster parents, they are going to feel that that is how society [has] to live. But we are talking about strengthening family. By strengthening family that means we work with the parents to protect children. But some parents say when your colleague came, because I was Black, she didn't hear me, she assumed that I am a bad person. Because I talked to her or to him and because I am Black, she thought I was violent. But you know Black people, when we talk, we are loud [sighs]. That means by having a Caucasian who is scared of a Black parent, I can talk about a wrong judgment because when a person, it can be a Caucasian, it can be a Black, when he is upset, for sure, he would be loud, but for a Caucasian being loud to him is like more of violent but as a Black I do understand easily that when one is loud, they gonna calm down, it doesn't mean that it gonna continue.

Tonto, a Black male worker, expressed concern that inadequate cultural and racial awareness among some workers leads to apprehensions and placements that are avoidable:

> So, racism is a big deal because I have found, there are social workers who would just go into the pretence of these and apprehend Black families on something that wouldn't have been an apprehension, if these families were not Blacks. For instance, schools have been calling us, that children don't bring good lunches to school. Like can they define what they call "good lunches." Because most of the food that we eat in Africa, we eat with our fingers … we eat with our fist, we eat spinach, it might look nasty to you but it is our traditional food. So, if my child is bringing spinach to school and you call that not a good lunch or his/her lunch is nasty or disgusting

is even an insult to my culture. But if these children had brought a pizza to school, it wouldn't have been a subject of investigation. So, with racism, it's just a big issue.

Another way that racism is enacted in Canadian child protection is via the assumption of incapability on the part of racialized parents (Antwi-Boasiako et al. 2022; Cénat et al. 2021; Cénat et al. 2023). In our study, we found that workers sometimes judged Black parents as mentally unfit because the workers failed to recognize unique cultural and racial ways of parenting. For example, in one case, a white worker described a Black mother as mentally sick because of how she had dressed in her own home:

> I have two or three cases at human rights, why, because the front worker, again was a Caucasian, he went and investigate a Black family. The Black parent said that there was a miscommunication, not because of language but a misunderstanding ... she was putting on her skirt because she was cooking and not that clean then the investigator stated she was mentally sick because of the way she was dressed. And for her, "I was at home doing my chore at home and I don't need to have makeups I don't need to be dressed."

In another case, a Black Jamaican parent's attempt to incorporate her cultural and religious values into her parenting practices was met with disrespectful response from a worker:

> There is a Black family, the case was transferred to me, that's how I know this. There was a family, and in the Caribbean family in Jamaica, I'm just finding this out, that when they have a baby, in the baby's crib at the foot they will normally put an open Bible and they leave it at the edge of the crib. And really, they just feel it's a way of protecting the baby when the baby is sleeping. We had a white Canadian worker visiting at the time and one of our policies is that in the crib, nothing should be in the crib, just the folded sheet and the baby. Not a blanket, not a pillow, not a book, nothing. The worker asked the mother to remove the Bible and she [the mother] explained what the Bible is for. The worker then later requested a psychological assessment on the mother.

The practice concern here is not the worker's demand that the Bible be removed from the crib, but the way in which the worker went about it. In a more respectful approach, the worker would have explained the policy to the mother and worked with her to find a way to preserve her cultural traditions without contravening the policy. It is particularly concerning that the worker requested a psychological assessment of the mother. Requesting a psychological assessment for a Black parent is another way of suggesting that they are not mentally fit to be a parent.

Leslie, a Sierra Leonean–Canadian father, also shares his frustration with child welfare services for disregarding his cultural values in parenting. Leslie lost custody of his child because he yelled at the child: "When a social worker came to my home … I was also accused of yelling at the child, which was considered as verbal abuse." It is a mistake to think that the efforts Black parents make to protect their children indicate verbal abuse or a lack of love or warmth. Indeed, Black parental control over their children, sometimes perceived as excessive by white standards, is inspired by parental care and love to protect Black children from a world that will harm and wound them if given a chance. Black parents often "control" their children to shield from the harsh realities of anti-Black racism and discrimination. They view giving children the freedom to make mistakes and learn from them as irresponsible parenting practices. In their view, the context of virulent anti-Black racism context means that Black children (regardless of age) do not have the luxury of making mistakes and learning from them (Ojo and Turner 2016). Every mistake by a Black child carries potentially disastrous consequences, including bodily injury, imprisonment or death.

Another area where there appear to be cultural misunderstandings is the question of language, specifically how certain words used frequently among Black immigrant communities convey a meaning different from when those words are used in white communities. For instance, the word "spanking" is not part of everyday vocabulary among many Black immigrant families, who alternatively use the word "beating" to describe what is generally understood as "spanking" in the white world. Moses, a Ghanaian-Canadian social worker, recounted a story in which a Nigerian father was arrested for threatening to "kill" his child. Of course, the father did not literally mean that he intended to kill his child. "I will kill you" is an overstatement emphasizing the father's displeasure with the child's behaviour. Maxine, a Congolese mother, clarifies the use of such language in Black immigrant communities:

> My mum use to call me "aku falobi," it's a Lingala language which in English it means "she will die tomorrow." She named me that because I was always sick as a child. So, if I'm fighting with my brother, my mother will say to my brother … "Let her be … akufa lobi … she will die tomorrow." I didn't die. Does this mean that she really wanted me to die tomorrow? No … she was telling them not to disturb me or fight with me because I do not have strength because all the time I am sick. That's how our parents talk back home. Sometimes when I misbehave my mum would say to me, "Today I'm going to eat you." Does this mean that she really wants to eat me? The answer is no.

The inability of some workers to differentiate words spoken literally and those spoken for emphasis within specific cultural and racial contexts leads to child protection interventions that could easily have been avoided. It is apparent from our study as well as other research (Bonnie et al. 2022) that many child welfare workers lack the racial and cultural knowledge and experiences required to appreciate and support the difficult decisions Black parents make every day to protect their children.

The increased presence of racialized minorities in Canada has heightened discussions around cultural and racial value differences between white Canadians and their racialized counterparts. Many racialized immigrant populations retain their cultural beliefs, traditions, values and world views when they relocate to Canada. As the Black parents in our study explained, they rely on these in their daily interactions and social relations including parenting practices (Adjei et al. 2018; Adjei and Minka 2018). Competing visions of protection and safety for children pose a challenge for workers committed to anti-racist, socially just practice with Black children, parents and families.

ANTI-RACIST CHILD WELFARE PRACTICE

Canadian child welfare legislation attempts to balance the protection of children from abuse and maltreatment with the rights of parents to raise their children and to abide by culturally distinct practices and expressions embedded in their ancestral roots (Ivan 2021). In practice, workers must safeguard the best interests of children while supporting parents to provide care to their children within their racial and cultural contexts. But as our conversations make clear, many practitioners struggle to take account of racial and cultural contexts and instead impose white middle-class standards in the assessment process. In doing so, workers omit information that is critical for accurate assessment and supporting the efforts of Black parents to safeguard their children. When workers include race and culture contexts and factors in the assessment of risk and harm, they provide clarification about what constitutes risk and harm within the specific context of Black parenting. Anti-racist practice requires that workers inquire about the cultural, racial and immigration/refugee context of parents when conducting any type of assessment, including initial safety assessments. Further, workers must understand the cultural and racial contexts of Black parenting practices to support Black parents to protect their children. Children are safest and most supported when parents and workers are jointly committed to these efforts.

The Need for More Black Workers

The Black child welfare workers that we interviewed routinely draw on their cultural and racial knowledge to address issues that arise between Black parents and child protection workers and to establish trust. More Black workers or other

Black-focused resources within child protection services would increase the availability of this knowledge and might facilitate the establishment of trusting relationships. Anita, a Black worker says:

> We do have support, like we do have some counselling program, especially I talk about Caribbean Black communities, where you take for all Blacks because the counsellor over there, they understand the culture, they understand the pattern. As I said when you work with a Black family it is easy because by your skin colour, they open door for you. If it's the parents, they are gonna take you as a son and they talk to you about the issue openly because there is that trust from your colour and you can easily bring them to an understanding point. That is why we prefer for a Black African community or family, we refer them to the Caribbean counselling program, which is given by the Tropicana, given by Black counsellors.

But services such as Tropicana are rare, and where they do exist are likely to have long waiting lists or restrictive criteria (Butler 2021; Cénat et al. 2021; Mohamud et al. 2021). In this context, Lizzy, another Black worker, advocates for more Black workers in child protection to enable more race-matching (i.e., workers share racial identity with the family being investigated) to reduce cultural or racial misunderstandings:

> Sometimes when you don't have the right match, the right cultural match, if it was a Jamaican worker that went there [referring to the case of Jamaican mother having a bible in the baby's crib], that conversation wouldn't even come out right. And if okay, maybe I'm not a Jamaican but maybe when I went and she explained oh no, you know, the Bible is to keep the child protected and I mean really, it's a baby so I'm probably gonna think maybe it's at the edge of the foot of the baby, there is probably nothing to it. But I would definitely not be asking for a psychologist for assessment (laughs) ... I think the agency [child protection service in Toronto] is really trying to really balance that out in terms of hiring more Black folks, in terms of paying attention to these issues. However, I think the match, I don't know how it goes through the list, how they give the different workers. But I think matching is crucial, looking at the person's history ... where they are from, what language they speak, all those, it's crucial. I know sometimes it gets so hectic around here that maybe they just go down the list, whoever has the less case will just get whatever, that needs to change, that needs to change, right.

Tonto, a Black worker, also supports race-matching in child protection services because of the need for trust between parents and child welfare workers:

> A Black family will sit me down and tell me their story, they are not comfortable to talk to a Caucasian because the issue of trust is a big deal as far as our profession is concern, the issue of trust is a big deal. People don't wanna talk to you because they don't want you to take information from them and use that information against them. But a Black family will easily trust a social worker who is a Black guy; they would sit you down and tell you. So as far as the issue of trust is concern, more Black social workers will be more advantageous to work with these Black families.

Recognizing that racial matching is not always feasible, Tonto advises his colleagues who are not Black but working with Black families to pay particular attention to the cultural and racial background of their clients to serve them effectively:

> You have to assume that most of the Black families are immigrants. Most of them are immigrants. They are either from Africa, from Asia or from the Caribbean. They are all immigrants. So, these professional social workers, they need to have detailed understanding of the cultural backgrounds of the family that they are assigned to. Anytime that they are given a file, they need to take their time and review the file. Know the background, know like who they are, have some detailed information about the family, before you even get involved with them. Because if you don't have this kind of knowledge about the family and you get yourself in there, I bet you, it will not be easy for you. Because sometimes establishing this rapport with these families becomes a big issue, because you don't understand them and you don't get along with them. Because even have a little knowledge about their cultural background, like anytime I have an African family, I may have felt at home, because I know that Africans irrespective of your country, we have some basic things in common. So, this background knowledge is important.

A Foundation for Anti-Racist Practice

Paterson and Hughes (1999, 608) argue that discrimination lies not only in barriers put before certain people but also in "corporeal and inter-corporeal norms and conventions," by which they mean the unwritten rules that apply to how individual bodies and their interactions with other bodies in certain spaces are perceived. Although child welfare laws, regulations, policies, assessment processes and procedures are on the surface colour-blind and culturally neutral, there is voluminous evidence that child welfare practices routinely impose white middle-class standards on Black families. This places Black families in a double bind. If they parent to white middle-class standards, they prepare their children for a world of illusions and fantasies, because a world in which Black children are given fair opportunity and their skin colour is not criminalized and pathologized remains a fantasy. On the other hand, if Black parents want to prepare Black children to survive and thrive in an anti-Black society, their parenting standards may be deemed to violate child protection standards. In other words, Black families face a child welfare system that is more likely to punish Black parents than to support them to protect Black children.

It is important to keep in mind that workers as well as Black parents contend with a child welfare system that, according to Sonia Mills-Minster, is "built on White supremacy, racism, and colonialism, which has led to the oppression of [Black and Indigenous] children" (CBC Radio 2016). But while Black parents recognize these realities, many of the workers they encounter do not. Workers must therefore commit to tackling the unconscious cultural racism that limits the ability of practitioners to understand parenting from the perspective of Black parents. Unconscious racism also limits practitioners' ability to see the ways in which child welfare legislation, policies and procedures are deeply embedded in the values, world views and culture of white society. These values and world views are routinely manifested in practice to the detriment of Black children, parents and communities. Given this, anti-racism and decolonial training for all child welfare workers is essential. In the absence of such training, workers should seek out opportunities to acquire knowledge about the effects of colonialism and racism on Black, Indigenous and racialized minority communities. For example, they can seek out relevant books, articles and films; review relevant websites; or attend open community events.

Most importantly, workers must listen carefully and openly to the experiences and perspectives of the Black parents with whom they are working. Such efforts may keep more Black children at home with their families.

Saying workers must educate themselves about the cultural and racial backgrounds of Black families does not mean Black families are a homogeneous group. However, there are shared histories of anti-Black racism, colonization and decolonization struggles, as well as cultural experiences that may be consistent among Black communities across Canada. A worker must first understand the impact of anti-Black racism on Black people's lived experiences. Such understanding can help workers gain a deeper understanding of how to work with Black families. Taking a colour-blind or culturally neutral approach — the idea that people's racial identity or colour differences are not important to understanding their experiences nor relating to them — can hinder workers' ability to notice the impact of anti-Black racism on Black families and their parenting practices. This usually requires that workers move out of their comfort zones and show authentic empathy and curiosity about how anti-Black racism and racial discrimination work. At the same time, workers must not rely on or expect Black service users to educate them about anti-Black racism because this shifts the focus of engagement from Black family needs to their own needs. Workers in general cannot fully engage and work with Black families if they are unwilling to confront their own racial and cultural world views, values, biases and privileges.

Workers should also be alert to how Black families use cultural resources and strengths such as spirituality, faith and religious values to deal with everyday systems of oppression. Whatever their own beliefs, it is important for workers to be open to the many ways in which spirituality and religion interplay with Black people's lived experiences. Black people are not asking workers to introduce them to spirituality and religious resources; they already have them. They are asking workers to recognize and respect these resources and their place in their lives.

Finally, race-matching may increase child welfare effectiveness in working with Black families. Workers and parents spoke several times about the trust needed to even begin deep conversations about parenting and family needs. In other professional services, such as counselling and therapy, racialized clients trust racialized counsellors than more white counsellors (Meyer et al. 2011; Ward 2005). For this reason alone, child protection services need to ensure more Black social workers are hired to work directly with Black families.

NOTE

1   All the parents' names are pseudonyms.

SUGGESTED READINGS

Adjei, Paul Banahene and Eric Minka. 2018. "Black parents ask for a second look: Parenting under 'White' child protection rules in Canada." *Children and Youth Services Review* 94.

Adjei, Paul Banahene, Delores Mullings, Michael Baffoe, Lloydetta Quaicoe, Latif Abdul-Rahman, Victoria Shears and Shari Fitzgerald. 2018. "The 'fragility of goodness': Black parents' perspective about raising children in Toronto, Winnipeg, and St. John's." *Journal of Public Child Welfare* 12, 4.

Bonnie, Nicole, Keishia Facey, Bryn King, Barbara Fallon, Nicolette Joh-Carnella, Travonne Edwards, Miya Kagan-Cassidy et al. 2022. *Ontario Incidence Study of Reported Child Abuse and Neglect-2018: Understanding the over-representation of Black children in Ontario child welfare services.*

Butler, Alana. 2021. "Low-income Black parents supporting their children's success through mentoring circles." *Canadian Journal of Education* 44, 1.

Cénat, Jude Mary, Pari-Gole Noorishad, Konrad Czechowski, Joana N. Mukunzi, Saba Hajizadeh, Sara-Emilie McIntee and Rose Darly Dalexis. 2021. "The seven reasons why Black children are overrepresented in the child welfare system in Ontario (Canada): A qualitative study from the perspectives of caseworkers and community facilitators." *Child and Adolescent Social Work Journal* 40, 3.

Clarke, Jennifer. 2012. "Beyond child protection: Afro-Caribbean service users of child welfare." *Journal of Progressive Human Services* 23, 3.

Ojo, Kike. 2016. *One vision, one voice: Changing the Ontario child welfare system to better serve African Canadians.* Toronto: Ontario Association of Children's Aid Societies.

REFERENCES

Adjei, Paul Banahene, Delores Mullings, Michael Baffoe, Lloydetta Quaicoe, Latif Abdul-Rahman, Victoria Shears and Shari Fitzgerald. 2018. "The 'fragility of goodness':Black parents' perspective about raising children in Toronto, Winnipeg, and St. John's."*Journal of Public Child Welfare* 12, 4.

Antwi-Boasiako, Kofi, Barbara Fallon, Bryn King, Nico Trocmé and John Fluke. 2022. "Addressing the overrepresentation of Black children in Ontario's child welfare system: Insights from child welfare workers and community service providers." *Child Abuse & Neglect* 123.

Block, Sheila, and Grace-Edward Galabuzi. 2011. *Canada's colour coded labour market*. Ottawa: Canadian Centre for Policy Alternatives.

Boatswain-Kyte, Alicia, Tonino Esposito and Nico Trocmé. 2020. "A longitudinal jurisdictional study of Black children reported to child protection services in Quebec, Canada." *Children and Youth Services Review* 116.

CBC Radio. 2016. "Ontario Children's Aid will collect race data to address overrepresentation." The Current. June 7, 2016. cbc.ca/radio/thecurrent/the-current-for-june-7-2016.1.3619776/june-7-2016-full-episode-transcript-1.3621302#segment1

CBC News. 2015. "Baltimore mom who smacked son during riots: 'I don't want him to be a Freddie Gray.'" April 28. cbc.ca/news/trending/baltimore-mom-who-smacked-son-during-riots-i-don-t-want-him-to-be-a-freddie-gray-1.3051954.

Cénat, Jude Mary, Sara-Emilie McIntee, Joana N. Mukunzi and Pari-Gole Noorishad. 2021a. "Overrepresentation of Black children in the child welfare system: A systematic review to understand and better act." *Children and Youth Services Review* 120.

Cénat, Jude Mary, Pari-Gole Noorishad, Konrad Czechowski, Joana N. Mukunzi, Saba Hajizadeh, Sara-Emilie McIntee and Rose Darly Dalexis. 2021b. "The seven reasons why Black children are overrepresented in the child welfare system in Ontario (Canada): A qualitative study from the perspectives of caseworkers and community facilitators." *Child and Adolescent Social Work Journal* 40, 3.

Cénat, Jude Mary, Pari-Gole Noorishad, Seyed Mohammad Mahdi Farahi Moshirian, Wina Paul Darius and Robert J. Flynn. 2023. "Reasons for admission to service and overrepresentation of Black youth in the child welfare system in Ontario, Canada: Does race matter?" *Child Abuse & Neglect* 140.

Clarke, Jennifer. 2012. "Beyond child protection: Afro-Caribbean service users of child welfare." *Journal of Progressive Human Services* 23, 3

Cole, Desmond. 2022. *The skin we're in: A year of Black resistance and power*. Toronto: Doubleday Canada.

Cooper Brathwaite, Angela, Dania Versailles, Daria Juüdi-Hope, Maurice Coppin, Keisha Jefferies, Renee Bradley, Racquel Campbell, Corsita Garraway, Ola Obewu, Cheryl LaRonde-Ogilvie et al. 2022. "Tackling discrimination and systemic racism in academic and workplace settings." *Nursing Inquiry* 29, 4.

Craven, Julia. 2015. "Dear White America: Toya Graham Is Not Your Hero." *Huffington Post*. April 30, 2015. huffpost.com/entry/toya-graham-hero-mom_n_7175754.

Dei, George, Jerry Sefa, Josephine Mazzuca, Elizabeth McIsaac and Jasmin Zine. 1997. *Reconstructing 'drop-out': A critical ethnography of the dynamics of Black students' disengagement from school*. Toronto: University of Toronto Press.

Dunn, T. 2018. "In deadly encounters with Toronto police, more than a third of victims are black." *CBC News*. April 5, 2018. cbc.ca/news/canada/toronto/police-deaths-blacks-data-1.4599215.

Eisen, Arlene. 2014. "Operation Ghetto Storm: 2012 Annual Report on the extrajudicial killings of 313 Black people by police, security guards, and vigilantes." *ProudFlesh: New Afrikan Journal of Culture, Politics and Consciousness* 10.

Fekete, Elizabeth. 2006. "Enlightened fundamentalism? Immigration, feminism and the right." *Race and Class* 48, 2.

Giroux, Henry A. 2015. "Taking notes 48: America's new brutalism: the death of Sandra Bland." *Philosophers for Change*.

Gosine, Kevin, and Gordon Pon. 2011. "On the frontlines: The voices and experiences of racialized child welfare workers in Toronto, Canada." *Journal of Progressive Human Services* 22, 2.

Greenbaum, Bryant. 2014. "Child welfare system rigged against black families." *Toronto Star*. December 11, 2014.

Henry, Annette. 2015. "'We especially welcome applications from members of visible minority groups': Reflections on race, gender and life at three universities." *Race Ethnicity and Education* 18, 5.

Ivan, Gabriela. 2021. "Child protection in Canada and England: a comparative analysis." *Journal of Policy & Law* 14.

King, Bryn, Barbara Fallon, Reiko Boyd, Tara Black, Kofi Antwi-Boasiako and Carolyn O'Connor. 2017. "Factors associated with racial differences in child welfare investigative decision-making in Ontario, Canada." *Child Abuse & Neglect* 73.

King, Robin Levinson. 2015. "Baltimore woman called 'mother of the year' after cursing son who took part in riots." *Toronto Star*. April 28, 2015.

Maynard, Robyn. 2017. "Canadian education is steeped in anti-black racism." *The Walrus*. November 29, 2017.

Mennen, Ferol E. and Maura O'Keefe. 2005. "Informed decisions in child welfare: The use of attachment theory." *Children and Youth Services Review* 27, 6.

Meyer, Oanh, Nolan Zane and Young Il Cho. 2011. "Understanding the psychological processes of the racial match effect in Asian Americans." *Journal of Counseling Psychology* 58, 3.

Mohamud, Faisa, Travonne Edwards, Kofi Antwi-Boasiako, Kineesha William, Jason King, Elo Igor and Bryn King. 2021. "Racial disparity in the Ontario child welfare system: Conceptualizing policies and practices that drive involvement for Black families." *Children and Youth Services Review* 120.

Moisi, Dominique. 2010. *The geopolitics of emotion: How cultures of fear, humiliation, and hope are reshaping the world*. New York: Random House.

Naber, Nadine. 2006. "The rules of forced engagement: Race, gender, and the culture of fear among Arab immigrants in San Francisco post-9/11." *Cultural Dynamics* 18, 3.

Ojo, Kike and Tana Turner. 2016. *One vision one voice: Changing the Ontario child welfare system to better serve African Canadians. Practice framework Part 2: Race equity practices*. Ontario Association of Children's Aid Societies.

Ontario Human Rights Commission. 2018. *OHRC interim report on Toronto Police Service inquiry shows disturbing results*. Toronto: Ontario Human Rights Commission.

Parliament of Canada. n.d. *The "spanking" law: section 43 of the Criminal Code*. https://lop.parl.ca/sites/PublicWebsite/default/en_CA/ResearchPublications/201635E.

Paterson, Kevin and Bill Hughes. 1999. "Disability studies and phenomenology: The carnal politics of everyday life." *Disability & Society* 14, 5.

Phillips, Doret, and Gordon Pon. 2018. "Anti-black racism, bio-power, and governmentality: Deconstructing the suffering of Black families involved with child welfare." *Journal of Law*

& *Social Policy* 28.

Pitts Jr., Leonard. 2015. "An angry mom, yes — but a fearful one, too." *Miami Herald*. March 6, 2015.

Pon, Gordon, Kevin Gosine and Doret Phillips. 2011. "Immediate response: Addressing anti-Native and anti-Black racism in child welfare." *International Journal of Child, Youth and Family Studies* 2, 3/4.

Raza, Ali. 2022. "Being Black in School: Peel students open up about the racism they face in the classroom." *CBC News*. April 13, 2022. cbc.ca/news/canada/toronto/peel-students-racism-panel-1.6408851.

Sinha, Vandna and Anna Kozlowski. 2013. "The structure of Aboriginal child welfare in Canada." *International Indigenous Policy Journal* 4, 2.

Sinha, Vandna, Nico Trocmé, Cindy Blackstock, Bruce MacLaurin and Barbara Fallon. 2011. "Understanding the overrepresentation of First Nations children in Canada's child welfare system." In *Child welfare: Connecting research, policy, and practice*, edited by Kathleen Kufeldt and Brad McKenzie. Waterloo: Wilfred Laurier University Press.

Spivak, Gayatri. 1999. *A critique of postcolonial reason: Toward the history of the vanishing present*. Cambridge: Harvard University Press.

Statistics Canada. 2022. *Canada at a glance 2022*. Ottawa: Statistics Canada.

Teelucksingh, Cheryl and Grace-Edward Galabuzi. 2010. "The impact of race and immigrant status on employment opportunities and outcomes in Canada." In *Health promotion and quality of life in Canada: Essential readings*, edited by Dennis Raphael. Toronto: Canadian Scholars' Press.

Trocmé, Nico, Della Knoke and Cindy Blackstock. 2004. "Pathways to the overrepresentation of Aboriginal children in Canada's child welfare system." *Social Service Review* 78, 4.

Ward, Earlise C. 2005. "Keeping it real: A grounded theory study of African American clients engaging in counseling at a community mental health agency." *Journal of Counseling Psychology* 52, 4.

Wijesingha, Rochelle. 2021. "Disparities in tenure and promotion outcomes among racialized and female faculty in Canadian universities." Doctoral dissertation, McMaster University.

Wilkins, Karin Gwinn. 2009. "Mapping fear and danger in global space: Arab Americans' and others' engagement with action-adventure film." *International Communication Gazette* 71, 7.

Winsa, Patty, and Jim Rankin. 2012. "Police Service Board decision on 'carding' stuns activists." *Toronto Star*. April 14, 2012. thestar.com/news/gta/2012/04/14/police_service_board_decision_on_carding_stuns_activists.html.

Wright-Kim, Jeremy and Laura W. Perna. 2023. "Gender and race-based differences in negotiating behavior among tenured and tenure-track faculty at four-year institutions." *The Review of Higher Education* 47, 1.

Chapter 10

"DEPORTATION IS DOUBLE PUNISHMENT"
The Neoliberal "Crimmigration" System

by Mandeep Kaur Mucina, Jessica Pratezina and Amira Abdel-Malek

CHAPTER FOCUS

This chapter examines social service practice with non-citizen former youth in care who are entangled in the child welfare, immigration and criminal justice systems. For the lives of these four women, precarious legal status construes them not as vulnerable young people in need of protection but as "deportable subjects" to be removed from the country. Their insights and those of their legal advocates demonstrate a neoliberal framework characterized by bureaucratic violence, a violence that often stems from the social institutions providing rights-based services to migrant communities and require them to move through strenuous processes that are often humiliating, triggering and constraining (Gren et al. 2024). These young noncitizens encounter many challenges in their pursuit of justice, including lack of advocacy support to gain citizenship while in care, frequently hindered by a "care-to-prison-to-deportation pipeline." Yet there are promising practices for child welfare professionals working within this system, particularly the advocates and practitioners that work to push and change the social institutions to consider the vulnerability the system puts noncitizen youth in care through.

QUESTIONS ADDRESSED IN THIS CHAPTER

1. What is bordering practice and how do child welfare systems participate in enforcing who is a deportable subject?
2. How do neoliberal practices create a dichotomy between "deserving" and "undeserving"?
3. How do bordering practices influence the rights, privileges and social supports accessible to Non-Citizen Former Youth in Care (NCFYC)?
4. What are examples of bureaucratic violence in the child welfare and carceral systems?
5. What does trauma-informed practice look like with NCFYC?

THE "OTHER" CHILDREN IN CHILD WELFARE CARE

Abdoul Abdi, a former child refugee, experienced a tumultuous journey through Canada's child welfare and criminal justice systems. Arriving in Canada at age six with his aunt and sister, Abdoul and his sister Fatouma were soon placed in the care of social services in Nova Scotia (*Abdulkader Abdi v.* MPSEP et al. 2018; Jones 2020). Abdoul and Fatouma's childhoods in Canada were marked by instability as they were shuttled through multiple foster homes. Abdoul recalls as many as thirty-one placements. As an adult, Abdoul faced imprisonment and potential deportation to Somalia after serving a four-and-a-half-year sentence for various criminal charges. However, a federal court judge halted his deportation, a decision that followed the federal government's decision to drop the case. Abdoul's story highlights deep-seated issues within Canada's child welfare, criminal justice and immigration systems (Bergen and Abji 2020). Far from an isolated incident, his case mirrors the struggles faced by many children who live in Canada with precarious status. Abdoul's story hit major media sites. Many asked if his story was an isolated case, or whether there are gaps in child welfare policies and systems that could have prevented a former youth in child welfare care from being slated for deportation.

The Canadian child welfare system has struggled to responsively address the complex needs of immigrant families, children and young people. There is little comprehensive data on the demographics of immigrant children in care, making it difficult to direct policies and develop programs to meet their needs. This is especially concerning considering the increasing number of refugee and immigrant families in Canada. In 2023 Canada had over 500,000 new permanent residents and 2.5 million temporary residents, representing 6.2 percent of Canada's population (Statistics Canada 2022). The United Nations High Commissioner for Refugees (UNHCR) has reported an unprecedented level of global displacement, with over 108 million people displaced as of 2022, marking the highest levels in forced displacement in recorded history (UNHCR 2024). In 2017, Canada ranked as the ninth-largest recipient of asylum seekers worldwide (Office of the Auditor General 2019). In Canada, an asylum seeker (also called refugee claimant) is a person who has fled their home country due to persecution and formally applied for refugee protection within Canada, but whose claim has not yet been decided by the Canadian immigration authorities (Canada Council for Refugees 2024). Canada continues to experience a high influx of refugee claims, with over forty thousand claims processed by the Canada Border Services Agency in 2023 (Government of Canada 2024). In 2021 over one in five people in Canada (23 percent) were born abroad, with a significant proportion of residents, approximately one million, being non-permanent residents (Statistics Canada 2022).

In recent years there has been an increase in both academic and popular attention toward the institutionalized discrimination experienced by racialized and Indigenous children and families involved with child welfare (Cénat et al. 2021; Sinclair 2016). At the same time, little interest has extended to the precarious experiences of immigrant children and young people engaged with child welfare, the majority of whom are also racialized, and the ways in which social policies, immigration laws and the carceral system perpetuate harm. Even less research has considered what happens when these young migrants age out of care.

Youth age out of care when they reach the age of majority, which is eighteen or nineteen depending on the province/territory in which they reside. Once aged out, they are not eligible for care services and often the loss of support and resources is sudden (Woodgate et al. 2017). Along with this abrupt shift and often having experienced the instability of multiple foster and group homes, these youth may encounter myriad challenges, including homelessness, poverty and mental health issues, particularly post-traumatic stress disorder, and substance use (Doucet et al. 2022). Their precarious socioeconomic position and lack of social support can increase their susceptibility to criminal involvement and being targeted by police and the prison system. This transition can be particularly challenging for noncitizen youth, who in addition to lacking a stable support system, may find themselves without access to consistent housing or employment. They are made more vulnerable by their unclear immigration status, which can lead to harsh legal consequences including the threat of deportation if they are charged with a crime (Barker et al. 2014; Mucina and Lash-Ballew 2024).

Described as "a growing 'crimmigration system'" by Bergen and Abji (2020, 42), a kind of pipeline can be traced from involvement with child welfare, to prison and finally to deportation. Bergen and Abji describe how "the child in 'care' is reframed from victim to a threat to the Canadian population due to criminality and noncitizen otherness" (40). Unlike citizen children who may be seen as needing rehabilitation, these "other" children are reframed from being young people in need of protection to problems that must be excised from the country.

Few frontline workers and advocates, including social workers, lawyers and health care professionals, receive support or training to address the needs of those living with precarious status. Child welfare legislation across Canada offers minimal direction to those supporting noncitizen children and youth who become permanent wards of the state. In the absence of clear policies, frontline workers may lack the preparation and skills needed to work effectively and compassionately with immigrant children youth and their families and may not understand the implications of youth leaving state guardianship without citizenship.

The experiences of four noncitizen former youth in care (NCFYC) and five legal advocates who supported the NCFYC to fight their deportation orders illustrate the systemic racism of these principles and practices in action. To challenge the "crimmigration system," we must confront the systemic racism, practices and ideologies that surround the liminal experience of this population. To foster more equitable and just approaches to working with NCFYC, we must take note of the most basic practice failures that all these former youth experienced: no one (including social workers, lawyers and judges) asked about or considered their permanency in Canada; no one asked whether they were citizens; no one asked whether they had their immigration papers; and no one asked for or listened to their migration story. In this chapter, you will hear from the four NCFYC and their advocates as they share their insights on the systems that impact youth with precarious status and offer ways to challenging the system to shift and change. We have used pseudonyms for each of the participants in this study to maintain anonymity and confidentiality. The names of the four NCFYC are Summer, Spring, Fall and Winter.

BORDERING PRACTICES IN THE IMMIGRATION, CHILD WELFARE AND CARCERAL SYSTEMS

Global neoliberalism as an economic and political ideology emphasizes the importance of free-market capitalism and deregulation (Wilson 2017). Hallmarks of this perspective include: the view that individuals (not society) are responsible for the shape of their lives; privatization of public services; and the belief that free markets are the most efficient way to allocate all social and economic resources (MacLeavy 2016). Similarly, government should apply market-driven principles to social policies, prioritizing economic growth and efficiency over welfare, equality and justice (Cooper 2020). Social programs, from this perspective, are designed to serve the interests of the free market by creating "productive" members of society who contribute to economic growth (Fenton 2021; Krysa et al. 2017).

Neoliberalism also impacts migration experiences (Bhuyan et al. 2017). For example, Canada uses a points-based system to determine who is eligible for immigration, with a newcomer's economic potential being one of the main selection criteria (Krysa et al. 2017). Potential newcomers to Canada are viewed almost exclusively in terms of their economic utility and contribution to society, encompassing both how they might be productive workers while also considering the potential risk that they could drain social resources and contribute to criminalized behaviour (Roberts 2016).

Neoliberal policies have created a disconnect between economic participation and social-political membership for many migrants. Bhuyan et al. (2017, 349) argue that conditional status, which is often granted to temporary migrants such as refugee claimants, is precarious, making migrants vulnerable to economic insecurity, loss of access to social and health services and deportation. The disconnect between how migrants are brought into Canadian labour markets and what they have access to as members of our society is often invisible to Canadian citizens who live with the privilege of permanent status. Neoliberal policies and practices have resulted in a significant portion of the labour force being comprised of temporary workers, refugee claimants and undocumented migrants, all of whom experience precarious migration conditions (Marsden 2012). For example, Canada has seen a 150 percent increase in temporary foreign workers over the past ten years (Statistics Canada 2023). Temporary foreign workers are a class of noncitizen immigrant workers who have clear and significant restrictions, especially regarding where and when they can work. They have no political representation and unequal access to social and economic benefits. The push to increase temporary foreign workers is aimed at supporting a free-market, economic agenda (Roberts 2016).

Neoliberal principles of market efficiency and individual responsibility also shape child welfare practice both at the level of social policy and at the level of professional social work practice. Under a neoliberal framework, child welfare systems often prioritize cost effectiveness and measurable outcomes at the expense of addressing the deeper, complex needs of children and families (Fenton 2021). The focus on individual responsibility shifts attention away from the systemic issues and inequalities that contribute to child welfare problems, instead placing the onus on families to navigate and resolve their challenges without government support (Cooper 2020). Ultimately, the goal of neoliberal child welfare systems is for youth to no longer be dependent on the state but to be "independent" and "productive" members of society.

THE NEOLIBERAL DICHOTOMY OF UNDESERVING VERSUS DESERVING

The neoliberal framework creates a dichotomy between those who are considered "deserving" and "undeserving," particularly in the context of access to supports and services. Those seeking help are compelled to demonstrate their eligibility, effectively proving their worthiness for support (Fenton 2021). Demonstrating worthiness includes being a citizen, both in the sense of legal status and in the sense of cultural belonging (Mitchell 2016). In this dichotomy and in a neoliberal era, immigrants that don't fit the mould of contributing effectively to Canada's market economy, and those who are perceived as "not quite real Canadians," are not deserving of the care that should be reserved for "legitimate" citizens (Roberts 2016, 210). When a migrant engages in criminal behaviour, they become doubly unworthy and thus deportable. As one advocate shared:

> But — and then, even more pronounced when you're not a citizen. Cause it's again a secondary reason to not have to care … Not only do I not have to care about you cause you're a criminal, you're not even my criminal. You're someone else's problem or criminal.

The implementation of bordering practices exacerbates this situation by segregating individuals into categories that differentiate between the rights, privileges and access to resources for citizens and noncitizens and the continuum of precarious status that exists between these two dichotomies. In other words, bordering practices determine not only who belongs and how they might move about, but how deserving they are of rights and services. For noncitizens in care, deep-seated issues in the child welfare system heighten their risk of deportation, as they face multiple forms of structural violence, including family separation, abuse in care and an increased likelihood of imprisonment (Bergen and Abji 2020; Mucina and Lash-Ballew 2024). Speaking about her experience of trying to understand the consequences of not having citizenship, Spring explains:

> You don't have that choice, being a minor. And if your parents, if they leave you alone, like me? Then you don't have the choice to say, hey, I want my citizenship. You know? I didn't even know — I was a kid! I didn't know how to say "Okay, can you get my citizenship?" or "I need citizenship." That wasn't even on my mind!

Winter describes an experience of accessing medical care while framed as an undeserving noncitizen:

> Like people treat you totally different. Like, the doctors ... I remember one doctor looked right at me, she checked me and everything and then she started yelling at me because I told her, "You're not going to get paid, not till I get my citizenship and then you can get paid." She's like, "Well I'm not checking you and I don't care what happens, you can go to outpatient."

Youth who have precarious immigration status are labelled a "risk identity," casting them as threats to national security and characterizing them as undeserving of support and protection (Bryan and Denov 2011). Once a young migrant becomes involved in the carceral system, they can be viewed as especially risky and doubly undeserving of rights and supports. The impact of this is starkly evident in the case of noncitizen youth, who, if convicted of a crime and sentenced to more than six months, face automatic deportation under the 2013 Faster Removal of Foreign Criminals Act. This Act triggers deportation even for those who have lived in Canada since childhood and as wards of the state. As Bergen and Abji (2020, 40) write, "the threat of the stranger/noncitizen other is imposed without any understanding of the state's own responsibility or failure to protect or integrate its 'own' child." One advocate explains:

> They [Canada Border Services Agency] say that the essential social contract ... the promise that, that non-citizens make is that they won't commit a crime. And while I agree that criminal offenses are a violation

of the social contract, it's a pretty narrow way of looking at that social contract ... if you're going to take that social contract analysis, there was no awareness of Canada's own failures as part of that.

INDIVIDUAL RESPONSIBILITY AND "PRODUCTIVE" MEMBERS OF SOCIETY

Neoliberalism creates abstracted individuals divorced from their unique context — independent, self-regulated decision-makers who must reap the consequences of their actions, for good or for ill (Mackenzie and Louth 2020). Linked to what is often called a "just world theory" (Stroebe et al. 2015), people are thus rewarded for hard work and following the rules. Consequently, poverty or crime are understood to be about personal responsibilities and moral failings rather than the result of structural determinants and systems of oppression (Roberts 2016). The failure to acknowledge the structural forces and barriers that can push former youth in care into criminal activity, particularly after a childhood spent in state care, is particularly damaging for noncitizen former youth in care.

Neoliberalism has brought with it a rise in what Cunneen (2015) calls "responsibilisation," a perspective that holds individuals, families and communities as primarily accountable for their own safety, economic security and overall well-being, thus relieving the state of these responsibilities. Often connected to social conservatism, this perspective drives policies that reduce public spending on social programs and in turn expects individual families to fill the void from the lack of services (Cooper 2020). For example, reducing (or eliminating) funding for child care programs is paired with a social narrative that it is the parents' (mainly mother's) responsibility to care for children at home. In this context, there is a convergence of family values with neoliberal rhetoric advocating for reduced government involvement in social services. When these families are unable to offer the required support, both neoliberal and socially conservative narratives attribute the shortcomings to individual or family failure.

For noncitizen former youth in care for whom the absence of familial support systems combines with inadequate state resources to leave them highly vulnerable this is especially detrimental. As one legal advocate explains:

> We devalued you all the way along by just letting you be in a system that's abused you and told you you're less than and then put you in prison because like you're at fault for all of these things and then at the end of the day we're just going to send you away because actually you're that low.

NCFYC are seen as personally responsible for the systemic problems they face. Moving through what has been described as a "care-to-prison-to-deportation pipeline" by Heather Bergen and Salina Abji (2020), they are deemed undeserving of social support, imprisoned and eventually deported. This trend has been noted across Canada, the United States, United Kingdom and Australia (Cunneen 2015). The narratives of NCFYC show how immigration status and criminality become entangled and used to justify dehumanizing treatment. Spring's experience of being hospitalized after receiving her deportation order poignantly illustrates this:

> They said I was a danger to the public, a danger to myself, and a flight risk ... was shackled, and chained up to the bed as well, and [upon recounting this to a lawyer later] she wasn't pleased about that at all. I was so sick, like I wasn't even criminally charged with anything. Like, they were treating me like I was a criminal, right? Like I already did my time. I'm a foreign national, I wasn't there on charges. I was there — like, I really felt victimized.

A primary goal of neoliberalism is making productive members of society. Because neoliberalism is a market-oriented way to think about what it means to succeed, the primary value of an individual comes from their ability to contribute economically (Roberts 2016). A newcomer's economic potential is the main selection criteria for immigration (Krysa et al. 2017), and Canadian policy views immigration as a means of improving the economy (Government of Canada 2017; Roberts 2016). Krysa and colleagues (2017, 484) write, "Those who are accepted to Canada are expected to become productive citizens. Productive citizens are understood as those who participate in the labor market and contribute to the economic growth of Canada." Similarly, the purpose of the justice system is to turn a criminal into an (economically) productive member of society. Rationalized as protecting Canadian borders and interests, the state polices these "unproductive" foreigners to the point that deportation is an almost inevitable outcome.

AUSTERITY AND INEQUITY

Neoliberal austerity measures aim to reduce government spending and often involve cuts to public services, social programs and welfare provisions (Rogowski 2021), supports that are mostly for disadvantaged people. The primary objective is to shift the responsibility for social care from the state to individuals and families (Cooper 2020). For example, when families come up against systemic limitations like poverty or disability that inhibit their ability to provide for their children, child welfare services may become involved, an interference that is often punitive and reactionary. Families are, in essence, punished for being unable to protect their children from the effects of state divestment (Bergen and Abji 2020).

Austerity measures create increasingly underfunded social services. Refugees and immigrants often find themselves categorized as undeserving and excluded from most social programs and state services. These exclusions contribute to an increased risk of poverty and can lead to involvement with the child welfare system, where immigrant and racialized families are overrepresented (Pottie et al. 2015). A legal advocate states:

> We are having a housing crisis ... an affordable housing crisis in Halifax and a food bank crisis because so many refugees are living in such abject poverty that they are using our food banks and using our affordable housing because we are not caring for them properly .... You know we are criminalizing poverty, we are criminalizing race, we are criminalizing addiction, we are criminalizing mental health, and we are criminalizing trauma.

A noncitizen youth who ages out of the child welfare system will almost certainly face challenges accessing affordable housing, mental health resources and educational opportunities. For these young people, the state becomes a pseudo-family, a relationship that is severed through the process of aging out of care. With this, there is what one advocate calls "a huge access to justice problem because of the ways that we fund, or don't fund, legal services in this country." The need for support through the legal processes of immigration and the carceral system, especially for NCFYC, are also pronounced. A legal advocate explains:

> It's ... something that should be well resourced and funded, and funded by you know, legal aid ... but asylum seekers and refugee claimants are not eligible for most of these services.

To say that young people involved with the child welfare system receive inadequate care because of divestment and underfunding would be an understatement. Foster care is itself a form of adverse childhood experience (Humphrey and Van Brunschot 2018). Young people in state care in Canada experience significantly lower rates of high school completion (Trocmé et al. 2019) and poorer mental health (Dubois-Comtois et al. 2021). Considerable research has found that those who age out of care struggle with income, housing stability and health, among other indicators (Doucet et al. 2022; Dubois-Comtois et al. 2021; Gypen et al. 2017). Children involved with the child welfare system are also disproportionately represented in the criminal justice system (Yang et al. 2020). Should these young people also become involved in the criminal justice system, they are seen first as a threat rather than as a human with inherent rights and viewed as doubly undeserving of limited resources (Nath 2022). The neoliberal impact on social, health and educational services creates a precarious environment for NCFYC. Summer describes a system that failed to protect them while in care, pushed them towards drugs, sex work and criminality and ended with attempts at deportation:

> I didn't have any type of good role model around me ... I was living on the edge doing drugs, prostituting and still providing for myself ... I'm pimping myself out but that money, I'm not using to buy drugs, I'm paying my rent with that and I'm living off of that.

Spring shares:

> I was in and out of juvenile detention centres ... I didn't know any better. I was just thinking it was cool to be, do crime, and uh, when I turned 18, I stopped doing crime ... I became addicted to drugs and the drugs kind of, I did crime to fill my drug habit, right? So ... I should have gone to treatment, instead of gone to jail, but that's what we're dealing with now.

BUREAUCRATIC VIOLENCE AND ITS CONSEQUENCES

Neoliberal policies exacerbate bureaucratic violence through inefficient and impersonal systems. Neoliberal policies often entail overwhelming practitioners with administrative tasks (Rogonwski 2018). Gren et al. (2024) describe the violence inflicted on refugees moving through multiple social systems that degrade, humiliate and often place them in life-threatening situations after they have been declared refugees seeking asylum in Western nations like Canada. Excessive bureaucracy generates a ceaseless busyness for practitioners and advocates, compelling them to engage in countless trainings, constant reporting, auditing, compliance-related tasks and the challenging process of reapplying for program funding, which is often competitive and non-recurring (Morley and O'Bree 2021). The discretionary practices embedded in these bureaucratic positions of power over communities who are desperate for support can lead to a type of violence that is difficult to touch or name.

The narratives of NCFYC are marked by the violence this bureaucracy inflicts. These systems not only limit access to justice but cause harm. Bureaucracy decontextualizes a young person from their life history, oversimplifies the application of law and uses a punitive and individualist approach to address complex social problems. One advocate explains:

> The way that you have to fit somebody's story into the legal test, it sometimes doesn't work, and the process is awful.

Insights shared by NCFYC reveal a lack of consideration for their personal histories, struggles and the complicated contexts of their lives. Despite having spent a significant portion of their lives in Canada, these individuals find themselves reduced to "foreigners." The oversimplified categorization illustrates the dehumanizing impact of bureaucratic language. Spring reports:

> And, like I've been here for 27 years, and they didn't give a flying rat's ass. They didn't care that I had history, I had a life. They didn't care that in Ontario, I was there for my whole life. They didn't care that I was troubled.

The punitive nature of bureaucratic systems becomes apparent as NCFYC recount instances where they felt judged and condemned. Meetings with CBSA (Canadian Border Services Agency) officers and attempts to seek assistance from family workers for immigration issues were marked by a lack of empathy. These youth report few opportunities to present their side of the story, and yet faced immediate judgments with severe consequences. Spring explains:

> When it finally came down to it, they automatically found me inadmissible to Canada, from 5 questions. Which were: What's my first and last name, what's my birthdate, where was I born, am I a Canadian citizen, and was I charged with a federal offense. And once I'd answered all those questions, they said I was inadmissible to Canada, and I was up for deportation.

Spring shares:

> I tried to reach out to this family worker for immigration, and I guess she was off, and I didn't find that out for two months. And then I met with a CBSA officer, and I didn't know what kind of meeting I was walking into, and she wanted me to tell her my whole life story in the matter of an hour. And she judged me instantly and found me guilty that day.

The assessments and decisions made by lawyers, judges, police, border agents and others do not consider circumstantial, historical, political and sociocultural contexts. Consequently, any accountability is disproportionately placed on the NCFYC.

The state's bureaucratic imperative, driven by a need for simplistic administrative schemas and a monopoly of coercive force, often results in bureaucratic violence (Graeber 2012). For NCFYC, government agents and bureaucrats engage in bureaucratic violence by placing all the blame/responsibility for their lives on their young shoulders. By dismissing social and systemic alternatives they clearly expose the injustice of designating a NCFYC as deportable. But there are alternatives.

CRITICAL APPROACHES TO PRACTICE WITH NCFYC

Bergen and Abji (2020, 40) propose that social workers have a responsibility to disrupt the process by which the state "'adopts,' jails, and then deports young people." Legal advocates and the NCFYC themselves highlight areas where workers can do just that. The former youth in care and their advocates we talked to had clear suggestions and recommendations for how the system could have supported them and policies that could be changed so that NCFYC are not moving through a welfare-justice-deportation pipeline. All the young people interviewed for this study were able to fight their deportation with the tireless work of advocates.

Training about Immigration Law

Canadian social work education has not adequately prepared professionals for the complexities of working with NCFYC. For example, child protection workers are not typically aware of the immigration status of the youth on their caseload and report a lack of confidence when working with migrant children, youth and families (Maiter and Leslie 2015). Child welfare policies across Canada currently provide minimal guidance to those working with migrant families or noncitizen children and youth who become permanent wards of the state. The absence of clear policies for handling individuals with mixed and precarious immigration status can leave frontline workers unaware of the consequences for NCFYC.

Legal advocates we interviewed called for increased awareness and collaboration across sectors. It will likely fall to child welfare workers to educate not only themselves but judges, lawyers and CBSA agents about the realities facing NCFYC. As social workers, we are often well placed to do that because we have the incredible privilege to hear people's stories of survival, humanity and resilience that many in the interlocking systems do not see. One advocate talked about her role as an advocate "appealing to the human in every person she encountered," especially those who deemed her clients as not worthy of humanity:

> I did it in every turn at every turn. Whenever I encountered someone within the system. I tried to get them to know her, rather than just a name … Because I feel like, yeah, we have systems that we all uphold, but once you, as a human being hear and know someone's story, it's harder. It's harder to uphold your bureaucracy.

As well, social workers must be prepared to inform clients about legal processes, providing them a sense of agency and a voice to navigate the system. One legal advocate states:

> The process is awful. And so, when I say you can use the legal process to empower people … the best you can do is give them a sense of agency in the way that they have to interact with the system. And at least use the opportunity to give them a voice.

Trauma-Informed Practice

Advocates call for not only more education about the law, but for training for social workers, lawyers, judges and border service agents to better understand and respond to the complex needs of NCFYC with trauma-informed practice across systems. Recognizing how trauma can impact the way people navigate systems allows for the practitioner to be led by the client. Workers also need to think about how not to replicate practices that trigger people to be retraumatized in the process. One advocate poignantly states:

> We need so much better trauma informed practice. Like real trauma informed practice, not just checkbox trauma informed practice in ... across every one of these systems.

This approach requires framing every individual's story with compassion, recognizing the full context of their experiences. Often actions like engagement in drug trafficking are crimes of survival, and practitioners across disciplines are urged to consider alternative perspectives and understand the systemic pressures that lead to these behaviours. Above all, there is a need to engage the humanity and human rights of young noncitizens who become entangled in the child welfare and carceral systems. This is done through deeply listening to the narratives of these young people and bringing their own voices to the fore and then going that extra mile to research how to fill in the gaps of what is missing in these policies and practices. An advocate reflects:

> The difference between a lawyer who cares and knows nothing and a lawyer who doesn't care but knows a lot is that the lawyer who cares but knows nothing will actually do research and try to do a good job on it.

Seeking Knowledge of Immigration Status

Overwhelmingly, the former youth in care talked about the lack of knowledge and understanding they had about their immigration status. As one advocate stated, "Both the lawyers and the judges involved in the criminal justice system need to know, or need to ask, about a person's status before they suggest and accept a plea." Not having this knowledge meant that when NYCFC faced criminal charges, their lawyers would often encourage them to plead guilty for the crimes, regardless of the context in which these criminal acts occurred. The NCFYC talked about pushing back on the system if they knew their incarceration would lead to their deportation. Yet, their court appointed lawyers were not providing NCFYC legal advice on how to proceed with their criminal charge, without knowledge of their immigration status and the long-term impacts this will have once they exit incarceration. Winter put it eloquently:

> For immigration ... for the system ... when a person is going through the immigration and they are in court, your judge should do his background, the lawyers ... should do background checks. If the person tells you

she's adopted, you should do a background check, because if she is adopted that means she might not have her citizenship, so you can give her a chance or give her a different sentence. I could have done a different sentence so I wouldn't have went to federal, I would have just done a year or almost a year in provincial, but he didn't do that. He didn't do his research, he just thought I was a crackhead and a drunk and ... did not care. And that's what a lot of lawyers do. They don't want to listen to anybody, and I think that the government needs to change, they need to change that policy.

"DEPORTATION IS DOUBLE PUNISHMENT ... EXILE SENTENCE SHOULDN'T EVEN EXIST ANYMORE"

The migrant justice network Solidarity Across Borders (Yiu 2013) describes deportation as "double punishment ... the unjust policy used against non-citizens who face deportation after already being punished by the criminal justice system." One of the advocates we talked to powerfully stated its heavy impact:

> The potential for deportation is so psychologically damaging for people sometimes that some people have even called it a worse form of persecution, like it is just incredibly stressful and anxiety producing to be in that situation where people are in limbo and in limbo in a precarious situation where they don't have access to the same services and they aren't granted the same rights, basically, as others.

The impact of living with the potential for deportation is a tremendous burden on the lives of the former youth in care who spoke with us. For them, it is by far the most difficult part of moving through these systems. As they described, to be potentially removed from their community supports, children and family to a country where they may not even have memories and from which they escaped violence and displacement was an incredibly scary future for them to imagine. One of the NCFYC, Winter, describes it as, "everything is closing in, you know, like your whole life is closing in." Both advocates and NCFYC ask that exile or deportation be entirely removed as an option for former youth in care.

Abdoul and Fatouma, who instigated so much public knowledge of the realities of NCFYC, initiated a lawsuit against the province of Nova Scotia and the Nova Scotia Home for Colored Children for the oppressive and abusive experiences they encountered in care (Jones 2020). Their bravery in doing so has led to many changes in the provincial child welfare systems, including a policy shift to the Nova Scotia Child and Family Services Act requiring social workers to record a child's citizenship when a child enters the care of the state and to reassess the child's status at least every ninety days (Luck 2019). Recently, Senator Mobina Jaffer tabled Bill-S235, which seeks to automatically provide Canadian citizenship to noncitizen youth who have been in Canada for at least a year before leaving foster care. Advocacy efforts like these not only provide hope for systemic change but inspiration for youth in care that their stories can inspire change for the future. In the words of Fatouma Abdi (cited in Jones 2020), "I want to change this because this can't happen to anybody else. What happened to me has happened, and I'm here now, but I don't want it to happen again."

"THEY SHOULD TREAT YOU LIKE A HUMAN BEING"

Being at "home" within a nation-state involves drawing borders and boundaries, marking some as "belonging" and others as "outsiders" (Yuval-Davis et al. 2018). Through bordering practices, the state determines who belongs and who does not. Neoliberal policies are foundational in this process. Designating immigrants as "deserving" and "undeserving" means that some, particularly NCFYC, find themselves doubly marginalized, facing deportation not only due to criminality but also as a consequence of being perceived as outsiders in the social order. Austerity measures compound these challenges, as government divestment places the burden of care on families, often leaving NCFYC without support. The neoliberal emphasis on personal responsibility obscures the systemic forces that contributing to NCFYC involvement in the criminal justice system. Bureaucratic violence, stemming from neoliberal efficiency measures, decontextualizes NCFYC experiences, oversimplifies legal applications and employs a punitive approach. The failure to consider circumstantial and historical contexts places undue accountability on these young people who, very often, have only known Canada as their home and the state as their parent.

Promising practices involve disrupting adoption, incarceration and deportation processes through increased collaboration, education and trauma-informed practices across social sectors. The narratives of NCFYC and their advocates underscore the urgent need for a compassionate and rights-based approach to this work that acknowledges the humanity of these individuals and centres a holistic and collaborative effort to dismantle the barriers faced by NCFYC. Spring shares:

> They shouldn't treat you like a criminal. They should treat you like a human being. And that is one thing I want to say. They need to treat people like human beings and not like criminals.

SUGGESTED READINGS

de Finney, Sandrina and Mandeep Kaur Mucina. 2021. "The End of the Tunnel: Girls' Marked Bodies in the Canadian Transcarceral Pipeline." *Girlhood Studies* 14, 3.

Rampersaud, Marsha, Kristin Swardh and Henry Parada. 2024. "Child Welfare, Immigration, and Justice Systems: An Intersectional Life-Course Perspective on Youth Trajectories." *Laws* 13, 3.

Rogowski, Steve. 2021. "Neoliberalism, Austerity and Social Work with Children and Families: Challenges and Critical/Radical Possibilities." *Critical and Radical Social Work* 9, 3.

REFERENCES

Abdulkader Abdi v. MPSEP et al. 2018. FCC 733.

Barker, Brittany, Thomas Kerr, Gerald Taiaiake Alfred, Michelle Fortin, Paul Nguyen, Evan Wood and Kora DeBeck. 2014. "High Prevalence of Exposure to the Child Welfare System Among Street-Involved Youth in a Canadian Setting: Implications For Policy and Practice." *BMC Public Health*, 14.

Bergen, Heather and Salina Abji. 2020. "Facilitating the Carceral Pipeline: Social work's Role in Funneling Newcomer Children From the Child Protection System to Jail and Deportation." *Affilia: Journal of Women and Social Work* 35, 1.

Bhuyan, Rupaleem, Daphne Jeyapal, Jane Ku, Izumi Sakamoto and Elena Chou. 2017. "Branding 'Canadian Experience' in Immigration Policy: Nation Building in a Neoliberal Era." *Journal of International Migration and Integration* 18.

Bryan, Catherine, and Myriam Denov. 2011. "Separated Refugee Children in Canada: The Construction of Risk Identity." *Journal of Immigrant & Refugee Studies* 9, 3

Canadian Council for Refugees. 2024. "Background Information About Refugees." ccrweb.ca/en/information-refugees.

Cénat, Jude Mary, Pari-Gole Noorishad, Konrad Czechowski, Joana N. Mukunzi, Saba Hajizadeh, Sara-Emilie McIntee and Rose Darly Dalexis. 2021. "The Seven Reasons Why Black Children are Overrepresented in the Child Welfare System in Ontario (Canada): A Qualitative Study From the Perspectives of Caseworkers and Community Facilitators." *Child and Adolescent Social Work Journal* 40, 3.

Cooper, Melinda. 2020. "Neoliberalism's Family Values: Welfare, Human Capital, and Kinship." In *The Nine Lives of Neoliberalism*, edited by D. Plehwe, Q. Slobodian and P. Mirowski. Verso.

Cunneen, Chris. 2015. "Surveillance, Stigma, Removal: Indigenous Child Welfare and Juvenile Justice in the Age of Neoliberalism." *Australian Indigenous Law Review* 19, 1.

Doucet, Melanie M., Johanna K.P. Greeson and Nehal Eldeeb. 2022. "Independent Living Programs and Services for Youth 'Aging Out' Of Care in Canada and the US: A Systematic Review." *Children and Youth Services Review* 142.

Dubois-Comtois, Karine, Eve-Line Bussieres, Chantal Cyr, Janie St-Onge, Claire Baudry, Tristan Milot and Annie-Pier Labbé. 2021. "Are Children and Adolescents in Foster Care at Greater Risk of Mental Health Problems Than Their Counterparts? A Meta-analysis." *Children and Youth Services Review* 127.

Fenton, Jane. 2021. "The 'Undeserving' Narrative In Child and Family Social Work and How it is Perpetuated By 'Progressive Neoliberalism': Ideas for Social Work Education." *Societies* 11, 4.

Gordon, Elyse. 2013. "Under-served and un-deserving: Youth empowerment programs, poverty discourses and subject formation." *Geoforum* 50.

Government of Canada. 2017. *Canada-British Columbia Immigration Agreement.* canada.ca/en/immigration-refugees-citizenship/corporate/mandate/policies-operational-instructions-agreements/agreements/federal-provincial-territorial/british-columbia/canada-british-columbia-immigration-agreement-2010.html.

Government of Canada. 2024. *Asylum claims by year - 2023.* canada.ca/en/immigration-refugees-citizenship/services/refugees/asylum-claims/asylum-claims-2023.html.

Graeber, David. 2012. "Dead zones of the imagination: On violence, bureaucracy, and interpretive labor: The Malinowski Memorial Lecture, 2006." *HAU: Journal of Ethnographic Theory* 2, 2.

Gren, Nina, Dalia Abdelhady and Martin Joormann. 2024. "Unmasking the Impact of Bureaucratic Violence." *Refuge: Canada's Journal on Refugees* 39, 2.

Gypen, Laura, Johan Vanderfaeillie, Skrallan De Maeyer, Laurence Belenger, and Frank Van Holen. 2017. "Outcomes of Children Who Grew Up in Foster Care: Systematic Review." *Children and Youth Services Review* 76.

Humphrey, Tamara, and Erin Gibbs Van Brunschot. 2018. "Accumulating (dis)advantage: Do Social Bonds Mediate the Relationship Between Multiple Childhood Adversities and Persistent Offending?" *Journal of Developmental and Life-Course Criminology* 4.

Immigration and Refugee Board of Canada. 2023. *Claims by country of alleged persecution - 2022.* https://www.irb-cisr.gc.ca/en/statistics/protection/Pages/RPDStat2022.aspx.

Jones, El. 2020. "'There Was No Care' Fatouma Abdi is Suing the Province. Today, She is Ready to Tell Her Story." *Halifax Examiner,* September 2, 2020.

Krysa, Isabella M., Albert Mills and Salvador Barragan. 2017. "Canadian immigrant guidelines on how to become productive members of society: A postcolonial analysis." *Equality, Diversity and Inclusion: An International Journal* 36, 6.

Luck, Shaina. 2019. "Abdoul Abdi's Case Changes N.S. Policies on Children in Care: Social Workers Now Have Power to Apply for Canadian Citizenship on Children's Behalf." *CBC Nova Scotia Investigates,* January 22, 2019. cbc.ca/news/canada/nova-scotia/abdoul-abdi-child-welfare-nova-scotia-policy-change-1.4979208.

MacLeavy, Julie. 2016. "Neoliberalism and Welfare." In *Handbook of Neoliberalism,* edited by Simon Springer, Kean Birch and Julie MacLeavy. Routledge.

Mackenzie, Catherine, and Jonathon Louth. 2020. "The Neoliberal Production of Deserving and Undeserving Poor: A Critique of the Australian Experience of Microfinance." *Social Policy and Society* 19, 1.

Maiter, Sarah, and Bruce Leslie. 2015. "Child Welfare Systems and Immigrant Families." In *Child Welfare Systems and Migrant Children: A Cross Country Study of Policies and Practice,* edited by Marit Skivenes, Ravinder Barn, Katrin Kriz and Tarja Pösö. Oxford University Press.

Marsden, Sarah. 2012. "The New Precariousness: Temporary Migrants and the Law in Canada." *Canadian Journal of Law and Society/La Revue Canadienne Droit et Société* 27, 2.

Mitchell, Katharyne. 2016. "Neoliberalism and Citizenship." In *Handbook of Neoliberalism,* edited by Simon Springer, Kean Birch and Julie MacLeavy. Routledge.

Morley, Christine, and Charlie O'Bree. 2021. "Critical reflection: An imperative skill for social work practice in neoliberal organisations?" *Social Sciences* 10, 3.

Mucina, Mandeep K. and Abigail Lash-Ballew. 2024. "Narratives From Non-Citizen Former Youth in Child Welfare Care Fighting Crimmigration and Deportation." *International Journal of Migrant and Border Studies.*

Nath, Nisha. 2022. "Curated hostilities and the story of Abdoul Abdi: Relational securitization in the settler colonial racial state." In *A World Without Cages,* edited by Sharry Aiken and Stephanie Silverman. Routledge.

Office of the Auditor General. 2019. *Report 2: Processing of Asylum Claims*. oag-bvg.gc.ca/internet/English/parl_oag_201905_02_e_43339.html.

Pottie, K., G. Dahal, L. Hanvey and M. Marcotte. 2015. "Health profile on immigrant and refugee children and youth in Canada." *The health of Canada's children and youth: a CICH profile*.

Roberts, Dorothy J. 2016. "Race and neoliberalism." In *Handbook of Neoliberalism*, edited by Simon Springer, Kean Birch and Julie MacLeavy. Routledge.

Rogowski, Steve. 2018. "Neoliberalism and social work with children and families in the UK: On-going challenges and critical possibilities." *Aotearoa New Zealand Social Work* 30, 3.

———. 2021. "Neoliberalism, austerity and social work with children and families: Challenges and critical/radical possibilities." *Critical and Radical Social Work* 9, 3.

Sinclair, Raven. 2016. "The Indigenous child removal system in Canada: An examination of legal decision-making and racial bias." *First Peoples Child & Family Review* 11, 2.

Statistics Canada. 2022. *Focus on geography series, 2021 census of population*. www12.statcan.gc.ca/census-recensement/2021/as-sa/fogs-spg/index.cfm?Lang=E.

Statistics Canada. 2023. *Economic and Social Reports, October 2023*. www150.statcan.gc.ca/n1/pub/36-28-0001/362800012023010-eng.htm.

Stroebe, Katherine, Tom Postmes, Susanne Täuber, Alwin Stegeman and Melissa-Sue John. 2015. "Belief in a just what? Demystifying just world beliefs by distinguishing sources of justice." *PloS one* 10, 3.

Trocmé, Nico, Tonino Esposito, Jennifer Nutton, Valerie Rosser and Barbara Fallon. 2019. "Child welfare services in Canada." In *National systems of child protection: Understanding the international variability and context for developing policy and practice*, edited by L. Merkel-Holguin, J.D. Fluke, & R.D. Krugman. Springer.

UNHCR: The UN Refugee Agency. 2018. "Forced displacement above 68m in 2017, new global deal on refugees critical." unhcr.org/news/news-releases/forced-displacement-above-68m-2017-new-global-deal-refugees-critical.

———. 2024. "Refugee statistics." unrefugees.org/refugee-facts/statistics/.

Wilson, Julie. 2017. *Neoliberalism*. Routledge.

Woodgate, Roberta L., Oluwatobiloba Morakinyo and Katrina M. Martin. 2017. "Interventions for youth aging out of care: A scoping review." *Children and Youth Services Review* 82.

Yang, Jennifer, Evan McCuish and Raymond Corrado. 2021. "Is the foster care-crime relationship a consequence of exposure? Examining potential moderating factors." *Youth violence and juvenile justice* 19, 1.

Yiu, Cera. 2013. "What is double punishment?" *Solidarity Across Borders | Solidaridad sin fronteras*. solidarityacrossborders.org/en/solidarity-city/solidarity-city-journal/what-is-double-punishment#:~:text=Double%20Punishment%20is%20the%20unjust,by%20the%20criminal%20justice%20system.

Yuval-Davis, Nira, Georgie Wemyss, and Kathryn Cassidy. 2018. "Everyday bordering, belonging and the reorientation of British immigration legislation." *Sociology* 52, 2.

Chapter 11

DECOLONIAL TRAUMA-INFORMED SCHOOL-BASED PRACTICE
Hearing the Voices of Refugee Newcomer Parents

by Mehmoona Moosa-Mitha

CHAPTER FOCUS

Every year, Canada admits a significant number of refugees. For example, from 1980–2017, it admitted over a million refugees (UNHCR n.d.a), with numbers increasing every year. From 2016 to 2021, 218,430 new refugees were admitted as permanent residents (Statistics Canada 2022). Thus, school-based social workers and child welfare workers can expect to encounter refugee newcomer parents and their children in practice.

This chapter centres the voices of fourteen Syrian refugee newcomer parents to describe some of the challenges that refugee parents, and their children, face. Central to these challenges is trauma, a significant mental health issue present in refugee newcomer populations as in the case of Syrian refugees. Within a decolonial analysis of trauma, however, trauma is not understood only as a one-time cataclysmic event occurring in faraway places, such as the country they flee from, but rather as ongoing due to repeated experiences of exclusion that refugee newcomers experience in societies in which they resettle. The typical practice with people experiencing such trauma stems from bio-medical approaches. These approaches do not reflect refugee newcomers' experiences with trauma. Based on Syrian parents' perceptions of traumatic experiences facing their children, I make recommendations for decolonial trauma-informed practices that are social justice oriented.

QUESTIONS ADDRESSED IN THIS CHAPTER

1. How might we understand trauma in the lives of refugee newcomer children, and why is a decolonial approach needed?
2. How do racism and Islamophobia impact refugee newcomer families with school-age children?
3. What concerns do refugee newcomer parents have about misperceptions of themselves, and their children, made within school settings?
4. What concerns do refugee newcomer parents have about school curriculum, particularly SOGI (Sexual Orientation and Gender Identity) curriculum?
5. How can decolonial trauma-informed practice be implemented in ways that consider the concerns of parents?

DECOLONIAL PERSPECTIVES ON TRAUMA

Trauma is usually understood within a bio-medical lens as related solely to mental suffering as it impacts brain functionality (Bond and Craps 2020, 12). Decolonial notions of trauma however take a "socio-genic" perspective in understanding trauma. Fanon (2005; 2008) defined the socio-genic conceptualization of trauma as paying attention to the social context and lived experiences of people living with trauma. Fanon worked as a psychiatrist in the French occupied country of Algeria and attributed much of the trauma that he saw in his clients to colonial violence, rather than understanding trauma as resulting from a singular and catastrophic event as it is generally understood. In this alternative approach, trauma is seen as emanating from structural and social violence, often with the state as a significant perpetrator of this violence. In the 1980s, feminist and anti-racist theorists and activists analyzed acts of violence such as domestic violence, police brutality and racism as being traumatic (Agathangelou 2019, 245). Critical theorists of trauma (that include decolonial and critical race feminists) insist on using the terms trauma and violence together to connote this significant relationship between the two (Wathen and Varcoe 2023).

Thus, refugee newcomers are viewed as having been traumatized not only by singular instances of violence, such as civil war in the country they originate from and from which they are forcibly expelled, but also by ongoing exclusionary practices like racism, ableism and patriarchy, which are experienced as everyday violence (Craps 2013). A decolonial view of trauma also challenges views of trauma that assume other countries, particularly those in the global south, are unsafe, while countries of the global north, such as Canada, are a "safe haven." This overlooks settler-colonial violence as well as other forms of social exclusion that characterize Canada (Moosa-Mitha 2022b).

REFUGEES IN CANADA

The United Nations defines refugee as "someone who has been forced to flee his or her country because of persecution, war or violence. A refugee has a well-founded fear of persecution for reasons of race, religion, nationality, political opinion or membership in a particular social group" (UNHCR n.d.b). For a person or family to be recognized as a refugee in Canada, they must apply for refugee status to the Immigration and Refugee Board. To qualify for refugee status, a person must provide evidence that they have a well-founded fear of persecution for reasons of race, religion or any of the UNHCR factors, by their country of origin and are therefore unwilling to seek protection from this country (Immigration and Refugee Board of Canada n.d.). Under the Universal Declaration of Human Rights, to which Canada is a signatory, everyone has the right to seek asylum from persecution in other countries by asking for refugee status in another country deemed safe (United Nations n.d.c).

Canada had received less than 2 percent of the refugee claimants from the 104.8 million displaced people in the world in 2021 (Carling 2023), though this percentage is greater than that of other Western countries (UNHCR n.d.c). Since 2015, when the civil war in Syria broke out, a significant number (44,645) have been Syrian refugees (Statista n.d.). Research demonstrates the presence of trauma among Syrian refugees upon arrival into Canada (Gleeson et al. 2020). Post-migration studies indicate that mental health is a growing issue among Syrian refugee newcomers living in Canada (Al-Hamad et al. 2023; Aldiabat et al. 2021; Drolet et al. 2020). Newcomers have identified racism and Islamophobia, isolation, estrangement from their own cultural milieu and contending with Canadian cultural mores, particularly its individualist nature, as significant strains on their mental health (Agroam 2021).

On a practical level, lack of affordable housing is a nationwide issue that particularly impacts refugee newcomers who are simultaneously struggling to get on their feet in Canada, find good jobs and learn English (Woods 2022; Iqbal and Magbouleh 2021; Bhattahcharyya et al. 2020; Kuo 2020). The Syrian parents who spoke to me explained that the lack of adequate housing is more than not having a comfortable place to live, it also compromises their well-being and that of their children:

> I believe that the first difficult thing we faced was finding a place to rent, as it was hard, and we had to stay in the hotel for almost 2 months. Once I left the hotel, they gave me a house to stay in, but this house had many issues; first it was full of mice, second, it was on the third floor, and I have 2 kids. But thanks god finally I was given a new place to live in which I will be moving to at the end of this week.

Another parent spoke to the effect of housing difficulties on their children:

> One of the major difficulties that I faced was moving between almost four houses because each house had a problem, such as the first house didn't have windows, and we had asthma, so we had to apply to a different place. Also, when we ended up being here in Victoria, we had to move to different places for other reasons as sometimes the landlords want their house back, or they want to sell it out. Eh, I would say my kids' emotions and feelings were affected because we kept moving to different places, which resulted in moving them to different schools, and for sure, they had to find new friends. One of my kids got really attached to his friends, so it wasn't easy for him to move out and find new friends. Also, this affected his academic performance.

Another parent echoed similar sentiments:

> I had mentioned before to the ICA [Inter-Cultural Association] the major problem was in renting a place. When they asked me to mention what are the issues we are facing, and they asked me to mention everything that is going on with us. I had complained about the same things, but honestly, nothing had changed. I was renting a two bedrooms house that has *no kitchen* [emphasis added], and I have been in this situation for almost 6 years. I couldn't get government housing to this day, and I would say that this situation is very difficult for me because two of my kids are staying in the same room and they are not feeling comfortable.

Added to the initial trauma of becoming a refugee are these sorts of practical challenges, meaning that aspects of life in Canada contribute to ongoing trauma in the lives of refugee children and youth.

SCHOOLS, REFUGEE NEWCOMER CHILDREN AND ONGOING TRAUMA

School plays a significant role in resettlement of refugee newcomer youth in Canada (Nakhaie et al. 2022); it is where children and youth spend most of their waking hours socializing and getting an education. Schools also constitute a site of racism, including Islamophobia, which along with other forms of social exclusion and violence differentially impact refugee newcomer children and youth (Bakali 2017; Elkassem 2023; Guo et al. 2021; Miled 2020; Walker and Zuberi 2020; Zulfikar 2016). The concerns identified by the Syrian parents echo these findings. Parents pinpointed Islamophobia as a significantly damaging factor in their children's lives. Parents felt excluded from understanding or participating in the school's curriculum. Parents also experienced school staff treating their parenting styles with suspicion, producing anxiety in their children and impacting their children's mental health.

Racism and Islamophobia as Significant Issues in Families' Lives

Islamophobia "targets expressions of Muslimness or perceived Muslimness" (All Party Parliamentary Group on British Muslims 2018, 50). Islamophobia is also intersectional. Muslim girls experience different forms of discrimination than do Muslim boys. Many parents spoke about their children reporting experiences of Islamophobia at the hands of their peers at school. One parent noted that experiences of Islamophobia initiated by other youth was not universal but rather school specific:

> I have three older children and three young children. My older children didn't face any problems at school. Even when it came to praying time, they [teachers, administrators] were cooperative, and [my children] were given a place to pray. But my middle children faced serious racism, especially when I moved to [X] school. One time my young daughter, who is 13 years old, had a conflict with one of her classmates, as he kept bothering her because she was wearing a hijab. Also, he accused her that she was the reason for the events of September 11 [9/11 attack on New York twin towers by jihadists], but my daughter wasn't even born yet at this time. So, my daughter is really suffering now at school because of her hijab, and this has affected her feelings and emotions.

Two other parents narrated how their daughters were affected upon hearing that their hijabi friend was attacked on the school bus and had her hijab torn off:

> *Parent 1:* My daughter is constantly scared, and she started to feel that she will be facing the same situation whenever she goes out alone. Especially when she is on the bus.
>
> *Parent 3:* This caused our daughters to start to hate wearing hijab. Especially my daughter, I started to feel that she fears wearing hijab. I can feel there is a source of fear for her when it comes to hijab-wearing, as she is scared that someone will abuse her or hit her.

Trauma and fear are closely interconnected phenomena (Huggett 2019). Islamophobia has a high incidence among young Muslim refugee newcomers at schools in Canada (Elkassem 2023; Beydoun 2023; Farooqui and Kaushik 2022). Experiencing Islamophobia results in feelings of fear that is experienced as traumatic (Elkassem 2023; Beydoun 2023; Farooqui and Kaushik 2022; Khan 2021). Moreover, Islamophobia is intersectional with hijabi-wearing young women and Black Muslim youth, particularly young males, experiencing more intense forms of this racism (Elkassem 2023; Emon 2023).

According to the parents with whom I spoke, their children reported that their teachers knew about the racism that they were experiencing but did not do anything about it — and in some instances, teachers themselves were openly racist:

> As for my children, they were so happy at the school that they used to go to near my house, as even the teachers there and the principal really liked them. They used to have a very good relationship with them. My children used to wake up actively to go to this school. But after I moved them to [X] school, I found that there was huge racism from both the students and the teachers. My kids don't like to go to school anymore.

> Sometimes teachers are the ones who are getting racist against our children not only the students. Like my daughter told me I ask the teacher several times about a question, and she would never answer. Like she is ignoring her … So, my daughter now can feel the discrimination when the teacher answers students that are not wearing hijab and ignores my daughter's question because she is wearing hijab.

As this parent attests, while some teachers hold anti-Muslim biases, other teachers exhibit a capacity for empathy and a willingness to learn how to counter Islamophobia (Ennab et al. 2024; Elkassam 2023; Ahmed 2021). Several studies show that Muslim students are more likely to experience higher stress levels, anxiety and feeling targeted when discriminatory behaviour comes from teachers rather than if that behaviour comes from students (Abu Khalef et al. 2023). As one parent reported, this can lead to children's unwillingness to go to school, which in turn may have long-term effects on their future as well as their current sense of well-being. Parents also described discrimination by teachers that had its basis in their children's ethnicity/race as it intersected with their immigration status, as in this example:

> I would say mostly this happens in the school. For example, when children are playing with each other and one of them intentionally hits his friend, if the boy that was hit is Canadian, then they will talk to the kid and ask him to write an apology. Like they will make it a big issue. But if the kid that was hit is from the Middle East, then they won't make it as big a deal. I believe the reason is that we don't speak English very well and we can't go and discuss it with them, which results in making us feel guilty, and we are the ones who should apologize. The right of our child is lost. And this thing happens continuously.

Cultural and Social Marginalization as Exclusionary Social Practices

Parents reported experiences of racism and discrimination that add to the other aspects of cultural and social marginalization for their children. For example, schools fail to include the culture of their children in the curriculum, which often makes no mention of Middle Eastern culture. Parents reported feeling concerned that, as a result, their children would lose their sense of identity and cultural values:

> So, I would say the challenges that are facing us as parents are different from the ones that are facing our children as they are facing more challenges every day through the situations they are going through, and what is resulting is in losing their identity or value imbalance. Parents want their children to be within certain values, and at the same time the children want to integrate into society, and this is hard on them as they are facing a culture shock. Also, there is a contradiction between what parents want and what children face and live within schools. Children are wondering if they shall carry the values that they learned from their parents, or if they should be among the values of Canadian society, so this is really causing a big conflict for them.

Many parents reiterated apprehension over their children losing their cultural values. When refugees have already experienced material, emotional and psychological losses, they see their cultural capital as something precious that they bring with them that contributes to their sense of well-being (Massing et al. 2023). Parental anxieties over the potential loss of culture must be understood in this context.

Exclusionary practices that position Eurocentric ideas, values and beliefs as central and normative inevitably result in the positioning of other cultures as inferior, and can leave children feeling confused, with lower self-esteem and reduced motivation to do well at school (Mahfouz and Anthony-Stevens 2020). It can also lead to communication breakdown between parents and children:

> Well, she is not telling me [why her daughter refuses to wear her hijab] but every time I approach her with this subject, she will say later. I don't want to wear it now. I talked to her a lot about it, and I had explained to her that this is our religion and not wearing it is against our morals, religion, and principles. Then her answer will be later, I will be wearing it myself without any pressure from you. I believe that maybe one of her friends had faced a racist situation for wearing a hijab and that's why she is refusing to do this now. Also, I believe that they should talk about it at the school and tell the students not to discriminate against each other based on hijab, religion, or anything, and to teach the students to respect

each other's religion and traditions. And they shouldn't criticize each other based on any of these issues. It's freedom, they should be free to wear what they want.

Students in schools where their culture is not recognized report feeling socially marginalized and that they lack a sense of belonging (Elkassam 2023; Emon 2023). The parents with whom I spoke recognized the need for their children to have a sense of belonging and spoke to the positive outcomes that occurred when schools reflected some of their cultural practices as well.

School Curriculum Viewed as a Threat

Parents spoke passionately about the education that their children received. They were concerned about not understanding the pedagogical approaches used by teachers in Canada nor did they understand what was being taught. As one parent said: "For us, we hope that we can know what our children are learning at school." Other refugee newcomer families from Arabic-speaking backgrounds have also expressed the desire for greater involvement with the school (Cranston et al. 2021; Cureton 2020). Parents also critiqued the pedagogical approach to education their children were exposed to at school:

> My complaint is about the education system as it is not strict ... For example, my daughter told me that there are some of the students sleep during class, and no one tells them anything, or students leave and come as they want. So, we don't feel that there is prestige for the teacher, but I know I can't change anything as this has been the education system for a long time.

Pedagogical styles here in Canada vary from those in the Middle East, where children are more likely to learn by rote, have more homework and where teachers tend to enforce a stricter disciplinarian regime (Barek 2020; Fakih 2020).

The primary source of concern for the parents, however, had to do with differing cultural values between those that the parents held and those that the school was reported to espouse:

> I found out that they are teaching them about gays, which is not accepted by our religion, or traditions. And I am afraid that my kids will be influenced by what they are learning at school. Also, they are getting conflicting ideas between what is being taught at school and what is being taught at home .... to be honest, if that situation remains the same, then I won't send my kids to school anymore, as I prefer them to become ignorant than learning things that is against our religion and concepts.

Similarly, another parent complained: "This thing [LGBTQ+] is against our traditions and our religion too. So, we are afraid that if kids keep hearing about these things, then this will open their eyes to these things, and it would make them accept it as a normal thing."

The social background from which the parents are speaking must be contextualized to avoid reaffirming already existing stereotypes that assume all Muslims are anti-gay (Kugle 2010; Ahmadi 2011). Canada has also witnessed a growing "home grown" anti-SOGI (sexual orientation and gender identity) movement of late. Made up largely of right wing, conservative white Christians and community members, this movement objects to resources being made available in classrooms that are inclusionary of and reflect the lived realties of 2SGLBTQ+ students (Wong 2023). Their argument against 2SLGBTQ+ inclusionary education is that it infringes on their religious beliefs and the freedom to practise those beliefs, which are largely anti-2SLGBTQ+ (Hollinger 2019). Anti-SOGI movements in Canada are gaining momentum within a socio-political context in which the Canadian state is increasingly acknowledging the equality rights of 2SLGBTQ+ people. However, the anti-SOGI sentiments of refugee parents arise from a different socio-political context and must be understood within that context.

Middle Eastern families arrive in Canada from societies that are highly repressive against 2SLGBTQ+ community members. These repressions are rationalized on faith grounds by the governing regimes but are often in fact based on cultural patriarchy and compulsory heterosexism inculcated by the Western countries (France, Britain and Italy) who colonized the Middle East. Present-day Middle Eastern societies have continued these colonial practices, though they may not have existed as such prior to colonization, using Islam as the rationale for doing so (Kugle 2010; Ahmadi 2011). In fact, it is the normative culture in Middle Eastern societies that tends to be homophobic. Muslim scholars and activists as well as 2SLGBTQ+ Muslims actively resist homophobic interpretations of Islam as erroneous, even if it comes from their own community members (Kugle 2010).

It is fair to say that there is an overlap between what the parents explained about their faith-based objections to 2SLGBTQ+ positive curriculum and the Canadian anti-SOGI movement. However, there are also important differences. Refugee newcomer parents spoke to the anxiety that is produced by their lack of familiarity with the curriculum. They are not sure what is being taught in 2SLGBTQ+ sex-positive classes and already feel like their own culture is socially marginalized. This adds to their anxiety, leading them to believe that their children are being persuaded to adopt non-heterosexual identities and other forms of gender diversity. Members of the Canadian anti-SOGI movement, on the other hand, are very familiar with school curriculum and are not so much concerned with their children becoming 2SLGBTQ+ as they are that the curriculum breaches their right to be *anti*-2SLGBTQ+ (Hollinger 2019). Theirs is a majoritarian position that is rejecting an inclusionary stance towards a marginalized population. In the case of the Muslim parents in this study, it is the majoritarian position on an issue to which they have not previously been exposed, and before which they feel powerless as a minority to influence, that fuels their anxiety. While there is certainly an overlap between the two groups, the social contexts that informs each group's responses to 2SLGBTQ+ communities are markedly different.

Several parents expressed a desire for some say in the curriculum that their children are being taught, and wanted to know how to exercise their rights in relation to this curriculum:

> For example, I got an email for the rainbow day at my son's school, but other than that, I am not receiving any emails. I could say that things have changed from the first time we came to Canada. I believe they don't have the right to teach our kids about sex and other stuff, and they should leave it to us, as we know how to teach our children about sexual life, and we know what is appropriate to learn and what is not. Briefly, I could say that we can't stop them from teaching these things at school, but we have the right to know and refuse to send our children on these days.

Education is a provincial issue in Canada, and in BC parents are guaranteed certain rights, such as the right to allow their children to opt out of sex-positive education classes if they so wish, or to be informed of the curriculum content of such classes (Nash and Browne 2021). However, in the absence of any kind of dialogue between parents and teachers, parental rights over their children's education tend to be overlooked, and parents in this study stated that they did not know what their rights were.

The parents were aware that their children sometimes avoided sharing information with them. When one parent stated, "As sometimes, our kids won't come and tell us what they have learned because they feel scared of telling us," there were several nods by other parents showing agreement with this sentiment, attesting to a mutual feeling that their children were simply not sharing what was being taught at school on this subject. While all children negotiate anxieties and confusion around sex education, refugee newcomer students are often also negotiating the clearly negative stance that their parents have towards it. Refugee newcomer students from Middle Eastern backgrounds who may identify as or be curious about 2SLGBTQ+ are likely to feel particularly caught in the crossfire between school sex education curriculum and parental attitudes towards it.

School Suspicions of Parenting Approaches

There was a high degree of agreement among the parents that the school staff generally found their parenting styles wanting. As one parent forcefully remarked:

> Well, one time, we faced a problem with my son's school, as they were luring my son to tell them things they wanted, such as asking him if he was being hit at home, and then they wrote things as they wanted. After, we were asked to come to the school. When we went there, they told us that our son had confessed that he was being hit at home, and they found this after asking him some questions.... I got mad and told them to stop using a manipulative way to hear what they want, and just to prove things against us, and pretending that this is for my son's good.

Another parent reported:

> They believe that our children had come from a strict family, and they were not treated in a nice way. They picture us as only an executioner, and we treat our children in a cruel and unfair way. The first thing they teach our children is how to call the police or the family protection center. Also, they gave them their numbers. They picture everything that parents do or say as rebuking their children.

Another parent spoke of similar experiences of having their children's behaviours interpreted as symptomatic of lack of parenting abilities:

> My young daughter, as you know, likes to hug people she likes, so one time she hugged her teacher because she likes her. But the school sent us an email saying that our daughter needs love, and she lacks tenderness and love in her life. So that was a funny reaction, and my husband asked them: "How can a five-year-old kid have a lack of love?" and we are wondering why they didn't think that our daughter was expressing her love for her teacher.

These concerns of the parents are not unusual. Other refugee newcomer parents have reported that their parenting styles were always regarded with suspicion by school staff when they differed from Canadian parenting norms (Massing 2023; Iqbal and Maghbouleh 2021; Yoryor 2018; Dumbrill 2009). This Eurocentric bias results in an overrepresentation of child welfare interventions in the lives of children from refugee backgrounds. Child welfare interventions often have a traumatic effect on refugee newcomer parents, who report feelings of high anxiety due to their lack of familiarity with the child welfare system and fears that such interventions will result in their children being taken away from them (Wilson et al. 2020).

DECOLONIAL AND ANTI-RACIST TRAUMA-INFORMED SCHOOL-BASED CHILD WELFARE PRACTICE

Understanding Trauma as a Practice of Coloniality

Decolonial notions of trauma acknowledge and pay attention to the social and structural context that results in trauma rather than being solely focused on the individual, psychological effects of trauma (Moosa-Mitha 2022a; 2020). Practices of coloniality such as racism, cultural marginalization, parental loss of power in influencing school curriculum and the accompanying confusion experienced by their children, as well as teacher bias and stereotypes are the main sources identified by the parents as resulting in experiences of trauma in children. Decolonial trauma-informed school-based child welfare practices therefore need to address structural and systemic exclusionary practices, particularly as they occur within the school system.

Acknowledging Asymmetrical Power Relationships in Canadian Society

Masson and Smith (2019) point out that the colonial context of settler-colonial societies such as Canada needs to be acknowledged in order to understand and address trauma in relation to Indigenous and racialized people. Neoliberal economies that characterize settler-colonial societies, and are not outside of practices of coloniality, produce class and racial stratification. Material deprivations such as extreme poverty, as Lerner (2019) has pointed out in relation to Indigenous communities, can reinforce collective trauma. As I discussed earlier, extremization of poverty, Islamophobia and white supremacist thinking that privileges Western ways of knowing and doing over other cultural practices are the context within which trauma is produced and experienced.

While school-based child welfare workers may not be able to directly address the socio-political context of settler societies such as Canada, they can influence the school environment where these asymmetrical relationships are reflected, assumed and practised. They can, for example, ensure that they engage in conscientization activities alongside direct child welfare practices with individual refugee newcomer child and youth experiencing trauma. These conscientization practices could take the form of professional education programs with teachers to better understand the socio-political context that forms the daily realities of refugee newcomer parents and their children.

Working with Community: Islamophobia as Collective Trauma

Masson and Smith (2019, 17) argue for a decolonial definition of trauma that centres the collective nature of trauma over individualist bio-psychological–oriented views of trauma. One form of collective trauma experienced by many communities is particularly relevant to parents in the present study. According to Masson and Smith, this collective trauma results "[w]hen people hold exclusive values, norms and mental images of another group that is the result of stereotyping and fits into the idea that a particular group is suspect or cannot be trusted."

To respond to this trauma, school-based social workers must also work as community social workers by making strong connections not just with the families of students living with trauma but by making connections within community, through attendance at community events or invitations for community Elders to attend specific school events. Im and Swan (2022) speak to the necessity of social workers letting the community take the lead in teaching them about community understandings of mental health, its relationship to culture and traditional ways to address healing in their communities. It is important that child welfare workers also examine their own biases against Muslim communities, particularly in relation to Muslim women who choose to wear a hijab. Studies have shown a tendency for social service workers to hold similar biases as those found in the wider population (Moosa-Mitha 2022b).

Culturally Safe Practices

Decolonial theorists understand that culture is political and not just as it is normatively understood in sociological terms as representing customs and rituals. Culture is a world view that acts as a guide in everyday life and informs both the epistemological and ontological foundations of people's life trajectories. Decolonial political definitions of culture are derived from the colonial or settler-colonial context. The cultures of Indigenous and colonized peoples everywhere were the targets of outright elimination, as in the case of Indigenous communities in Canada where the holding of powwows was criminalized or denigrated as inferior to Western cultural practices that were viewed as civilizational (Moosa-Mitha and Wallace 2020).

Islamophobia is a modern extension of colonial times when cultural prejudice against Muslims (as colonial subjects) was used to rationalize economic and other forms of material subjugation (Mbembe 2017). Post-colonial theorists such as Said (1978) challenged these cultural prejudices and their material consequences, locating their roots in colonialism. Said named these practices in which the figure of the Muslim was constructed in the West as "savage" or as an existential threat to Western civilization as "orientalism."

The parents in this study clearly saw the necessity of drawing upon their own cultural resources to prevent and protect their children from the trauma of racism and cultural bias against Muslims. One parent responded to the question of how schools could address the various difficulties they had: "They could teach Arabic at schools so kids could feel that there is something from their culture, and their country. Even if it is going to be for a short time but at least they could feel that others care about them and respect their culture."

Culture is recognized as a source of resiliency (Raghavan and Sandanapitchai 2024). For example, Muslim youth who identify as transgender identify their religion as a protective factor for them in resisting trauma, even when their own community use it as a rationale for exclusionary practices (Etengoff and Rodriguez 2022). Similarly, some parents consider cultural integration as an important resource to bring down barriers to integration as well as parental involvement in schools (Zaidi et al. 2021). Indigenous communities also recognize the integral role that culture plays in addressing and protecting Indigenous youth from living in trauma (Moosa-Mitha 2022a).

Another parent spoke eloquently to the positive effects on their children's mental health due to cultural recognition from the school:

> Last Ramadan [X] school made shirts for Muslim students that has a sentence saying: "Ramadan Mubarak" and that was nice! In addition, they made simple gifts for each kid on Ramadan, even though Muslim students were fasting. Also, on Eid, they made a nice celebration with a BBQ that has different kinds of halal food such as hotdogs, burgers, and much more. I had made falafel and most of the Canadian students left the non-halal food and started to eat our food ... so that would be nice if most schools do the same thing.

It is essential for school-based child welfare workers to know more about the cultural festivals of Islam and understand the meaning and significance these have in the lives of students. Moreover, it is important that cultural knowledge and awareness is reflected in the spatial and pedagogical aspects of the school system. Such initiatives directly counteract Islamophobic as well as orientalist biases of non-Muslim students and introduce decolonial practices as a part of child welfare work.

Suspicion about the parenting styles of families from the Middle East needs to be recognized as reflective of practices of coloniality that continue to view non-Western cultural practices as inferior rather than different. Parents do not have innate knowledge of parenting practices that come with the birth of their children. Child rearing is a social practice and reflects the sociocultural milieu in which children are raised. Upon arrival in Canada, a different set of expectations are in play and child rearing practices such as physical punishment and rules around hugging are very different from those in the Middle East. Cultures change and evolve. The developing understanding of the harms that children experience because of physical punishment gradually changed the culture and laws of Canada over time. Rather than treating them as indifferent to their children's welfare, parents from Middle Eastern countries must be afforded time and support to similarly change their beliefs and behaviour. Workers engaging with newcomer families have to hold themselves open to providing support across a range of possibilities these families may encounter, including their children's interest in the 2SLGBTQ+ community. When working with families and young people who want to adopt non-heterosexual or gender identities that diverge from their cultural and religious beliefs, workers can uphold the importance of their cultural and religious identities while affirming the significance of integrating minority sexual or gender identities. Providing this support may require seeking consultation from or referring to relevant sources, such as local or national 2SLGBTQ+ organizations.

Bridging Familiarity with School Curriculum

A significant finding of this study was the extensive anxiety that these parents expressed about school curriculum. Notably, other studies report similar parental reactions, particularly in relation to sex-positive curriculum (Wood et al. 2021). Rather than dismissively stereotyping this reaction from parents as simply anti-gay or homophobic, decolonial trauma-informed school-based social workers can play a role in bridging parents with teachers and school staff so that parents can develop a better understanding of the curriculum, including their rights in relation to deciding what their children learn around sex education.

The narratives of the parents show a disconnect between what is taught at schools and parental perceptions of the curriculum. Parents believed that schools were encouraging their children to be gay, whereas schools see the curriculum as enhancing diversity and literacy about sex and sexual orientation (Bozcam 2021). Parents in this study and other ones clearly express the desire and need to be engaged with the school system and have a voice in it (Cranston et al. 2021; Cureton 2020). It is important that school-based social workers facilitate the dismantling of the barriers that parents experience in interacting with the school system and encourage school staff to build relationships with the parents.

Like all social workers, workers in these situations need to navigate the practice challenge of working across difference in ways that preserve empathy, dignity and respect even when their clients hold values or beliefs with which they may strongly disagree or even find reprehensible. For example, social workers who work with victims of intimate partner violence routinely encounter women who remain committed to their violent partners even in cases of life-threatening abuse, often blaming and berating themselves for causing the violence inflicted against them. Practice approaches that involve judging these women or challenging patriarchal beliefs they may hold are very unlikely to be experienced as supportive. Alternatively, a social worker's ability to create and maintain a respectful, empathic connection and exhibit genuine curiosity about these behaviours and beliefs can open space for victims to develop new understandings. Similarly, social workers encountering anti-SOGI parents are free to maintain their own pro-SOGI values, while attending to the relational processes from which they can better understand the context of refugee parents' misgivings about SOGI curriculum and provide parents with opportunities to change their perceptions of SOGI. Finally, workers must ensure that they maintain empathy, dignity and respect even in the absence of any attitudinal change.

COLONIALITY AND SCHOOL SOCIAL WORKERS

Social workers must view trauma not as a bio-medical issue but rather as one that requires a socio-genic approach aligned with a decolonial understanding of trauma. Decolonial trauma-informed child welfare practices need to be situated within the context of the coloniality that marks racialized people and newcomer refugee families' experiences of trauma.

Practices of coloniality have traumatic effects, both systemic and individual, on the lives of refugee newcomer youth and their families. A decolonial response to trauma therefore must be grounded in understanding and challenging colonial child welfare practices by acknowledging asymmetrical power relationships that exist in colonial-settler societies such as Canada. Child welfare practitioners also need to be skilled in anti-Islamophobic practices, by acting as a bridge that facilitates cultural recognition within school systems while familiarizing refugee newcomers with the pedagogical cultural expectations of Canadian schools.

SUGGESTED READINGS

Ahmed, Asma. 2021. "Muslim Youth Yearning for Normal Lives." *Annals of Social Studies Education Research for Teachers* 2, 1.

Ahmadi, Shafiqa. 2011. "Islam and Homosexuality: Religious Dogma, Colonial Rule, and the Quest for Belonging." *Journal of Civil Rights and Economic Development* 26.

Bozcam, Emel Seven. 2021. "An Analysis of Canadian Educational Policy for Syrian refugee Children from a Social Work Perspective." Master's thesis, Dalhousie University.

Dumbrill, Gary C. 2009. "Your Policies, our Children: Messages from Refugee Parents to Child Welfare Workers and Policymakers." *Child Welfare* 88, 3.

Williams, Monnica T., Anjalika Khanna Roy, Marie-Paule MacIntyre, and Sonya Faber. 2022. "The Traumatizing Impact of Racism in Canadians of Colour." *Current Trauma Reports* 8, 2.

REFERENCES

Abu Khalaf, Nadin, Ashley B. Woolweaver, Roslyn Reynoso Marmolejos, Grace A. Little, Katheryn Burnett and Dorothy L. Espelage. 2023. "The impact of Islamophobia on Muslim students: a systematic review of the literature." *School psychology review* 52, 2.

Agathangelou, Anna M. 2019. "A Conversation with Emma Hutchison and Frantz Fanon on Questions of Reading and Global Raciality." *Millennium: Journal of International Studies* 47, 2.

Agroam, Floranda. 2021. "Syrian Refugees in Canada Transition to Resettlement: Through the Perspectives of Housing, Income, Female Resettlement, and Mental Health." *Major Research Papers* 14.

Ahmed, Asma. 2021. "Muslim Youth Yearning for Normal Lives." *Annals of Social Studies Education Research for Teachers* 2, 1.

Ahmadi, Shafiqa. 2011. "Islam and homosexuality: Religious dogma, colonial rule, and the quest for belonging." *Journal of Civil Rights and Economic Development* 26.

Al-Hamad, Areej, Cheryl Forchuk, Abe Oudshoorn and Gerald Patrick Mckinley. 2023. "Listening to the voices of Syrian refugee women in Canada: An ethnographic insight into the journey from trauma to adaptation." *Journal of International Migration and Integration* 24, 3.

All Party Parliamentary Group on British Muslims. 2018. "Islamophobia defined: The inquiry into a working definition Islamophobia." March 13, 2024.

Aldiabat, Khaldoun M., Enam Alsrayheen, Catherine Aquino-Russell, Michael Clinton and Roger Russell. 2021. "The lived experience of Syrian refugees in Canada: A phenomenological study." *The Qualitative Report* 26, 2.

Bakali, Naved. 2017. "Islamophobia in Quebec secondary schools: Inquiries into the experiences of Muslim male youth post-9/11." In *Muslim students, education and neoliberalism*, edited by M. Mac an Ghaill and C. Haywood. Palgrave Macmillan.

Barek, Hiba. 2020. "Exploring the experiences of high school Syrian refugee students with interrupted formal education and their teachers in ELD classrooms." Doctoral dissertation, University of Western Ontario.

Beydoun, Khaled A., and Nura A. Sediqe. 2023. "Unveiling: The law of gendered Islamophobia." Cal. L. Rev 111.

Bhattacharyya, Pallabi, Sally Ogoe, Annette Riziki and Lori Wilkinson. 2020. "In Search of a 'Home': Comparing the Housing Challenges Experienced by Recently Arrived Yazidi and Syrian Refugees in Canada." *Applied Psycholinguistics* 41, 6.

Bond, Lucy, and Stef Craps. 2020. *Trauma: The new critical idiom*. London: Routledge.

Bozcam, Emel Seven. 2021. "An Analysis of Canadian Educational Policy for Syrian refugee Children from a Social Work Perspective." Master's thesis, Dalhousie University.

Carling, Jørgen. 2023. "The Phrase 'Refugees and Migrants' Undermines Analysis, Policy and Protection." *International Migration* 61, 3.

Cranston, Jerome, Shauna Labman and Stephanie Crook. 2021. "Reframing Parental Involvement as Social Engagement: A Study of Recently Arrived Arabic-speaking Refugee Parents' Understandings of Involvement in Their Children's Education." *Canadian Journal of Education* 44, 2.

Craps, Stef. 2013. *Postcolonial witnessing: Trauma out of bounds (Vol. 2)*. Basingstoke: Palgrave Macmillan.

Cureton, Ashley E. 2020. "Strangers in the School: Facilitators and Barriers Regarding Refugee Parental Involvement." *The Urban Review* 52, 5.

Drolet, Julie, Gayatri Moorthi, Lisa Elford, Amanda Weightman, Dania El Chaar, Esra Al Saadi, Careen Khoury and Erin Smith (eds.). 2020. "The Alberta Syria Refugee Project: Understanding Trauma and Resilience in Refugee Resettlement" In *A National Project: Syrian Refugee Resettlement in Canada*, edited by L.K. Hamilton, L. Veronis and M. Walton-Roberts. Quebec: McGill-Queen's University Press.

Dumbrill, Gary. 2009. "Your Policies, Our Children: Messages from Refugee Parents to Child Welfare Workers and Policymakers." *Child Welfare* 88, 3.

Elkassem, Siham. 2023. "Muslim Youth Experiences in a Visceral Islamophobia and Anti-Muslim Racism Context." Doctoral dissertation, Memorial University of Newfoundland.

Emon, Anver M. (ed.). 2023. *Systemic Islamophobia in Canada: A Research Agenda.* Canada: University of Toronto Press.

Ennab, Fadi, Sharifat Makinde and Janet Nowatzki. 2024. *Young Women's Experiences of Anti-Muslim Racism in Schools.* CCPA (Canadian Centre for Policy Alternatives).

Etengoff, Chana, and Eric M. Rodriguez. 2022. "'At its Core, Islam is About Standing With the Oppressed': Exploring Transgender Muslims' Religious Resilience." *Psychology of Religion and Spirituality* 14, 4.

Fakih, Fatima. 2020. "Exploring the School Experiences of a Syrian Refugee Student in a Windsor, Ontario Secondary School: A Case Study." Master's thesis, University of Windsor.

Farooqui, Jannat Fatima, and Archana Kaushik. 2022. "Growing Up as a Muslim Youth in An Age of Islamophobia: A Systematic Review of Literature." *Contemporary Islam* 16, 1.

Fanon, Frantz. (ed.). 2005. *The Wretched of the Earth.* New York: Grove Press.

____. 2023. "Black Skin, White Masks." In *Social Theory Re-Wired*, third edition, edited by W. Longhofer and D. Winchester. New York: Routledge.

Gleeson, Christina, Rachel Frost, Larissa Sherwood, Mark Shevlin, Philip Hyland, Rory Halpin, Jamie Murphy, and Derrick Silove. 2020. "Post-migration Factors and Mental Health Outcomes in Asylum-seeking and Refugee Populations: A Systematic Review." *European Journal of Psychotraumatology* 11, 1.

Guo, Yan, Srabani Maitra, and Shibao Guo. 2021. "Exploring Initial School Integration Among Syrian Refugee Children." *International Migration* 59, 6.

Hollinger, Dennis P. 2019. "Religious Freedom, Civil Rights, and Sexuality: a Christian Ethics Perspective." In *Religious freedom, LGBT Rights, and the Prospects for Common Ground*, edited by W. Eskridge and R. Wilson. Cambridge University Press.

Huggett, Betsy. 2019. "Fight, flight or freeze: Your body's defense mechanism." *TEDx Talks.* July 26, 2019. https://www.youtube.com/watch?v=_GiOGobZKLI&t=3s.

Im, Hyojin, and Laura E.T. Swan. 2022. "'We Learn and Teach Each Other': Interactive Training for Cross-Cultural Trauma-Informed Care in the Refugee Community." *Community Mental Health Journal* 58, 5.

Immigration and Refugee Board of Canada. n.d. "Chapter 4 - Grounds of persecution - Nexus." https://www.irb-cisr.gc.ca/en/legal-policy/legal-concepts/Pages/RefDef04.aspx.

Iqbal, Maleeha, Laila Omar and Neda Maghbouleh. 2021. "The fragile obligation: gratitude, discontent, and dissent with Syrian refugees in Canada." *Mashriq and Mahjar: Journal of Middle East and North African Migration Studies* 8, 2.

Kugle, Scott Siraj al-Haqq. 2010. *Homosexuality in Islam: Critical Reflection on Gay, Lesbian, and Transgender Muslims.* England: Oneworld Publications.

Kuo, Ben C.H., Lais Granemann, Avideh Najibzadeh, Riham Al-Saadi, Monira Dali, and Bayan Alsmoudi. "Examining Post-migration Social Determinants as Predictors of Mental and Physical Health of Recent Syrian Refugees in Canada: Implications for Counselling, Practice, and Research." *Canadian Journal of Counselling and Psychotherapy* 54, 4.

Lerner, Adam B. 2019. "Theorizing collective trauma in international political economy." *International Studies Review* 21, 4.

Mahfouz, Julia, and Vanessa Anthony-Stevens. 2020. "Why trouble SEL? The need for cultural relevance in SEL." *Occasional Paper Series* 43.

Massing, Christine, Needal Ghadi, Daniel Kikulwe and Katerina Nakutnyy. 2023. "Refugee background families' engagement in schooling across migration contexts: a community cultural wealth perspective." *Diaspora, Indigenous, and Minority Education.*

Masson, Francine, and Linda Harms Smith. 2019. "Colonisation as collective trauma: Fundamental perspectives for social work." In *The Routledge handbook of postcolonial social work*, edited by Tanja Kleibl, Ronald Lutz, Ndangwa Noyoo, Benjamin Bunk, Annika Dittmann and Boitumelo Seepamore. Routledge.

Mbembe, Achille. 2012. "Metamorphic thought: the works of Frantz Fanon." *African Studies* 71, 1.

Miled, Neila. 2020. "Beyond Men to Surveil and Women to (Un)veil: Muslim Youth Negotiating Identity, Home and Belonging in a Canadian High School." Doctoral dissertation, University of British Columbia.

Moosa-Mitha, Mehmoona, and Bruce Wallace. 2020. "Lessons Learnt on Designing a Community-Based Participatory Research Study on Trauma: A Qualitative Study With Arabic Speaking Refugee Newcomers and Their Service Providers." *The Canadian Journal of Action Research* 21, 2.

Moosa-Mitha, Mehmoona. 2022a. "Understanding experiences of people with pain within newcomer, refugee and Indigenous populations: A decolonial analysis." *Pain BC*, February 16, 2022. https://painbc.ca/health-professionals/webinars/understanding-experiences-people-pain-within-newcomer-refugee-and.

____. 2022b. "Decolonial Ethics as a Framework for Anti-Islamophobic Social Work Praxis." *International Journal of Social Work Values and Ethics* 19, 2.

Nakhaie, Reza, Howard Ramos and Fatima Fakih. 2022. "School Environment and Academic Persistence of Newcomer Students: The Roles of Teachers and Peers." *Journal of Teaching and Learning* 16, 1.

Nash, Catherine J., and Kath Browne. 2021. "Resisting the mainstreaming of LGBT equalities in Canadian and British Schools: Sex education and trans school friends." *Environment and Planning C: Politics and Space* 39, 1.

Raghavan, Sumithra, and Priyadharshiny Sandanapitchai. 2024. "The relationship between cultural variables and resilience to psychological trauma: A systematic review of the literature." *Traumatology* 30, 1.

Said, Edward. 1978. *Orientalism*. New York: Pantheon Books.

Statista. n.d. "Number of Syrian refugees in Canada as of 2021, by entrance category." statista.com/statistics/555329/number-of-syrian-refugees-in-canada-as-of-by-entrance-category/.

Statistics Canada. 2022. "Immigrants make up the largest share of the population in over 150 years and continue to shape who we are as Canadians." www150.statcan.gc.ca/n1/daily-quotidien/221026/dq221026a-eng.htm

United Nations High Commissioner for Refugees (UNHCR). n.d.a. "Refugees in Canada." unhcr.ca/in-canada/refugees-in-canada/.

____.n.d.b. "What is a Refugee?" https://www.unrefugees.org/refugee-facts/what-is-a-refugee/.

____.n.d.c. "Universal Declaration of Human Rights." https://www.un.org/en/about-us/universal-declaration-of-human-rights.

Walker, John and Daniyal Zuberi. 2020. "School-aged Syrian refugees resettling in Canada: Mitigating the effect of pre-migration trauma and post-migration discrimination on academic achievement and psychological well-being." *Journal of International Migration and Integration* 21, 2.

Wathen, Nadine and Colleen Varcoe. 2023. *Implementing Trauma and Violence-Informed Care: A Handbook*. Toronto: University of Toronto Press.

Wilson, Samita, Sarah Hean, Tatek Abebe and Vanessa Heaslip. 2020. "Children's Experiences with Child Protection Services: A Synthesis of Qualitative Evidence." *Children and Youth Services Review* 113.

Williams, Monica T., Anjalika Khanna Roy, Marie-Paule MacIntyre and Sonya Faber. 2022. "The Traumatizing Impact of Racism in Canadians of Colour." *Current Trauma Reports* 8, 2.

Wong, Jackie. 2023. "Don't kid yourself about 'parents' rights.'" *The Tyee*. September 20, 2023. thetyee.ca/Opinion/2023/09/20/Who-Are-1-Million-March-4-Children-Fighting-For/.

Wood, Jessica. Alexander McKay, Jocelyn Wentland and Sandra E. Byers. 2021. "Attitudes Towards Sexual Health Education in Schools: A National Survey of Parents in Canada." *The Canadian Journal of Human Sexuality* 30, 1.

Woods, Karli. 2022. "Public Policy Brief Through the Federal Government: The Social, Civic, and Cultural Integration of Resettled Refugees in Canada and Germany." *Federalism-E* 23, 1.

Yoryor, Isaac. 2018. "How We Can 'Bell the Cat': African Canadian Perspectives of the Canadian Child Welfare System." *Journal of Law and Social Policy* 28, 2.

Zaidi, Rahat, Christine Oliver, Tom Strong, and Hanan Alwarraq. 2021. "Behind Successful Refugee Parental Engagement: The Barriers and Challenges." *Canadian Journal of Education* 44, 4.

Zulfikar, Teuku. 2016. "'I feel different though': Narratives of Young Indonesian Muslims in Australian Public Schools." *Cogent Education* 3, 1.

Chapter 12

TAKING CHILDREN'S RESISTANCE EVEN MORE SERIOUSLY
A Response-Based Approach to Children Who Have Experienced Violence

by Kineweskwêw (Cathy Richardson) and Shelly Dean

CHAPTER FOCUS

Grounded in response-based practice, the authors explore children as spirited, responding agents, not as passive recipients of life. Children yearn for dignity, resist against violence and other forms of adversity, respond to and understand fairness, create safety in all ways that they are capable of and seek justice.

Children are always seamlessly part of the circle of Kaska women and Elders. The circle opens with a prayer, and their little hands join with the strong hands next to them as they hear the words of prayer spoken in their language and then translated into English by an Elder. The talking stick is passed to the children equally, opening the circle in a good way and inviting them to share. Natalie is only four years old, and she looks to her mother, unsure of what to say. "Tell them what you dreamt about," her mother suggests. Natalie immediately smiles and responds, "I dreamed about her," and she points to Julie. Everyone in the circle laughs, and Natalie's grin grows even bigger. She has a special bond with Julie, who is a visitor on her land and plays with her for hours. They make up games and imagine themselves drinking magic potions. It is the highest honour to be the subject of a child's dream, and Julie acknowledges this by quietly touching the palm of her hand to her heart and gives Natalie a nod. Natalie experiences the ease of equality within the circle, where power is shared and never abused. Natalie's bond with Julie is secured, witnessed and honoured. Without disruption, the talking stick moves to the next person. Natalie listens as the Kaska women share, one by one, their laughter, despair and outrage. They are speaking primarily about colonial violence on their land — violence against their people, animals and waters.

Within the circle, Natalie plays as the women speak. Sometimes she is alone, and sometimes she is engaged with other children. She is always listening. When she becomes tired, she sleeps, sprawled out across her mother's lap. When she is hungry, someone gets her the food that she likes. Everyone seems to know that she likes the wrapper pulled back just enough so that she can eat, and not so much that she will get her fingers sticky.

It is not a Kaska belief that children should be prevented from overhearing adults on matters of the heart. Nor is it a belief that the suffering of adults, expressed through tears and stories, will harm a child. Natalie's movement between her mother, her grandmother and her great-grandmother isn't the result of reading about attachment theory. Kaska Dena women would chuckle, respectfully, at such a suggestion. They might say that Natalie is Kaska, and this is the history of her people. They might say that she is the future, and that she must understand who she comes from, where she comes from and what has happened as a result of colonization. They might say this is what it means to be "attached."

QUESTION ADRESSED IN THIS CHAPTER

1. How should we understand children's social interactions, particularly in situations of violence?
2. How do children orient towards safety and dignity, for themselves and others?
3. What role does the social responses of others, including professionals, play in the behaviour, safety and dignity of a child?

THE DEVELOPMENT OF RESPONSE-BASED PRACTICE

The set of methods and ideas now known as response-based practice (RBP) took shape in the early 1990s as a specialized approach to interpersonal violence. The original working group was Nick Todd, Linda Coates and Allan Wade. Nick was working at the Calgary Women's Emergency Shelter, primarily with men who had been abusive. Linda was doing a PhD in Psychology at the University of Victoria, specializing in micro-analysis of social interaction. Allan was working in private practice as a family therapist, with adults and children who had been subjected to or committed violence, while doing a PhD in Psychology at the University of Victoria, specializing in micro-analysis of social interaction in the same group as Linda Coates.

From the outset, founders Allan Wade, Linda Coates, Nick Todd, and later Cathy Richardson and Shelly Dean, worked inductively, "from the ground up," with a primary focus on the realities reported by service users. RBP also draws on several lines of practice and research: brief and systemic therapy traditions; social justice and feminist-informed practice; micro-analysis of social interaction; critical discourse analysis on the connection between violence and language (e.g., colonial and legal discourse); and research and practice experience on the quality of institutional responses.

Early on, we found that many of the methods we had inherited stemmed from unfounded assumptions and were unsuited to addressing interpersonal violence. Although adults and children invariably respond to and resist violence, they are widely portrayed as passive and self-destructive. Although violence is with rare exceptions deliberate, offenders are widely portrayed as hapless people who are driven or caused to commit violence by forces they do not understand and cannot control. Although violence is a unilateral act by one person or group against another, it is widely portrayed as a mutual act, for which victim-survivors and offenders share responsibility (Dutton 2006; Kelly 1988; Maruna and Butler 2013; Reynolds 2014; Scott 1990; Todd 2000; Todd et al. 2004; Walker 1984).

The Orcas Society, which includes Duncan BC–based counsellors, psychologists, activists, educators and a psychiatrist (Cheryle Henry, Mary Shivel, Jenny Horne, Dr. Robin Routledge, Allan Wade, Heather Ferris and others), provided a rich context for the development of RBP. On a purely volunteer basis, Orcas Society members organized training with leaders in the brief and systemic therapy fields and, with the proceeds, created a platform for local colleagues to develop and share their work. For several years, the Orcas Society hosted a series of local and low-cost events under the name "Violence, Language and Responsibility," which extended the community and energized the development of RBP.

The Calgary Women's Emergency Shelter (CWES) (FearIsNotLove) has been involved in the development of response-based practice from the outset. Nick Todd was joined by Gillian Weaver-Dunlop and Cindy Ogden in developing response-based work with men who have been abusive. CWES produced two key documents, "Choosing to Change" and "Honouring Resistance." Indigenous Elders and colleagues such as Gillian Harris, Fran Tait, Donna Moon and April Buffalo Robe generously shared their cultural and practice knowledge and played an important role in shaping RBP from the outset. For guidance and inspiration over the past twenty-five years, we are particularly indebted to Ann Maje Raider and Kaska Dene youth and Elders centred in southeastern Yukon.

Métis scholar and family therapist Cathy Richardson, who had a strong interest in analysis of child protection practices and Indigenous families, joined the group in 1998. Shelly Dean, also a family therapist, with background in leadership and supervision and direct service work with children who had been subjected to violence and other forms of adversity, joined the group in 2005. Today, RBP is used in cross-practice settings (e.g., child protection, mental health, victim services, shelters/refugees, policy, research, education) where violence is an issue.

Over time and through these many collaborations, RBP has come to be defined by several axioms that guide practice and research/analysis:

- Adults and children (i.e., victims-survivors) invariably respond to violence, overtly or covertly, depending on the dangers and opportunities present in specific situations.
- Complex forms of suffering and resistance are responses to violence and the quality of social network and institutional responses and cannot be adequately encoded in a language of effects, impacts or reactions.
- Dignity is central to individual and collective well-being. In response to humiliation, such as violence, people work to preserve and reassert their basic human dignity and the dignity of loved ones.
- Violent actions are with rare exceptions deliberate. Violent actions are a chosen course of action in a context.
- Violence is social. It is committed within a social interaction. Consequently, careful analysis of social interaction is an indispensable part of analysis and intervention.
- Violence is unilateral, not mutual, in that it consists of actions by one person or group against another person or group.
- Accurate language is essential. Language can be used to (a) conceal or reveal violence; (b) obscure or reveal offender responsibility; (c) conceal or reveal victim-survivor responses and resistance; and (d) blame and pathologize or contest the blaming and pathologizing of victims-survivors.
- Social network and institutional responses are directly connected to the tactics of resistance and the strategies of violence and a matter of constant concern for both victims-survivors and offenders.

These principles and understandings apply to working with people of all ages, including very young children.

Over the past ten-plus years, RBP has continued to develop in terms of response-based conceptualizations around children and their social interaction. This includes interaction that involves violence, where children are the targets and responders, by adults or other children. This analysis can inform child protection work, all aspects of family law, ideas about child development and violence in families, variously called intimate partner violence, family violence or domestic violence. None of these terms clearly elucidate who is doing what to whom, and how victims-survivors respond to and resist the violence. We find that children are always engaged in understanding the situation that they and those they love are in; negotiating safety; and supporting and protecting their non-abusive parents or adults.

As well, the world has changed considerably in the past decade. Earth and communities in most parts of the world are now experiencing ecological disasters in some form or another. Climate change and unpredictability means that children are growing up in a kind of "eco-anxiousness," worrying for the future. The pornography industry has successfully gained access to children's lives and their sacred spaces of play, targeting them to no end of detriment, sometimes leading to child perpetration on other children. Parents, counsellors and social workers must face the realities of ever-increasing and changing forms of violence. Social media use has become all-pervasive, and many parents have lost the ability to maintain control over what their children are exposed to. Children experience many images that are difficult to process and integrate, largely because the images are shocking and violent and do not line up with the higher human aspirations for a safe and socially just world.

Additionally, Canada has had to reckon with the discovery of child graves, the bodies of Indigenous children discovered underneath former residential school buildings. Perhaps these children are calling on Canadians to examine this genocidal history and to explore settler-Indigenous relations in this post–Truth and Reconciliation Report era.

CONCEPTUALIZING CHILDREN'S RESISTANCE TO VIOLENCE

We make the assumption that children are always responding to and resisting violence, broadly defined to include physical, sexualized, emotional, psychological and spiritual violence. They are active, interactive and purposeful in many ways of protecting, escaping, withdrawing, despairing, raging or becoming highly attentive to some things while not attentive to others. This view challenges many of the current discourses that dominate child protection and welfare work, where children's behaviour is assessed, diagnosed and medicated as a mental health disorder. Often, children's behaviour has been assessed without a contextual analysis of their experience of violence. There are important points that we address in this chapter:

- A child's action and behaviour must always be considered in context.
- Given that a child's responses and acts of resistance to violence are very often understandable in context, misdiagnosing children (i.e., categorizing responses/resistance to violence as a symptom of illness or dysfunction) is a threat.
- A child's resistance typically holds some logic in relation to the particular people and forms of violence involved.
- Children's responses are oriented towards increasing safety and dignity for themselves and often for others.
- A child's inclination to protect others, including parents, is understandable and not pathological.
- Children are targets of the pornography industry. There is increasing evidence of children harming other children in sexualized ways (Tener and Katz 2021). They themselves are also victims.

Keeping children's lives in their situational context is imperative for understanding and promoting the dignity and well-being of children. One of our central tasks is to restore meaning to acts of resistance which may have been decontextualized, so they fit back into the world of children, into social interactions and into a world where violence against children can be contested on moral, ethical, developmental and rights-based grounds.

When we refer to violence, we are speaking of the force and will that are enacted upon another being with the intent to harm, limit or humiliate them. Resistance refers to activity in which any action or energy is expended for the purposes of maximizing safety or maintaining dignity in the face of violence and/or humiliation. Resistance encompasses a wide range of activities, from wishing, breathing (deeply, quickly, shallowly), longing, sighing to moving, running or trying to outsmart. Violence is understood as unilateral, social and deliberate. Responses to violence, either by the victim-survivor or by others, have the potential to restore dignity and minimize harm, or they can do the opposite. In a response-based framework, it is generally understood that responses to violence are "small acts of living" (Goffman 1963), which are understandable within their context and are embedded with and in human dignity.

In the dominant discourse from the DSM-5 (Diagnostic and Statistical Manual of Mental Disorders, fifth edition), descriptors such as insomnia, depressed mood, persistent worry or diminished pleasure quickly take on the meanings like depression or anxiety disorder. Following this discourse creates significant consequences for young victims of violence, often in the form of a secondary assault — a diagnosis of mental illness. The use of the DSM-5 diagnostic discourse to pathologize young victims of violence by defining their responses as in need of changing means that their efforts to protect themselves, others and their dignity in the face of violence are misunderstood.

To assist children, adults need to intervene in ways that directly address violence, both the history and the imminent threat of it. The treatment trend towards diagnosing and medicating children's symptoms of outrage against their mistreatment is a further assault on their dignity. Much of what is considered child psychiatric illness could be considered both as a misdiagnosis and a social construction. Statistics clearly indicate that the outcomes for young people are not meeting anyone's objectives: neither are the kids safe nor are the professionals who care for them satisfied. According to Ubelacker (2017), "A study by the Institute for Clinical Evaluative Sciences found almost 12 percent of kids and youth with attention deficit hyperactivity disorder, or ADHD, were prescribed antipsychotics like Risperdal, Zyprexa and Seroquel." Not only is there a lack of evidence regarding the efficacy of these medications for ADHD, but there are also clearly known risks that they cause to children. For example, side effects include an average weight gain of nineteen pounds and a risk of developing childhood diabetes (Ubelacker 2017). Most antipsychotic medications prescribed to children are for "off-label" uses, which means that they are being used in a way that has not been reviewed or authorized by Health Canada. Further, most children in the provinces reviewed are not receiving regular follow up testing through laboratories (Chen et al. 2018). We say in Canada, "Every Child Matters." We are striving to create communities, systems and institutions where children themselves will claim that this is true.

SEEING THE WELLNESS OF CHILDREN THROUGH THE SLIGHTEST DETAILS

> I didn't know where my mom was, but she hadn't come home for a couple of days. When there was an aggressive knock on the door, I knew it wasn't good. I was only 6 years old, but I thought it through. I thought … If I was a cop or a social worker and I was expecting a kid to be inside, I bet he'll peek out the curtain to see who's banging on the door. So, for that reason, I didn't let myself peek. I knew they expected me to, and I wouldn't do it. They came back a couple of times, and I wouldn't let myself peek and didn't open that door. I wanted to, but I wouldn't let myself. I just hid in the corner of the kitchen for … I don't know … a couple of days. They finally caught me because I left the house to go to the internet café. (Former youth in care).

Children respond to violence against their mothers, themselves, their siblings and others whom they love in a wide variety of ways. They respond to violence itself, and to the humiliation that is created from it. In fact, many children describe the humiliation of violence as the most injurious impact. The sting of humiliation is an affront to their dignity and creates the most lasting pain. Their responses to the fear and danger of violence are quick, careful, protective and can range from slight actions to grand gestures. We must pay attention to a six-year-old who says, "I thought it through" and give it the same credence as the more obvious action of "hiding in the corner of the kitchen for a couple of days." It is often the unseen, unnoticed, silent responses of thought, prayer, holding breath while carefully listening, or making an oath to themselves that their children will never have to experience what they live through, that indicates the steady action that children are taking when someone around them is violent. Children of all ages demonstrate the ability to respond to and resist violence in ways that appropriately matches their circumstances.

In the response-based framework understanding of children's responses to violence, a contextual analysis guides assessment, interviews and documentation. Family systems, school settings, peer systems and other surroundings form an analysis that includes the context, the social interactions, the offender actions along with specific forms of adversity, their responses and resistance to violence, the social responses they've received and their responses to the social responses. To neglect the full range of contextual and interactional details surrounding violence and other forms of adversity is to risk completely misunderstanding the child. Theories or assessments that do not consider the full context of a child who has suffered, will likely be defined with mental illness and behaviour disorder. These assumptions have a direct impact on the social responses that children receive from professionals, family members and their other important social relationships.

Children are social actors and prefer action talk; their choices of behaviour, including silence, can be understood as a social achievement in the most troubling circumstances. They choose an action, or an inaction, that is very often logical to them in the context of their lives. These choices are most often guided by their private logic, which is not always revealed, and so their behaviour is easily misunderstood and frequently pathologized (see page 238).

IT TAKES A SAFE VILLAGE

Seeking to understand children and youth is everybody's business. Working with young people responding to violence, abuse or adversity is a community responsibility. Parents, grandparents, aunts and uncles, teachers, coaches and other community members have a great deal to contribute. If it takes a village to raise a child, as the saying goes, it takes a coordinated, safe and intentional village to respond helpfully to children and youth who have experienced any form of violence, danger or fear.

It would be tragic, then, if family and community members felt unqualified for this task, as though the job of helping youth was for specialized professionals only. Mental health and community service professionals have key roles to play. Professional knowledge is important but should not be seen as superior to the knowledge of family and community members. Furthermore, meeting youth where they are at may require less talk, attention to interaction, willingness to set aside a therapeutic agenda and genuine curiosity. The actions and interactions of young people, including the decision to not speak, may reveal the private logic that is resisting a specific form of distress.

This is not to devalue professional knowledge, but rather to highlight the existing knowledge of youth, families and communities that is too often undervalued. After all, criminal justice and mental health professionals cannot claim to have solved the problem of child and youth mental health, specific forms of violence against women and children or to have developed effective ways of working with children and youth.

When a young person wakes with a nightmare, it is a family member or parent figure who responds. In recovering from violence or specific forms of terror, children benefit most from what healthy families and communities already provide: safety, security, warmth, clarity, consistency, love, fun, activity, work, home, structure, culture, engagement. Professionals are, at best, collaborators within the child's family system. Perhaps these ideas are best expressed by Anne Maje Raider (2022) of Liard Aboriginal Women's Society:

> For the longest time, I did not feel the term residential school survivor defined us in any way. What I witnessed was resistance and children upholding each other's dignity and grace. The word "survivor" denotes the suffering and overcoming of the suffering. Yes, I witnessed pain and suffering from the absence of culture and the pain of separation and loneliness for a sense of belonging. What I witnessed was how children used their resistance and dignity to overcome ongoing, devastating suffering.
>
> It is so powerful and important to remember this because the whole purpose of the prison camps euphemistically called "residential schools" (they cannot be considered residences or schools) was to humiliate us and destroy our humanity. They took us from our families. They tried to isolate us from one another, to stop brothers and sisters from being together, to turn children against one another. But we did many things to preserve our dignity. We always found ways to disobey, to get together, to break through the isolation. We did not let them destroy our humanity. We took care of one another.

ATTACHMENT: THE TU CHO CIRCLE

Observing young children in a circle of Kaska women is not a scientific study. It isn't evidence based, and describing it is not intended to compete with the abundant information available for parents and professionals to read on the topic of attachment theory. It is simply a guest's observation of the Kaska way — devoid of theory and rich with acumen. Renowned family therapist Virginia Satir once stated, "We need four hugs a day for survival. We need eight hugs a day for maintenance. We need twelve hugs a day for growth" (O'Brien Institute 2022). This quote can be found throughout attachment parenting literature, which promotes nurturing touch, feeding with love and respect, engaging in nighttime parenting, providing constant, loving care, and positive discipline. Touch is undoubtedly desired by both children and adults for a sense of connection and well-being. How much and from whom is highly contextual. For young Natalie, twelve hugs within an hour, from many people, would be considered normal. For her grandmother or great-grandmother, twelve hugs might only happen with certain people, in certain settings and over a certain amount of time. Too much would simply be, well, too much. When someone grows up in a foster home or a prison camp, touch can take on a different meaning. Perhaps it would be better stated that we need safe people around us, and safe caregivers, to hug freely.

Many Indigenous people have been told that they are not capable of attachment because they attended prison camps and therefore did not experience the love of a parent. But the love of their parents and community clearly and repeatedly happened before, during and after their abduction. They have been punished, nonetheless, not for the absence of their parents' love but for the absence of government accountability for the violence done to them and their families. The punishment has been further violence in the form of their own children being removed into a government-run foster system, justified once again by the colonial code of relationship (Todd and Wade 1994). Indigenous children disproportionately represent children in foster care in Canada. Less than 10 percent of Canada's children are Indigenous, and over 50 percent of children in Canada's foster care system are Indigenous children (O'Brien Institute 2022). The colonial code (Todd and Wade 1994) is expressed routinely in a three-part message:

1. You are deficient (heathen, savage, falsely conscious, submissive, passive, internally oppressed, helpless, cognitively distorted and afraid).
2. I am proficient (critically conscious, expert, professional, closer to god, empowered by the state).
3. Therefore, I have the right (duty, sacred obligation, authority) to perform certain operations upon you (prescribing, advising, educating, assessing, praying, counselling, legislating, apprehending) for your own good.

Many Indigenous women have come to believe this message. But if academics, experiments such as the "strange situation," and theorists were removed from ideas about attachment, it might become a practice of commonsensical, intuitive parenting. There is strong evidence that even in the worst circumstances, Kaska women have always been capable of attachment to their children.

> And that's what I've been trying to teach my grandchildren. I just want to share one story about my granddaughter that just passed. We went up to the mountain when she was four years old, she walked all the way up from the river and when we get to the tent, she was so tired, she said, "I'm so tired Dad, pack me" and her dad had all her candies, her sweets and blankets and her clothes, so he couldn't pack her. "We're almost there, baby, we're almost there," he said. Once we reached the top, she forgot all her pain, she forgot everything, she was just out running around all over the mountains and the next day there was a whole group of us, it was

Rose and her family, her mother and father. The only one that stayed down by the lake, was my dad and my youngest boy Randy, stayed with him. The rest of us, all of us went in the mountains and I talked to her —she wanted to pull some flowers, and I tell her "No, don't pull flowers, don't pull roses, they're there for a reason." I tell her, "Do not step on it, do not break it." It's just a wrong thing to say to a four-year-old kid. Because when we were walking, she made sure I didn't step on any flower. Everybody left us behind, they went over the mountains, we were the last one to go over. She watched where I stepped. And there was no fear, you know, when you're out in the bush. Why is respect so important when you're out in the bush? Because everything knows you, the animals know you. I've never feared anything when I'm on the land, even the grizzlies, the bears, the wolves, everything. I talk to them, even when I'm alone. I see them, I just tell them which way to go, and us we're going our own way. They listen too — so that's what happens when you learn to respect everything on land. (Leda Jules, personal communication)

When a precise recipe is created for something like human attachment, there will necessarily be an absence of context. If we were to consider it to be true that people need twelve hugs a day for growth, then we would also believe that those who don't receive twelve hugs a day will not be capable of meaningful growth. For children who grew up in foster homes or prison camps, hugs were not necessarily freely, or safely, given. In fact, they may have been rare, or dangerous for many people. And yet, we hear stories of sisters who sneak into the kitchen from their beds at 5:00 a.m. before anyone else is awake, just to hold each other close. That may be the only "hug" they snuck that day, but the closeness and warmth of each other will last until they meet in that kitchen again. The context matters.

RESPONSE-BASED CONTEXTUAL ANALYSIS

Effective interventions in cases of violence depend on accurate and detailed information. Violence and resistance are not enacted in the abstract but in second-by-second detail in actual social interactions. The social-cultural context, the immediate social-physical setting and the actual or possible responses of others are crucially important to understanding perpetrators' actions and victims' responses, including those of children. Further, how service users make sense of these realities varies tremendously.

Conversations provide an opportunity to explore these factors in a manner that upholds dignity and promotes safety. We refer to this process as "contextualizing." It is a process of moving past abstractions and generalizations into the exploration of

FIGURE 12.1. Response-based contextual analysis

Source: Wade, Coates, Richardson and Sonnah, 2014.

particulars. As Aimé Césaire (1950, 24) articulated in "Discourse on Colonialism," detailed analysis involves the consideration of "all the particulars ... the deepening of each particular, the coexistence of them all." The opposite of contextualization is abstraction, the process of moving away from particulars into category terms, generalizations, theories of causation and so on. The process of abstraction is widely used in psychology and psychiatry to conceal particulars, including excluding the resistance of victims/survivors and the efforts of offenders to overcome and suppress that resistance. Instead, victims/survivors are given certain personality traits or disorders said to pre-dispose them to being abused.

Below is a simple map of the interconnected factors — particulars — that practice and research show are immediately relevant and, arguably, indispensable to any specific and grounded analysis in cases of violence. This map can be used as a guide for interviewing and for critical analysis of matters such as supervision, expert reports in family law and daily documentation.

The purpose of response-based contextual analysis is to grasp events as much as possible on their own terms, with a minimum of theory. Only when we look plainly at social and material realities can we begin to appreciate the nature and meaning of events for the people involved, the forms and situational logic of their responses and how we can best respond.

Violent acts are committed in specific social and material contexts, in specific social situations within those contexts and through specific actions by one person, the offender, against another, the victim. The "victim" responds to the offender's actions and to salient aspects of the social situation such as the presence or absence of others. Others who are present respond as and after the violence is committed. Authorities (e.g., police, child protection) and members of social networks (e.g., friends, family) respond later, if and when they learn of the violence. The victim and offender respond to these social responses. Close analysis of these factors, and the interplay between them, is essential to socially just interventions. Contextual analysis explores the relationship between the micro, the unique elements of individual cases, and the macro, the larger social and material realities connected to individual cases: "We speak in generalities and live in details" (Coates 2018).

Actual and possible social responses are a constant concern for victims-survivors and offenders in cases of interpersonal violence, including children. Research and practice experience show that the quality of responses by social networks and institutional actors is strongly correlated with the level of victim distress in the short and long term and is closely connected to the likelihood of victim disclosure. Victim-survivor responses to offenders depend in part on the victim's view of actual and possible social responses. For example, if the victim is isolated and knows no one will be able to step in to help, open defiance may be the least viable form of resistance. Rather, a victim may resist covertly to get through the assault and work for safety and autonomy quietly and secretly to avoid even more extreme violence. In these situations, resistance may exist in the privacy of a victim's mind, and in the subtle, crafty and covert actions that avoid the attention of the perpetrator.

> A nine-year-old child stood in the doorway, watching their grandfather scream at their grandmother, and then throw her to the ground. The child ran upstairs and locked themself in the bathroom. They found their grandfather's toothbrush and scrubbed it around the inside of the toilet. They carefully dried it off and replaced it where they found it. Later that night, they sat in the hallway, watching their grandfather brush his teeth through the open bathroom door, with lips slightly curved — not quite a smile.

Covert resistance can be the most viable (e.g., least life-threatening, safest for children) form of resistance over long periods of time, depending on social responses, related structural conditions (e.g., poverty, racism, immigration status) and the strategies used by the offender. Ongoing covert resistance is less an indication of the victim's personality or awareness or readiness than it is a recognition of the realities at work in the situation. Covert resistance can be a way of protecting other victims within a family.

Social responses are therefore a key part of the concrete particulars in specific cases. To comprehend and acknowledge the victim's situational and private logic — how the victim interprets and responds in situ to the offender during and after assaults and other forms of abuse, and sometimes before — it is necessary to ask specific questions to learn about social responses. This is an enquiry into a context of complex relationships and institutional practices. The response-based conceptual framework guides our analysis, our questions and our report templates. It is a philosophical orientation that leads one to look here, in the direction of proficiency, protection of self and others and the bonds that motivate behaviour rather than a set of steps designed to look there, toward deficiency and pathology.

The following example is from Lucy, who was eight years old at the time. She is describing her experience of protecting herself, while also trying to protect her mom from her father's violence. This conversation was in the context of sharing her views in a family law dispute and has been provided with full consent. Names and identifying details have been changed.

> L: When he gets started, my mom gives me a signal and I have to go upstairs …
>
> S: What kind of a signal?
>
> L: Umm. She points up the stairs with her thumb.
>
> S: Where do you go … once you get upstairs?
>
> L: I go to the bathroom. It's the only room we have with a locking door.
>
> S: Was that your idea, or your mom's idea?
>
> L: That was my mom's idea. That's where I always go.
>
> S: What do you do when you're in the bathroom?
>
> L: I flush the toilet over and over and over so that I can't hear what he is saying to her. But if I hear things crashing, I go to the door and make sure I can hear sounds coming from my mom, so I know she's alive.
>
> S: So, it sounds like you have a system? Like … you flush the toilet over and over and over to drown out the noise, but in a way … you're still listening … just in case he becomes even more dangerous, and your mom gets really badly hurt or even killed … you believe he might kill her?
>
> L: I know he will kill her one of these times. The last time it happened, I heard him throw her down the stairs. I could tell that's what he did, because I could hear her falling and screaming. I thought … I can either run to my bedroom, climb out the window and down the tree, run across

the yard and down the back alley, and then it's only a block to the police station and I can try and get some help for her. Or … I can just run out of the bathroom and down the stairs and try to stop him, to make sure she's ok all by myself.

S: So … what did you do … how did you decide?

L: I ran downstairs. I knew I wouldn't have time to run and get help if she was really hurt and he's never hurt me … only her … so I was pretty sure he wouldn't throw me down the stairs. I was right, he was scared when he saw me and ran out the front door. How does someone change so fast from beating up my mom to stopping like that … just stopping?

There is nothing new in the fact that adults and children resist violence and other forms of oppression. Resistance is as real and "factual" as violence. This means that detailed accounts of victims' resistance should be routinely visible in all institutional settings, particularly those that respond to cases of violence and to the people involved. Effective intervention begins with accurate analysis of the facts on the ground, with a minimum of theory. Detailed accounts, in context, allow seemingly small acts to become understandable as resisting violence. Random acts have purpose:

- a mother pointing her thumb
- a child choosing to enter the bathroom
- a child flushing the toilet
- the exact time that a child chooses to leave the bathroom, and where she goes

"Going elsewhere" in your mind can be understood as a memory, or a way of withstanding torture. Symptoms of mental health or behavioural challenges can be understood as appropriate sadness, worry, anger and fear. Lucy shared her mother's fear, because each understood his rage and they feared for themselves and one another. Her mother shared, "When you are truly afraid of someone and know what they are capable of, you do not want to challenge them or anger them for fear of unleashing what you know they could do. The only thing I could do, while waiting until it was safe enough to get out, was protect my daughter as much as possible."

A year after Lucy's mother escaped, Lucy had court-ordered supervised visits with her father. The first account of these visits is from the supervisor's report. The second account includes Lucy's responses and resistance to her father and the supervisor.

First account

He arrives 10 minutes early for the supervised visit.

He jokes with the receptionist, and then enters the playroom and asks the supervisor about her weekend.

He is inside laughing and joking with the supervisor. She laughs along with him at a joke he told her.

Together with the supervisor, they get up excitedly as his daughter slowly enters the room.

He speaks loudly and moves toward her, "I missed you, honey!"

The supervisor moves beside the girl and nudges her slightly in the direction of her father.

He bends down, looking her in the eyes and smiling, and asks her how she and her mom have been doing this week.

He reminds her that school is almost out, and that he would love to take her on a vacation this year!

Wouldn't she love to go on an adventure, to a sunny country with an ocean and beaches?

The supervisor exclaims that this sounds magical, and that "every child dreams about swimming in the ocean with dolphins."

He waits about 3 minutes while his daughter goes to the washroom. He jokes with the supervisor about his ex-wife.

She returns and they sit together on the couch. He speaks to her in a loud voice, "I'm sorry that your mother is putting you through this, baby. You don't deserve it. We should be able to go outside and play together, alone! This is bullshit!"

The supervisor puts her hand on his shoulder but doesn't say a word.

He says, "I know, I know. It just isn't fair … I love her so much …."

Second account

He arrives 10 minutes early for the supervised visit.

She sees his car in the parking lot when she arrives with her mother and begins to cry. She doesn't want to get out of the car.

He jokes with the receptionist, and then enters the playroom and asks the supervisor about her weekend.

Her mom tries to assure her that she will be safe, and that the supervisor will not leave her alone. She is biting her nails so close to the nail bed that blood is running down her fingers.

He is inside laughing and joking with the supervisor. She laughs along with him at a joke he told her.

The girl gets out of the car and enters the building. She believes that if she doesn't go to these visits, which have been ordered by the judge, her dad will kill her mom.

Together with the supervisor, the father gets up excitedly as his daughter slowly enters the room.

She notices that the supervisor and her father are friends, because the supervisor looks at him and smiles. This scares the girl.

He speaks loudly and moves toward her, "I missed you, honey!"

He has never called her "honey" before. She doesn't like it, and she moves to the side. She knows he is doing it to convince the supervisor that he is a good and loving father.

The supervisor moves beside the girl and nudges her slightly in the direction of her father.

The girl stiffens and doesn't know what to do. Now she knows for sure that they are on the same side and that she is not safe in here. Her dad has convinced this woman that he is good, the way he convinces everyone.

He bends down, looking her in the eyes and smiling, and asks her how she and her mom have been doing this week.

The girl whispers, "Fine." He's not supposed to ask about her mom, and he knows that. Why isn't the supervisor stopping him? Why can't that woman see that his mouth smiles, but his eyes are mean? The girl knows he is scaring her on purpose.

He reminds her that school is almost out, and that he would love to take her on a vacation this year!

She doesn't answer him.

Wouldn't she love to go on an adventure, to a sunny country with an ocean and beaches?

She knows that he is telling her that he can take her away from her mom and never bring her back. He's told her that before.

The supervisor exclaims that this sounds magical, and that "every child dreams about swimming in the ocean with dolphins."

She says that she has to go to the bathroom. She knows she can hide in there for 3 minutes without causing suspicion. It's her only break in the hour.

He waits about 3 minutes while his daughter goes to the washroom. He jokes with the supervisor about his ex-wife.

She can hear them laughing together as she walks back to the playroom from the bathroom. They are friends.

She returns and they sit together on the couch. He speaks to her in a voice that is too loud. "I'm sorry that your mother is putting you through this, baby. You don't deserve it. We should be able to go outside and play together, alone! This is bullshit!"

She looks at the floor. Tears are running down her face. She bites her nails and her fingers are bleeding. She is thinking, "I am not your baby. I am not your honey. I am not your daughter anymore." She is silent.

The supervisor puts her hand on his shoulder but doesn't say a word.

She did not stop him from scaring her or threatening her or yelling at her. She is on his side. If he has the chance, he will kill her mom.

He says, "I know, I know. It just isn't fair … I love her so much …."

She watches the clock. The second hand hits the 12 and she gets up. She doesn't look back. It's Tuesday. She has freedom until Thursday, when this will happen again.

WHAT A CHILD IS OR ISN'T DOING RATHER THAN WHAT A CHILD OUGHT TO DO

We continue to broaden our understanding of what young people do when they are victimized by others, which is revealed through a series of interactions between victim(s) and perpetrator(s). What happens after experiencing violence is closely connected to the social responses that are perceived and received by both perpetrators and victims of violence. What has happened, what is happening and what a child's greatest hopes might be — these are the questions that we seek to understand, as they form the foundation of an analysis and helping practice. Perhaps Pippi Longstocking says it best as she articulates what a child is or isn't doing, rather than what others believe they ought to do:

> You understand, Teacher, don't you, that when you have a mother who's an angel and a father who is a cannibal king, and when you have sailed on the ocean all your whole life, then you don't know just how to behave in school with all the apples and ibexes (Lindgren 1950, 58–9).

YOU DON'T SAY: CHILDREN WHO CHOOSE SILENCE

by Shelly Dean

You don't ever say …

I know what to do.
I protect myself as well as I can, and I protect the people I love.
I am not broken.
I know how to talk, I know how to smile, I know how to stay quiet.
I make many, many decisions.
I don't say.
That the fairies lifted me to the ceiling until the danger was over.
I know that they will say I'm crazy.
They might tell me the fairies aren't real.
Even if my life depends on them.
The fairies are the only place I am believed, protected, and guided.
Their response is my salvation.
That is real.
I won't say.
Where I hid when I ran away
It isn't because nobody asked.
It isn't because I didn't think they could take it, if I told
It's because I won't make my mother cry with the truth.
I can't say.
What the kids did to me on the first day of school
And on each day that followed …
I don't have to say the words to my sister.
She saw my face, and gently wiped it clean before anybody else came home.
She won't tell dad.
I don't say.
A word about what is happening at home.
They say, "tell someone if you need help."
I don't know who 'someone' is?
'Someone' doesn't sound safe, or private, or a person who will change anything.

'Someone' might make everything worse.
You don't ever say …
It means something that I despair against the smell of alcohol.
I long for the days that weren't filled with haunted smells and sickly sounds.
What I despair against is what I long for.
I know things.
I've promised myself a different life.
You don't say …
It makes sense that I would protect my mother.
That I sit there, atop the stairs, waiting … and watching …
Knowing that nobody is safe.
I was told it isn't a child's job to look after their parent.
But it isn't a job.
It's love.
What else am I supposed to do?
You don't say.
Space to speak freely means you won't force me to tell.
My privacy is my dignity, and I get to choose who, and when.
That means you won't force me to stop something I do.
or start something I don't need.
Maybe "I don't know" means "I can't say."
Maybe … of course I know.
People ask … why didn't I say something?
I did say!
They did not hear but turned away.
I said it again.
They said I should not hurt anyone.
I knew I did not matter.
My dancing eyes changed.
They became slow and watchful.
And I said nothing at all.
That says everything.

ACKNOWLEDGEMENTS

We wish to acknowledge all the children, youth and former children who have taught us, and continue to teach us what to pay attention to. They teach us of the many harms that come from diagnosing, medicating and other forms of misunderstanding done by those who are charged with serving the health and well-being of children and families. As a former youth from Canada's foster care system stated, "They said I have attachment disorder. Really, I have a life disorder. I attach accordingly." She was referring to growing up without meaningful relationships or lasting and trustworthy adults in her life.

SUGGESTED READINGS

Carr, Alan. 2009. "The Effectiveness of Family Therapy and Systemic Interventions for Child-Focused Problems." *Journal of Family Therapy* 3.

Kelly, Liz. 1988. *Surviving Sexual Violence*. Minneapolis: University of Minnesota Press.

Maxwell, Krista. 2017. "Settler-humanitarianism: Healing the Indigenous Child-Victim." *Comparative Studies in Society and History* 59.

Överlien, Carolina and Margareta Hydén. 2009. "Children's Actions When Experiencing Domestic Violence." *Childhood* 16, 4.

Reynolds, Vikki. 2008. "An Ethic of Resistance: Frontline Worker as Activist." *Women Making Waves* 19.

REFERENCES

Aimé Césaire. 1950. *Discourse on Colonialism*. New York: Monthly Review Press.

Chen, Wenxin, Monica Cepoiu-Martin, Antonia Stang, Diane Duncan, Chris Symonds, Lara Cooke, et al. 2018. "Antipsychotic prescribing and safety monitoring practices in children and youth: a population-based study in Alberta, Canada." *Clinical Drug Investigation* 38.

Coates, Linda, Shelly Dean, Catherine Richardson and Allan Wade. 2014. *Response-based Contextual Analysis in Cases of Violence*. Unpublished manuscript.

Coates, Linda. 2018. "Masterclass Language and Violence." *Insight Exchange*. December 6, 2018. youtube.com/watch?v=gnlHFDoHyG0.

____. 2022. "You Don't Say: Children Who Choose Silence." Unpublished.

Dean, Shelly, K. McIntosh and Cathy Richardson. 2021. *Stanley on the Shoulders of Giants: How Children Respond to Violence*. Tellwell Talent.

Dutton, Don. 2006. *Rethinking Domestic Violence*. Vancouver: UBC Press.

Goffman E. 1963. *Stigma: Notes on the management of spoiled identity*. New York, NY: Simon and Schuster.

Kelly, Liz. 1988. *Surviving Sexual Violence*. Minneapolis: University of Minnesota Press.

Lindgren, Astrid. 1950. *Pippi Longstocking*. New York: The Viking Press.

Maruna, Shadd and Michelle Butler. 2013. "Violent Self-narratives and the Hostile Attributional Bias." In *Behavioural Analysis of Crime: Studies in David Centre's Investigative Psychology*, edited by Donna Youngs. Ashgate Publishing Ltd.

O'Brien Institute for Public Health. 2022. "Response to High Number of Deaths of Indigenous Children in Child Intervention Services." University of Calgary.

Reynolds, Vikki. 2014. "Resisting and Transforming Rape Culture: An Activist Stance for Therapeutic Work with Men Who Have Used Violence." *The No to Violence Journal*.

Scott, Joan C. 1990. *Domination and the Arts of Resistance*. New Haven: Yale University Press.

Tener, Dafna, and Carmit Katz. 2021. "Preadolescent Peer Sexual Abuse: A Systematic Literature Review." *Trauma, Violence, & Abuse* 22, 3.

Todd, Nick, and Allen Wade. 1994. "Deficiency, Domination and Psychotherapy." *The Calgary Participator* 46.

Todd, Nick, Allan Wade and Martine Renaux. 2004. "Coming to Terms with Violence and Resistance: From a Language of Effects to a Language of Responses." In *Furthering Talk: Advances in the Discursive Therapies*, edited by Sally McNamee, Thomas Strong and David Pare. Boston: Springer.

Todd, Nick. 2000. "An Eye for an I: Response-based Work with Perpetrators of Abuse." *Men's Crisis Service*, Calgary, AB. Unpublished paper.

Ubelacker, Sheryl. 2017. "Ontario children and youth with ADHD often prescribed antipsychotics, study finds." *CBC News*. January 18, 2017. cbc.ca/news/canada/toronto/ontario-children-and-youth-with-adhd-often-prescribed-antipsychotics-study-finds-1.3942049.

Wade, Allan. 1999. "Resistance to Interpersonal Violence: Implications for the Practice of Therapy." Doctoral dissertation, University of Victoria.

Wade, Allan. 2018. "Knowledge Keeper and Expert Hearing on Child and Family Welfare Winnipeg Day 5." *National Inquiry for Missing and Murdered Women and Girls*. October 5, 2018. facebook.com/MMIWG/videos/634127340347801/.

Walker, Lenore. 1984. *The battered woman syndrome*. New York: Springer.

Chapter 13

CALLING ALL WARRIORS

Indigenous Social Workers Fighting Inequity Within the Child Welfare System

by Carolyn Peacock and Brooke Lightning-Montour

CHAPTER FOCUS

In this chapter, we share a story of a frontline experience that we believe has important teachings for new frontline social workers. It is written in a storytelling format as Carolyn has always been a storyteller, and because we choose to honour the process of Cree storytelling rather than write in an academic format. We share our story of a particular situation that we faced and refer to some of the literature that supports our work. We use these and other questions to guide our critical assessment of the current state of reconciliation and its impact, if any, on the child welfare system and to help guide our thoughts.

QUESTIONS ADDRESSED IN THIS CHAPTER

1. How does anti-Indigenous racism play out in the age of reconciliation?
2. Does a divide remain between social workers who work on the reserve as opposed to off reserve?
3. What are the roles of Western and non-Indigenous attachment theories in anti-Indigenous racism in child welfare?
4. How can workers resist ongoing anti-Indigenous racism in child welfare and other social work practice areas?

WHO WE ARE

Carolyn

My name is Carolyn Peacock, and I am from the Enoch Cree Nation in Alberta. I am a mother of four and grandmother of thirteen. I have worked in child welfare on reserve since 1988. After graduating with my college diploma in social work and continuing my education journey with my BSW and then MSW, I became a director of First Nations Child and Family Services for two delegated First Nation agencies in Alberta on reserve beginning in 1995. I was asked by my friend and sister of my heart Jeannine Carrière to once again write a chapter for the third edition of *Walking This Path Together*. For this latest chapter, I have asked my friend and colleague Brooke Lightning-Montour to join me. We have worked together for the last eleven years, and she is the assistant director of Kasohkowew Child Wellness Society, which is the agency where I am currently director. She will succeed me when I retire, and it has been my honour to be her teacher. I have learned so much from her. Brooke is truly a person who walks her talk, and I believe that she has helped me become a better social worker and person.

Brooke

My name is Brooke Lightning-Montour, and I am Cree from the Samson Cree Nation. My social work journey began in 2008, and I have had the privilege of working alongside Carolyn for the last eleven years. Together we have worked through some of the most tragic and heart wrenching cases. I have learned so much from her strong spirit. Her hope is infectious. She has been a leader in the social work field for over forty years, a feat that not only shows in her work but also in her character. It is said that it is in times of adversity and change when true character is revealed, and such is the case with Carolyn. It is my honour to share any insights I may have with future social workers.

THE AGE OF "RECONCILIATION"

In 2015, Canada's Truth and Reconciliation Commission issued 94 Calls to Action specific to child welfare (TRC 2015b). Since then, federal and provincial/territorial governments have taken various steps towards reconciliation in child welfare. For example, in 2020 the federal government passed a new law, Bill C-92, An Act respecting First Nations, Inuit and Métis children, youth and families, intended to reduce Indigenous disproportionality in child welfare (Government of Canada n.d.); the province of Alberta subsequently produced twenty-six recommendations for policy changes. Yet it is our experience that there are many disparities between these formal commitments to reconciliation and what policy dictates to First Nations community child welfare agencies in Alberta. The challenges of resolving these disparities and contradictions fall most heavily on the shoulders of Indigenous social workers.

In previous editions of *Walking This Path Together*, Carolyn described the challenges of working within her Indigenous community as the director of an Indigenous child welfare agency, trying to be a "good" social worker while striving to do what is right by your people (Peacock 2009; Carrière and Peacock 2015). These challenges still exist and are now compounded by added pressure to reconcile the damages created from past systems. With limited resources and amid Alberta's mounting racism and resistance to acknowledge our people's inherent rights, we as Indigenous social workers press on to support our people in a good way. But there will always be dissension in this context until we have total control of child welfare legislation in our nations.

Many social workers enter this field filled with the hope that they can change the world. Indigenous social workers do not enter this field to be "good" social workers. We get into this field to do what is right. Because we are expected to walk between two worlds, it is inevitable that those two worlds will not only intersect but often contradict, leading to feelings of personal discord or internal conflict. Perhaps we were naïve in thinking that we could embrace provincial policies and work with the province to make changes for our people. This could not be further from the truth. Colonialism is rooted in systems and institutions designed to "remove the Indian from the child," as per Prime Minister John A. Macdonald's intentions so many years ago. According to Hanson et al. (2020), "from the 1990s onward, the government and the churches involved — Anglican, Presbyterian, United, and Roman Catholic — began to acknowledge their responsibility for an education scheme that was specifically designed to 'kill the Indian in the child.'" With this in mind, we ask ourselves: is reconciliation just another stop over on this inevitable journey towards assimilation? Are we contributing to the harm inflicted on our people's most cherished gifts from the Creator?

In our years of working with foster parents, we have met many who are conscientious and caring and open their homes to legitimately give a child a better option than having no home and no family experience. However, not all foster parents are drawn to a higher emotional calling. In our experience, there are some foster parents who gainfully work the system to manipulate the needs of the children in their care so as to ensure that they as foster parents receive the maximum payment available. This is clearly not in the best interest of the child or children, many of whom are left with a lifetime of stigma, poor self-esteem and doubt, all of which may contribute to depression and possibly death. Often these same foster parents neglect the basic needs of the children they are supposed to protect for their own personal gain. Clearly these sorts of people should not be licensed to operate a foster home for any child, Indigenous or otherwise, and it is the task of social workers and the agencies they work for to ensure that they do not become, or do not continue to be, foster parents. The story we tell in this chapter is about how, in the midst of "reconciliation," Indigenous workers in an Indigenous agency were, despite their best efforts, unable to protect an Indigenous youth from a foster parent such as those described — a foster parent unable to care for Indigenous children in loving and child-centred ways.

APPROACHING INDIGENOUS CHILD WELFARE

It is our belief that child service systems are stacked against Indigenous children and families in many ways. For example, it is our experience that attachment theory, as described below, continues to be used to assimilate Indigenous children into white settler culture. One erroneous view that supports assimilation is that our children have greater success when they are cared for by non-Indigenous caregivers. Similarly, there is a pervasive belief that the emotional bonds that formed between a child and their primary non-Indigenous caregiver is sufficient for their well-being. Although we do not dispute that emotional bonds are important between a child and a caregiver, the quality of those bonds must be assessed to determine whether they are healthy or toxic. Our observations and interactions with the foster parent we discuss in this chapter lead us to conclude that they have taught the foster children to deny who they are, and that being Indigenous is negative. The foster parent has also taught them that traditional practices of smudging and praying are witchcraft and that Indigenous people "get high" from the smoke when we smudge with sweetgrass. Our lived experiences are consistent with a long line of policies intended to "take the Indian out of the child."

The Role of Attachment Theory

White Western theories about attachment are dominated by the ideas of John Bowlby and Mary Ainsworth (Ainsworth and Bowlby 1991), who classified the type of attachment an infant or child has formed based on their responses, typically to one caregiver. Indigenous concepts of connection to culture, family and community of origin conflict with attachment theory. While attachment theory focuses on the bonds formed between individuals, especially in infancy and childhood, the Indigenous concept of connection emphasizes the broader web of relationships that shape a person's identity and experiences throughout their life (Smith 2012). In a comparison between these two frameworks for child welfare practice, it is evident that Indigenous connection theory emerges as the logical concept for Indigenous children in terms of its depth and holistic perspective. Indigenous children have a kinship system that must not be ignored by non-Indigenous caregivers.

Western notions of attachment primarily emphasize the impact of early caregiving experiences on an individual's psychological development and attachment style and the significance of early relationships in shaping an individual's emotional well-being and ability to form healthy relationships in adulthood (Ainsworth and Bowlby 1991; Fear 2017). Although attachment bonds maybe an important factor in human development, they are not the only factor. Indigenous theories such as connection or connectedness encompass all aspects of the human experience; emotional, spiritual, physical and mental bonds are all equally important. Too often with Indigenous children in care there has been an underlying assumption that they are better off away from any Indigenous influence. In our experience, attachment theory has been used to sever kinship connections for Indigenous children. Finestone (2023, 207) states:

> It is, for instance, important to determine how one can decolonize "attachment theory" so that the framework for healthy attachment is not based in the desire to either reproduce (or mimic) the supremacy of the biological/nuclear family, and instead is shaped by an intention to emplace Indigenous children within networks of loving and self-determining kin (human and more-than-human). However, in a context where an Indigenous child is on the cusp of removal, the urgent need to make use of imperfect theories as a means of being heard, understood, and taken seriously by the Powers That Be represents a strategic avenue towards refusal in colonial conditions.

In the case of the non-Indigenous foster parent with whom we worked, attachment theory became the underlying focus of a judicial trial as the "colonial condition." Throughout the trial, there was an unwillingness to acknowledge any connections that the children in question had with their culture, birth family and community of origin. In many instances, representatives of the judicial system and the child welfare system called the foster parent "mom." During the trial, the focus became about whom the children were attached to and any other argument or theory was negated, further solidifying the colonial condition that has been long held within Canada's judicial system. Traditionally, one of the principles shared by Elders regarding child-raising and the best interests of a child was the idea of strong connection to one's identity, as children need to know their identity, culture and language. These are passed down from generation to generation (Wahkohtowin 2021). This world view was not only not supported during the trial we experienced, but it was also not even explored.

What those who subscribe to Western attachment theory do not acknowledge is that there are deeper bonds, cellular and spiritual, that set Indigenous connection theory apart as a logical concept for Indigenous children in care. Unlike attachment theory, which is limited in scope, connection theory recognizes the influence of cultural heritage, extended family dynamics and community support systems as some of the diverse factors that shape an individual's identity and experiences. This Indigenous world view and child development theory support the idea that these elements contribute significantly to an individual's sense of self, resilience and overall well-being. Connection theory also focuses on the importance of ancestral ties, language and environment as positive influences for child and youth development (Neckoway et al. 2007; Carrière and Richardson 2009).

The concept of connection to culture, family and community of origin recognizes that human development is not solely determined by one's individual attachment relationships but also by the broader sociocultural context in which they grow and thrive (Absolon 2010; Neckoway et al. 2007; Carrière and Richardson 2017). Connection encompasses the bonds formed with family members, cultural traditions and the community at large. It acknowledges that these multifaceted connections influence an individual's values, beliefs and sense of belonging, extending beyond the early caregiver-child attachment. Connection honours who this child was before they were apprehended as well as the birth family, community and nation that this child has come from. A connection approach should be established policy for Indigenous children in care to resolve further harm to Indigenous communities (Blackstock 2001, 2016; Sinclair 2017). It provides a framework to Indigenize our thoughts and actions into active healing processes that simultaneously decolonize and Indigenize (Absolon 2010).

THE FOSTERING STORY

Our involvement with the foster parent began when she called the youth's caseworker in our agency. A youth and his siblings had been placed by a previous caseworker in an off reserve foster home that contracted their services to the Alberta government. The foster parent demanded that we pick up our male youth or she would drop him off at our office. We picked him up and, because he was placed in the home as part of a sibling group, we removed both him and his sister from the home. When they were picked up by their caseworker the boy, who was fourteen years old at the time, was in diapers. Both youths had very poor physical hygiene and their clothes were filthy and too small for them. The clothing needed to be disposed of as the odour could not be washed out. Both of the youth had been home-schooled by their foster mother and isolated from their family and community with no contact with their kinship circle. We believe that this was done to control them and to hide that they were not the high special needs kids the foster parent was making them out to be. In fact, after we moved them, their personal hygiene immediately improved. The youth commented that they loved their new clothes and the food and mostly they loved going to school and being around other youth. It should be noted that the youth was out of diapers within a week.

This foster parent's neglect of the emotional, social and spiritual needs of these youth was concealed for far too long. Her isolation of the youth, primarily through home-schooling them, hid them from any external scrutiny. The children had minimal contact with their broader community of origin, further exacerbating their isolation. She removed them from public school and decided to home-school them without the agency's knowledge. When their behaviours became too much for her to handle, she demanded that we immediately come and take the children. Had there been open communication, regular meetings or openness to suggestions on how to collaborate on the upbringing of the children, most of the concerns would not have occurred.

As we stated earlier, the steps taken by the foster parent seemed calculated to obscure the fact that the children should not be categorized as "special needs." In Alberta, special needs designations typically come about through assessment by a team of professionals, including psychologists, educators and medical experts. However, in this instance, it appears that the assessment might have been compromised or misrepresented by the foster parent. Responsibility for monitoring the children fell under the purview of the foster care agency yet their oversight failed to detect the ongoing neglect. Our decision to move the children to a new home was imperative to ensure their well-being. The new caregivers provided a stark contrast to the former foster parent, offering a nurturing environment that prioritized the children's cultural heritage and educational needs. Despite the trauma of a sudden placement change, these youth did not express a desire to return to their previous foster home, indicating the depth of their maltreatment.

Within a couple of weeks of the move, the foster mother requested visits with both children, which our agency denied. Due to the extent of the neglect the youth experienced in her care we felt it was not conducive to their well-being to have her visit with them. She then submitted an "Administrative Review," a procedure that allows caregivers and/or children in care to request a review of a decision made by Alberta Children's Services. The administrative review panel upheld our agency's decision. When someone disagrees with a decision Alberta Children's Services makes, they have an opportunity to file a complaint with the Alberta Appeals Secretariat, otherwise known as the "Appeal Panel." The foster parent called the Alberta Children's Advocate who immediately filed a complaint with the Appeal Panel. The panel then referred the matter to the statutory director, who requested that we work out details of visitation with the foster parent. Carolyn agreed to try mediation, although the agency's past experiences with the foster parent is that she always agreed to these sorts of processes, but then did not follow through. We generally try to use the least intrusive measures possible. In this situation, however, it was challenging due to the foster parent's resistance or refusal to follow through on previous agreements.

Neither the remedial discussions with the statutory director nor at the Appeal Panel determined a resolution. Hence, we were ordered by a judge to continue to allow the visits. It was determined by the judge that we needed to honour the relationship that had developed between the youth and their foster parent because they had spent considerable in her home. The judge's argument was that the emotional bonds these children had developed with her were first and foremost over other considerations. When we argued that the concealed neglect had to be considered, the judge interpreted this as bullying by the children services department against the foster parent. The judge not only refused to listen to our side of the story but went so far as to state that we were vilifying white people. The issues of neglect and spiritual abuse that surfaced after we moved the youth from her care were continuously denied. We therefore insisted that the visits with their previous caregiver be supervised.

When the visits began, so did the complications. For example, we had planned the visits to occur outdoors at a local park. However, the foster parent made excuses as to why this was not suitable and proceeded to take both youth back to her home and refused to return them. She kept them for three days longer than the agreed time. We requested assistance from the Ministry of Children Services Crisis Unit, local RCMP and Ministry staff but to our dismay, none would assist us in having the children returned. No reasons were given. The request for assistance was simply ignored. On the third day of her refusal to return them, we had no choice but to get an apprehension order to have the youth returned to the agency's care and to the home in which we had placed them. Following this incident, the statutory director, the foster parent's legal counsel and the youth's counsel provided by the advocate's office, all supported the foster parent despite the evidence that she had breached her agreements with the agency by over-keeping them. The various individuals and agencies supporting the foster parent provided reasons for this support that often seemed to prioritize the stability of the foster home over the children's cultural heritage. Some argued that the foster parent had provided a structured environment, emphasizing the children's attachment to the foster parent as paramount. Others believed that the children's high needs designation justified their placement in the home, despite any neglect of their physical, social or spiritual needs.

In the foster parent's emails to our caseworker, we discovered to our shock that she had contacted the youth's psychiatrist to transfer previous prescriptions of tranquilizers to her pharmacy prior to the visit occurring. The pharmacist provided the medication to her on the basis of the rapport they had previously established, and because she misrepresented herself as the youth's legal guardian. The foster parent had no legal authority to call the psychiatrist to request medication. Typically, foster parents require the consent of a director to discuss a foster child's situation with a psychiatrist treating the youth, and only legal guardians are authorized to consent to medications administered to children. We also believe that the absence of community involvement and consistent visitation from the caseworker further solidified her negative stance about their cognitive abilities. The fewer people who saw the youth, the easier it was for the lies about their cognitive inabilities to become the truth.

Following the over-keeping of the children, Carolyn received a call from the statutory director asking if we were going to follow the court order regarding the visits with this foster parent. This call occurred despite the foster parent's very concerning behaviours in over-keeping and in requesting medication that she did not have the authority to request or receive on behalf of the children. Carolyn replied that we were trying to return to court to have the order varied. However, following that telephone discussion, the statutory director revoked Carolyn's delegation authority specifically regarding these youth on the basis that Carolyn was defying a direct order given by the statutory director.

Delegation authority is typically given to directors of children's services agencies under Alberta's Child, Youth and Family Enhancement Act. That authority is then subdelegated by agency directors to frontline workers. In this case, delegated authority was revoked for the two youth only but not for the other two hundred plus children for whom Carolyn is responsible. When he returned the youth to the foster parent's care, the statutory director contravened procedures and processes that he is required to follow both in our agency services agreement with Alberta and in the Act.

In our view, the statutory director's actions appeared to prioritize optics over the critical needs of Indigenous children in care. Instead of addressing the systemic issues and concerns raised by the community regarding the neglect of cultural heritage and ancestral ties, the director seemed more focused on maintaining a facade of efficiency and stability within the foster care system. By downplaying or dismissing the grievances brought forward by the Indigenous community, the director's approach underscored a concerning disregard for the well-being and cultural identity of the children under their care. This emphasis on appearances rather than the substantive needs of Indigenous youth reflects a systemic failure to prioritize the rights and dignity of marginalized communities within the child welfare system.

Attachment or Connection?

The situation we describe highlights a concerning pattern where multiple agencies and individuals, including parts of the legal system, disregard the concerns raised by the First Nations involved. It raises questions about whether these agencies are influenced by entrenched beliefs about attachment or possibly even by underlying racist attitudes that downplay the importance of preserving Indigenous identity and cultural connections.

The events surrounding the youth caused us to reflect on how attachment theory was used in this situation. While mainstream attachment theory may provide valuable insights into the significance of early emotional bonds, the concept of connection to culture, family and community of origin is, we think, the logical theory due to its more encompassing nature. Connection to origins recognizes the multifaceted influences that shape an individual's identity and experiences, emphasizing the importance of cultural heritage, extended family relationships and community ties. By embracing this holistic perspective, we gain a deeper understanding of human development in the interconnected web of relationships which contribute to our well-being and sense of belonging in the world.

Furthermore, we believe that Indigenous connection to origins promotes a more comprehensive understanding of human relationships and development than white Western theories. Indigenous theory acknowledges that attachment bonds are just one facet of a person's interconnected existence, which is deeply intertwined with cultural, familial and community ties. This holistic perspective encourages us to appreciate the richness and complexity of human experiences, valuing the interplay between attachment relationships and the broader connections that define our sense of self and belonging. The actions of the larger human services systems put in place to not only protect its citizens but also to uphold best interests for the child negated these beliefs and perspectives.

During this situation it became clear to us that that there is a hidden set of rules for Indigenous people and/or agencies that does not apply to non-Indigenous people and/or agencies. We experienced the blatant disregard of the connection to origin for Indigenous families and their children. How can this be, we wondered, when this very system has made promises to reconcile these systemic discriminations and prejudices?

In the area of child welfare, legislation that controls child worker action has not substantially moved towards anything approximating reconciliation. In Alberta, the child welfare system still defines good social workers as those who are compliant with rules that fail to recognize the unique needs of Indigenous children. Rather than follow rules, we need to do what is right by Indigenous children and their families.

RECONCILIATION — WHAT DOES IT REALLY MEAN?

Reconciliation has become a catch phrase that is typically used to placate Indigenous Peoples rather than to make significant strides in reconciling past systems. Despite public statements committing to reconciliation, the Alberta government continues to operate under the same rules and regulations that applied prior to these commitments being made, rules and regulations that continue to oppress our people.

Rather than being viewed as a good or compliant social worker according to Western child welfare systems, we need to do what is right by the people we work alongside. We believe that an anti-oppressive approach supports us to "do right." Anti-oppressive theory influenced our decision-making in this foster parent situation. Here are two anti-oppressive practice principles that we observed and experienced:

1. Be prepared to carry the images and stories of the children and youth. They will always be with you. You will ask yourself if they are having a good life and how things worked out. We can hear something or see another child who resembles a child we have worked with, and we are taken back. We have been in contact with a lot of children and youth who have become adults and there have been some good stories and some not so good.
2. Hold what you know in confidence. Even if you leave the field, remember that what you know is confidential for the rest of your life and not just while you worked with children and families. In these positions, we often unknowingly and progressively become "profilers," and we need to be cautious of our judgments against people who may be innocent. This is particularly so for social workers who deal with various types of people in trauma. Judgment is a trap that all longtime social workers sustain while in active practice. We also need to recognize when we ourselves are using unhealthy ways to cope. Lateral violence, gossip and political differences can be used to hurt each other. This must stop. Walk away, say no and don't participate in it or encourage it.

Based on our interactions with her and our practice knowledge, we believe that the foster mother manipulated the children's behaviours so that she could continue to receive higher funding under Alberta's special needs foster care rates. She isolated the youth from everyone, home-schooling them so no one could see how they were being cared for. These children never went to school, they never passed a grade, they had no friends and they were not allowed to go anywhere. She created fears in the youth so that they feared their home of origin, their Indigenous community and our agency. Preying on their self-worth, she maliciously taught them that it is not positive to be Indigenous or to practise traditional praying and smudging with sweetgrass or other medicines. These are acts which some see as the most extreme forms of racism (Rose 2021). Such acts also serve another purpose. Adam Barker (2021) conducted research on settler colonialism and the legacies of the colonial institutions and practices used to disadvantage Indigenous people and communities. He explains how problematizing Indigenous people as pathological takes the focus away from colonial and systemic issues by labelling Indigenous people as the problem instead.

Both cultural connection to origins and careful planning play pivotal roles in the well-being and development of children in care. For children placed in foster homes or residential facilities, maintaining a strong tie to their cultural heritage is essential for several reasons. First, it provides a sense of identity and belonging, helping them to understand who they are and where they come from. This connection can boost their self-esteem and self-worth, as it reinforces their unique cultural background. Moreover, cultural connection to origins can act as a source of emotional support. It offers a bridge between the child's past and present, creating stability in an otherwise tumultuous life. This continuity can help them navigate the challenges they may face in the children services system with a stronger sense of self and purpose. Planning for children in care should encompass their cultural needs and aspirations. Careful consideration of their background and heritage must be part of the placement process. This includes selecting caregivers who are culturally respectful and humble. They must be able to provide an environment where the child's customs, traditions and language are respected and celebrated. When we create opportunities for the child to engage with their culture through activities, events or connections with their extended family we not only honour their heritage but also the community or nation they come from.

Over the years the foster parent we described never brought the children to any cultural activities within the community. She always made excuses as to why they couldn't visit their home community. Even though a home study was ordered by the judge, the foster parent remained defiant and tried to control both how the home study was conducted (including refusing to let the Safe Home Study writer see the youth alone) and how the cultural connection plan is implemented.

This case is a notable example of how Indigenous concepts of family and community connections are ignored by larger government systems. As Indigenous social workers we must thoughtfully plan and make paramount cultural connections for children in care for their overall well-being and successful transition into adulthood. It empowers them to embrace their identity, fosters strong-spiritedness and enhances their sense of belonging, ultimately providing them with a stronger foundation for a brighter future.

HAVE GOVERNMENT SYSTEMS RECONCILED WITH INDIGENOUS COMMUNITIES?

Our experiences with government systems and provincial judicial systems are that they are far from reconciling with Indigenous communities. As we shared our experiences over the past few years with many child welfare professionals involved with this terrible, abusive and oppressive foster parent situation, it has been very difficult to understand the open discrimination and racist acts we witnessed. We noticed that more racism directed at us after the discovery of the mass graves of children in the grounds of the former Kamloops Residential School. It was shocking for us to see, hear and feel the racist pushback; even when nothing racist was said, the culture of silence about challenging racism was evident.

At present, we are also witnessing First Nations developing their own child welfare legislation as part of "reconciliation." Louis Bull First Nation was the first nation to do so in Alberta. Although they continue to pave the way for First Nations that wish to enact their own child welfare law, we believe it is too early to know what impacts Bill C-92 has had or will have. Many delegated First Nation Agencies are waiting for a national funding model to support their own legislation. Our agency is moving along this path by reviewing the new Act. Our agency has also partnered with Wahkohtowin Law Lodge to conduct community research that will help spell out a legal way forward.

Reconciliation is complex and multifaceted. It can refer to different things in various contexts, but generally, it involves the process of healing and rebuilding relationships between individuals or groups that have been divided or harmed by conflict, discrimination or other forms of injustice (TRC 2015a; Wagamese 2019). Whether reconciliation is a reality or a fairytale depends on the specific circumstances, the commitment of the parties involved and the actions taken to address the underlying issues. In this foster parent case, reconciliation was reduced to a buzz word or passing fad, something to be checked off a list when human services are dealing with Indigenous people or complex issues. There seems to be no real action taken by government systems, certainly not beyond the now obligatory land acknowledgements that is offered everywhere. Reconciliation must involve acknowledging past wrongs, seeking forgiveness and also hard work towards achieving mutual understanding, empathy and cooperation. It may involve addressing historical injustices such as racism or colonialism and finding ways to rectify them (Tuck and Wang 2012). It is not a tool that should be used to vilify all non-Indigenous people, rather it is a concept offered to even the playing field for those of us that are oppressed from such systems. Matheson et al. (2022, 2) state:

> Colonization as it is recapitulated in current times meets the key criteria of Article II of the UN Convention on Genocide. The intergenerational effects of historic and ongoing systemic racism have had considerable implications for the health and well-being of Indigenous Peoples (Article IIb).

CURRENT RECONCILIATION IN CHILD SERVICES

We believe that we are on the cusp of some major changes in on-reserve child welfare services. The current chaos in child welfare across Canada must change. We are all guilty of failing Indigenous children. There must be a more collaborative and coordinated way of providing services and provincial laws, regulations and policies have to articulate with federal funding. As of December 2022, Indigenous children represented 74 percent of all children in care in Alberta (CBC 2023). Alberta Children Services has answered this crisis with a "permanency push": caregivers are being pushed to apply for private guardianship to bring down the number of children in care. This initiative has been undertaken without proper notice being given to either the First Nations or the biological families of these children. For those of us who have been in the field for so long, it is time to acknowledge the uncomfortable truth that despite our best intentions, we have been responsible for the removal and displacement of children and failing to bring them back to their families and communities. We must change our practice and policies.

Reflecting on reconciliation in the context of our experience with this foster parent, we offer these practice considerations, which keep in mind that all of us, Indigenous and non-Indigenous, are impacted by colonialism and its harmful beliefs:

1. *Complexity:* Reconciliation is a challenging and ongoing process that requires effort and commitment from all parties involved. It may take years or even generations to achieve meaningful reconciliation and it may never be fully realized in some cases. Trust your gut! If something does not feel right, follow that instinct. The situation we describe could have been avoided had we not been so trusting with the foster parent. Just because a child is in a long-term placement does not mean that the placement is appropriate for them.
2. *Reality vs. Fairytale:* Whether reconciliation is a reality or a fairytale depends on the extent to which individuals and societies are willing to confront and address the root causes of division and injustice. While reconciliation may seem idealistic or unattainable in some situations, there are numerous real-world examples where reconciliation has made significant progress, such as post-apartheid South Africa or post-genocide Rwanda (Matheson et al. 2022). We must keep pushing for Indigenous ideals, values and beliefs to be accepted as just as valid mainstream white Western ideals, values and beliefs.
3. *Persistent Racism:* Racism is a deeply ingrained and systemic issue. Achieving reconciliation in the context of ongoing racism requires a multifaceted approach that includes education, policy changes, legal reforms and community engagement. It is important to acknowledge that reconciliation does not mean ignoring or downplaying ongoing racism but rather addressing it head on.

4. *Moving Forward:* To move on in the face of persistent racism, it is crucial to take concrete actions to undo it. This includes implementing anti-racist policies, fostering dialogue and understanding among diverse groups, promoting education about the history and consequences of racism and supporting initiatives that aim to rectify past injustices.
5. *Individual and Collective Responsibility:* Reconciliation is not solely the responsibility of marginalized communities. It requires the active engagement of the individuals and institutions who actively perpetuate racism. It is important for people of all backgrounds to recognize that they have a role in dismantling racist systems and working towards a more equitable society. Reconciliation is a challenging and ongoing process that will vary in its success depending on the specific circumstances and the commitment of those involved. While it may be difficult to achieve complete reconciliation, it is possible to make meaningful progress by addressing the root causes of division and injustice.

No matter how much many Canadians would like to believe that racism is not a part of Canada, this is simply not true. Racism remains an enduring and deeply ingrained issue, persisting despite significant progress such as the Truth and Reconciliation Commission and other social justice efforts. While overt forms of racism may have declined, more subtle and systemic manifestations continue to affect individuals and communities. To address these enduring challenges, it is essential for individuals, communities and institutions to engage in ongoing self-reflection, education and proactive efforts to combat racism and promote equality for all.

How Can Ongoing Anti-Indigenous Racism in Child Welfare and Other Social Work Practice Areas Be Resisted?

We have compiled a list of several practice standards that we think social workers, Indigenous or not, should hold sacred when delivering services to children in care:

1. *Capacity building for parents and families in implementing motivational factors for the health and well-being of First Nations families*: Building the capacity of families and their children and youth means protecting and supporting the Indigenous family system and social network. Family group conferencing is one method of implementing this standard.
2. *Strengthening the extended family and kinships systems through contextual value systems provides continuity and sustainable relationships*: Raising children and youth in healthy and nurturing environments and communities is a collective and collateral responsibility. Social connections and networks are foundational for Indigenous child welfare programs. When

we begin to strengthen the extended family and kinship systems, we are not only recognizing that connection theory is a valid theory for practice, but we are also respecting the value system that was in place prior to contact. Federal and provincial governments have violated and traumatized Indigenous Peoples continuously since colonization through the Indian Act and measures such as residential schools and, currently, the child welfare system. There has always been an underlying belief that Indigenous Peoples had to engage in their own colonization and assimilation to make them into contributing members of society. This case has not only highlighted this belief, but it has also solidified the need for active decolonization measures. We as social workers need to do more to uphold the dignity of the people that we work so hard to advocate for.

3. *Traditional healing and problem-solving approaches are the strength of Indigenous families and communities*: Practice standards for safe and sustainable relationships for families and their children and youth are based on cultural values and heritage. Traditional healing such as counselling by Elders in their communities can be offered to the children and families.

4. *Community and cultural competencies of holistic healing practices*: First Nations need to identify and implement community and cultural competencies for decision-making processes and interventions. Holistic healing programs, supports and services assist us to utilize a collateral approach to family enhancement and protective services. This means that we can work with a diversity of colleagues to engage in casework practice, family violence, addictions, traditional healing, counselling, therapy, community awareness and parenting programs.

We also wish to highlight some recommendations for practice that we have observed to be beneficial for Indigenous children and families. Carolyn developed these to assist frontline practitioners entering the child welfare field:

1. *Mentors*: It is critical that students and new workers find at least two or three mentors in their field of practice (child welfare, education, health, justice, etc.). I personally have learned more from my many mentors over the years than I ever learned from my professional training. I was very fortunate to be able to work with and learn from some of the best social workers with many years of experience. They taught me the "how" of putting theory into practice; the "how to" in working with clients; work ethics; social work ethics in daily practice; and the Indigenous practice standards they incorporate into their daily practice. I learned from watching, listening and asking questions (even when I thought they were dumb questions). My mentors were there to guide me through my learning. My

mentors have included supervisors and colleagues from different fields of practice and from diverse cultural backgrounds. Some I keep in contact with; others I continue to give credit to for what they taught me. Other mentors came from the academic world, professors and colleagues whom I will always admire for their "academic smarts," their writings and their partnerships in program development. As an Indigenous director, I was able to put into practice approaches that reflect First Nations standards. None of this would have happened without one special mentor's belief that we could develop programs to change the way we provide services to our children, families and communities.

2. *Networking*: I believe that to do the work we are expected to do in social work, we need to have contacts in all kinds of other professions. Part of our responsibility as social workers is to ensure we are referring our clients to competent professionals.

3. *Continuing competency*: Ongoing learning, reading current articles, attending workshops and classes, participating in conferences, joining your professional association and writing papers are all essential parts of continuing your own learning while you are in practice.

4. *Self-care*: There are many ways to practice self-care including counselling, traditional healing, attending ceremonies, writing, smudging, praying, going to sweats, keeping a journal and debriefing stressful situations with supervisors and colleagues.

5. *Professional responsibility*: Learn your job description, personnel policies and all other policies that apply to your job, including relevant legislation, regulations, standards, codes of ethics, codes of conduct and anything else that pertains to the job that you are being paid to do. Follow up is essential. Never assume something has been done. Follow up to ensure that commitments to children and families are met.

6. *Humour*: Many Indigenous people have a great sense of humour. Cree people (and I would say most Indigenous people in Canada) have mannerisms that we use daily in communicating with each other and we don't even realize we are doing it, such as lip-pointing and saying "chuu, ma, wah-wa, chaa"! We are great storytellers, and we like to tease each other in fun and joke and laugh with each other. We also love to give nicknames in our language or other names that have a story behind them. (PS Mine is Susie ... long story!) We love to play in a safe sober way. I encourage you to laugh, play and have some fun. Our work is hard enough!

7. *Volunteer*: Join a committee through your work or professional interest, in your community, provincially or nationally. Volunteer at a local woman's shelter, hospital, or Elder's home. Your time will be appreciated.

8. *Self-evaluation*: Question your own practice, ask yourself the tough questions, change what you are not happy with and learn from your past mistakes. Develop work plans and to-do lists, and ask for feedback from coworkers, supervisors and mentors.
9. *Common sense*: Common sense is "sound practical judgment." Using practical judgment in your everyday practice promotes efficiency in decision-making. It helps find the balance in communication, problem solving, policy, theory and practice. Use it wisely. Without common sense, nothing makes sense.
10. *Intuition*: Tuning into your intuition, your "gut feeling," will help guide you in most situations. Your intuition can give you an advance warning when a situation arises that may require you to act. Intuition comes from your personal and professional experiences and can be either a positive or negative feeling. Our Elders encourage the use of intuition in their teachings. In our practice, intuition is an important ingredient in decision-making and using it wisely, consciously and responsibly provides us with an effective tool in whatever we do.
11. *Assessment*: The three most important things I learned in my social work education were assessment, assessment and assessment! It is important when working with individuals in all kinds of practice, and especially child protection, to have your own good assessment approach in addition to those required by provincial child welfare ministries or Indigenous child and family service agencies. Take the time you need to complete your assessment. Be thorough. The more information you collect, such as that found in whole person assessments, the more you will be able to assist the individual and family to make good decisions about what change is needed and who needs to do what, as well as what resources in the community could assist in the situation. Whole person assessments are the vision and the work that comes from it is the transformation. It seems to fit better with our day-to-day realities on reserve and the way we have incorporated our traditional teachings into our practice.
12. *Relationships*: Build healthy relationships with the people you work with and with other professionals. You can accomplish this by treating others the way you would want to be treated — with respect and non-judgment. Be honest, trustworthy and fair. Do what you say you are going to do. Walk your talk. Maintain your relationships in a good way through contact and friendliness. Be genuine about what you can commit to.
13. *Supervision*: In any work setting, taking and making quality time for supervision will benefit your practice. Find and develop a supervision process that fits your job description. Supervision provides focused, rational

guidance and direction for the workplace. Formal supervision with a supervisor should occur at least once a month. Go prepared with notes, develop your own supervision file to bring with you and be prepared with goals that are specific, measurable, achievable, realistic and time related. Be open to constructive feedback, both receiving and giving it; learn and change what you can.

14. *Practice from your heart*: Always remember who you are working with and how you are working. The children and families you work with should never be your "cases"; they are your people. Treat them with respect and do not assume you know everything about their lives.

15. *Voices are our strength*: Culture to us means a whole way of life, beliefs, language and how we live with one another and Creation. This is the interconnectedness of the elements — culture, spirituality and ethics. I trust in the guidance of our Elders and our traditional ways. I strongly believe that things work out in many instances because we follow cultural protocols and consult with the Elders. We have learned to listen and really hear what they are trying to tell us through their stories and their vision of what could and should be. I believe the strength to do what we had to do came from their prayers and being entrusted with the responsibility of caring for our most precious gifts: our children. As Indigenous social workers, we have the responsibility to acknowledge that many of us have been raised, taught and learned from the teachings and that as we mature in practice, we will accept what we know as Indigenous Knowledge.

HOPES FOR A BETTER FUTURE

We call on all emerging social workers to rise to the work on reconciliation because our children are counting on you. We have a very long way to go, and as a coworker asked, "What does that really mean? Is it a reality or a fairytale and how do we move on if racism still exists?" We believe we move on as we have since the closing of the last residential schools when we stood up and said "ENOUGH." We took the initiative to get and be healthy; heal; learn; get educated; and embrace our languages, traditions and culture in our communities. We are a strong-spirited people. We need to continue to work towards a better future for our children. As our friend and hero Dr. Cindy Blackstock stated, "moral cowardice diminishes children while moral courage uplifts them" (2001, 35).

Let us find our moral courage to uplift our children together. Aiy hiy.

SUGGESTED READINGS

Blackstock, Cindy. 2019. "Indigenous Child Welfare Legislation: A Historical Change or Another Paper Tiger?" *First Peoples Child & Family Review* 14, 1.

Brittain, Melisa and Sarah Auger. 2020. "(Dis)placed Indigenous Youth and the Child Welfare System Learning Guide for Professionals Working with Indigenous Youth." *Faculty of Education*, University of Alberta.

Faculty of Law, University of Alberta. 2019. "Bill C-92: The Good, the Bad and the Unknowns – A Panel Discussion with Cindy Blackstock and Hadley Friedland." YouTube. November 7, 2019. youtube.com/watch?v=I7tMq0ta0D0.

First Nations Child & Family Caring Society. 2024. "Reformed Approach to Child and Family Services." Ottawa.

Sinclair, Raven. 2016. "The Indigenous Child Removal System in Canada: An Examination of Legal Decision Making and Racial Bias." *First Peoples Child & Family Review* 11, 2.

REFERENCES

Absolon, Kathy. 2010. "Indigenous Wholistic Theory: A Knowledge Set for Practice." *First Peoples Child & Family Review* 5, 2.

Ainsworth, Mary S., and John Bowlby. 1991. "An Ethological Approach to Personality Development." *American Psychologist* 46, 4.

Blackstock, Cindy. 2001. "Wanted: Moral Courage in Canadian Child Welfare." *First Peoples Child & Family* Review 6, 2.

Barker, Adam J. 2021. *Making and Breaking Settler Space: Five Centuries of Colonization in North America*. Vancouver: UBC Press.

Bowlby, John. 1969 (1982). *Attachment and Loss, Volume 1: Attachment*. New York: Basic Books.

Carrière, Jeannine, and Carolyn Peacock. 2015. "Practising from the Heart: Living and Working in Indigenous Communities." In *Walking This Path Together: Anti-racist and Anti-oppressive Child Welfare*, second edition, edited by Jeannine Carrière and Susan Strega. Winnipeg: Fernwood Publishing.

Carrière, Jeannine, and Cathy Richardson. 2009. "From Longing to Belonging: Attachment Theory, Connectedness and Indigenous Children in Canada." In *Passion for Action in Child and Family Services: Voices from the Prairies*, edited by Ivan Brown, Sharon McKay and Don Fuchs. Regina: Canadian Plains Research Centre.

____. 2017. *Calling Our Families Home: Métis Peoples' Experience with Child Welfare*. Vernon: J.Charlton Publishing Ltd.

CBC News Online. 2023. "74% of Youth in Care in Alberta are Indigenous. Here's What 2 of Them Had to Say." April 2, 2023. cbc.ca/news/indigenous/indigenous-youth-child-welfare-1.6796576.

Fear, Rhona M. 2017. *Attachment Theory: Working Towards Learned Security*. London: Karnac.

Finestone, Erika. 2023. "Making Kin/Unmaking the Colony: Indigenous Refusal in the Era of Colonial Child Removal." Doctoral dissertation, University of Toronto.

Government of Canada. 2020. *An Act respecting First Nations, Inuit and Métis children, youth and families* (S.C. 2019, c. 24). laws.justice.gc.ca/eng/acts/f-11.73/index.html

Government of Canada. n.d. "Reducing the Number of Indigenous Children in Care." sac-isc.gc.ca/eng/1541187352297/1541187392851

Hanson, Erin. 2009. Updates and Revisions by Daniel P. Gamez and Alexa Manuel. 2020. "The Residential School System." *Indigenous Foundations*. indigenousfoundations.arts.ubc.ca/residential-school-system-2020/.

Matheson, Kimberly, Ann Seymour, Jyllenna Landry, Katelyn Ventura, Emily Arsenault and Hymie Anisman. 2022. "Canada's Colonial Genocide of Indigenous Peoples: A Review of the Psychosocial and Neurobiological Processes Linking Trauma and Intergenerational Outcomes." *International Journal of Environmental Research and Public Health* 19, 11.

Neckoway, Raymond, Keith Brownlee and Bruno Castellan. 2007. "Is Attachment Theory Consistent with Aboriginal Parenting Realities?" *First Peoples Child & Family Review* 3, 2.

Peacock, Carolyn. 2009. "Practising from the Heart." In *Walking This Path Together: Anti-racist and Anti-oppressive Child Welfare Practice*, first edition, edited by Susan Strega and Jeannine Carrière. Winnipeg: Fernwood.

Rose, Jarrett Robert. 2021. "Decolonizing Western Psychedelic Consciousness: The Therapeutic and Social Implications of Indigenous Plant Medicine Knowledge." *Canada Watch* (Summer).

Sinclair, Raven. 2017. "The Indigenous Child Removal System in Canada: An Examination of Legal Decision-making and Racial Bias." *First Peoples Child & Family Review* 11, 2.

Smith, Linda Tuhiwai. 2012. *Decolonizing Methodologies: Research and Indigenous Peoples*. New York: Zed Books.

Truth and Reconciliation Commission of Canada (TRC). 2015a. *Honouring the Truth, Reconciling for the Future: Summary of the Final Report of the Truth and Reconciliation Commission of Canada*. Ottawa: Truth and Reconciliation Commission of Canada.

___. 2015b. *Truth and Reconciliation Commission of Canada: Calls to Action*. Ottawa: Truth and Reconciliation Commission of Canada.

Tuck, Eve and Wayne Yang. 2012. "Decolonization is Not a Metaphor." *Decolonization: Indigeneity, Education, and Society* 1, 1.

Wagamese, Richard. 2019. "Reconciliation." *Facing History and Ourselves Canada*. facinghistory.org/en-ca/resource-library/reconciliation.

Wahkohtowin Law and Governance Lodge. 2021. *Onekihikomawiwin: Good Child Rearing Analytical Framework Report*.

INDEX

Abdi, Abdoul and Fatima, 183, 195–6
Absolon, Kathy, 27–8
addictions, 190
    personal experiences of, 108–9, 191
    support with, 116, 257
aging out of care, 36, 83, 87–8, 94, 184, 190
Alberta, 126
    child welfare legislation/processes in, 243–4, 248, 250–1, 254
    foster care experiences in, 247–50, 252
    Indigenous children in care, 7–8, 128, 255
    kinship care in, 122, 129
    Métis Nation of, 124–5
Alfred, Taiaiake, 115
Anderson, Jackie, 114–16
Anderson, Jordan River, 9–10, 88
Anderson, Kim, 32
Anita (Black female social worker), 171, 175
anti-Black racism,
    in Canada, 162–6, 168–9, 172
    child welfare context of, 162, 164–5, 173, 176–7
    by police/schools, 161–3
    see also Black children; Black parents
anti-colonialism, 142
    social worker commitment to, 65–6, 122–3, 157
anti-Muslim racism, 167–8, 205; *see also* Islamophobia
anti-oppressive living, 18, 27–30, 33
anti-oppressive practice (AOP),
    centring/praxis of decolonization, 27–8, 30, 33, 61
    commitment to, 123, 134–5
    elements of, 20, 23, 27–8, 252
    as Indigenous-centred, 18, 27–8, 30, 123
    Indigenous teachings for, 26, 28
    living, *see* anti-oppressive living
    Medicine Wheel and, 22–3, 28
anti-racist approaches, 66
    anti-oppressive practice and, 28, 123, 134–6, 160, 256
    in assessment/documentation/record-keeping, 62, 64, 77–8, 134, 162
    child welfare, 5, 11, 36n1, 160–2, 174
    social work teaching of, 6–7, 65, 176–7
    trauma-informed, 201, 211
Aotearoa/New Zealand, 67, 110–11; *see also* Maori
apprehension, child, 247
    Black, 160–1, 163, 171
    calls for standards in, 9, 11, 36n1
    higher rates of Indigenous, 9, 35, 86, 128
    kinship/community, 132, 145, 156
    Sixties/Millennium Scoops and, 45, 86, 128
    social worker involvement in, 117, 144, 156, 229, 249
    support organizations without, 85, 118
Assembly of First Nations, 9–10, 88–9
assessments, 7, 195
    awareness of racial/power dynamics in, 134, 152, 162, 171–2, 174, 229
    of children's responses to violence, 224, 226–7
    decolonial/anti-racist/Indigenist, 64, 73–8, 93–4, 171, 174–6, 259
    Family Group Conference, 112, 115–17
    mainstream child welfare practice, 33, 62–3, 73–7, 171–3, 192, 248
    risk-oriented safety, 72, 75–7, 111–12
    standardized, 61–4, 73–4, 76–7, 174
assimilationist agendas, 27
    awareness of, 11, 123, 244–5
    government/church, 8–9, 23–4, 107, 142, 257
    Indian Act, 42, 53, 85–6
    residential school, 24–6, 30, 51, 68–9, 127
    resistance to, 34, 110, 125
    social work(er)/child welfare, 9, 67–70, 86, 128–9
assumptions,
    on children's responses to violence, 222, 224, 227

critical examination of, 20, 28, 30–1, 64, 208
about Indigenous Peoples, 31, 52, 148, 246
racist, 31, 68–9, 148, 171–2, 201
social worker, 156–7, 176, 211, 258, 260
attachment (theory),
Kaska Dene women and, 220–1, 229–30
rebuilding, 107, 109, 116
settler versus Indigenous notions of, 228, 230, 245–51
austerity, 189, 196
Australia,
child welfare processes in, 129, 135, 188–9
settler-colonial context of, 67, 69
A Way of Life, 18, 20–1, 24–7, 35
AYIT program, see Youth in Transition program(s)

Bear's Den (FGC program), 114
beloved community, notions of, 28
best interests, children's, 170
anti-oppressive/Indigenous critiques of, 33, 36n1, 78, 174, 244, 251
individualized versus collective view of, 70–2, 90, 246
mainstream social work/colonial view of, 5, 69, 94
Bill C3 (Gender Equity in Indian Registration Act), 52–3
Bill C-31 (An Act to Amend the Indian Act), 51–3, 55
Bill C-92 (An Act Respecting First Nations, Inuit, and Métis Children, Youth and Families), 35, 77–8, 125, 157, 143, 254
Bill S-3 (An Act to Amend the Indian Act), 53
Black children,
above-average performance expectations, 164, 166–7
discipline of, 161–2, 164–70, 173
overrepresentation in child welfare, 5–6, 72, 77, 169–70
parental discipline of, 161–2, 164–70, 173
preparation for racist society, 160–2, 164–70, 173, 176–7

Black child welfare workers,
experiences of, 162, 164, 171–2, 175–7
race-matching of, 175–6, 178
support for Black families, 162, 171–2, 174–8
Black parents,
discipline of children, 161–2, 164–70, 173
experiences of, 161–2, 165–70, 173
language use/differences, 173–4
non-Black social worker interactions/perceptions and, 160, 171–3, 177–8
practices of, 160, 165–70, 176–7
state intervention against, 162, 168, 172
teaching of "pseudo-suffering," 165–6
Black people,
assimilating white values, 27, 167, 176
assumptions about, 68, 160, 164, 166–7, 171–3
parenting for survival, 160, 164, 167–8, 176–7
police violence against, 161–4, 170
social worker lack of awareness about, 170–3, 177–8
systemic racism impacts on, 6, 160–1, 164–71, 204
see also anti-Black racism
Blackstock, Cindy, 28–9, 260
Bopp, Judie (*The Sacred Tree*), 29–30, 34
boys,
discrimination facing Muslim, 204–5
misperceptions of Black, 163, 165, 168, 170
mistreatment in care, 147, 247
residential school labour of, 4, 50
Britain, 208
child welfare practice impacts of, 63, 66, 68–9, 77
imperial policies of, 3–4, 42, 62–3
relations with former colonies, 62–3, 66–8, 77
British Columbia, 19, 46, 141, 209, 222
Representative for Children and Youth, 34, 147
Brooks, Rayshard, 161, 163
Bruyere, Gord, 35

Calgary Women's Emergency Shelter (CWES), 221–2

Calls to Action, TRC, *see* Truth and
    Reconciliation Commission
Campbell, Maria, 123
Canada, 213
    anti-Black racism in, 162–6, 168–9, 172
    child welfare in, 19, 28, 68–72, 153, 183
    immigration/asylum/refugee issues in,
        183–7, 191, 202–7
    Indigenous people living in, 43, 128, 229
    neoliberal policies in, 70
    poverty in, 44
    settler-colonial context of, 24–5, 66–8,
        211–12, 246
Canada Welfare Council, 9
Canadian Association of Social Workers
    (CASW), 9
Canadian Charter of Rights and Freedoms,
    52, 71
Canadian Human Rights Tribunal, 9–10, 89
capitalism, 24–5, 66–7, 185
Castile, Philando, 161, 163
Catholicism, 63, 68, 127, 168, 244
ceremony/ies,
    banning of, 25–6, 42, 85
    in child welfare processes, 73, 84, 95–6
    child/youth participation in, 45, 49, 90,
        95, 99, 124
    decolonization and, 100, 109–10, 258
    Family Group Conference, 110, 112–13,
        115–19
    governance through, 25
    understanding of identity and culture via,
        31, 33–4, 49, 90, 95, 115
Césaire, Aimé, 231
Child and Family Services Act,
    Nova Scotia, 195
    Ontario, 86, 92
children,
    Black, *see* Black children
    concerns about morality of, 4, 24, 68–9
    education levels in Canada, 5, 62, 84–5,
        97
    home, 3–4, 63
    Indigenous, *see* Indigenous children
    as labourers, 4, 25, 63, 69, 251
    protection of, *see* protection, child
    responses to violence, 213, 220, 222–8, 234
    rights of, 5, 19, 71–2, 76, 86, 250

Children's Aid Societies, 5, 84, 92, 96, 108
child rescuers, 68–9, 73
child welfare systems,
    anti-Black racism in, 162, 164–5, 173,
        176–7
    anti-racist approaches, 5, 11, 36n1,
        160–2, 174
    assessments in, 33, 62–3, 73–7, 171–3,
        192, 248
    in Canada, 19, 28, 68–72, 153, 183
    deportation, involvement in, 182–4, 188,
        192–3
    disproportionality in, *see* disproportional-
        ity in child welfare
    documentation in, 33, 62–4, 74–6, 226
    Eurocentrism of, 63, 66, 68–9, 77
    families, approaches to, 62–3, 69–70,
        73–7, 127–9, 245
    Indigenous, *see* Indigenous child welfare
    inequities in, 68–73, 76
    institutions, 90, 92, 108, 144, 147–9
    lack of funding/resources, 86–9
    neoliberalism impacts on, 62, 64, 70–1,
        73, 186
    policies, *see* policies, child welfare
    practices, *see* practices, mainstream child
        welfare
    racism in, 6–7, 14, 68–9, 148, 162–8,
        171–7, 205
    social order maintenance and, 5, 63, 196
    statutory, *see* statutory child welfare
        system
Christianity, 51, 208
    civilizing missions and, 3, 25, 69
    residential schools and, 48–50, 63, 96,
        107
    settler-colonial frameworks and, 66, 85,
        96
churches, 127, 244
    facilities for underage mothers, 4
    residential school involvement, 8, 47–9,
        63, 85, 107
civilizing missions,
    education/residential school, 26, 49, 51,
        63
    legislation, 107
    social work, 3, 25
Clark, Stephon, 161, 163

class,
    child welfare concerns and, 4, 73
    inequities, 5–6, 64–5, 148, 163, 186, 211
    values of white middle, 73, 108, 134, 174–6
    working, 25, 148
Coates, Linda, 221
Cole, Desmond (*The Skin We're In*), 163
colonization,
    by British, 3–4, 42, 62–3, 66–8, 77
    capitalist expansion in, 24–5, 66–7
    civilizing mission of, 3, 25–6, 49, 51, 63, 107
    family impacts of, 73, 95, 106, 160, 251
    four levels of, 106–7
    harm from policies, 41–2, 85–8, 107–8, 257
    Indigenous communities versus, 23–6, 50–5, 106–8, 212, 250
    Indigenous resistance to, 3, 67, 77–8, 143
    Indigenous women versus, 6, 41–2, 78, 229
    influence on child protection, 62, 86–7, 90, 95–6, 127
    policy inequities, 9, 14, 54, 71, 89
    power relations of, 26, 41, 142, 211
    racism as basis of, 23
    recordkeeping as technology of, 62–4, 131–2
    trauma from, 10, 24–5, 41–3, 66, 85–8, 107–8, 257
    violence of, 24, 41, 47–8, 51–4, 257
    see also settler colonialism
community/ies,
    2SLGBTQ+, 208–9, 214
    children's integration in Indigenous, 72, 91–2
    children's separation from, 8–9, 48, 67–9, 87–90, 148–9
    child welfare challenges facing, 23, 64–5, 76–7, 246–8, 250–5
    colonizer aims to break up, 25–6, 50–5, 106–8, 212, 250
    cultural, 10–11, 129–30, 173–5, 211–13, 245–7
    culture and tradition as essential to, 34–5, 48–9, 89–93
    Family Group Conference model and, 109–13, 115–19
    fostering/deepening relationships with, 30–4, 74, 92, 123–7, 131, 256–60
    loss of, 63, 128, 134, 195
    personal responsibilities to, 123–5, 127, 129–30, 135–6
    poverty of, 45, 211
    racism impacts on BIPOC, 6–7, 170–1, 177, 211–12, 255
    self-governance, 10, 21, 25–6, 36n1, 78, 157
    services based in, 10–1, 153, 227
    social worker commitment to, 28–31, 92, 108–9, 155–6, 211–12, 244
    support for/care of young people, 5, 92–100, 131–3, 227–9, 250–2
Couchie, Alyssa, 23
Creator, 29
    children as gifts from, 30, 32, 98, 131, 244
Cree-Dene communities/people, 41, 45, 107
Cree communities/people, 9, 45, 54, 109, 114
    language transmission, 46, 50, 106, 258
    Métis kinship, 122, 130
    Sixties Scoop investigations, 107
    storytelling in, 242–3
criminalization, 134
    assumptions of Indigenous, 4, 69, 89, 212
    in child welfare law, 72–3, 75, 162
    stereotypes of Black, 166, 177
    susceptibility to, 184–6, 189–90
criminal justice system, 227
    child welfare system involvement and, 182–3, 188–90
    deportation struggles, 186–7, 194–6
"crimmigration" system, 184–5
critical race lens, 160, 201
culture, Indigenous,
    community, 10–11, 129–30, 173–5, 211–13, 245–7
    decolonizing approach emphasizing, 21, 27–9, 65, 140, 212–13
    focus on specific, 90–1, 100n2, 134
    importance for youth, 34–5, 48–9, 89–93, 94–8
    lack of connection to, 86–7, 89–90, 95–6
    participation in, 45, 49, 90, 95, 99, 124
    settler-colonial disruption of, 10–11, 23–6, 108

understanding identity through, 31,
  33–4, 49, 90, 95, 115
Cyr, Gale, 21

day schools, 26, 85, 107
Dean, Shelly, 221–2, 238
decolonial approach,
  anti-oppressive practice and, 27–8, 30,
    33, 61
  in assessments/documentation, 62–4,
    77–8, 93–4, 171, 174–6, 259
  to child welfare, 5, 18, 20–1, 27–9, 65, 140
  Indigenous service providers', 142–3,
    151–3, 155–7
  need for training in, 177, 257
  political definitions of culture with,
    212–13
  to trauma, 200–1, 211, 213–14
decolonization,
  of attachment theory/connection, 246–7
  ceremonies and, 100, 109–10, 258
  critical consciousness and, 114, 116,
    118–19
  as event and process, 114
  Family Group Conference model supporting, 105, 114, 118–19
  personal journeys of, 105–6, 110, 118–19
  settler state resistance to, 67, 142–3, 153
  struggles in Canada for, 66, 151, 177
Dene communities/people, 41, 45, 107,
  119n2, 222; *see also* Cree-Dene
  communities/people
deportation,
  child welfare system involvement and,
    182–4, 188, 192–3
  fighting, 184–5, 190–2, 194–6
  neoliberal policies and, 185–7, 189
Dhillon, Jaskiran, 142
disability, 5–6, 88–9, 111, 189
discrimination, 114
  anti-Black, 164–5, 173, 177
  anti-Muslim/Middle Eastern, 167, 204–6
  concept of, 176
  in Indian Act, 52–3
  Indigenous children/families facing,
    9–10, 19–20, 88, 109
  institutional promises to address, 251,
    253–4

  systemic, 76–7, 127–8, 184
dispossession, 23
  Indigenous, 65–7, 98, 148–9
disproportionality in child welfare, 149
  Black children's, 5, 72, 160, 163–4, 170
  Indigenous children's, 7–8, 83–5, 122,
    128, 229, 243
  mental illness and, 5–6
  poverty and, 5–6, 71–2, 148
  practices, 20, 73, 190, 192
documentation, 163
  decolonial/anti-racist/Indigenist, 77–8,
    231
  embedded inequities in, 33–4, 61
  mainstream child welfare practice, 33,
    62–4, 74–6, 226
duty to report, 150–3

education, 76, 190, 222
  2SLGBTQ+ inclusivity versus religious,
    207–9
  anti-racist/decolonial, 7, 99, 106, 110,
    127, 177, 211
  Canada's levels of child/youth, 5, 62
  change as basis for, 27–8, 143
  children's entitlement to, 73, 131
  Eurocentric/assimilationist, 4, 25–8,
    91–2, 127, 229, 244
  loss of Indian Status with, 50–1, 54, 84–5
  post-secondary, 84–5, 97
  racism in, 163, 203, 211, 255, 260
  sex, 209, 214
  social worker mainstream, 31, 33, 90–1,
    193, 196, 255–7
  support for Indigenous, 36n1, 46–9, 54,
    78, 93, 248
Elders, Indigenous, 55, 108
  child-raising guidance, 132, 246
  Family Group Conference model
    involvement, 112–19
  Medicine Wheel/teachings of, 22–3, 109,
    123, 257–60
  sharing of knowledge/experiences, 32–5,
    74, 106, 212, 222
  youth growth/connections with, 84–5,
    90, 94–5, 97–100, 130
enfranchisement,
  government reasoning for, 51–2

Indian Act policies on, 39–42, 47, 55
loss of rights for women with, 50–1
eugenics, 4

Fallon, Barbara, 7–8
families,
    anti-oppressive practice and, 19–20, 27–30, 32–3, 251–2
    assessment/documentation of, 73–8
    awareness of different, 6, 213–14
    Black, 7, 162, 168, 170–2, 174–8
    care for children within, 31–3, 255–60
    children's removal from, 8, 25–6, 34, 50–2, 86, 107–8
    child welfare system involvement, 6, 10–11, 69, 122, 141–5
    colonization impacts on, 73, 95, 106, 160, 251
    colonizer aims to break up, 25–6, 30, 63, 95, 228
    culturally appropriate programming for, 7–10, 36n1, 86–90, 93, 212–13
    having unique strengths/relationships, 112, 257
    immigrant/refugee, 183–4, 190, 193, 196, 207–8, 213–15
    Indian Act impact on, 39, 47, 50–2, 54, 107
    Indigenous, 8–9, 25–7, 33–5, 141–4, 147–56, 257
    kinship care in, 122–3, 129–33, 135–6, 147–56
    legislation on Indigenous, 35, 77–8, 125, 157, 143, 254
    mainstream child welfare approaches to, 62–3, 69–70, 73–7, 127–9, 245
    neoliberalism impacts on, 186, 188–90
    nuclear, 6, 246
    poor, 4, 6–8, 63, 71–2, 148–9, 163
    reclaiming/reconnecting with, 41, 70–2, 113–16, 135, 212
    social worker power dynamics with, 20, 27–32, 255–60
    systemic racism facing, 6–7, 19–20, 43, 47, 160, 184–5
    urban Indigenous, 5, 87
    violence, responses to, 223, 227–9
    see also Family Group Conference model

Family Group Conference (FGC) model, 105, 110
    Bear's Den, 114
    experiences in/teachings from, 114–19
    four stages, 111–13, 115–17
    values and elements of, 112–13, 118–19
    as wise practice, 107, 113–14, 118–19
Fanon, Frantz, 201
federal government, 9, 24, 71, 255
    assimilationism of, 8–9, 23–4, 53–4, 107, 142, 257
    colonial policies, harm from, 41–2, 85–8, 107–8, 257
    deportation cases, 183, 192, 195
    legislation, child welfare, 4, 10–11, 35, 71–2, 91–4, 243
feminist-informed practice, 201, 221
Finestone, Erika, 246
First Nations Child and Family Caring Society, 28
    human rights complaints, 9–10, 19–20, 88–9
First Nations Child and Family Services (FNCFS), 9–10, 19
food insecurity, 43–5, 71, 115, 190
foster care, 75, 127, 171
    experiences in, 41, 96, 183–4, 190, 229–30, 247–50
    Indigenous overrepresentation in, 5, 7–8, 19, 86–7, 229
    kin/community, 36n1, 87, 133–4, 145–7
    non-Indigenous placements, 8, 69, 86–7, 117, 244–50, 252–5
    public versus private systems, 84, 87–9

Gage, Kendra, 141–2, 154
gender, 5
    child welfare concerns and, 4, 6
    diversity, 208, 214
    policies related to, 52, 73
    see also sexual orientation and gender identity movement; transgender youth
genocide, Indigenous, 119n2, 254–5
    agendas/policies of, 8, 43, 47, 63, 224
    child welfare involvement in, 36n1, 67, 69
    cultural, 23–6, 108
Gina (Nigerian-Canadian mother), 165–6
girls, 204

labour of, 4, 50
violence against, 18, 21
Giroux, Henry, 163
Graham, Toya, 161
grandparents, 124, 163, 232
  attachments with, 98, 109, 221, 226, 228–9
  caring for children, 19, 35, 49, 131–4, 145
  enduring colonial policies, 41–2, 47, 52, 98
  Family Group Conference model, 112
  knowledge sharing from, 105, 109, 119, 126–7
  residential school attendance, 27, 128
  resilience of, 34, 46, 126
guardianship, 255
  child protection assessment changes in, 62, 69, 72
  policies for care, 75, 162, 249–50
  state, 134–5, 147, 184

Hamelin, Tammy, 114–16
Hannah (Black mother), 167–8
Hardlott, Susan, 42, 45
Hart, Michael, 73, 111
Hokowhitu, Brendan, 24
home children, 3–4, 63
homelessness, 29, 89, 105, 109, 184
hooks, bell (*killing rage*), 27–8
housing,
  inadequate Indigenous/immigrant, 8, 44–5, 115, 202–3
  youth, 36n1, 71, 84, 98, 184, 190
Hulitan, 141–2, 144, 149; *see also* Journeys of the Heart program
Hul'qumi'num Mustimuhw teachings, 26, 28–9

immigrants,
  children's removal from parents, 4, 63
  complex needs of, 183–4
  neoliberal (un)deservingness, 186, 189–90, 196
  white cultural misunderstandings about, 173–4, 176, 184
immigration system,
  noncitizen former youth in care in, 182–90, 192–4
  restrictive Canadian, 68, 185, 187
  social worker training on, 193
  status limitations in, 184, 187–9, 193–5, 205, 232
Indian Act,
  amendments to, 47, 52–3, 86, 127
  banning of ceremonies in, 25, 85
  child welfare impacts, 86, 127
  colonial violence through, 24, 41, 47–8, 51–4, 257
  enfranchisement policies/loss of Status via, 39, 42, 50–4, 85
  implementation and governance through, 24, 85–6, 107
  Métis communities and, 92
  residential schools and, 25, 39, 42, 47, 55, 85–6, 127
Indian hospitals, 2, 10, 45–6, 55
Indian and Northern Affairs, 9–10
Indigenizing lens, 18, 20–1, 28, 73
Indigenous-centred approaches,
  anti-oppressive social work practice, 18, 27–8, 30, 123
  systems of community care, 122
Indigenous children,
  child welfare experiences, 7–10, 45–50, 128, 255
  community integration, 72, 91–2
  discrimination against, 9–10, 19–20, 88, 109
  as gifts from Creator, 30, 32, 98, 131, 244
  grandparents caring for, 19, 35, 49, 131–4, 145
  importance of relationships with, 31–5, 72, 91–2, 255–60
  inequities facing, 5, 60–2, 68–70, 73
  Métis, *see* Métis children and youth
  overrepresentation in child welfare, 7–8, 19, 83–7, 122, 128, 229, 243
  percentage of child population, 5, 7–8, 86
  placements, 7–8, 69, 87, 90, 128
  relationships with parents, 32–5, 45, 127–8, 131–3
  removal from families, 8, 25–6, 34, 50–2, 86, 107–8, 245–7
  responses to violence, 213, 220, 222–8, 234
  well-being of, 5, 11, 35, 85, 226, 256

Indigenous-led child welfare, 96
    anti-oppressive practice and, 18, 27–8, 30, 123
    decolonial approaches of, 142–3, 151–3, 155–7
    history of, 22–6, 28
    Indigenous community involvement in, 10–11, 117–18, 155–7, 256–7
    legislation for, 9, 157
    service provision, 78, 85, 140–6, 149, 154, 244
    workers, 30, 127, 144–51, 155, 243–4, 251–3
Indigenous parents, 19, 48
    anti-oppressive practice with, 27, 29, 151–2, 256
    blocked from passing on culture, 49–50
    child welfare assessments of, 62–3, 68–9, 108–9, 145–8, 152–4
    culturally appropriate programming for, 9, 95, 256–7
    Family Group Conference model and, 105, 111–12, 114–17
    Indian Act Status and, 53–4
    poetry about, 56, 238–9
    poverty and child welfare involvement, 63, 68–9, 71, 88–9, 98
    relationships with children, 32–5, 45, 127–8, 131–3
    residential school discipline versus, 9, 24, 47–50
    settler-colonial stereotypes of, 8–9, 24–5, 34, 149
    social worker lack of understanding of, 95–6, 145–8
Indigenous Peoples,
    assumptions about, 31, 52, 148, 246
    attempted assimilation of, 8–9, 23–6, 30, 51, 68–9, 107, 142, 257
    civilizing missions for, *see* civilizing missions
    colonization and, *see* colonization
    culture, *see* culture, Indigenous
    discrimination facing, 9–10, 19–20, 88, 109
    dispossession, 23, 65–7, 98, 148–9
    enfranchisement, *see* enfranchisement
    inadequate housing, 8, 44–5, 115
    population percentage, 8, 43, 128, 229
    resistance of, *see* resistance, Indigenous
    rights of, 5, 21, 23, 64–5, 92, 244
    violence facing, 24, 41, 47–8, 51–4, 85–8, 107–8, 257
inequities, 74
    child welfare process, 68–73, 76
    colonial policy, 9, 14, 54, 71, 89
    neoliberalism and, 62, 70, 189
    for youth in care, 60–2, 68–70, 73
infant mortality, Indigenous, 43–4
institutional settings,
    assessment and documentation in, 63–4
    harshness of residential school, 25, 43, 49–50
    Indigenous service providers in, 155–7
    racism in, 6–7, 28, 147–9, 162–3, 184, 256
    surveillance in, 144, 147
    settler-colonial violence in, 66, 68, 77, 182, 244, 252
institutions,
    children sent to, 4, 43
    child welfare, 90, 92, 108, 144, 147–9
    inability to change, 90, 92
    Indigenous-led, 21, 90, 129
    responses to violence, 222–3, 226, 232–4
    state-funded, 140, 142–3
Islamophobia, 167–8, 202–5, 211–15
Jackson (Black father), 166–7
Jackson, Suzanne, 146–7, 149
Johnnie, Delmar (Seletze), 29
Johnston, Patrick, 8, 45, 107
Jordan's Principle, 9–10, 36n1, 71, 88–9
Journeys of the Heart (JOH) program, 144–6, 154

Kaska Dene women, 220–2, 228–9
Kelm, Mary-Ellen, 52
Kemble, Tibetha, 8–9
Kimelman, Edwin (*No Quiet Place*), 108
kinship,
    animal/nature, 26, 31–2, 126
    care arrangements, 87, 111, 116–17, 122–3, 134–5
    developing relationships of, 99, 130–3, 155, 255–6
    differing concepts/systems of, 129–32, 134

loss of Indigenous children's, 245–7
Western models of, 129–30, 133, 157
see also wahkohtowin
Knowledge Keepers, 14, 97, 260
  child welfare assessment input, 74
  Family Group Conference model and, 109, 113–16
  support for youth, 32, 84–5, 98
Krysa, Isabella, 189
kwum kwum skwuluwun, 28–9

Lac La Ronge All Saints Indian Residential School, 45–9
land, 230
  decolonizing approach and, 21, 65, 123–6, 130, 135–6
  focus on economic productivity of, 24
  Indigenous removal from, 4, 10, 43–4, 63, 86–7, 134
  loss through Indian Act, 50–4, 85
  programming based on the, 97, 109, 115–16
  settler-colonial control of, 24, 27, 66–7, 148
  social worker awareness on Indigenous, 31, 65, 97, 220
  see also dispossession
Landertinger, Laura, 8
law, child welfare,
  federal, 10–11, 18, 25, 93, 193, 229, 243
  Indigeneity/kinship in, 122, 174, 244
  policy approaches, 54, 71–3, 78, 91, 150, 213, 254
  racism/harm in, 6–9, 32–5, 66, 127, 184, 191, 251
  reforms, 36n1, 85–8, 162, 176–7, 254–5
  worker awareness of, 63–5, 73–4, 76–7, 144, 184, 258
  see also statutory child welfare system
law, family, 223, 231, 233
listening,
  in assessment process, 64, 74, 177
  familial, 126, 220, 226, 233
  importance of social worker, 55, 97, 162, 194, 258–60
  lack of professional, 184, 195, 249
Little Bear, Leroy, 118

Longstocking, Pippi, 237
Lucy (eight-year-old experiencing violence), 233–7

Macdonald, John A., 24, 244
MacDougall, Brenda, 130–1
maltreatment, 63, 174, 248
  investigations of Black child, 162, 170
  investigations of Indigenous child, 7, 19, 71–3, 153–4
Ma Mawi Wi Chi Itata Centre (Winnipeg), 110–11, 113–18
Manitoba,
  Indigenous children in care, 7, 9–10
  infant mortality in, 43–4
  Métis communities in, 124–5, 131
  provincial failure on children's care, 108
  residential schools in, 107, 119nn2,3
Maori, 110–11
Maracle, Lee, 26–7
McIvor, Sharon, 52–3
Medicine Wheel, 21–3, 28, 34–5, 94
mental health issues, 131, 213
  disproportionate child welfare involvement, 6, 70, 89, 95, 184
  immigrant/refugee, 189–90, 200–4
  racist assessments of, 172–3, 212
  responses to violence as, 224–7, 234
mentors, 21
  Family Group Conference, 110–19
  social workers finding, 257–9
  youth connection with, 91, 94, 97, 100
Métis children and youth, 5, 43
  apprehension into care, 86, 107–9, 122
  community connection/services for, 92–3, 114, 123–5, 136
  kinship care, 122, 126–7, 129–32, 134–6
  legislation covering, 10–11, 35, 78, 125, 243
Middle Eastern people,
  curricular/pedagogical differences facing, 207–9
  discrimination facing, 167–8, 205–6, 213
Millennium Scoop, 6
  settler-colonial violence through, 10, 30, 45, 86, 122, 128–9
Ministry of Children and Family Development (MCFD), 141, 145–8, 150–4, 157

Missing and Murdered Indigenous Women and Girls, National Inquiry into, 21
    Calls for Justice, 18, 36n1
Moffat, Tina, 44
Mohawk people, 35, 97, 105–6
Moore, Percy Elmer, 44
morality, 32, 166, 188, 206, 225, 260
    concerns about children's, 4, 24, 68–9
moral reform, *see* social reformers
Mother Earth, relationship with, 22, 26, 31–2, 126
Murray-Lichtman, Andrea, 6

Natalie (Kaska Dene child), 220–1, 228
nation building, settler-colonial, 67–8, 70
nation-states,
    post-colonial/neoliberal, 66, 77, 196
    settler resistance to decolonization, 67–8
neglect, 128, 162
    cases of, 4, 111, 150, 248–50
    investigations into, 8, 71–3, 152–3
neoliberalism,
    aims/values of, 185–6, 188–9, 211
    bureaucratic violence of, 182, 191–2, 196
    child welfare practice under, 62, 64, 70–1, 73, 186
    immigration policy under, 182, 185
    individual responsibility and, 90, 188, 196
    public policy under, 69–70, 76, 188–90
    (un)deservingness under, 186, 196
Niijkiwendidaa Anishnaabekwewag Services Circle,
    catchment areas, 83–5, 96–7
    experiences at, 94–5, 98–100
    operational challenges, 89, 96–7
    see also Youth in Transition program(s)
    noncitizen former youth in care in, 182–90, 192–4
Nova Scotia, 183, 195
nursing, Indigenous careers in, 46–7, 50, 55

Ojibway communities/people, 91, 107–8, 114
Oji-Cree communities/people, 107, 114
Ontario, 77, 100n2, 192
    child welfare involvement in, 5–6, 87, 170
    Indigenous children in care, 7–8
    provincial policy shifts, 85–6, 88, 91, 93–4, 96–7
    racism in, 96, 163
    youth transition programming, *see* Youth in Transition program(s)
Orcas Society, 222

patriarchy, 6, 201, 208
    child welfare policy reinforcement of, 6, 214
    hetero, 63, 73
    Indian Act reinforcement of, 41, 51
Paul, Minnie, 39, 41, 45–50
placements, 96, 183
    agency/field, 6–7, 157
    Black children/youth, 160, 171
    decisions about, 90, 133–4, 147, 248–9, 253–5
    Indigenous children/youth and, 7–8, 69, 87, 90, 128
    kin, 122, 128, 133
police, 150, 201, 210
    anti-Black violence/profiling by, 161–4, 169–70
    noncitizen youth and, 184, 189, 192
    responses to household violence, 232–3
    targeting of Indigenous people, 47, 78, 85
policies, child welfare,
    crises/contestation in, 19–20, 64–5, 143–4, 243
    harm from, 6, 11, 14, 24, 247
    Indigenous children/families in, 30–5, 63–5
    Indigenous-led, 10, 77–8, 157
    neoliberalism and, 70–3, 185–6
    racist, 6, 26–7, 34, 135, 177, 255
    settler-colonial basis for, 5, 14, 27, 39, 67
    Sixties Scoop, *see* Sixties Scoop
    social worker reflection on, 27, 72–4, 172, 244–5, 255–9
    transition from care, 93, 96–7
    Westernized versions of kinship, 129–30, 133
policies, settler state,
    assimilative, 8–9, 23–4, 47, 123, 129–30
    development of, 55, 70, 77, 92
    enfranchisement, *see* enfranchisement
    immigration, 68–70, 183–6, 189, 193–6

neoliberalism and, 70-3, 188-9, 191
residential school, see residential schools
violence of, 10, 24-5, 42-3, 66
see also Indian Act
Porter, Tom, 105-6
post-traumatic stress disorder (PTSD), 107, 109, 184
Potlatches, banning of, 25-6
poverty, 40, 109, 232
   disproportionate child welfare involvement, 5-6, 36n1, 68-76, 148-9
   health impacts from, 44, 184
   Indigenous Peoples and, 8, 11, 34, 50, 128, 211
   industrial schools and, 3-4, 63
   kinship care and, 134-5
   neoliberalism and, 70-1, 90, 163, 188-90
power relations,
   anti-oppressive analysis of, 20, 26, 33, 134
   asymmetrical, 20, 109, 211, 215
   colonial, 26, 41, 142, 211
   Indigenous teachings on, 30, 35, 116, 220
   social worker-family, 20, 64, 134-6, 153
   white/settler dominance in, 6, 26, 55, 157, 191
practices, mainstream child welfare,
   anti-oppressive, see anti-oppressive practice
   assessment in, 33, 62-3, 73-7, 171-3, 192, 248
   cultural awareness in, 7-11, 33-4, 36n1, 86-90, 93, 212-13
   discriminatory, 9-10, 19-20, 76-7, 127-8, 184, 204-6
   documentation in, 33, 62-4, 74-6, 226
   with Indigenous families, 19-20, 27, 31-2, 73, 190, 192
   neoliberalism impacts on, 62, 64, 70-1, 73, 186
   racist, 6-7, 14, 68-9, 148, 162-8, 171-7, 205
   settler-colonial basis for, 5-6, 14, 61-3, 66, 68-9, 77
   social worker reflection on, 27, 30-5
   solidarity in, 2-3, 64-5, 77, 155, 157
protection, child,
   anonymity in, 153-4
   assessment/documentation processes in, 62, 71-5, 154, 172, 224, 259
   colonial influence on, 62, 86-7, 90, 95-6, 127
   different concepts of, 151
   duty to report, 150-3
   legislation/policy on, 71-3, 78, 85-7
   poverty and investigations on, 6, 147-8
   racism in, 134, 152, 162, 171-4, 193, 229
   response-based practice and, 222-3, 232
   risk assessment for concerns of, 71, 111, 141
   shifting policy/practice on, 14, 85-7, 90-2, 96
   surveillance in, 140, 154
Protestantism, 63, 68
provincial/territorial governments, 141
   collaboration issues with, 9-10, 78, 91-4, 96, 244, 253-7
   inadequate resource provision, 10, 86-90, 92-4, 226
   Jordan's Principle, 9-10, 36n1, 88
   legislation, child welfare, 72-5, 78, 84-6, 127, 195-6, 243
   in Sixties/Millennium Scoop, 9, 86, 108

race, 28
   child welfare concerns and, 4, 73, 128, 148, 174
   criminalization of, 190, 202
   discrimination based on, 9-10, 164-7, 173, 177, 205
   matching based on, 175, 178
   stratification based on, 5-6, 23, 64, 163-4
racialized communities, 174, 211, 215
   disproportionate child welfare involvement, 11, 71-3, 163, 172, 184, 190
   racialized social workers and, 177-8
   stereotypes of, 6-7, 68-70, 142, 148-9
racism,
   anti-, see anti-racist approaches
   anti-Black, see anti-Black racism
   anti-Muslim, see anti-Muslim racism
   in assessments/documentation, 134, 152, 162, 171-3, 174, 229
   assumptions, 31, 68-9, 148, 171-2, 201
   in Canada, 24-5, 66-8, 162-9, 172, 211-12, 246

in child protection, 134, 152, 162, 171–4, 193, 229
as colonialism's ideological rationale, 23
community impacts of, 6–7, 170–1, 177, 211–12, 255
disproportionate child welfare involvement, 5–6, 72, 83–5, 122, 128, 160–4, 170, 243
institutional, 6–7, 28, 147–9, 162–3, 184, 25
internalized, 27, 29, 127
in legislation, 6–9, 32–5, 66, 127, 184, 191, 251
in policies, 6, 26–7, 34, 135, 177, 255
in practices of child welfare, 6–7, 14, 68–9, 148, 162–8, 171–7, 205
preparation for, 160–2, 164–70, 173, 176–7
in schools, 163, 203, 211, 255, 260
systemic, 6–7, 19–20, 43, 47, 160–1, 164–71, 204
Raider, Anne Maje, 222, 228
reconciliation, 114
in child welfare services, 243, 254–5, 260
concept of, 254
lack of settler government action on, 10, 135, 141, 243, 254
systemic discrimination and, 244–5, 251
see also Truth and Reconciliation Commission
recordkeeping,
citizenship, 195–6
as colonial technology, 62–4, 131–2
decolonial/anti-racist/Indigenist, 62, 64, 77–8
embedded inequities in, 61, 76
in mainstream child welfare practice, 74–5
refugee newcomer parents, 200
cultural marginalization/recognition, 206–8, 211–15
housing difficulties, 202–3
racism/Islamophobia facing, 203–6, 211–13
school curriculum concerns, 203–9, 214–15
refugees, 4, 125
assessment of, 174
close child supervision, 170, 207–9
concept of, 202
cultural marginalization/recognition, 206–8, 211–15
families of, 183–4, 190, 193, 196, 207–8, 213–15
growth in Canada, 185–6, 200, 202
housing difficulties, 202–3
school curriculum concerns, 203–4, 207–9, 214–15
social/state program exclusion, 189–91, 201, 206–8
Syrian, 200, 202–3
trauma/racism faced by, 183, 201, 203–6, 211–13
see also immigrants
reserves,
assumptions about, 30–1
children taken from, 30, 107–8, 247
disconnection from, 87, 92–3
government jurisdiction over, 54–5, 85–6
forced removal onto, 10, 42–3, 85
inadequate funding for, 19, 92
Indian Status and living on, 51–2, 54–5, 86
service provision for, 19, 141, 243, 254–5, 259
residential schools,
assimilationism of, 24–6, 30, 48–51, 68–9, 127
child labour/discipline at, 4, 9, 24–5, 43, 47–50
Christianity and, 48–50, 63, 96, 107
civilizing mission of, 26, 49, 51, 63
cultural genocide through, 23–6, 108
Indigenous family breakdown via, 8, 25–6, 34, 50–2, 86, 107–8
mandatory attendance at, 25, 47, 85, 98, 107, 128
policies pertaining to, 24, 55, 85–6, 107
poor education in, 25, 50
survivor stories, 47, 49, 55–6
violence of, 24–5, 45–50, 63, 86, 127–8, 257
resilience,
anti-oppressive/decolonizing approach and, 21, 33

building youth/family, 33, 94, 98, 109
cultural elements contributing to, 43, 89, 94, 213, 247
Indigenous Peoples', 31, 34, 42–3, 126
trauma/violence response and, 42, 45–6, 107, 118, 193
resistance, children's, 230
covert, 223, 232–3
response-based, 223–8, 230–3
silence as, 226–7, 237–8
trauma/violence and, 213, 220, 223–8
resistance, Indigenous,
in child welfare processes, 143–4, 146–7, 150–7
to colonial systems, 3, 67, 77–8, 143
to enfranchisement, 52
as essential for survival, 34–5, 126
to settler state sole sovereignty, 67
worker solidarity with, 77–8, 143–4, 150–7
response-based practice,
contextual analysis, 230–7
development and axioms of, 221–3
framework of, 224–7
Rice, Tamir, 161, 163
Richardson, Cathy, 135, 221–2, 231
Rita (service provider), 150–1
Reinhold, Kurt, 161, 163
rights,
Charter, 52, 71
children's, 5, 19, 71–2, 76, 86, 250
defence of, 48, 196, 225, 250
human, 70, 77, 89, 172, 190, 194–5, 202
Indigenous inherent, 21, 23, 64–5, 92, 244
individualized versus collective view of, 26, 71–2, 132
legislation, 9–10, 50–2, 174, 202, 244
loss via Indian Act, 42, 48, 50–5, 85, 93
(non)citizenship, 187, 190
parental, 174, 209, 214
treaty, *see* Treaty Rights, loss of
Royal Canadian Mounted Police (RCMP), 47, 50, 55, 249

Sabbas-Watts, Priscilla, 154
Said, Edward, 212
Saskatchewan, 10
experiences of Indigenous children in, 45–50
Satir, Virginia, 228
schools,
cultural marginalization/recognition in, 206–8, 211–15
curriculum/pedagogy concerns by parents, 203–9, 214–15
racism/Islamophobia in, 203–6, 211–13
residential, see residential schools
see also education
Scott, Duncan Campbell, 24
security, 115, 185, 188
Indigenous children's/youth, 5, 14, 71, 91, 228
settler state/national, 66–7, 70, 168, 187
Seletze, *see* Johnnie, Delmar
self, 233, 251–3
importance of knowing in practice, 30, 95–7, 123–4, 247, 258–9
Medicine Wheel work on, 22–3
self-determination,
barriers to, 51, 65, 143
decolonizing approach emphasizing, 21, 28, 32, 109, 246
governance policies on, 36n1, 66–7, 77–8
Indigenous rights to, 54, 64, 112, 142–3, 154–5
settler colonialism,
Canada's context of, 24–5, 66–8, 211–12, 246
child welfare policy influence of, 5, 14, 27, 39, 67
child welfare practices and, 5–6, 14, 61–3, 66, 68–9, 77
Christianity and, 66, 85, 96
disruption of Indigenous culture, 10–11, 23–6, 108
institutional harm from, 66, 68, 77, 182, 244, 252
intentional harms and violence of, 42–3
land, control of, 24, 27, 66–7, 148
nation building, 67–8, 70
racism as basis of, 23
social worker analysis of, 6, 23–5, 67, 127–8, 150–2, 251
stereotypes of Indigenous Peoples, 8–9, 24–5, 34, 149

violence, 10, 41–3, 66–7, 85–8, 107–8, 122, 128–9
sexism, 63, 76, 160
　hetero, 208
sexual orientation and gender identity (SOGI) movement, 208, 214–15
Simon, Mary, 35
Simpson, Audra, 67
Sixties Scoop,
　evolution to Millennium Scoop, 6, 45, 86
　origin of phrase, 8, 45, 107
　policy of, 9, 55, 107
　racist underpinnings of, 6, 128–9
　traumatic legacy of, 10, 105–8, 122, 129
Skye's Legacy: A Focus on Belonging (BC Representative for Children and Youth), 34
social reformers, 3, 68
social workers, 40
　anti-oppressive practice of, *see* anti-oppressive practice
　assumptions of, 30–1, 72, 153–4, 157, 171–3
　awareness of power relations, 20, 27, 34–5, 146–7, 150–2, 251–2
　Black, *see* Black child welfare workers
　encountering violence/trauma, 224, 226, 252
　Indigenous/Métis, 30, 127, 144–51, 155, 243–4, 251–3
　need for self-reflection, 22–3, 30–1, 65, 212
　practice standards/recommendations for, 255–60
　questions/exercises for, 27–9, 55, 146–7, 153–4
　school-based, 200, 212–14
　training on citizenship/immigration issues, 184–5, 192–6
social work profession, 186
　assimilationism in, 9, 67–70, 86, 128–9
　complicity in settler colonialism, 6, 67, 127–8, 150–2, 251
　emphasis on Euro-Western objectivity, 33–4, 76–7, 90
　genogram work, 119
　relationships with children/families, 32–3, 144–5, 164, 212–14
　understanding of racism/white supremacy in, 6–7, 36n1, 135, 146–8
solidarity, 41, 161
　in social work practice, 2–3, 64–5, 77, 155, 157
Solidarity Across Borders, 195
sovereignty,
　barriers to, 65, 156
　decolonizing approach emphasizing, 21, 28
　Indigenous rights to, 64, 156
　settler state, 66–7
special needs designation, 89, 247–8, 252
Spivak, Gayatri, 143, 156–7, 164
Spring (noncitizen former youth in care), 187, 189, 191–2, 196
standardized assessments, 61–4, 73–4, 76–7
Stanley-Jones, Aiyana, 161, 163
Status, Indian,
　court cases/legislation for, 52–4
　future generations' loss of, 53–4, 85
　urban youth and lack of, 87, 92–3, 96, 100
　women's loss of, 50–2, 55, 85
statutory child welfare system,
　involvement in, 71, 141
　policy approaches of, 71–3, 78, 150
stereotypes, 208
　anti-Black, 166–8
　anti-Indigenous, 31, 96, 124
　in school settings, 211–12, 214
sterilization, women's, 4, 45
storytelling, 98, 193, 242
　Elder teachings through, 32, 106, 260
　Indigenous use of approach, 39, 41, 49, 73, 85, 258
　residential school survivor, 47, 49, 55–6
strengths-based models, 21, 31–2, 95
Strong-Boag, Veronica, 68
Summer (noncitizen former youth in care), 190–1
Sundances, 25, 118
Sweat Lodges, 84, 99, 109, 115, 118, 258

Taylor, Breonna, 161, 163
teachers, 253
　biases by school, 168, 205, 210–12
　child welfare assessments and, 74, 164

Index 277

connection with ancestors, 47, 49, 98, 126–7, 136
curricula/pedagogies of, 206–12, 214
parents as, 160, 165–6, 168–9, 229
transition youth, 95, 99–100, 227
untrained/unhelpful, 50, 204–7
teachings, 36n1
 anti-oppressive/anti-racist, 6–7, 18, 65, 126–7, 176–7
 Elders', 22–3, 84, 106–9, 123, 257–60
 Family Group Conference, 114–19
 Hul'qumi'num Mustimuhw teachings, 26, 28–9
 lack of, 51, 147, 237
 language, 25–8, 34–5, 46, 50, 90, 126
 Medicine Wheel, 21–2, 34–5, 94
 traditional, 20–1, 26–8, 30–4, 95, 115–16, 124
 wahkohtowin, 122, 125, 127, 130–2, 254
temporary migrant parents, 68–70
Todd, Nick, 221–2
Tonto (Black male social worker), 171–2, 175–6
transgender people, 29, 213
transition, youth in care, 253
 challenges facing, 96–7 184
 experiences in, 89, 94–5, 97–100
 principles to support, 93–4
trauma,
 from colonial policies, 10, 24–5, 41–3, 66, 85–8, 107–8, 257
 decolonial approach to, 200–1, 211, 213–14
 family, 25–6, 30, 63, 73, 95, 228
 from Indian Act, 24, 41, 47–8, 51–4, 86, 127–8, 257
 institutional, 66, 68, 77, 182, 244, 252
 intergenerational, 31, 90, 98–9, 114–15, 118, 156, 254
 responses to, 42, 213, 220, 223–8
 socio-genic, 201, 215
 see also post-traumatic stress disorder; trauma-informed practice
trauma-informed practice, 93, 119, 153, 193–6, 214–15
treaties, 23–4, 42, 66
 obligations under, 51, 67
Treaty Rights, loss of, 53–4

Truth and Reconciliation Commission reports,
 Calls to Action, 9, 11, 18, 243
 era after, 135, 224, 256
 findings/assertions of, 19, 23–5, 47, 86, 127
Tu Cho Circle, 228–30
Tuhiwai Smith, Linda, 63

UNICEF, children/youth well-being snapshot, 5, 71
United Nations, 254
 Convention on the Rights of the Child, 70–1
 Declaration on the Rights of Indigenous Peoples, 77
 decolonial/nation-state framework, 66
 on refugees, 183, 202
United States,
 BIPOC parenting in, 161–3, 168
 child removal in, 69, 107–8
 noncitizen former youth in care in, 188–9
 settler-colonial context of, 67
urban areas, 98
 children/youth in, 5, 100n2, 114, 124
 Indigenous service provision in, 114, 127, 141
 Indigenous youth experiences in, 31, 52, 87–89, 92–3

violence,
 children's responses to, 213, 220, 222–8, 234
 child welfare policies, 4, 6, 11, 14, 24, 63, 247
 colonial, 24, 41, 47–8, 51–4, 257
 domestic, 201, 223
 family responses to, 223, 227–9
 against girls, 18, 21
 institutional, 66, 68, 77, 182, 244, 252
 law, child welfare, 6–9, 32–5, 66, 127, 184, 191, 251
 neoliberalism and, 182, 191–2, 196
 police anti-Black, 161–4, 169–70, 232–4
 residential school, 24–5, 45–50, 63, 86, 127–8, 257
 settler state policies and, 10, 24–5, 41–3, 66–7, 85–8, 107–8, 257

Sixties/Millennium Scoop, 10, 30, 45, 86, 122, 128–9
   against women, 18, 21, 45, 128, 214, 227

Wade, Allan, 221–2
wahkohtowin, 122, 125, 127, 130–2, 254
Waziyatawin, 114
wellness, 164
   colonial system barriers to, 65, 71–2, 89, 107, 188, 202–5
   cultural/community connection and, 92, 99, 123, 206, 228, 245–54
   Family Group Conference model and, 112–13, 118
   four levels of, 109–10
   holistic, 105, 223, 225, 256
   Indigenous children/youth, 5, 11, 35, 85, 226, 256
   see also Family Group Conference model
white society/settlers, 29, 44, 249
   anti-Black violence of, 160–1, 163–4
   Black parenting in, 160–2, 164–70, 173, 176–7
   child welfare system rooted in, 31, 162, 170–4, 176–8
   Indigenous subjugation for, 25, 48
   nation building of, 3–4, 68
   theories of attachment, 245, 251
   values/norms of, 27, 73, 124–5, 174, 255
white supremacy,
   control over resources and, 6, 27
   Indigenous assimilation and, 24–5, 69, 73, 128, 211, 245
   racism interplay with, 6, 65, 163–4
Whitton, Charlotte, 4
Winter (noncitizen former youth in care), 187, 194–5
women,
   Indigenous, *see* women, Indigenous
   Muslim, 204, 212
   violence against, 214, 227
women, Indigenous,
   fighting colonial patriarchy, 6, 41–2, 78, 229
   loss of Status, 50–3, 55, 85
   service provision/support for/by, 84, 144, 220–2, 228–30
   violence against, 18, 21, 45, 128

Yellow Bird, Michael, 114
youth,
   building resilience, 33, 94, 98, 109
   ceremonies, participation in, 45, 49, 90, 95, 99, 124
   Elders, connections with, 32, 84–5, 90, 94–5, 97–100, 130
   housing for, 36n1, 71, 84, 98, 184, 190
   importance of culture for, 34–5, 48–9, 89–93, 94–8
   inequities facing, 60–2, 68–70, 73
   legislation covering, 35, 77–8, 125, 157, 143, 254
   mentors for, 91, 94, 97, 100
   Métis, *see* Métis children and youth
   placements for, 7–8, 69, 87, 90, 128, 160, 171
   security of Indigenous, 5, 14, 71, 91, 228
   transition programs for, *see* transition, youth in care
   urban Indigenous, 31, 52, 87–89, 92–3, 96, 100
   see also noncitizen former youth in care; Youth in Transition program(s)
Youth in Transition (YIT) program(s), 88
   challenges with, 96–7
   Circle of Courage model, 94
   experiences in, 89, 94–5, 97–100
   launch of, 83–5